Tolkien's Cosmology

Tolkien's Cosmology

Divine Beings and Middle-earth

 Sam McBride

The Kent State University Press
Kent, Ohio

Contents

Introduction

Seeking the Divine in Middle-earth

hortly after publishing *The Two Towers,* J. R. R. Tolkien admitted his annoyance at two strands of criticism by early reviewers: first that the book lacked religion, and second that it lacked female characters. The second of these two annoyances, and Tolkien's assertion that an absence of female characters "does not matter," prompted my analysis of Tolkien's views on gender in my book with Candice Fredrick, *Women Among the Inklings: Gender, C. S. Lewis, J. R. R. Tolkien, and Charles Williams.* I now turn to the first of these annoyances, that critics found "no religion"[1] in *The Two Towers.* My book has its foundation in answering the following question: why should Tolkien feel annoyed by critics who find no religion in his tale?

This question begs another one: what prompted Tolkien to think *The Two Towers,* and *The Lord of the Rings* in general, *does* contain religion? If based solely on the evidence provided by the story itself, I agree with the early critics. The story portrays no religious characters: no priests, no prophets, no shamans. It includes no religious sites: no churches, no altars, no holy ground. Middle-earth's residents show no religious practice: no rites or rituals, no sense of worship, no prayers (or at least nothing overtly identified as prayer). Flieger adds that Tolkien's work "has no miracles, no holy hermits, no Grail, no didactic allegory."[2] Even Tolkien admitted that few Hobbits engage in prayer or worship, and then only those with strong connections to Elves.[3] Indeed, a reading of Tolkien's story suggests the author successfully created a world lacking religion; readers might agree with early critics, such as Moorman, that "Middle-earth . . . is the stark, basically pessimistic world of the [Norse] sagas in which God does not intervene in human conflicts."[4]

This doesn't make the book purely naturalistic; in fact, authors such as Caldecott write of Tolkien as "one of the greatest spiritual writers of our time."[5] Glimpses of a metaphysical reality do appear. Gandalf's power comes from somewhere, and not apparently some vague force, ā la *Star Wars*. Elves who leave Middle-earth go somewhere, and *across the sea* seems to be someplace inaccessible to non-Elves; in addition, that journey appears one-way, with no return. These elements "show providential planning at work," according to Ellwood.[6] Furthermore, evil appears obviously metaphysical in *The Lord of the Rings*. The Eye of Sauron is not a device or machinery, like the One Ring; instead, the Eye seems a metaphor (or perhaps metonymy) for a metaphysical power. Additionally, the story conveys a strong ethic: evil is clearly evil, and thus should be opposed. Sauron, the primary antagonist in the story, is obviously not the source and origin of evil, but only its current primary exponent, just as Gandalf is a representative of good.

A clearly developed ethics and hints of metaphysical reality suggest more than meets the eye in Middle-earth. Pearce asserts, "Those who fail to see the far-off gleam of evangelium in Tolkien's work are those who are not looking for it."[7] But an awareness of metaphysical cosmos, whether on the part of characters or readers, is not the same as basing behaviors on an awareness of the divine, which could serve as a simplified definition of religion. What Middle-earth lacks is "the machinery of orthodox piety," as Urang describes it,[8] not a metaphysics. Brawley explains this state of affairs by suggesting the book offers "a connection to the numinous," which in turn provides readers "the *experience* of the holy [but] without relying on traditional religious motifs."[9] Similarly, Madsen finds in *The Lord of the Rings* "religious feeling . . . without ritual, revelation, doctrine, indeed without God."[10] Religious effects, Brawley and Madsen insist, without actual religion.

One could speculate that Tolkien felt upset over the criticism of "no religion" in his book solely because the criticism implies that his book *ought* to contain religion. Yet why should readers expect religion to appear within the story? First, Tolkien firmly embraced Catholicism; it would be unsurprising if elements in *The Lord of the Rings* reflect the Catholic theology Tolkien loved and admired. Second, he formed a strong friendship with C. S. Lewis, the foremost Christian apologist of the twentieth century. Like Tolkien, Lewis created a fictional world (Narnia) with characteristics borrowed from mythology and medieval Europe; Lewis's stories, however, contain enough Christian symbolism to verge on Christian allegory. Considering the extent to which the two men thought themselves like-minded, one might expect Tolkien's work to parallel Lewis's.

Furthermore, Tolkien's nonfiction writings, including his scholarly essay "On Fairy-stories" (a foundational text for theorizing fantasy literature), openly embrace theism; Bossert argues that Tolkien followed the teachings of Pope Pius X that a scholar should not "divorce his academic persona from his religious persona."[11] Tolkien himself acknowledges spiritual dimensions of his writing, finding even in Lembas a reference to the sacred Eucharist. Christianity, Tolkien told one correspondent, "can be deduced from my stories." He added that he felt no compulsion to make his fiction fit with Christian orthodoxy, though at the same time he did intend a consonance between the two.[12] As Ring summarizes, "Middle-earth can best be interpreted on the basis of an underlying layer of Christian concepts . . . in Tolkien's writing, the supposition of which is supported by his friendships and non-fiction works."[13]

Equally important, Tolkien relies on characteristics of epic literature in his story. He frequently alludes to characters and tales long past, suggesting an underlying mythology. To a first-time reader, this name-dropping may feel distracting, but it leaves an impression of a deeper, richer history behind the story. Of course, the presence of the divine forms a major element in epic literature and mythology. As a product of the British educational system, Tolkien knew well the tales of the Greek gods and goddesses, and as a specialist in ancient Scandinavian languages, he loved the Norse and Icelandic sagas. Thus, the apparent lack of religious elements in Tolkien's story might surprise readers, since divine beings form an expected element of the genre. All these factors contributed to early critical surprise that *The Lord of the Rings* lacked a religious dimension.

𝒥 *Searching for* Valasse

Despite the critics' observations, Tolkien certainly felt that he *did* incorporate religious elements into *The Lord of the Rings*. The central conflict, Tolkien explained, concerns God's right to honor from his creation. Though not an allegory, he added, the tale uses religious concepts and assumes a "natural theology" for its characters.[14] Many readers perceive traces of this "natural theology"; Dickerson notes the "strong sense in *The Lord of the Rings* and even in *The Hobbit,* that the Wise of Middle-earth—especially Gandalf and Elrond—have a faith in a power higher than themselves. . . . [T]here is both a seen and an unseen in Tolkien's Middle-earth: both a material plane and a spiritual plane."[15]

To grasp the extent and characteristics of that "spiritual plane" with its "natural theology," however, one must immerse oneself in the massive quantities of Middle-earth material Tolkien wrote besides *The Lord of the Rings.* These materials reveal the scope of Tolkien's work as *subcreator,* as a writer who "dared to build / Gods and their houses out of dark and light."[16] Tolkien believed the impulse to create imaginary worlds itself evidences metaphysical reality; humans create because they are made in the image of a creator.[17] Many of the writings that serve as a background to *The Lord of the Rings* are overtly religious; that is, they show the presence of the divine, *valasse* in Tolkien's invented Quenya,[18] and the responses of created beings to divine beings. Exploring Tolkien's legendarium will show the cosmological structure of Middle-earth, but also reveal moments in *The Hobbit* and *The Lord of the Rings* when the metaphysical impacts the physical.

The approach I embrace here, examining the totality of Tolkien's Middle-earth-related writings in search of a coherent cosmology, differs from a productive strand of Tolkien criticism, that of tracing developments in Tolkien's stories over the course of the fifty-five years he wrote them. Rateliff, for example, in *The History of the Hobbit* argues that the world of *The Hobbit* differs from the world of *The Lord of the Rings.* The One Ring, a mere magic ring in the earlier book, shows few signs of developing into an obsession for Bilbo or into an object that might lead to the downfall of the free world. Gandalf of the latter story is "ennobled" in contrast with "the wandering wizard who flits in and out" of *The Hobbit.* Blurring the distinction between the two books, Rateliff argues, may cause readers to "make assumptions that may not be justified, and bring things to *The Hobbit* that simply aren't there."[19] Of course, one can push Rateliff's argument further: the Gandalf who scratches a mark on Bilbo's door at the beginning of *The Hobbit* differs from the Gandalf who commands the attention of three intersecting armies at the end of the book. And the reader who returns to *The Hobbit* after reading *The Lord of the Rings* will not be the same reader,[20] nor will she or he see Gandalf the same way. The books simply can't be exclusively discrete, cut off one from another.

I risk committing the sin of overreading Tolkien's texts precisely because it enriches my reading experience of the entire legendarium, in the same way as perceiving the development of Tolkien's stories over time, but with different results. Examining the chronological transformations allows insight into the creative process; examining the connections that exist among the texts allows insight into the mythology. It permits one, for example, to learn more about the Gandalf (or Gandalfs) who inhabits the books. Gandalf practices magic, and I agree with Tolkien that magic presumes access to a divine power. Thus, tracing Gandalf's connections to the god(s) of Middle-earth will provide a fuller picture of Gandalf, even if Tolkien had not developed that full picture when he first conceived the character. Ultimately, Tolkien held a high opinion of Gandalf; though describing him as testy and avuncular in his relationship to Hobbits, Tolkien claimed for Gandalf a unique authority and high dignity.[21] Tolkien held this view not simply because of Gandalf's role within *The Lord of the Rings,* but because of the character's position in the larger legendarium.

Scull and Hammond warn of the dangers of my approach: "it is dangerous to quote from texts of different dates and to assume that statements necessarily have equal weight."[22] And indeed such a venture can put a critic in the position of using Tolkien as an authority against Tolkien. Yet I note (only half ironically) that Tolkien viewed his own writings in the manner I embrace. Visitors, especially in the 1960s, heard Tolkien speak of events in Middle-earth as if they existed "with as much reality as the French Revolution or the Second World War."[23] Tolkien described his compositional process as discovering preexisting stories, rather than inventing, adding that he felt compelled to find connections among the tales. He compared finding such connections to a complex game, almost addictive in its power to engross him.[24] One aspect of the game, as Apeland points out, involves pretending his writings form "an authentic mythological tradition."[25]

As a rule for his game, Tolkien believed that a mythology ought to make coherent sense. Finding rational explanations for situations and for character motivations within a mythology displays a desirable level of consistency.[26] Systematizing the cosmology of his stories formed a primary focus of Tolkien's efforts following *The Lord of the Rings.* To examine, more or less systematically, *valasse* within the corpus of Tolkien's work thus plays along with Tolkien; this book is a search for *valasse* in Tolkien's writings.

In a sense, this book forms a systematic theology of Tolkien's fictive world; of course, since that world is fictive, this book lacks the serious tone of most systematic theologies. And I trust no reader would foolishly base his or her personal religious beliefs on those Tolkien invoked for his subcreation. The purpose of this study is solely to read Tolkien closely on matters of *valasse,* to better understand and appreciate Tolkien's fiction, rather than to understand our own reality. My project takes to heart an observation Tolkien deleted from a manuscript of *On Fairy-Stories* regarding study of primitive societies: a cursory examination of such peoples discovers their stories; digging deeper finds their mythology; digging deeper still reveals their underlying philosophy.[27] Applying this to the social structures of Middle-earth, the pleasure reader of *The Lord of the Rings* appreciates the story's adventures; the Tolkien devotee digs into *The Silmarillion* to discover the myths underlying *The Lord of the Rings;* my book will seek an inner knowledge of Middle-earth metaphysics. As the Elf Rúmil claimed in an early section of *The Book of Lost Tales,* Tolkien's initial expression of the First Age of his legendarium, the stories of the Elves are so "knit together" with the stories of divine beings that to understand any one story, readers must grasp the broader history and cosmology into which that story fits.[28] By extrapolation, then, I argue that the stories of Hobbits and the end of the Third Age, since they intersect the stories of the Elves (and Dwarves and Ents), equally need the full cosmology of Middle-earth to do them justice.

✿ Outline

Tolkien's Cosmology traces the work of divine beings from prior to the creation of Middle-earth to its prophesied final fulfillment. Chapter 1, "Tolkien's Cosmogony and Pantheon," examines the creation story of Middle-earth as well as the beings responsible for developing and sustaining the world. Tolkien narrates a divine assembly of angelic beings singing before Eru Ilúvatar, the sole god of the legendarium. The resulting music involves more than sound, but instead forms a collaborative precreation, anticipating and prefiguring the world. Eru shows the assembly a vision of the music translated into story, then transforms the vision into reality. Some of the angelic beings choose to enter that reality, thus becoming the Valar, the world's caretakers and a pantheon for the residents of Middle-earth. Because the one true god of Middle-earth distances himself from his creation, leaving the Valar as his most visible representatives, the resulting cosmology is *monotheistic polytheism* (a world, technically monotheistic, in which multiple created divine beings serve as de facto gods).

Chapters 2 through 4 read the primary Middle-earth texts, *The Silmarillion, The Hobbit,* and *The Lord of the Rings,* as well as the tangential documents published in *The History of Middle-earth* and elsewhere, to trace divine involvement from the entrance of the Valar into the material reality to the end of the Third Age. The second chapter, "The Valar in the World," briefly highlights the Valar's earliest work to prepare the world for Elves and Humans, and the earliest interactions between the Valar and sentient beings of Middle-earth, as narrated in *The Silmarillion* and related writings. In these texts the Valar serve as characters, openly interacting with the Elves and, to a lesser extent, Humans.

The next two chapters consider the work of the Valar and Maiar during the Third Age, specifically in regard to the era's tumultuous climax, the War of the Ring. Chapter 3, "Divine Intervention in the Third Age: Visible Powers," considers representatives of the Valar at work in *The Lord of the Rings*. The most obvious divine beings operating in the story are the Istari, the Wizards, of whom Gandalf plays the most important role. Gandalf's work, death, and resurrection show his faithful subservience both to the Valar and to Eru Ilúvatar. The mysterious Tom Bombadil resists categorization, since his origins (within Middle-earth) remain unexplained; at the same time, he reflects both physical and metaphysical reality, and thus adds additional insight into the function of divinity in the Third Age. So, too, do the High Elves, Elrond and Galadriel; while not divine beings themselves, they exhibit special powers, promote knowledge of the Valar, and model the ethic of good over evil.

Chapter 4, "Divine Intervention in the Third Age: Invisible Powers," uncovers evidence of the Valar's involvement in the War of the Ring. While *The Lord of the Rings* (excluding its appendices) references the Valar only occasionally, Tolkien left hints in the text that more powerful beings influence events. The chapter first looks at two obvious sources of power, Sauron and Gandalf, who influence other beings from a distance. Subsequently, the chapter searches for moments in *The Hobbit* and *The Lord of the Rings* that suggest divine intervention by the Valar from an even greater distance.

Chapters 5 through 7 examine important cosmological issues topically: the problems of evil, death, and the end of the world. Chapter 5, "The Problem of Evil in Arda," uncovers the nature of evil by analyzing some of its unique dimensions within Tolkien's legendarium. To allow the good Valar a space in which they might learn from experience, Tolkien introduces *folly*, a space in which morally good beings make wrong choices that bear consequences without quite falling into evil. Second, evil lacks unity; while evil rebels against good, the habit of rebellion fosters mutiny against authoritarian rebel leaders. The most challenging aspect of evil in Tolkien's writings concerns the Orcs, who have no apparent possibility of redemption from evil. Almost as challenging in today's world is Tolkien's association of evil with technology.

Chapter 6, "Death," examines the various meanings of *death* in Middle-earth. For most created beings, death involves the separation of spirit and body; yet Tolkien embraced a belief in the immortality of the soul, and thus a dead being does not cease to exist, but transitions from one state into another. In Tolkien's metaphysics, this transition also involves a change in geography or cosmology. The chapter also considers some of the complications Tolkien's stories bring to death: the half-dead and the undead.

The final chapter, "Eucatastrophe, *Estel,* and the End of Arda," brings together a concept for which Tolkien coined a term and prophecies of the end of Middle-earth. *Eucatastrophe,* the unhoped-for sudden turn in a story (and in reality, which is itself a story), produces the consolation of the happy ending, which Tolkien attributes to divine intervention. Eucatastrophe serves as a structural element within Tolkien's tales, but also hints at a cosmic significance; only the highest power, Eru Ilúvatar, can bring about a final happy ending for Middle-earth, permeated as it was with evil. The chapter examines prophecies that assume such an ending for the world of Tolkien's creation, and the need for *estel,* or hope, on the part of created beings.

Source Materials

A difficulty for any study of divinity involves determining which texts claiming insight into divinity bear authority. My study will consider *The Hobbit, The Lord of the Rings,* and *The Silmarillion* as sacred texts in the study of Middle-earth's cosmology, and will assume for them a coherent (if sometimes contradictory) metaphysics. As such, I use each text to inform readings of the other two, much as biblical scholars may read the Old Testament in light of the New, or consider the Old Testament prophets in relation to Kings and Chronicles. From this perspective, I treat the volumes of posthumously published works as nonspurious apocrypha; that is, as long as texts don't blatantly contradict Tolkien's three primary works, they are authoritative. And those that do introduce contradictions remain worth noting (though space precludes an examination of all Tolkien's cosmological contradictions and revisions).

The most important of Tolkien's writings on the mythology of Middle-earth, *The Silmarillion,* reflects Tolkien's most profound metaphysical considerations, according to Christopher Tolkien.[29] Purdy describes the book as "a totally unique work. . . . [T]he attempt of a single man to do in a single lifetime what in the normal order of things is done by an entire culture over a span of centuries—create a mythology."[30] Its mythological style makes it the most widely purchased unread book published under Tolkien's name. Flieger acknowledges it as "without doubt the most difficult and problematic of Tolkien's major works."[31] Shippey, applying litotes, describes it as "uncompromising."[32]

I suspect many *Lord of the Rings* fans purchase the book, desiring more information about Middle-earth. They presume the book will contain an extended adventure story as gripping as *The Lord of the Rings*. Yet stylistically and organizationally, *The Silmarillion* differs drastically from *The Lord of the Rings;* if the latter is epic in nature, akin to Beowulf or *The Odyssey*, then the former is more akin to the Bible (King James Version). It contains linked stories, but not an overarching narrative; it uses an artificially archaic language style; it invokes names (many of them surprisingly similar) at several times the rate of *The Lord of the Rings*. Besides the complexity of *The Silmarillion*, it presumes an equally convoluted history of composition. The narrative mixes revelations of historical and cosmological truths (sometimes received directly from divine beings) with speculations by the Elves, shared with humans who added their own interpretations,[33] and ultimately copied and commented on by Hobbits.

In addition to the mythology's internal and presumed historical complexity, external factors in Tolkien's work further complicate its study. *The Silmarillion* remained incomplete at Tolkien's death. Or rather, while Tolkien had not yet finished an approved final version by his death, he had nearly completed several competing versions earlier in his life. Many of these differing versions have been collated, annotated, and published by Tolkien's son, Christopher, in the twelve-volume *History of Middle-earth* series; altogether this material forms what Kruger calls a "Silmarillion complex,"[34] more often referred to as a legendarium. The series also includes other Middle-earth materials, not directly related to *The Silmarillion*, such as rough drafts of *The Lord of the Rings*.

All these materials have shaped this book, with the published *Silmarillion* (1977) in a privileged position as first to appear and most widely distributed. Granting authenticity to *The Silmarillion*, as I do here, brings its problems. First, while multiple versions of the *Silmarillion* stories were written prior to *The Lord of the Rings*, and were thus present in Tolkien's mind, none appeared publicly until two decades after *The Lord of the Rings* premiered; thus, for two decades readers could only speculate on the identities and operations of Middle-earth's divine beings, based on brief hints from *The Lord of the Rings* itself, the appendices to the third volume, Tolkien's comments in *The Road Goes Ever On,* and a few published interviews with the author. Lobdell has referred to speculation from this era as "see[ing] in a glass darkly,"[35] and indeed some Tolkien fans indulged in wild speculation about the natures of divine beings in Middle-earth. A 1961 essay by Fuller declared Gandalf "partly an enigma but . . . in essence a man";[36] a decade later Wright speculated that the Valar might be "creators, or lesser gods, or simply the highest ranks of elves with responsibility for Middle-earth";[37] Purtill confidently asserted in a 1974 book that Saruman was "at least ostensibly a man or elf-man";[38] two years later, Grotta's biography of Tolkien assured readers that "Sauron was a flesh and blood creature."[39] Publication of *The Silmarillion* refuted such assertions, answered a host of other questions, and raised still more.

A fundamental difficulty with privileging the published *Silmarillion* concerns the debate over its validity as a Tolkien book. Flieger says the book gives "a misleading impression of coherence and finality, as it if were a canonical text."[40] Kane's *Arda Reconstructed* reveals *The Silmarillion* as a composite of Tolkien's diverse writings from throughout the fifty-five-year period Tolkien worked at Middle-earth tales, poems, history, and languages. Kane uncovers the editorial hand of Christopher Tolkien, and finds the published *Silmarillion* unnecessarily deficient when compared with the source materials; those deficiencies include the number of important female characters and the quantity of philosophical speculation.[41]

In the decades following publication of *The Silmarillion,* Christopher Tolkien himself expressed regret for the treatment he gave some passages and his concatenation of drafts from diverse periods.[42] Christopher acknowledged introducing editorial changes to increase consistency of verb tense and forms of names; occasionally, he simply eliminated textual difficulties. In retrospect, he considered some of his editorial work inappropriate meddling with his father's writing, a defect that caused the son to question whether he should have constructed a text that appears to be a unified, finished book. Yet for most Tolkien fans, *The Silmarillion* has become "a fixed point of reference of the same order as the writings published by" Tolkien, as Christopher notes in the "Introduction" to *Unfinished Tales.*[43]

I choose to accept the published *Silmarillion* as the standard text on the First and Second Ages of Middle-earth, not because I wish to defend the published *Silmarillion* against the valid objections of Kane, Flieger, and others, but simply because I can't imagine any other version of *The Silmarillion* emerging that would more accurately reflect Tolkien's contradictory wishes. At the same time, some discrepancies between other sources and the standard *Silmarillion* will be noted.

Chapter 1

Tolkien's Cosmogony and Pantheon

n the beginning, Tolkien created Middle-earth. Yet three years passed between first writing that world into existence in 1916 and devising its creation story, around 1919. Forty-five years later Tolkien recalled writing his "cosmogonical myth"[1] after the Great War had ended, while employed as an etymological researcher for the *Oxford English Dictionary*. Thus, drafts of the stories that eventually became *The Silmarillion* already existed prior to creating the creation story. Tolkien's cosmogony did not make possible the chronologically subsequent narratives of Middle-earth; rather, the existence of those stories necessitated creating an appropriate cosmogony.

To people his creation myth Tolkien developed a pantheon of gods and goddesses reminiscent of the divine beings in Greek and Norse mythology. Yet Tolkien shaped his gods differently from those of authentic pagan myths. Tolkien's divine beings eschew control of Middle-earth's residents, and learn to avoid interfering with the decisions of lower beings.[2] They avoid the petty wrangling and soap-opera lusts of Greek mythology, and the bitter sense of impotence and impending doom of Norse myth. They are, in Burns's words, divine beings that "A man like Tolkien, born in Victorian times," could feel comfortable with: an "improved pantheon."[3]

In fact, Tolkien's gods and goddesses aren't really gods and goddesses at all; they lack divinity as an intrinsic element of self-existent natures. Tolkien's gods remain creatures, the "first creations"[4] of the real god of Middle-earth, Eru Ilúvatar. Little can be said of Eru; one early text describes him succinctly as an incomprehensible prime mover, though McIntosh argues persuasively that Tolkien viewed Eru's nature through "the biblically informed Christian Neoplatonism of . . . Augustine and Aquinas" as a "personal agent" rather than a vague life force.[5] *Eru* means *the One God;* Flieger notes the emphasis on *one* implies *one alone,*[6] existing in a category separate from all else. *Ilúvatar* translates as *Allfather,* and thus the Elves see Eru as the creator, the source of matter and life. Eru possesses the Flame Imperishable, through which reality can exist independently of Eru, though derived from him. Eru exists outside of time and physical reality, both of which he creates. Yet Elves believe he can enter into his creation, much as a singer might enter his own song, or a storyteller his own story, while simultaneously remaining outside it. Elves describe Eru as beyond measure. Existence stems from Eru, Tolkien explained, and thus is called Oienkarmë Eruo, translated by Tolkien as "The One's perpetual production" and "God's management of the Drama."[7]

God's, rather than *the gods',* management forms a bedrock principle of Tolkien's invented world; Middle-earth is decisively monotheistic. Yet Eru chooses to remain distant and invisible to Middle-earth, leaving his "first creations" as the visible sources of power; in the apparent absence of Eru Ilúvatar, the Valar play the role of de facto gods.[8] Thus the cosmology of Middle-earth can be described as *polytheistic monotheism.* Middle-earth is a monotheistic world in which its creator only rarely appears. While Eru may be omnipresent within the world in some metaphysical sense, he rarely reveals himself. Rather, he is mediated through his representatives, creatures bound within the world, yet powerful and holy enough to be called, in one Tolkien name list, pagan gods.[9] Residents of Middle-earth learn of Eru Ilúvatar almost exclusively through the gods. This chapter will examine Tolkien's creation myth and pantheon to establish the self-contradictory concept of *polytheistic monotheism* as the groundwork of Middle-earth cosmology.

✐ Creation

History parallels music in Tolkien's imaginary realm. It exists over time, includes overlapping strands, and involves periods of development, punctuated by climaxes. Tolkien uses music as the underlying metaphor of creation in the "Ainulindalë," "one of the most profound theodicies . . . ever written," in Williams's view.[10] According to the "Ainulindalë," Eru Ilúvatar creates spirit-beings with musical potential, training and instructing them in musical production, then listening to their ensemble performances, all as background to the creation of a reality completely separate from the purely spiritual realm of Eru and his spirit-beings. The idea of music forming creation goes back to Plato's myth of Er in *Timaeus,* but especially to Boethius's *On the Consolation of Philosophy;*[11] Tolkien directly references the medieval notion of the "music of the spheres," though "imaginatively and selectively," according to Eden, adapting it to his own purposes, and adding the biblical accounts of creation in both Genesis 1 and John 1.[12]

Tolkien conceives of creation within his legendarium as a collaborative event encompassed in three distinct but parallel phases:

1. the Music of the Ainur (the Great Music);
2. the Vision of the Ainur;
3. physical creation.

At the same time, the "Ainulindalë," as with most stories of origins, begs the question of what comes before phase 1. The story implies an ex nihilo creation prior to the beginning of Middle-earth. "There was Eru," begins the tale, who created the Ainur prior to making anything else.[13] Thus in a single sentence, Tolkien establishes the a priori existence of just one creator-god, who then devises spirit-beings possessing rationality as his first creation,[14] using a process of pure thought.

While Tolkien's cosmogony says little about what came prior to the creation of the Ainur, it does offer insight into the Ainur's activities prior to their collaboration with Eru in creating physical reality. Having thought divine creatures into being, Eru turns to speaking as a means of instructing them. Prior to the Great Music, the Ainur develop their musical skills under Eru's direction with little knowledge of any purpose behind their training. At first the Ainur sing monophonically. Tolkien's description of their musical development parallels the history of music within Western culture since the early Middle Ages: monophonic melodies sung solo or by small ensemble, eventually incorporating rudimentary harmony.[15] The earliest heavenly music resembles Gregorian chant at least in its limited complexity; the addition of harmony suggests developments such as organum in eleventh-century Europe, which combines a primary melody with a parallel or contrasting melody.

More important than the sound of the Ainur's first music is its derivative nature. Not just the Ainur, but the musical themes they sing come from Eru, who implements a surprising pedagogical methodology for teaching music. A typical approach for teaching a song to a choir untrained in reading music involves a leader first singing a phrase or melody with the choir repeating it. Yet Eru gives oral direction, "propounding to them themes," which they then sing.[16] The Ainur, in other words, provide a musical interpretation, not of a written score, but of a spoken description.

The purpose of this early singing of the Ainur remains obscure. Given the impact of their later Great Music, this early singing may be practice, preparation, rehearsal. Yet the text suggests two further dimensions. First, as the Ainur sing before Eru, he expresses satisfaction and joy; this image parallels Christian descriptions of a heavenly host singing praise to God. The singing implies worship as much as aesthetic pleasure.[17] Second, the singing connects to a broader education. The thought propounded to each Ainu (Tolkien's singular form for Ainur) reflects but one facet of the mind of Eru. As the Ainur listen to one another, they learn more of the mind of their creator. This deeper understanding underpins and enables the increasing musical complexity of their output.

Eru apparently intends a further purpose behind this slow musical evolution; gathering together before him all the Ainur, Ilúvatar "declare[s] to them a mighty theme," containing wisdom he has not yet revealed. The content overwhelms the Ainur, reducing them to reverent silence. Rather than silence, however, Eru desires participation. He instructs them to make "a Great Music," each Ainu adorning the provided theme.[18] The instruction parallels the approach of a jazz ensemble, agreeing on a structure (typically a melody and a harmonic sequence) and who will solo when, but then improvising. Or perhaps more accurately, Eru's instruction reflects the baroque practice of improvising ornamentation on a prewritten melody, combined with basso continuo accompaniment based on a chart of harmonic progressions. Hart describes such music as "free and spontaneous ornamentation."[19] Improvisatory musical practices result, in theory, in spontaneous expression such that participants do not know precisely what notes their fellow musicians will play.

Most free improvisation exists within boundaries (limitations of a specific musical instrument; a performer's ornamentation tendencies; what worked well in rehearsal). Such is the case in the Great Music of the Ainur. The narrator of the "Ainulindalë" implies that the singers' voices possess individual qualities, some sounding like specific instruments, others contributing to a sound like a vocal choir. Furthermore, Eru instructs his Ainur to suggest their own thoughts by means of embellishments. Since each Ainu's musical expressions reflect some specific and limited part of the mind of Eru, each Ainu's contribution to the Great Music is idiosyncratic, limited by his or her own experience. The sum total of the singing provides a more complete reflection of the mind of the creator than that available to any one Ainu. Knight calls the Ainur in their singing "contributors to a great free collective improvisation."[20]

Yet to instruct the Ainur to embellish the theme with their individual *thoughts* implies more at stake than just music. Such a moment foregrounds that music in the narrative serves as metaphor, illustrating a concept that lies beyond the minds of created beings within a space/time continuum. Even given that Tolkien's is a fictional reality, a secondary world, the Music of the Ainur can hardly be music in the sense that we use the term today (or even in the same sense that Elves or Hobbits use the term in *The Lord of the Rings*); a later phase of the creation process shows that the Ainur have not yet experienced physical reality. There cannot be music (at least not as a phenomenon Humans can understand) where there is no air (or other physical medium) through which vibrations can transmit. Furthermore, Humans cannot conceive of music without time, and the events of the Singing of the Ainur take place prior to the creation of time (a statement that reveals the limitations of language in describing cosmological reality).[21] Thus music functions as a trope for something beyond Human (or Elven) comprehension. Naveh notes that "The music of the Ainur is clearly supposed to be abstract, celestial music played in the Void and intended for Ilúvatar's ears; thus, it certainly does not resemble any music known to humanity today or in any previous era. But despite its abstract nature, the description of the music is full of much more earthly concepts and images."[22]

An early version of "The Music of the Ainur" suggests a divine being told the creation story to the Elves; one can imagine this divine being describing the experience as music to make the experience comprehensible. Such a supposition foregrounds the inability to authenticate creation tales since, by definition, no storyteller could have been present except for the creator(s). As Nagy observes, in Tolkien's legendarium, "the ultimate authenticating force is always only implied: one can never actually reach it in a text, since it is embedded deep in the texture of culture."[23]

The extramusical dimension of "The Music of the Ainur" reveals Tolkien's scholarly orientation. As a specialist in languages from Medieval Europe, Tolkien knows the concept of *musica universalis,* or the music of the spheres. Rather than literal sound, this music serves as metaphor for the harmonious intercooperation of the elements of the universe: the stars, planets, and sun, which were thought to have profound mystical yet mathematical relationships. Tolkien's friend C. S. Lewis describes the medieval worldview as one in which, celestially speaking, "everything has its right place, its home, the region that suits it, and, if not forcibly restrained, moves thither."[24] Eden reads Middle-earth's history as "a huge mythological parable of Boethius's three types of music," not only singing and vocal music, but also "the harmony of the four elements, the four seasons, and . . . the movement of the celestial bodies."[25]

Events following the Music's dramatic final chord, ending phase 1 of creation, show the music's metaphorical nature. Eru presents a vision of something new, unknown, yet recognizable: physical reality developing through time. The vision, phase 2 of the creation process, reveals a movie-like image of a world, "globed amid the void,"[26] that appears separate from the Ainur and even from Eru, yet within which the Ainur recognize their own contributions. That vision reveals winds, light, colors; iron, stone, silver, and gold; and most impressive, water. The flow of the Ainur's music foreshadows the evolution of the world within the vision, and the different voices of the Ainur represent natural elements and processes.

The vision, in other words, depicts the Music of the Ainur; it forms Eru's translation of abstract musical form and melody into a story of physical reality. The Ainur realize the vision embodies more than just sound in praise of Eru; it is prophetic of a story yet to come. Eden describes this vision as "a sort of 'predetermined' cinematic preview," while Sammons calls it "visible history." Yet the vision surpasses the Music, revealing greater purpose than the Valar had grasped while performing. The vision, McIntosh suggests, "embodies the essential truth" of Eru more completely than the music does as a mere foreshadowing.[27]

Within the vision's physical substances, the Ainur find an intriguing surprise, an element they have not sung: sentient though material beings, whose presence within the vision-world stems solely from a melody introduced by Eru, without elaboration by the Ainur. The purpose of the Great Music then becomes clear: to prepare a place in which those sentient beings can live. The Ainur have unwittingly sung into existence a world for these beings. Dubbed the Children of Ilúvatar, the beings seem "strange and free,"[28] reflecting yet another previously hidden aspect of Ilúvatar's mind. The Children, Elves, and Humans, become the primary protagonists of Tolkien's stories.

Excepting the Children of Ilúvatar, the world within the vision reflects Eru's themes as elaborated by the Ainur; it forms, Klinger suggests, "an atemporal matrix" that "contains the entirety of time and space."[29] The Music of the Ainur determines, to some extent, the course of events of this vision; it becomes "the pattern for and the agency of creation," as Flieger says.[30] But while given a glimpse of that story, the Ainur lack a full understanding of its ending; Eru stops the vision before it reaches the music's final climax.[31] This lack of certainty about endings, as well as ignorance as to the natures of sentient beings (particularly their free wills), prevents the Music from functioning as a completely deterministic fate.

The Origin of Evil

Phase 2 of the creation process also reveals the consequence of complications that arise during the initial Singing of the Ainur, complications that will significantly impact the world when it comes to be in phase 3. Because the music of each individual Ainu influences the development of the vision, the freedom Eru grants the Ainur allows the possibility of abuse. And indeed, one Ainu chooses to interpolate alterations from his own imagination,[32] incompatible with the theme propounded by Eru. This Ainu, Melkor, sits at the left hand of Eru as the most gifted and powerful of the Ainur; Melkor is "eldest in the thought of Ilúvatar."[33] Yet despite his place atop the highest rank of the Ainur, he desires a greater role: to be like Eru, not simply in his image; he wishes to create, rather than to elaborate themes provided by his creator. Furthermore, Melkor neglects the comradeship of the Ainur, going by himself into the Void, hoping to acquire the Imperishable Flame;[34] Melkor mistakenly imagines the Imperishable Flame as a substance apart from Eru, rather than an element of Eru's own nature.

Spending so much time alone contributes to Melkor devising thoughts of his own. In short, he rebels. Yet lacking the power to create that which he thinks, Melkor does little with his thoughts, until the Great Music. Then, when he inserts his own thoughts into the singing, he produces discord within sounds Eru intends as harmony.[35] Discord becomes associated with Melkor, just as the Medieval world associated the tritone with the devil.[36] To use the analogies developed earlier, Melkor becomes a jazz saxophone player inserting an atonal melody into the ensemble, or a Baroque harpsichordist independently modulating to a different key. In contrast with Greek mythology, in which Discord is a goddess, Middle-earth mythology posits discord as a consequence of stepping outside the boundary appropriate to a created being. Discord produces effects: some of the Ainur grow depressed hearing Melkor's thoughts. Some stop singing while others change their music to make it compatible with Melkor's; a darker music results, reflecting the darkness of the Void wherein Melkor traveled. Like ripples in a pool emanating from a dropped pebble,

Melkor's discord spreads, overpowering the themes originally enunciated by Eru, which in turn become lost amid cacophony.[37]

Eru, of course, perceives Melkor's additions, and even understands his motives; as Tolkien notes, "No mind can . . . be closed against Eru."[38] Finally Eru introduces a new theme with its own beauty; the resulting theme and countertheme suggest sonata form.[39] But as the Second Theme gathers power and sweetness,[40] Melkor's discord continues to overpower it. Thus, Eru introduces yet another theme, less grand than the previous two, a quiet ripple of sound, but Melkor's discord cannot overpower it. The two strands of music fight one another: Eru's, beautiful though sorrowful; Melkor's, emphasizing braying trumpets endlessly repeating a few notes. While Melkor's music attempts to overwhelm Eru's, instead its best notes reappear within Eru's Third Theme; as Melkor's discord asserts itself more boldly, it unwittingly discovers itself sublimated within Eru's melody.[41] As these two themes contest, Eru brings the music to a close with one climactic chord, "deeper than the Abyss, higher than the firmament, more glorious than the Sun, piercing as the light of the eye of Ilúvatar."[42]

The narrative of Melkor's discord within the Music of the Ainur reinforces the story's purpose: communicating the incomprehensible to limited beings. The story necessarily personifies Eru by depicting him dependent on time and subservient to cause and effect. Eru's reactions to Melkor's discord, first smiling, then weeping, position him as just another character within a story, caught up in forces larger than himself. Yet if Tolkien's assertion that *nothing was hidden from the mind of Eru* includes the actions of his created beings, then Eru must have known in advance of Melkor's discord and its impact on the music. Elam words this problem succinctly: "One shouldn't . . . see the ostensible reaction of Ilúvatar as being affected by the discord, for he has presumably known that it should arise even before the Ainur were created."[43] Eru's reactions, therefore, must be playacting, or personifying a purely spiritual phenomenon.

Regardless of whether Eru responds genuinely or figuratively to Melkor's rebellion, the discord produces real effects in phase 2 of creation. The vision of physical reality incorporates both the discord and Eru's subsequent themes. As a result, the Ainur view the effects of Melkor's pride and presumption. Water, for example, the substance that most delights the Ainur, takes on new dimensions; Melkor's blaring cacophony introduces extreme heat and cold into the vision-world, resulting in snow, mists, clouds, and rain.

Yet these natural phenomena are not innately evil. As the Ainur recognize, the phenomena possess beauty. Melkor does not intend beauty when he introduces discord, as seen from two factors: (1) its sound—Melkor's discord opposes harmony; (2) its effect—some Ainur grow depressed and quit listening to the music altogether. Yet the vision presents Melkor's discord within a context, a vision-world in which Melkor's efforts are counterbalanced by the singing of those Ainur who remain faithful to Eru's original themes, and by the underpinning power of Eru himself. Those factors work together to dilute the effects of discord, to transform those effects into something good, though unintended by the singer of discord. By this, discord can be understood as evil yet subordinate to good. Ilúvatar announces this fact at the closing of the Music of the Ainur, telling Melkor he will ultimately learn that by pursuing rebellion, he instead aids Eru in creating new and unforeseen beauty; by attempting rebellion against Eru, Melkor inadvertently serves Eru.[44]

While evil produces inadvertent beauty, it also produces more evil. An early version of the "Ainulindalë" focuses primarily on its negative effects: Melkor's extremes of terror, sorrow, wrath, and evil produce Elvish and Human pain and cruelty, merciless cold and hopeless death.[45] Perhaps Tolkien removed this dire prophecy in later versions to avoid diminishing the enthusiasm of the Ainur for the vision they have witnessed.

The relationship between Melkor's discord and the Children of Ilúvatar remains unclear at this stage. The Children embody the Third Theme of Eru, introduced late in the proceedings and not elaborated by the Ainur. Hood assumes that the First Theme of the Music pertains to "lands and environment and animals,"[46] more or less corresponding to the first five and one-half days of creation as described in Genesis 1. The Second Theme, in contrast, is Eru's countermove against Melkor's discord, embellished by faithful Ainur and contested by the discord it opposes. The Third Theme, operating without Valian embellishment but in opposition to the discord, suggests a central role for Elves and Humans in the battle against evil while also implying that the Children will remain foreign to the Ainur.

Tolkien's story of the origin of evil parallels the Judeo-Christian view. Evil traces back to one rebel, created good, who falls and then spreads evil to others. The Judeo-Christian myth, however, posits a world initially free of the influence of evil. Satan brings evil into a pristine, unfallen environment; when Humans fall, Earth becomes infected by evil as a consequence. In Tolkien's myth, in contrast, evil is "subcreatively introduced," such that rebellion and discord are destined as part of the environment even prior to its physical creation.[47] Thus evil will impact the residents of Eä, regardless of whether they themselves experience a fall.

Tolkien insists on a hierarchical inequality between Eru Ilúvatar and Melkor, which allows the blame for rebellion to fall on Melkor while denying him innate creativity. The evil impact of Melkor's discord arises "through him but not by him."[48] Melkor's power to induce discord into the Singing of the Ainur stems from Eru. Thus, Eru asserts, even prior to the creation of material reality, the world will experience a happy ending (eucatastrophe; see chapter 7) despite the appearance of evil. Sorrow, misery, wickedness, and terror will ultimately speak to Eru's glory; in the long run, sentient creatures will agree that discord enriches the life and history of the world, making it "so much the more wonderful and marvelous."[49] Yet Crabbe asserts that Eru remains the only being who understands how "the great design is unified, how everything has its origin in himself and contributes to his own greater glory";[50] since Eru refrains from communicating that understanding (perhaps because sentient humanoids, and perhaps even the Valar, cannot fathom it), creatures need to accept the theological assertion by faith, or doubt that any such understanding is possible.

🍃 *Creation and the Ainur: Monotheistic Polytheism*

The divine collaborative creative process thus far involves two stages: a choral production by the Ainur under the direction of Eru Ilúvatar, and a vision induced by Eru that enacts the previous music. The vision serves as visual prophecy, or seeing history in advance, which the Ainur experience relatively passively. By the end of phase 2 a mental construct of physical reality has been previewed by the Ainur, though the universe has not yet come to be. During the vision, many of the Ainur become enraptured by its beauty and caught up in its developments. When Eru removes the vision, the Ainur feel unrest. Their love of the vision causes them to wish it to be. Thus Eru, speaking the word *Eä!, Let It Be,* brings physical reality into existence. Tolkien likens the transition as one from *story* to *history*.[51] McIntosh suggests that the three-part division underlying creation, "Music to Vision to Reality," parallels "intelligible essence or abstract form, to a story, to an existing, mind-independent reality."[52] This primeval creation first appears as a clouded flame in the distant void;[53] in fact, Eru places the Flame Imperishable within it, the element out of himself that causes something to emerge from nothing.

This new creation takes the name that Eru speaks to generate it: Eä, the material universe. *Eä* is separate from *Ilu* (a root of Ilúvatar) which, according to Tolkien, means *all that is*. Eä involves all of nature, while Ilu encompasses nature plus spirits and souls. Within Eä are both space and matter, that which residents of Middle-earth consider reality; Tolkien describes Eä as secondary reality, in relationship to Eru, who is the primary reality.[54] Matter has formed a (flat) world, called Arda, and centered within Arda is the continent Middle-earth.[55]

This phase 3 of creation apparently begins the flow of time. *The Book of Lost Tales* describes time as "unbreakable fetters," which even the Valar cannot loosen. The flow of time makes possible the history of Arda, which embodies the Music of the Ainur and its resulting vision; said another way, the Ainur perceive that the Great Music is in essence a rehearsal for the production of the history of Arda. Yet the Music does not rigidly determine this new world; the Ainur do not simply sit back and observe the inexorable unfolding of their earlier singing. Rather, many of the Ainur, those enamored of the vision,[56] wish to exist within temporal and physical reality to shape the elements most compatible with their Eru-given natures. Ilúvatar grants their wish, though with the caveat that on entering Arda, they cannot leave it until Arda's history has come to its end, until the great final chord. Thus, these Ainur, in Shippey's words, choose to "bind themselves within the world."[57]

The Silmarillion's narrator describes this as a division among the divine beings. Some Ainur remain with Ilúvatar, in heaven (for lack of a better term), those who wish for no further participation in fulfilling Eru's plan. The Ainur who enter Arda leave the direct presence of Eru and enter physical reality. These Ainur, called Valar and Maiar, become separated not only from the heavenly Ainur, but to some extent from Eru himself. They exist solely within Eä, bound to material reality until Eä, as with the Music of the Ainur, reaches its conclusion. The Valar can recall memories of their prior existence and of the Vision of the Ainur, but otherwise have no access to that which was prior to and outside of time. Within time the Valar may mentally revisit the past and return to the present, without appearing to have moved at all. But they cannot move forward into the future, which they perceive only to the extent that the Vision has revealed it. This implies two alternate realizations of the history of Eä: within the universe, the Valar experience the linear progression of history; outside the universe, Eru and the remaining Ainur perceive past, present, and future simultaneously and continuously.[58]

Tolkien came to view the Valar as angelic creatures, comparable in power to mythological gods. They are *the Authorities,* since their power stems from Eru, who bequeathed them godlike power and knowledge appropriate for their positions. At the same time, they lack the complete omniscience and all-powerfulness of their creator; instead, they remain subordinate to and dependent upon him. The Valar are completely knowable to Eru, but they can only perceive his mind if Eru reveals it to them.[59]

The history of divine intervention within *The Silmarillion, The Hobbit,* and *The Lord of the Rings* shows primarily Valar, rather than Eru Ilúvatar, influencing the course of events. The structure Ilúvatar imposes on the world pushes him into the background, "offstage" as Birzer describes it, functioning as a "silent partner," according to Garbowski;[60] if not for the presence of the Valar, Eru might appear deistic, setting the world in motion and then passively watching it unfold.[61] Delegating authority to the Valar suggests Eru wishes to be mediated rather than directly present to his creation. Tolkien's earliest version of his mythology explains Eru's relationship to his creation with a simple cosmological summary: "Ilúvatar is the Lord for Always who dwells beyond the world; who made it and is not of it or in it, but loves it."[62] Only a handful of times in the history of Middle-earth does Ilúvatar make an obvious appearance, and then not to Humans or the masses of Elves. Instead, the Valar and Maiar represent divinity to the sentient life-forms of Middle-earth, and then only to a select few, primarily Elves. To learn of Ilúvatar, a resident of Middle-earth must be taught by the Valar, or by one of the Valar's students.

Eru positions himself as distant, "immensely remote," from Arda and its affairs, a situation significantly unlike the Judeo-Christian concept of God intimately involved in Earth's sustenance.[63] With phase 3 of creation, after speaking material reality into existence, "Eru takes a back seat," as Rosebury puts it.[64] Yet this is a "feigned absence" since Eru retains the freedom to enter Eä at will and to influence its events.[65] Not bounded like the Valar by the space/time of Eä nor by the Music of the Ainur, Eru remains (as Tolkien said in a very different context) "that which governs and is above the rules."[66] At the same time, Hutton notes, "the chance that Ilúvatar himself is directing events is only mentioned in retrospect, as a faint but cheering possibility."[67] As a result, the Valar become the apparent powers of the world, resembling Norse gods, according to Shippey, "in their relative independence, differing natures and fields of action, and the limitations on their power."[68] In essence, Burns adds, Eru "soon fades from the main narrative tale, becoming more a figurehead than a participant, and the Valar—in spite of reassurances to the contrary—now seem in charge."[69]

Thus, Tolkien's mythology contains "elements of apparent polytheism,"[70] according to Hart. Tolkien's cosmos, though definitively monotheistic, has as its focal point a world that appears populated by many gods. Said more intellectually (by Rosebury), Tolkien's legendarium imagines the history of the world as "a fulfillment of creative purposes which proceed both directly from God and Mediately from him, through the sub-creativity of created beings."[71] This differs radically from the Judeo-Christian tradition, which posits that God created the universe, and apparently without delegating activities to lesser powers. This difference in origins impacts the beings that dwell within such a universe; while Tolkien's universe is monotheistic, his world, Arda, seems polytheistic. The Valar, Tolkien said, function as gods imaginatively but not theologically.[72]

Burns sees this as Tolkien "granting equal standing to opposing ideals," though she also notes the Valar's decrease in god-likeness over the evolution of Tolkien's legendarium, becoming *gods* rather than *Gods*.[73] Agøy attributes the transformation Burns describes as recovery from "a Romantic project" that came to seem too pagan. Tolkien slowly reconciled his earliest work with Christianity as he shifted from story-telling to "working out in detail the philosophical and metaphysical framework in which they existed."[74] Tolkien himself articulates a desire to provide his world with beings comparable to the gods of mythology but which would seem acceptable to adherents of Christian orthodoxy.[75]

Tolkien's discomfort with his own creation emerges throughout the six decades he elaborated his mythology. The narrator of the "Valaquenta" calls the Valar by the somewhat ambiguous term *the Powers of Arda,* but then admits that Humans "often called them gods,"[76] a phrase open to multiple meanings. First, the term may be appropriate and correct: the Valar are truly gods, though in a subordinate sense because they derive their authority from Eru, the One. Or perhaps the Valar are only gods so-called; Eru's distance positions the Valar in the role of gods (at least to Humans, if not Elves). But third, the phrase can imply that Humans call the Valar gods, but are wrong to do so; such an error positions Humans as idolaters, confusing the created with the creator. In a letter Tolkien provided a fourth possibility:

gods is the concept of the Valar "Englished";[77] since English lacks a word for *near-god* or *assistant god, gods* would need to suffice.

However, the Valar can be described as stand-ins for god: in another letter Tolkien claimed his legendarium has no proper gods, but the Valar are god-substitutes.[78] Flieger sums up Tolkien's conundrum by calling the Valar "limited god-figures," but far more influential than the Christian tradition recognizes for angels.[79] Furthermore, Pearce notes, Tolkien's acknowledgment that referring to the Valar as gods is both appropriate and inappropriate "manages to accommodate paganism as well as evolution within his mythology, making both subsist within Christian orthodoxy."[80]

With this context in mind, the phrase I apply, *monotheistic polytheism,* should be understood as subordinating the second term to the first. After the opening chapters of the "Quenta Silmarillion," only a few fleeting references remind readers that Eru Ilúvatar remains the ultimate divinity; following Fëanor's return to Middle-earth, the name of Eru Ilúvatar appears only rarely until the Akallabêth, at which time his overt intrusion into the history and cosmology of Arda leaves no doubt as to his superior authority. Yet as Tolkien's Silmarillion story unfolds, readers easily lose sight of Eru; one can understand why Humans, Dwarves, or Hobbits, perhaps even less-enlightened Elves, might see the Valar as gods and even fear them, and why enlightened Elves wish to admire and honor them. One version of the "Ainulindalë" sums up its themes by echoing the words of Proverbs 1:7 ("the fear of the Lord is the beginning of wisdom"): the story shows the Children of Ilúvatar as created beings within the flow of time, and "the Valar, the Powers of the World, contesting for the possession of the jewel of Ilúvatar; and thus thy feet are on the beginning of the road."[81]

Monotheistic polytheism gives Tolkien the mythmaker several narrative advantages. First, the existence of one ultimate divine creator fits comfortably with Tolkien's Catholicism. While Tolkien did not see inventing a purely polytheistic imaginary realm as sinful, his writings on subcreation suggest he viewed inventing an imaginary world as the highest honor Humans could offer to God, since Humans are subcreators in the image of a creator. No wonder Tolkien as mythmaker broke the mold of nearly all of Earth's non-Judaic mythologies to posit a monotheistic universe.

At the same time, Tolkien's familiarity with diverse mythologies would suggest several benefits from a polytheistic cosmos. Central to storytelling is conflict. In the Judeo-Christian tradition, angels, though fascinating in many respects, lack conflict (except for those that rebelled against God). Admittedly, when angels appear within a biblical narrative, they inspire awe and fear. Yet as characters in a plot they appear rather dull. Most Christian angelology posits angels as beings in harmony with one another (except for the great division of good versus evil) and happily subordinate to God, who is always immanent within his creation. Lacking a fallen nature, good angels experience no conflicts among themselves nor between themselves and God. But lack of conflict makes for dull stories.

By distancing himself from his creation, Eru forces the Valar to function on their own, learning through trial and error, and introducing the possibility of conflict even among the gods. Furthermore, Tolkien assigns individual Valar unique personalities,[82] allowing them to function as consistent and semipredictable characters. His earliest depiction of the Valar heightens this sense of conflict, with a god and goddess of war, Makar and Meássë, who revel in conflict and position themselves between Melkor and the Valar without embracing a clear allegiance to either side.[83] Tolkien's familiarity with mythology, Burns suggests, allows him to "rely upon a pantheon's dramatic interaction, as well as on a pantheon's traditional connection to the world it oversees."[84] While conflicts within Tolkien's pantheon never reach the ludicrous degree of strife found among the gods of Greek mythology, conflicts do contribute to gripping narrative.[85]

The Valar also lend divinity a sense of immediacy, at least within *The Silmarillion*. "The dealings between divine beings and Men and Elves are as direct and physical as those in Home," in the view of Wood, writing shortly after publication of *The Silmarillion*. "In this kind of world[,] religion, in the sense of formalized worship of a remote divine being (or beings) has no place."[86] Yet *remote* remains the proper word to describe Eru, Masson points out, since Eru "delegates the creation and government of Eä to subordinates."[87] Theologically, a distant though potentially immanent God parallels while augmenting the perspective of the Old Testament. As Glover notes, those rare moments when a distant God intercedes foreground "a radical discontinuity between a transcendent God and the world and reduces the cosmos itself to a dependent, penultimate status."[88]

While positioning the Valar as de facto gods, Tolkien appears uncomfortable using the term *gods* for created beings. As he revised "The Lay of Leithian," he substituted the word *Valar* for *Gods* in phrases describing their activities in Aman. Christopher Tolkien speculates that Tolkien wished to eliminate the word *Gods* from the text,[89] though Christopher doesn't speculate about his father's purpose. An examination of divinity in Middle-earth benefits from seeing the Valar simultaneously as creatures from a theological perspective and *the gods* from a literary perspective.

🍃 *The Middle-earth Pantheon*

Tolkien briefly discusses the individual Valar who choose to enter Eru Ilú-vatar's new creation at the end of the "Ainulindalë," at greater length in the "Valaquenta," and again briefly in the first chapter of the "Quenta Silmaril-lion." The topic appears important to his conception of his subcreation, even though only a portion of the fourteen Valar receive credit for active participation in later events. Chapters 3 and 4 of this book will search for moments in *The Hobbit* and *The Lord of the Rings* when the Valar's invisible influence can be traced. Understanding each Vala and his or her Eru-given nature will facilitate such discernment.

Tolkien complicates his fourteen Valar by superimposing upon them several intersecting dimensions and attributes: physicality, gender, familial relation-ships, marital relationships, age, and language. Physical embodiment is not essential to the Valar, who were conceived as spirits prior to the creation of the physical world. Thus, the Valar take on physical presences only because they wish to honor the body-dependent Elves and Humans, whom they foresaw in vision. The relationship between the Valar and their physical manifesta-tions approximates, according to the "Ainulindalë", the relationship between Humans and clothing: the manifestation contributes to their identities, but is unnecessary to their being. The Valar, in other words, humanize themselves, appearing like the Children of Ilúvatar, though with greater splendor; they appear taller than Humans (though not giants), but they are not incarnated (in the sense that Christians understand Jesus Christ). Their visible dimen-sions do not come from the elements of Eä.[90] Instead, the Valar "clothe them[selves] in their own thought,"[91] making their own avatars. Coombs and Read have suggested the Valar's embodiment "involves knitting together molecules and atoms to form a working physical body," a procedure that "places severe restrictions on the activities available to the Valar."[92] However, when the Valar choose not to reveal themselves, they can be present though unperceived among Elves.[93]

While the Valar are not restricted to embodied existence, choosing to self-embody places at least temporary restrictions upon them. Embodiment decreases the power and precision with which a Vala can communicate tele-

pathically, an ability Tolkien calls ósanwe; embodiment makes such communication slower and less precise. In comparison with Elves and Humans,
a Vala can fully control its body; the Valar's mental powers operate more
effectively than those of embodied beings.[94]

Tolkien says (via the Elf scholar Pengoloð) that Eru's rules (axani) regarding
the Valar's operations within physical reality remain unknown to the Children
of Ilúvatar; apparently no rule forbids embodiment or its enjoyment. But either
a rule or a natural consequence of embodiment decrees that a spirit choosing
self-embodiment will experience the same needs as naturally incarnate beings.
Furthermore, possessing a body becomes habit-forming. The more a Vala
uses its body, the more the Vala relies upon it, especially if the divine being
indulges in bodily pleasures, such as drinking and eating; Tolkien briefly added
"begetting or conceiving" to this list, but then added that the Valar don't do
things such as begetting, and only eat and drink at festivals.[95]

But despite not procreating, when the Valar wish to appear materialized,
they do so in a gendered manner; they take "upon them forms some as of male
and some as of female." This wording suggests no biological gender (since
they lack biology), but only a gender-compatible appearance. Yet Tolkien
complicates this interpretation by asserting Eru-given gendered natures for
the Valar, even when disembodied. That gendered identity preceded their
entrance into Eä; Tolkien describes gender distinction as "difference of
temper" assigned by Eru at the Ainur's creation.[96] *Temper* in this context
suggests "mental constitution" or "habitual disposition."[97] Gender, Tolkien
implies, is as much a state of mind as it is a physical, chemical, or genetic
manifestation. It expresses physically an element of a Vala's spiritual nature.[98]
Watkins considers this "no inherent sexual gender, but in its place . . . a
predisposition toward a particular characteristic gender."[99] Thus Vala and
Valier represent, not male or female, but masculinity and femininity necessary,
in the view of Sly, "to a creativity based on the model of sexuality, but . . .
associated with particular spheres of influence."[100] While Vincent speculates
that the self-created nature of Valian avatars might allow cross-dressing, that
"a 'female' Valar could choose to wear a 'male' body much as a woman might
choose to wear a pair of trousers,"[101] Tolkien's writing suggests neither essential nor apparent gender ambiguity among the Valar.

Tolkien's depiction of Valian gender overlaps with that of his friend, C. S.
Lewis, in the second book of Lewis's space trilogy, *Perelandra* (a similarity
pointed out by Purtill in 1974[102]). When Lewis's hero, Elwin Ransom (based
loosely on J. R. R. Tolkien), meets the Oyarsa (or chief angels) of Mars

and Venus, they appear masculine and feminine, consecutively, though not because of apparent sex organs. Rather, Lewis's narrator suggests, masculine and feminine are categories that divide all creation, not just living beings. Instead of seeing gender as a mental or social construct that has accumulated around sexual difference, *Perelandra* depicts sexuality reflecting a preexisting categorical divide. Perhaps Tolkien influenced Lewis on this subject; at the very least, Lewis certainly read Tolkien's Silmarillion mythology prior to writing *Perelandra*. While I've found no direct reference to an Inklings discussion of gender as a spiritual concept, what *Perelandra* refers to as "the real meaning of gender,"[103] it seems a fair inference that Lewis and Tolkien discussed this topic.

Gender differences among the Valar allow familial and marital relationships. Seven Valar are masculine (the Valar proper) while seven are feminine (termed Valier). Tolkien pairs twelve of the Valar as spouses, while seven are related as siblings. Tolkien first speculated that spousal unions preceded the Valar's entrance into Eä, but later implied that such unions only occurred with the creation of Arda; one text describes the female Vala Varda as "taking female form [and becoming] the spouse of Manwë" only after entering Eä.[104] In contrast with Greek mythology, the Valar exhibit no temptation to incest, polygamy, or adultery; in fact, they display few sexual tendencies at all, with their procreation limited to "blameless, fruit-and-flower" varieties, in Burns's view.[105] Tolkien's Valar behave in a consistently elevated manner compared with the gods and goddesses of most mythologies.

Tolkien offers little explanation of what it means for the Valar to be spouses, offering only a marginal comment to "The Annals of Aman" that the concept of *spouse* should imply "only an 'association.'"[106] Marriage may indicate just an appearance, much like the Valar's bodies, solely for the benefit of Elves and Humans, perhaps because Valar spouses exhibit compatible and complementary traits. Spousal complementariness may, in fact, be the primary basis for gender division; those Valier with spouses typically have traits that depend on their husband's traits for their completion (though the converse is not necessarily true). Burns sees Valier in general as "more static, far more focused on service and providing what others need"[107] than their masculine counterparts. At the same time, a version of "The Annals of Aman" claims equality with their male counterparts for the Queens of the Valar in both majesty and power. Perhaps one Valier gives insight into the meaning of spousal relationships among the Valar when she says (speaking of Elf marriages) "Fëa perceiveth Fëa and knoweth the disposition of the other, in marriage especially."[108] *Fëa,* the Quenya word comparable to *spirit*, defines the nature of the Valar in Arda; from this perspective marriage implies a spiritual bond between spirit-beings, which does not imply a sexual dimension that would require physical bodies.

Brother-sister bonds seem incompatible with beings who were not born; as Tolkien's son Christopher notes, Tolkien did not explain sibling and parent-child relationships in regard to the Valar. If Eru fathered the Valar, then all fourteen should be siblings. Perhaps the relationships function more structurally to suggest an Eru-given closeness and compatibility, no doubt also part of the Valar's tempers but somehow different from spousal compatibility. Tolkien describes the nature of the word *brother* as applied to Manwë and Melkor using the words *equipotent* and *coëval* in the mind of Eru.[109] This suggests a further distinction referenced but not explained in Tolkien's cosmology: age. Vána, for example, is Yavanna's "younger sister";[110] *younger* is a difficult concept to interpret considering that both Yavanna and Vána's origins as Ainur occurred prior to the initiation of the flow of time (though without the flow of time, the phrase *prior to* becomes meaningless).

Age relationships may imply that Eru intended specific contrasts between certain Valar. *Older* may denote greater knowledge or wisdom placed into one Vala by Eru, even if the Valar were created simultaneously (just as one twin may possess greater maturity than his or her sibling). With this in mind, all the relationships here described, sibling, spousal, gendered, may reference interconnections and similarities/differences that Eru input into the Valar at their creation. The words describing those interconnections may have been chosen by the Valar (or even by the Elves) to describe the reality in terms accessible to the Children of Ilúvatar.

Tolkien contradicts himself on the question of whether the Valar need, possess, or even use language. According to Tolkien's essay "Ósanwe-kenta," the Valar do not depend on language for communication, though a few have formed a habit of language use, in the same way that some consistently self-embodied. Another document, "The Lhammas," claims the Valar have possessed language "from the beginning," which might imply language as an innate quality bestowed upon the Ainur at their creation; contrarily, since Tolkien uses the word *Valar* rather than *Ainur*, the Valar might have acquired language only on entering Eä (which was indeed the beginning of time). On the one hand, "The Lhammas" reinforce the latter interpretation by asserting that the Valar "wrought their tongue" in Arda; on the other hand, "wrought" can mean *shaped* rather than *created*. However, Tolkien asserts that the Valar neither need nor possess a language.[111]

Another Tolkien document cites a lack of evidence regarding Valian language, but argues that language use would seem a philosophical necessity. Since the Valar embody themselves, they must have donned all characteristics of embodied sentient beings, otherwise embodiment would lack purpose; since language forms a primary characteristic of sentient embodied beings, the Valar must have created a language, which Tolkien names Valarin. At the same time, the Valar possess the ability to understand languages without needing to learn them. Thus, since Valarin is difficult for the Elves to acquire, the Valar choose to communicate with the Elves using Quenya, the Elves' own tongue, by which they reveal the story of creation using symbolism comprehensible to the Elves.[112]

The Silmarillion states categorically one hierarchy of relationships among the Valar, and hints at further comparative hierarchies. Eight of the fourteen Valar possess a higher rank than the remaining six, and are known as the Aratar, or the High Ones. Furthermore, some Valar possess greater power than others (a concept promoted primarily with masculine Valar), while some receive more reverence from the Elves (a concept associated primarily with the Valier). Tolkien does not strictly adhere to this system, and therefore no thorough ranking of the fourteen emerges. Yet each Vala embraces a special interest, a duty, power, responsibility, or province. Over these each Vala functions as Master, apparently recognizing one another's separate authorities; the Elf Voronwë notes that in the south of Beleriand, where vegetation is especially lush, Ulmo (the Vala of water) serves Yavanna (the Valier of life-forms).[113] This specialization of the Valar further suggests "the gods of pagan mythologies," according to Flieger, "since each has a separate function and most have as well a particular role in, or connection with, an element of the earth."[114] Yet the Valar's roles, according to Burns, represent "a fairer distribution of talents or powers [with] more kindly personalities and a higher moral tone" than, for example, among the Norse gods. At the same time, since the Valar exhibited "no excess, no cruelty, no evil of any kind," but instead embrace "Loyalty, dedication, and service," the Valar's attributes seem, in Burns's words, "more like occupations or positions than manifestations of natural forces or strengths."[115]

Along with each Vala's sphere of interest and distinct relationships to other Valar, each has multiple names. Tolkien refers to these as nicknames, since the Elves bequeathed the names rather than Eru or the Valar themselves. Ultimately, the Valar have identities, but "no 'true' names"; yet the names suit the identities since the names identify some central aspect of the Valar's being, purpose, or activity. Multiple names for a given Vala stem both from multiple aspects of the Vala's identity as well as the different languages that develop such nicknames.[116]

The fourteen Valar take positions hierarchically superior to a host of lesser Ainur, called Maiar, spirit-beings who, like the Valar, find their origin in Eru Ilúvatar's thought, but possess less power and authority than the Valar.[117] Maiar typically seem "more local, suggesting demigods or inhabiting spirits," according to Flieger.[118] Like the Valar, these lesser spirits possess gendered natures and assume bodily forms at will; some embrace appearances resembling plants or animals.[119] Ents and Eagles may be examples of such beings. Only a few Maiar receive names in the mythology, most commonly because they associate with one or more of the Valar, whom they assist or serve.

✒ Manwë and Varda

Manwë and Varda function as king and queen of the Valar. Manwë, "highest and holiest," the "viceregent of Ilúvatar,"[120] grasps most fully Eru's design; the world bears the title the Kingdom of Manwë. His righteous nature gives him little insight into evil, though Tolkien speculates that Eru granted Manwë a special ability to perceive revelations from Eru, and in turn Eru remains open to hear and respond to Manwë. Eru reveals his will to the Valar via Manwë's introspection; one text provides a dialogue between Manwë and Eru, in which the two spirit-beings speak directly to one another. Manwë alone of the Valar perceives what might be called alternate realities, or the long-term effects of what-could-have-been had Elven or Human free wills chosen other than they did. Manwë delights in air and everything associated with it: clouds, winds, breezes, the heavens and the color blue, but also birds, which obey his command.[121] He also appreciates poetry, trumpets, and music in general. One of his epithets, *Súlimo,* means *the breather* or *Lord of the Breath of Arda.*[122] Over time Tolkien transformed his depiction of Manwë into a silent ruler whose reign extends back into prehistory; as to later eras, however, Manwë "watches but speaks no more."[123]

Manwë's spouse, Varda, bears several epithets attributed to her by the Elves: Elbereth, Star-Queen, commonly rendered Lady of the Stars, and Gilthoniel, star-kindler. Larsen has traced the development of Varda through the evolution of Tolkien's mythology, noting that she functions primarily as a "stelliferous interior decorator" in the early writings; she evolved into a more powerful being as Tolkien wrote *The Lord of the Rings*.[124] Elves love and revere Varda more than any other Vala, in part because she created the stars that gave the Elves much joy at their first awakening in Middle-earth. Her face (or rather, the face she puts on as her avatar, one presumes) displays "the light of Ilúvatar";[125] light, therefore, is her special element, as air is Manwë's. Manwë and Varda's spheres of interest obviously connect: light needs air and space; stars need the heavens. The heavens, in contrast, do not in the same way depend on light, though utter darkness seems unpleasant (for creatures with the ability to see) and typically suggests evil in Tolkien's legendarium.

Manwë and Varda rarely part and seldom leave their primary residence. From a literary standpoint, Tolkien suggests, Manwë should refrain from adventures; "The Government is always in Whitehall," he observes. Staying at home lends suspense to the unfolding events of Middle-earth; if the king himself goes to war, he risks the possibility of defeat, an inappropriate condition for a being with the cosmological status of Elder King. Manwë's aloofness from war may terminate at the Last Battle destined to end the world.[126]

Together Manwë and Varda augment one another's powers. Manwë's vision increases in Varda's presence, providing him the ability to see across great distances, through darkness and mist. Conversely, Varda in Manwë's presence hears more distinctly voices sounding far to the east. Varda's ability suggests she listens to appeals for help, perhaps acting in response (though Tolkien depicts Varda as a silent listener, rarely speaking herself except to her husband).[127] Responding to appeals positions Varda as a Marian figure, one whom lesser beings might entreat. Manwë, too, reacts to what he sees from afar; while *The Silmarillion* depicts Manwë more active in the First Age of Middle-earth than in later eras, even in the Third Age, Tolkien notes, Manwë is "still not a mere observer."[128]

Manwë and Varda each retain a Maiar attendant; Eönwë serves Manwë as banner-bearer or sword-bearer,[129] while Ilmarë functions as Varda's hand-maid. Manwë also sends Eagles into Arda to observe and gather news; some manuscripts imply Manwë created the Eagles (and thus that they are mere birds), while others, including *The Silmarillion,* pose the Eagles as spirit-beings, probably Maiar, who serve Manwë in Eagle form.

🖋 *Ulmo*

While Manwë holds the title of Lord of the Breath of Arda, Ulmo embraces the name Lord of Waters. Ulmo has no spouse; "he is alone," as the "Valaquenta" poignantly describes him. Hierarchically, he is second in power to Manwë, and Manwë's closest friend prior to the creation of Arda. After the creation, however, he rarely associates with the other Valar. The Elves call him Dweller in the Deep. Ulmo makes music via horns fashioned from shells, but most often he speaks with a voice that sounds like water; one poem celebrating Ulmo (there named Ylmir) describes ocean sounds in terms that resemble the Music of the Ainur.[130]

Ulmo only rarely embodies himself. When he does appear to Elves or Humans, he takes the shape of a rising wave in human form, with a foaming helm and shimmering mail in shades of green and silver,[131] resembling the scales of a fish; additionally, he wears a dark green kirtle that, like his mail, shimmers "with sea-fire,"[132] held in place by a pearl belt. Ulmo's overall impression gives the beholder the sense of movement in deep water illuminated by light from bioluminescent deep-sea creatures.[133]

Of all the Valar, Ulmo most actively involves himself in the affairs of Middle-earth, constantly working to support Elves and Humans. Elves perceive Ulmo exerting influence throughout the continent, due to his position controlling the flow of rivers, springs, lakes, and fountains. In contrast with Manwë and Varda, who watch and listen to Middle-earth from afar, Ulmo, like water itself, flows throughout Arda. This continuous presence results in an intimate understanding of the world. Though Ulmo only rarely visits the realm of the Valar, he maintains some means of communicating with Manwë, sharing information that otherwise would remain hidden.[134]

Several Maiar associate with Ulmo. Salmar created Ulmo's seashell horns. Better known, Ossë and Uinen embody as spouses the ocean's yin and yang, governing waves, tides, and currents. Ossë, associated with the coastline, delights in storms and Manwë's winds. Tolkien variously describes Ossë as rebellious against Ulmo due to jealousy, as forming alliances with Mandos against Ulmo, and as simply antisocial. Ossë's enthusiasm for storms at times angers some of the Valar. His wife Uinen identifies herself more with the depths and prefers calm to her husband's storm; mariners appeal to her to restrain the wildness of Ossë. She also cares for the ocean's plants and animals, which are referenced metaphorically as Uinen's hair.[135]

✿ *Aulë and Yavanna*

Manwë and Ulmo identify themselves with air and water, two of the major elements of classical philosophy. Not surprisingly, a third Vala, Aulë, identifies with the substance of earth and the lore associated with it. The trio of Manwë, Ulmo, and Aulë formed Arda, with Aulë particularly responsible for shaping lands. Aulë embraces crafts such as weaving, woodwork, farming, animal husbandry, and chemistry, but especially lapidary work with gems and gold; yet Aulë lacks possessiveness, and thus he readily teaches others his skills.

Aulë wedded Yavanna, the Giver of Fruits. She created and protects plants, and appears tall, wearing a green robe before Elves and Humans, at times resembling a great tree. She symbolically takes root in her husband's element, the earth, but also connects with Ulmo's water, while Manwë's winds rustle her leaves. Elves refer to Yavanna as Kementári, Queen of the Earth, or Palúrien, the Lady of the Wide Earth. When tree-like, Yavanna resembles Yggdrasil, the cosmic Ash of Nordic mythology, though *The Silmarillion* depicts Yavanna as a character, actively engaging with the world around her, rather than an underlying structure supporting the world.

Several Maiar associate with Aulë and Yavanna, though not within *The Silmarillion*. *Unfinished Tales* connect Curumo, who becomes Saruman, to Aulë, and Aiwendil, who becomes Radagast, to Yavanna. Sauron may also have associated with Aulë prior to being perverted to evil by Melkor. Much as Manwë sent Eagles into Middle-earth, Yavanna sent the Ents, Shepherds of the Trees. The Ents may be spirits that reside in trees, or perhaps they have come to resemble trees over time.[136] Alternatively, *The Silmarillion*'s ambiguous wording suggests a theory that the Ents are Ainur called into Arda long after its creation.[137]

✿ *The Fëanturi, Their Spouses and Sibling*

Námo and Irmo, brothers known as the Fëanturi (Masters of Spirits), are more commonly known by the names of their domains, Mandos and Lórien, respectively. Mandos maintains the dwelling places of the dead, the Halls of Mandos; at Manwë's bidding, Mandos pronounces law, doom, and judgment, though often his pronouncements are Delphic.[138]

Tolkien classifies Mandos's pronouncements of dooms into three categories:

1. those from Manwë or from the Valar as a group; such pronouncements become binding even on the Valar, and thus some amount of time passes between the decision and its pronouncement.
2. those concerning the dead, who are under Mandos's authority; these decisions become laws, though pertaining only to individual cases or persons; also irrevocable, time passes between the decision and the pronouncement (at least ten Valian years in cases whether Elves should be allowed to reincarnate).
3. those that come from Mandos under his own authority, determining innocence or guilt resulting from events within Arda; Mandos, for example, judges the dead as to the manner of their deaths as well as their actions and characters prior to death; as a result, he determines the nature and the length of their waiting period within his halls post-death.

Mandos formulates decrees only after due consideration, and carefully examines deceased Children of Ilúvatar who have accumulated significant guilt while alive; thus, the Elves formed the saying, "Who among the Living can presume the dooms of Mandos?"[139]

Mandos possesses a perfect knowledge of both past and future, except for future actions initiated by Eru Ilúvatar that did not appear within the Music of the Ainur.[140] Mandos's alignment with the Music positions him at times in apparent conflict with Ulmo; Mandos embraces the Music as fate, often viewing it legalistically, while Ulmo views himself as an agent of Eru's actions that have been hidden from the other Valar. Mandos's spouse, Vairë, weaves "storied webs" that incorporate all the events of Arda. While Mandos remembers, Vairë records; she embodies history. Her webs, like tapestries, decorate the Halls of Mandos, which progressively expand with time as they include more webs, and more dead.[141]

Lórien (also called Olofantur) produces visions and dreams.[142] Early in the development of the legendarium, Tolkien wrote of Lórien as creator of Olórë Mallë, a Path of Dreams by which Human children in Middle-earth might experience visions of Aman, a concept Tolkien abandoned in later writings. Lórien keeps the most beautiful garden in Arda, where even the Valar come for refreshment among its plants and fountains. Supplementing the tonic aura, Lórien's spouse, Estë, functions as healer, physically, mentally, and spiritually. Estë sleeps by day on an island within her spouse's realm. At one point Tolkien conceived of Estë as the chief Maia,[143] but in

The Silmarillion she holds the status of Vala, with whom two Maiar are associated.

One of those Maiar, Melian, possesses a striking beauty, immense wisdom, and skill as singer of enchantments; she taught the Nightingales their song, though when she herself sings, all Valinor goes silent and even the fountains stop. Though a Maia, she was related to Yavanna even before the creation of Arda, which suggests that the Valar/Maiar hierarchy exists exclusively within Eä, rather than continuing a preexisting dichotomy among the Ainur. In Middle-earth she uses her power to preserve, establishing around Doriath a protective barrier that prevents entrance by undesirable elements. Melian's Elvish protégé, Galadriel, later mimicks Melian by establishing Lothlórien.[144]

Gandalf may also be a Maian follower of Estë, though Tolkien wrote ambiguously about this. *The Silmarillion* associates Olórin, wisest of the Maiar, with Estë. *The Lord of the Rings* briefly mentions Olórin in "The Window on the West" chapter of *The Two Towers*. Faramir quotes to Frodo words that Gandalf spoke on one of his visits to Minas Tirith, enumerating the various names assigned him throughout the lands of Middle-earth, including the phrase, "Olórin I was in my youth in the West that is forgotten."[145] Tolkien remains somewhat cagey regarding whether Gandalf-Olórin is the same Olórin mentioned as Estë's follower. One important essay on the Istari (the five Wizards mentioned in appendix B of *The Return of the King*) lacks the name Olórin; another document explicitly identifies Olórin as Gandalf, as does a 1971 letter.[146] Elsewhere Tolkien notes that some residents of Middle-earth toward the end of the Third Age believed Gandalf to be the last embodiment of Manwë. Tolkien expresses doubt about that belief, suggesting the Valar would send as emissary someone of equal rank with Sauron (that is, a Maia). But then Tolkien asserts authorial ignorance as to Gandalf's true identity. This study will presume Gandalf to be Olórin, in part because it adds layers of interest to a study of Middle-earth's cosmology; as Shippey notes, if Gandalf is the Maia Olórin, then he is essentially an angel, "very unlike the traditional image of an angel, with his long beard and short temper, but an 'angel' just the same."[147]

Nienna, sister of Mandos and Lórien, is the only Valier described hierarchically in *The Silmarillion* according to power, as "mightier than Estë." Her specialty involves mourning the ills of Arda, though hers is an other-oriented grief that produces pity and hope (qualities that she inspired in the Maia Olórin, who often visited her). Grief forms such an essential part of her being that her singing in the Great Music of the Ainur turned to lamentation; because Nienna wove musical expression of grief into the Great Music, grief became an essential element in Arda's unfolding. Yet since her nature encompasses grief, it must have preceded Melkor's introduction of evil into the Singing; in other words, Nienna perceived grief prior to having something to grieve. Her existence suggests anticipation or foreknowledge on the part of Eru Ilúvatar, as if he knew actions of his own created beings would produce a world in which grief would form a component. Like Ulmo, Nienna has no spouse, and only infrequently mixes with other Valar; while she has a dwelling place on the very edge of Arda, she spends most of her time in the Halls of Mandos, where the dead call to her.[148]

❦ *Tulkas and Nessa, Oromë and Vána*

Tulkas, the most powerful Vala in activities requiring strength, entered Arda last (fifteen hundred Valian years after the other Valar entered Eä), and he came with the express purpose of battling Melkor, at whom Tulkas openly laughs. Tulkas thus represents the positive dimension of violence in the battle of good versus evil, which Tolkien explains as unwillingness to compromise and preference for action over talk. Tolkien associates Tulkas with the Norse god Thor, even though Aulë more commonly uses a hammer.

Tulkas's spouse, Nessa, is a fast runner who loves deer and dancing on the green lawns of Valinor's rose gardens.[149] Tulkas and Nessa wedded at some point after Tulkas entered the world; Nessa's name, in fact, means *bride*, though Tolkien also translates her name as "she that has manlike valour or strength."[150] Thus she is a huntress, but, as Burns points out with irony, one "who never actually hunts."[151] Her names associate her with flowers (specifically pansies) and spring.[152]

Oromë, Nessa's brother, possesses less strength than Tulkas, but greater intimidation when roused to anger. His love of the hunt prompts him to breed the Mearas, the long-lived horses that the Noldorin Elves bring to Middle-earth as part of Fëanor's rebellion. In the early eras of Middle-earth history, Oromë rides his horse Nahar and hunts evil creatures in Middle-earth. Oromë trains the Maiar who associate with him to pursue Melkor's followers.

Oromë also has a passion for trees, a trait that might produce, among lesser gods, an awkwardness, since he marries Vána, the younger sister of Yavanna, the Valier of trees and other vegetation. Vána, the Ever-Young, associates with flowers blooming, birds singing, and the coming of spring.[153] Several Maiar connect to Oromë and Vána. Tilion and Arien become the spirits that guide the sun and the moon on their paths across Arda. Two others, Alatar and Pallando, become the Blue Wizards.

✍ Melkor, Sauron, Ungoliant, and Balrogs

The Silmarillion emphasizes that Melkor should not be considered one of the Valar, though Eru Ilúvatar intended such a role for him. Tolkien describes Melkor and Manwë as coeval, brothers in the mind of Ilúvatar. In fact, Melkor should have been the more powerful of the two (his name means "He who arises in might"),[154] but turning away from Eru progressively reduces him.[155] In Tolkien's earliest conception Melkor possessed a portion of all the Valar's powers, though due to his fall, he becomes the only Vala to experience fear. While intended as Manwë's brother, Melkor most resembles Aulë in thinking and strength. Melkor's centrality to the mythology grew in the post–*Lord of the Rings* decades as Tolkien's writings became ever more theological.[156]

Like the Valar, Melkor could, at first, choose to appear embodied. But unlike the Valar, Melkor has become bound by his body. His overpowering hatred weakened him, preventing his self-restoration. Ultimately, he lost the ability to modify his embodied appearance, as evidenced by his battle with Fingolfin. As Melkor became permanently attached to his embodied form, it fused into a highly unattractive appearance. Simultaneous with body dependence came reliance on physical weapons, particularly Grond, the Hammer of the Underworld.[157] Melkor has no spouse, in part because evil is barren. Melkor, Tolkien asserted, lacks the ability to procreate. Instead, Melkor has dissipated his power into his minions and into the elements of Middle-earth; when separated from his followers, he possesses no more power than any other Vala.[158]

Just as the Valar have unnamed Maiar associated with them, so, too, does Melkor; Tolkien once termed these the Umaiar. Melkor discovered that approaching a less powerful being with a forceful mind and will induces a sense of pressure and fear, which tends to close that mind to him. Thus, he chooses stealth and deceit to gain access to other minds through trust. The Maiar who first come under his influence already possess rebellious natures but lack Melkor's ruthlessness; such Maiar perceive Melkor's leadership potential in a rebellion against Eru. In contrast, uncorrupted individuals reject Melkor and close their minds to him, based on promptings from their consciences.[159]

Some Maiar who follow Melkor into rebellion apparently choose to continue in rebellion against all authority, even Melkor's, at least until he has proven his ability to contend with the Valar. Others side with the Valar until Melkor reveals his increasing strength; "The Annals of Aman" places some of those Maiar in "the voids of Eä." It further suggests the possibility that some Maiar may have been converted to Melkor's cause only after their coming to Aman, rather than in the Music of the Ainur. One manuscript similarly identifies many lesser beings (presumably Maiar) who willingly submit to him as he builds a fortress, Utumno, in the North of Middle-earth. *The Book of Lost Tales* describes spirit-beings with a natural tendency toward gloominess who reside in Mandos's realm. Melkor perverts these spirit-beings to their detriment during his imprisonment in the Halls of Mandos; one of these later serves as Melkor's herald.[160]

Sauron, the best known of the Ainur who submit to Melkor, becomes in the Second and Third Ages what Melkor had been in the First Age: the most powerful force of evil. While Melkor possessed greater native power than Sauron, Sauron inherits a world already infected with Melkor's evil. Though Sauron originally possessed less power than Melkor, Sauron focuses his power on one primary motive, to dominate the minds and wills of creatures, and on one primary object, the Ring of Power.[161] Yet, Sauron remains subordinate to Melkor, even paying at least lip service to him long after Melkor disappears from Arda. The "Valaquenta" associates Sauron with Aulë, whose knowledge of gems and crafts forms an ideal background to a ring maker.[162]

Ungoliant may have been a Maia associated with Melkor, as Abbott and Sookoo conclude.[163] If this speculation is correct, she may have been one of the Ainur who followed Melkor's lead in the Singing of the Ainur.[164] Bridoux interprets Ungoliant's passion for light to speculate that she may have served Varda. Apeland, however, claims Tolkien defined Ungoliant as "a name of the Primeval Night," and thus "the principle of Chaos and Old Night, the darkness before Creation, familiar from the pagan mythological traditions";[165] Apeland concludes that Ungoliant could not, therefore, have been a former Maia.

The Balrogs are very likely Maiar. Tolkien describes the Balrogs as primeval servants of Melkor, operating by means of destructive fire. In one narrative, Tolkien depicts a thousand Balrogs participating in a single battle, with more than forty killed in the attack leading to the fall of Gondolin. Tolkien even implies that Melkor had means of multiplying the Balrogs' numbers; later he revised his thinking to suggest only a handful of Balrogs ever existed, in the range of three to seven.[166] In the First Age the Balrogs served as Melkor's torturers, slave drivers, and warriors. *The Fellowship of the Ring* depicts a Balrog as shadow-like, in the shape of a Human, with fire as its essence.[167]

Spirits of flame reveals that the four classical elements are left incomplete among the Valar; Tolkien created no Vala of fire. Melkor may have been intended by Eru Ilúvatar as the fire god, as Shippey boldly asserts.[168] On at least one occasion early in crafting his legendarium Tolkien referred to Melkor with the adjective *fiery*, though he is also called the Vala of Iron.[169] Melkor's background suggests fire; he first entered the Void seeking the Flame Imperishable, but, according to the "Valaquenta," he then "descended through fire and wrath into a great burning, down into Darkness."[170] An early name list associates Melkor (at that time named Melko) with the Quenya word *velk*, translated as *flame*; at the same time, Melkor's name associates with cold, winter, and monster.[171]

Whether Melkor should have been Arda's Vala of fire, the existence of evil spirits of flame suggests the possibility of good spirits of flame. Indeed, Arien, the Maia given the task of guiding the sun, appears as pure fire when not seen as her avatar. *The Silmarillion* further describes her as a fire spirit who resisted Melkor's deceptions.[172] Such a statement implies that many, perhaps most, fire spirits became embroiled in Melkor's rebellion, perhaps because of a special affinity among them; such an affinity makes sense if Melkor, too, is a spirit of fire.

Gandalf also displays a special affinity with fire, wielding "the secret flame of Anor"[173] and best known among Hobbits for his fireworks. Gandalf augments his abilities with fire through use of the Elf-ring Narya; Tolkien's writings remain unclear as to whether the ring provides Gandalf's skills with fire, or whether instead he possesses such skills as part of his pre-Arda, Eru-given nature. Because Tolkien associates Anor with the sun, Gandalf's assertion before the Balrog on the bridge of Khazad-dûm suggests an affinity with Arien; perhaps both, along with the Balrogs, originally shared an affinity with fire.

The ways in which Tolkien complicates the Valar seem irrelevant to Melkor and his associates. The legendarium contains only two great female evil beings, Ungoliant and Shelob, both spider-like, and both associated with irrationality. Only physicality applies to Melkor and his followers, and in fact embodiment often traps both Melkor and Sauron, who eventually lose the ability to exist as pure spirits. While both experience a demise that transforms them back into a spirit nature, those transformations reduce both to apparent impotence.

✍ Conclusion

After personifying and humanizing the Valar as hunters, wrestlers, and dancers, as lords and ladies, and as spouses and siblings, the "Valaquenta" pulls back from anthropomorphism to explain their appearances as only that: appearances, making them comprehensible to the Elves; the avatars necessarily reduce the Valar's reality, as if their power and beauty can be perceived only when veiled.[174] The Valar remain mysterious, beyond comprehension by the creatures of Middle-earth, and thus, Tolkien implies, they remain beyond the comprehension of readers too. As *The Silmarillion* progresses from description in the "Valaquenta" to the narratives and histories of the "Quenta Silmarillion," the Valar appear less as beings and more as actors, supporting the subordinate life-forms of Middle-earth. The two images combine to reveal a fuller picture of the Valar, suggesting that just one mode of comprehension, either ontology (being) or deontology (doing), is inadequate without the other.

As divine beings acting within Eä, the Valar function as gods of Arda: they shape the Earth, much like the Hebrew Yahweh of Genesis chapter 1; they work and feast, much like the Greek gods in Hesiod's *Theogony;* they engage in battle as in the Norse Eddas. The "Ainulindalë" claims the Valar perpetually support all Arda with "minute precision"; as the powers of the world, they exist simultaneously as characters with wills, communicating and acting, and as the forces of nature: gravity, the energy of light, and the life force. "They are [Arda's] life and it is theirs."[175] In Kreeft's words, the Valar are "more than natural forces . . . , more than concrete individual superhuman persons . . . , and more than feelings, images or concepts within . . . thought, dreams, or imagination . . . , but they are the source and unity of all three."[176]

Yet with the Valar and Maiar in the foreground, Eru Ilúvatar disappears into the background, remaining all but invisible even to the Valar. "Of Aulë and Yavanna" records two moments in which Eru intrudes into the affairs of the Valar. In the first intrusion, Eru reprimands Aulë on his construction of the Dwarves; Eru speaks to Aulë directly, ultimately accepting Aulë's work and granting the Dwarves sentience. Later, as Yavanna foresees that those Dwarves will exhibit no love for trees except as firewood, she unburdens her heart to Manwë, who contemplates her words and enters a dream-like state. Manwë perceives himself immersed once again in the Singing of the Ainur, yet attending to many elements previously ignored.

As part of his vision, Manwë perceives Eru Ilúvatar's power sustaining the efforts of the Valar; Eru is the one true god, the deity behind the apparent deities. Manwë perceives Eru introducing unexpected elements that have re-mained hidden from the Ainur.[177] This opens the possibility that Eru himself intervenes in the history of Arda, sometimes in ways perceived by the Valar, sometimes unknown even to them. Tolkien's image of divine collaboration, of polytheistic monotheism, forms a cosmological structure unique among the mythologies of planet Earth.

Chapter 2

The Valar in the World

hile the story of Eä had been foreshown in the Vision based on the Music of the Ainur, it remains unclear exactly what Eru Ilúvatar creates when he speaks the material universe into existence and what the Valar find on entering time and space.[1] *The Book of Lost Tales* depicts Manwë and Varda flying through three levels of atmosphere to arrive at land masses already formed into continents, surrounded by seas, and meddled with by Melkor.[2] Later texts, in contrast, suggest that Eru's pronouncement of *Eä* only initiates phase 3 of the creation process; upon entering Eä, the Valar encounter what might be described as a primordial mess. The world they had come to love through the vision of the Ainur does not yet exist. All is darkness, unformed, and only "on point to begin."[3]

Tolkien's later description resembles his translation of the creation scene in "The Lay of the Völsungs": "unwrought was Earth, / unroofed was Heaven— / an abyss yawning."[4] At the beginning of time, the "Ainulindalë" suggests, the Valar begin a protracted period of labor, long before the appearance of the Children of Ilúvatar. An alternate version describes the Music of the Ainur as a foreshadow of what could be, indicating that the Valar will need to achieve what had been foresung.[5] As Garbowski words it, the Valar must "metaphorically roll up their sleeves"[6] and make the world into what they had witnessed in Eru's vision. Yet as Yavanna notes, the Vision did not last long and soon disappeared, so that Eru's full design remains unclear to the Valar.[7]

The Valar foresee that they cannot foretell the timing of two moments central to Middle-earth's future: the births of the Children of Eru, Elves and Humans. The Valar's anticipation of the Children highlights the extent of their ignorance, which negatively impacts both divine and material beings. Eru keeps the timing of the birth of his Children exclusively to himself, and gives little advance information about their natures. This secrecy foregrounds Eru's sovereignty over the Children, as well as over the Valar and Maiar, and reiterates the monotheistic nature of the universe. Yet Eru's absence, his apparent invisibility, creates circumstances in which the Valar seem to be the powers of Arda when those Children finally appear; Eru, in other words, uses his power as the sole god of the universe to sanction circumstances that will leave the Valar as the apparent multiple gods of Arda.

Positioning the Valar as the surrogate gods of Arda while providing them limited knowledge of the sentient material beings destined to inhabit that world leads, perhaps inevitably, to conflict, especially with Melkor's continuing influence toward rebellion. This chapter will examine the work of the Valar in forming Middle-earth as the destined home of the Children of Ilúvatar, and the interactions of the Valar with Elves and Humans throughout the First and Second Ages of Middle-earth. Knowledge of that divine intervention will explain the limited direct divine involvement in the Third Age, and uncover keys for finding invisible divine intervention in the War of the Rings.

The Valar's Continuing Creation

Rather than a sudden Genesis-like creation producing a fully-shaped Earth in a mere six days, Tolkien's later mythology implies long, slow, evolutionary development, though accomplished through the work of the Valar, whom Kane describes as "secondary creators," serving under Eru, the primary creator.[8] One pre–*Lord of the Rings* document (the "Later Annals of Valinor") suggests almost 20,000 Middle-earth years passed prior to the appearance of Elves. Elsewhere ("The Annals of Aman") Tolkien implies a number twice that size, 41,040 years. Yet Tolkien further complicates these numbers; "The Annals of Aman" suggests the Valar long worked to shape Eä even before entering it; Tolkien has described that work as demiurgic.[9] Since time begins only when the Valar enter Eä, their earlier work is both immeasurable and lasting no time at all.

The "Ainulindalë" and chapter 1 of the "Quenta Silmarillion" describe the Valar's earliest efforts as topographical and geological. The Valar shape mountains, valleys, and seas, subduing fire under the earth. At first, Melkor seems one of the Valar, expressing a desire to prepare Middle-earth for the arrival of the Children of Ilúvatar, specifically by bringing under control the extremes of hot and cold that his singing contributed to Middle-earth. Yet the narrator of *The Silmarillion* claims Melkor dissembles in this explanation, and that he harbors from the beginning a secret desire to dominate rather than serve. Thus, the early work of the Valar and Melkor soon encompasses a yin and yang of creation and destruction, as the Valar create structure while Melkor works to ruin it.[10] Crowe thus refers to Melkor as "the first and greatest of the unmakers of Arda."[11]

The description of this contradictory labor anthropomorphizes the Valar and Melkor: when the Valar shape land masses, Melkor causes their destruction; as they dig valleys, Melkor fills them in; as they create seas, "Melkor spill[s] them." Melkor "h[olds] sway with violence."[12] The description, though elevated in tone, compares to that of a spiteful child stomping on his playmates' sand castle (and indeed, this comparison appropriately suggests how low Melkor has stooped). Furthermore, the description sounds like a rapid process, as if one could sit along the sidelines as a bystander watching the Valar delve a valley and Melkor promptly filling it back in.

Yet other language, and the lengths of time described earlier, suggest a gradual process of shaping Middle-earth: "*slowly* nonetheless the Earth was fashioned and made firm."[13] The Valar's work, in other words, might resemble, or in fact be, natural processes; a mountain might be thrown down and a valley raised up through erosion and other natural causes. In this labor the Valar personify natural phenomena, as Tolkien describes in one theory of the origin of the Greek gods.[14] Within the context of *The Silmarillion,* the Valar function simultaneously as *beings* with whom Elves can interrelate, and *forces* that underlie the creation of Middle-earth. Later passages show the Valar continuing to underpin and influence natural substances. Ulmo, for example, as the Valar of water, remains more than just a being outside of water that relishes and controls it. Rather Ulmo in some sense *is* water, or resides throughout water. The Valar, Tolkien implies, cannot be reduced either to spirit-beings or earth-forces; they encompass both simultaneously, the divine presences that make true the observation during the Vision of the Ainur that "it seemed to them that [Arda] lived and grew."[15]

This role of continuous support for Arda's existence comes at a cost. Goñi sums up the closed nature of Eä, which "implies that Power must be applied to the modeling of creation until it reaches its completeness. Thus, as Creation is perfected, the amount of available Power diminishes even for the Valar."[16] In other words, the more energy the Valar put into Arda, the less energy the Valar have at their disposal (though Tolkien hints that Valar at rest recoup some of their energies). Tolkien uses a word for this long-term transformation of the Valar that he also applies to the Elves: *fading.* The Valar, he says, fade toward impotency as Arda becomes more precisely shaped. They resemble architects who become less and less important as a building nears completion.[17]

The Silmarillion's description of the Valar and Melkor's early work portrays good and evil as an unequal binary. The Valar (and thus ultimately Eru) receive credit for all work of creation, while all work of destruction is attributed to Melkor (and thus *not* to Eru, though it will ultimately, Eru claims, reveal itself as derivative from him and contributing to his glory). The Middle-earth pantheon contains no Vishnu, no single force encompassing both creation and destruction. Furthermore, the brief description of the Valar's and Melkor's work sounds as if Melkor completely eradicates the valleys and mountains shaped by the Valar, but a later passage (not to mention the existence of Middle-earth throughout Tolkien's writings) makes clear evil lacks the strength of good; "slowly *nonetheless* the Earth was fashioned and made firm."[18] In context *nonetheless* means *in spite of* Melkor's work of destruction.

Yet all aspects of the Valar's work in shaping Middle-earth feel the impact of Melkor's meddling; everything about Arda differs in some way from the Valar's original intention. Melkor takes a two-stage strategy in his efforts. First, he seeks to destroy or undo the Valar's efforts; yet if he cannot undo them, or if he feels he can use them to his advantage, he corrupts them. Middle-earth thus remains different from and less than the design of the Valar; Tolkien terms this *Arda marred.* At the same time, Melkor's work to destroy or corrupt steadily reduces his inherent power; said another way, Melkor's power becomes dispersed into the elements of Arda, to such an extent that Christopher Tolkien describes Middle-earth as the metaphysical parallel of Sauron's ring.[19] As with the Valar, the energy expended by Melkor in destruction and corruption reduces his available reserves of energy; just as the Valar fade, so, too, does Melkor.

The number of beings involved also contributes to the success of good over evil: fourteen Valar to one Melkor. At least some of the Ainur who joined their singing to Melkor's discord in the Music of the Ainur elect not to enter Eä; presumably they remain with Eru, and apparently in his good graces, forgiven if they have offended Eru, healed if Melkor has victimized them. According to one text, many of the Ainur, presumably Maiar, who enter Eä after joining with Melkor's singing, choose not (or at least not yet) to submit to his dictatorial leadership; such beings must either function along with the Valar in shaping Arda (and thus work in opposition to Melkor) or work independently, as minor rebels against both the Valar and Melkor. In fact, the dissonance produced in the Singing of the Ainur causes evil elements within Arda that do not result from Melkor's intention; "they [are] *not* 'his children,'" according to one text, and thus those evil beings hate Melkor as much as they hate the Valar.[20]

Though evil remains weaker than good, the contest between the two does not always clearly favor the Valar. One version of the "Ainulindalë" suggests Melkor's earliest work caused massive fires that filled Arda. The opening chapter of the "Quenta Silmarillion" describes the early conflict between the Valar and Melkor as a war, adding that for long it appeared Melkor would prevail. Only the arrival of the Vala Tulkas tips the power differential against Melkor, who flees into darkness outside Arda, resulting in a long era of peace, the Spring of Arda. Yet the conflict between Melkor and the Valar permanently etches the surface of Arda; the narrative "Of Tuor and His Coming to Gondolin" speaks of mountains surrounding that hidden city as carved by the Valar's hands in wars from Arda's earliest history, while *The Silmarillion* mentions mountains raised by Melkor in an effort to prevent Oromë from riding in Middle-earth.[21]

The Valar use the Spring of Arda to transform the continent of Middle-earth into a habitable realm, with specific Valar contributing based on their natures. Yavanna plants the seeds that she devised over long eons. Aulë produces two massive lamps, Illuin and Ormal, at Yavanna's request, presumably to provide the light needed to foster life. Varda fills Aulë's lamps and Manwë blesses them, producing biological life on Middle-earth; both plants (in particular, mosses, grasses, ferns, and trees) and animals appear (though neither flowers nor birds, or at least no singing birds; the first record of birds singing in Middle-earth occurs on the arrival of Melian the Maia, at about the same time that the Elves appear). The Valar produce a dwelling place for themselves (one account attributes its construction to Aulë) on the island Almaren in the midst of a large lake, which itself apparently lies in the middle of the continent.[22]

Having labored continuously, the Valar take a Sabbath rest to observe the unfolding of life-forms before them, to feast, and to celebrate the wedding of Tulkas and Nessa. During this period of unwariness, Melkor surreptitiously returns through the Walls of the Night with a host of like-minded though lesser spirits (presumably Maiar) to establish the fortress of Utumno in the far north.[23] The renewed presence of evil mars the Spring of Arda: plants begin to decay, rivers become clogged with weeds, swamps emerge with numerous flies, and animals become monstrously violent, with tusks and horns. Just as texts attribute creation to the Valar and destruction to Melkor, the narratives similarly associate birth and spring with the Valar and decay and death with Melkor; his return marks the end of the initial Edenic period of life's history in Middle-earth.

The battle resulting from Melkor's attack on the two lamps disturbs continents and oceans, marring Arda's symmetry. Melkor induces earthquakes and volcanic explosions, which further produce storms and tidal waves; some dry land sinks beneath the ocean, turning mountains into islands and creating new coastline. Bringing under control the resulting chaos prevents the Valar from pursuing Melkor, who retreats to Utumno; Melkor's work of destruction continues to unleash effects even after Melkor leaves the scene of battle.[24]

As the Valar regain control of the elements of Middle-earth, they develop a new strategy for their involvement in the world, a strategy that produces the cosmologic structure of the planet through the First and most of the Second Ages. Just as Eru Ilúvatar distances himself from his creation by remaining primarily outside the universe, the Valar choose to distance themselves from the continent of Middle-earth, where they know the Children of Ilúvatar will first appear. They wish to create a safe zone for intelligent life. Since they do not know precisely when or where the Children will appear, they fear that violent upheavals of the earth, as in their recent war with Melkor, might destroy the Children before their presence becomes known to the Valar.

So the Valar leave Middle-earth to establish a new realm in Aman, the continent to the west of their former residence. The resulting picture of physical reality, further expressed in "The Ambarkanta," suggests a more-or-less flat world within a spherical universe. The Walls of the Night, or Ilurambar, enclose the universe, Eä, forming a transparent barrier as clear as glass or ice but firm as steel; this barrier forms the boundary between material reality and that which remains outside (the "Ainulindalë" names the outside the Void, while another text names it the Eldest Dark).[25] The ban on the Valar's leaving Eä prohibits their crossing the Walls of Night, though Melkor may successfully cross it twice, once when Tulkas chases him out of Arda, and again on his secret return.

The sole gateway through Ilurambar is the Moritarnon, the Door of Night. *The Book of Lost Tales* describes the door as huge and black with pillars and lintel of basalt carved in the shape of dragons; smoke slowly oozes from the dragons' jaws. The unbreakable gates open only by means of a spell. Elves are forbidden to pass the Door, though no text suggests any feasibility of the Elves (other than Eärendil) even getting *to* the Door; passing through would allow Elf or Human to escape death and acquire knowledge not yet appropriate for the Children of Eru.[26] Within the Walls of the Night are three layers of atmosphere, Vaiya, Ilmen, and Vista (from outermost to innermost). Vaiya perhaps resembles deep space, though like water below and air above. Ilmen forms the stratum of stars, while Vista subdivides into a layer of clouds and a layer for birds' flight. At this stage of its development, Arda has neither sun nor moon.

Intersecting the sphere of the universe, a flat Earth consists of water surrounding multiple continents. The water between the Walls of the Night and the continents is the Outer Sea, or Ekkaia; the continents and oceans then form the world, Arda. Within Arda the western shore of Aman looks upon the Outer Sea, though its eastern shore faces Belegaer, also named the Great Sea of the West; across Belegaer lies the west coast of Middle-earth. Middle-earth deserves its name, in part, because it lies literally in the middle of Arda, between Aman to its west and an unknown continent to its east.[27] The name *Middle-earth* also connects Tolkien's legendarium to the medieval understanding of Earth "as placed between heaven and hell."[28]

While the "Ainulindalë" accounts for a vast creation, Arda remains its dramatic focal point. The Elves speculate that other worlds can exist and that other times may have existed, perhaps with their own sentient life-forms, their own creations and histories. But Arda, and the Children of Eru, are "the present concern of Eä," not because of Arda's innate importance, nor even because Arda houses the Children of Eru; rather, Arda gains importance as the site of Melkor's rebellion against Ilúvatar. One text describes Melkor as the most important exponent of revolution against Eru, not simply the chief influence of evil in Arda.[29]

Because the Valar cannot subdue Melkor, they fortify their new realm by building a tall mountain chain, the Pelóri, along the east coast of Aman; Tolkien identifies this work as the Valar's final demiurgic effort. Their expenditure of energy may be misguided, or perhaps actually bad; while it seeks to preserve, it implies a motive of selfishness, neglect, or (worse yet) despair. The Valar's desire to preserve the products of their work parallels the efforts of Elves such as Círdan, Elrond, and Galadriel during the Third

Age. At least one Vala, Ulmo, opposes the project. Yet Tolkien undercuts his criticism of the Valar by speculating that Elvish and Human thinking inherited Melkor's evil, and thus their cosmological suppositions reflect Melkor's lies.[30]

The Valar transform the region west of the Pelóri, Valinor, into their new realm. The first chapter of the "Quenta Silmarillion" describes a land replete with gardens, mansions, towers, and geographical features, all dutifully named (and often renamed in the various tongues of the Elves): Taniquetil (the mountain of Manwë and Varda, on which sit Manwë's throne and Varda's halls), Valmar (the Valar's city, filled with the sounds of bells), Ezellohar (a green mound, hallowed by Yavanna, before the western gate of Valmar); Máhanaxar (the Ring of Doom situated on Ezellohar, where the Valar sit upon thrones and hold council).[31] Furthest to the west Mandos establishes Halls where the spirits of dead sentient beings can dwell in rest. *The Book of Lost Tales* describes those halls as vast caves dug underground and even under the sea.

In Aman the Valar establish an uncorrupted paradise: unhindered by Melkor, trees and flowers do not wither and no life-forms experience death. Grapevines for wine production fill the valleys. Yavanna maintains pastures and wheat fields, while Oromë preserves an area of wild forest. Strange and beautiful creatures, unknown in Middle-earth, live in peace, since there are no predators; even the stones and streams receive a Valian blessing.[32] Aman remains what Middle-earth should have been, had Melkor not corrupted it.

The greatest creations of the Valar in Aman, and items central to the subsequent history of Elves and Humans, are the Two Trees of Valinor: Telperion and Laurelin. The light from the trees waxes and wanes in intensity and in opposing and overlapping schedules. The creation of the Two Trees marks the beginning of timekeeping in Arda. Estimates of the age of Middle-earth, therefore, are calculated backwards from the creation of the Two Trees, presumably by the Valar themselves. The Two Trees' liquid light marks the beginning of The Bliss of Valinor (which, according to the "Later Annals of Valinor," lasts one thousand years of Aman, roughly equivalent to ten thousand Middle-earth years).[33]

During The Bliss of Valinor, the Valar imitate the Children of Ilúvatar, whom they have foreseen in the Vision of the Ainur. Along with choosing appearances similar to Elves, they engage in other activities, such as festivals with eating and drinking. The "Quenta Silmarillion" reports times set for planting and harvesting, despite the absence of seasons (or at least the absence of winter). At harvest times the Valar themselves work at gathering Yavanna's fruits; Manwë hosts a festival at each harvest season, with the purpose of praising Eru Ilúvatar through music, song, and dance.[34]

🍃 The Valar and the Children of Ilúvatar

As befits a mythology, the narratives of the earliest eras of Elves and Humans show divine beings interacting with the Children of Ilúvatar. Oromë discovers the Elves as he hunts in Middle-earth. Even earlier, Varda sets constellations in the sky for the Elves' benefit; because they first experience the beauty of starlight when they awake, Elves venerate Varda. Both she and Manwë listen to and watch the doings of the Children of Ilúvatar from the holy mountain in Aman. Ulmo takes a more direct interest in Middle-earth, using its waterways as a means for perceiving all that occurs. Tolkien's diverse documents related to the history of the Silmarils show the Valar functioning as mythological gods.

But also as gods with serious limitations. While their battles with Melkor have already revealed the Valar as less than all-powerful, their interventions with the Children of Ilúvatar foreground the Valar's limitations; the Valar make serious mistakes in their decisions regarding the Children. Eru apparently wishes for the Valar to learn through trial and error, a decision with significant repercussions throughout the history of Arda. The Valar confess ignorance of the nature and future of the Children; Vairë observes that the Valar find Elves and Humans inexplicable. Tolkien adds that, at best, the Valar can draw conclusions through reasoning regarding actions stemming from the exercise of Elvish and Human free wills.[35]

Because of the Valar's ignorance, the legendarium consistently asserts that the Children of Ilúvatar should not worship the Valar as gods. The Valar do not deserve such worship, since they are created beings, not creators. As a result, the Valar are "elders and . . . chieftains" rather than masters over Elves and Humans.[36] *Elders* positions the Valar as older siblings, or members of a social structure who are privileged due to their extensive experience. *Chieftains* suggests instead a political leadership, authorized by heredity or group consensus. Combining the two suggests something more than adviser but less then ruler (since they are not masters). The mistakes made by these elders and chieftains with the Firstborn of Eru, the Elves, prompts the Valar to purposefully neglect Eru's Secondborn, Humans, when they finally appear.

Elves in the First Age

The Valar find their ability to function as Elders and Chieftains to the Elves hampered from the beginning. The Elves function as a primitive society in Middle-earth for 350 years before the Valar learn of their appearance. In the interim, Melkor harasses the Elves, perhaps even taking some captive. Melkor spreads a rumor of an unknown being called the Hunter or the Dark Rider, who presumably pursues and devours Elves. Thus, when Oromë finally discovers the Elves, some hide from him or flee, though others feel drawn toward the light of Aman, visible in Oromë's face. The Valar then take two decisive steps: in consultation with Eru, the Valar attack and restrain Melkor; then, apparently without consulting Eru, they summon the Elves to Aman. *The Book of Lost Tales* suggests the world would have been a better place, and the Elves a happier people, if the summons had not been extended;[37] Flieger terms the summons "an error in judgment."[38] In this case, the Valar's trial and error impact not just themselves but all the Elves and their descendants, and thus all Middle-earth; after witnessing the destruction of Beleriand during the First Age, for example, many Elves seek a return to a simpler life that they imagine might have been theirs had the Valar not revealed themselves.[39]

The summons results in divisions among the Elves. First, those who heed the summons (Light Elves, the Eldar) become distanced from those who do not (Dark Elves, the Avari); additionally, different rates of migration from the East toward the West split the Light Elves into three primary groups, the Vanyar, the Noldor, and the Teleri (though Tolkien also writes that the three groupings stem from much earlier, with the Elves' first awakening[40]). The divisions among the Elves serve well Tolkien the philologist, since they allow Elvish languages to evolve into variants, but divisions also emphasize the Valar's inability to predict the effects of their decisions.

In Aman, the Light Elves live under Manwë's protection. The Vanyar and Noldor gain direct access to the Valar, who function at this stage like mentors. Elves learn a variety of fundamental truths, including the story of the Music of the Ainur, because Manwë teaches it to Elf patriarchs in the earliest stages of Elf history.[41]

As often happens with teachers and parents, the Valar develop favorites. Manwë and Varda love most the Vanyar, whose king dwells in close proximity to Manwë on the Vala's holy mountain. Aulë and Mandos favor the Noldor; some, in fact, call themselves Aulëndur, which signifies Servant of Aulë. The Valar's favoritism, however, does not stoop to possessiveness or rivalry; instead, Manwë's favoritism stems from compatibility of disposition.

While the Vanyar learn special knowledge from their close relationship with Manwë, they share that knowledge with their friends the Noldor.[42] Aulë in particular teaches crafts, such as gem work, to the Noldor. The Valar welcome the Elves onto their lands and into their homes, though also granting the Elves territory to build their own city.

Perhaps the most significant instance of the Valar's inability to foresee the consequences of their actions involves their release of Melkor, following several ages of imprisonment within the Halls of Mandos. The decision, ultimately Manwë's, permits Melkor to interact with the Elves, spreading lies and innuendo, and ultimately instilling mistrust in the one Elf described (by Ulmo) as the greatest of all Elves: Fëanor. Fëanor's mistrust evolves over time into outright rebellion, despite the best efforts of the Valar to show him the error of his ways. His great speech before the Noldor, urging his kinspersons to join his rebellion, to revenge the death of Finwë, and to recover the stolen Silmarils, depicts the Valar as jailers; his effort to leave Aman results in the Kinslaying, which Tolkien refers to as war in heaven.[43]

The return of the Noldorin Elves to Middle-earth places the Valar into more traditional godlike roles in the later chapters of the "Quenta Silmarillion." While narratives of the First Age often assert that the Valar maintained a hands-off policy after the Noldor's return, the same narratives reveal continued Valian intervention. The creation of the sun and moon exemplifies the Valar's desire to aid the Elves of Middle-earth, while Fingon's rescue of Maedhros shows the Valar (or their representatives) responding to prayers from across the sea. At the same time, the story of the Children of Húrin shows the Valar unable or unwilling to interfere with Melkor's direct curse on Húrin's family. Additionally, Middle-earth possesses its own resident divinity in Melian, who becomes wife of Thingol and mother of Lúthien. Those roles often overshadow Melian's divinity, but the Valar no doubt understand that Melian remains faithful to Eru and thus indirectly supports the efforts of the Valar.

The most decisive action of the Valar, sending a host of Maiar and Vanyar to attack and overpower Melkor, leads to the end of the first Age. In this fifty-year War of Wrath the Host of the Valar enter Thangorodrim, where Melkor remains entrapped and fearful. He begs for pardon, but his feet are cut off and he is bound (with the same chain forged long previously by Aulë for Melkor's first imprisonment). Eönwë takes charge of the two remaining Silmarils from Melkor's crown, and the remains of that crown are fashioned into a ring around Melkor's neck.[44] Finally, "by the express command of Eru and by His power, [i]s Melkor thrown utterly down and deprived forever of all power to do or to undo."[45] With the removal of Melkor's direct influence over Middle-earth, the Host of the Valar return to Aman, apparently neglecting Middle-earth throughout the Second Age.

Humans in the Second Age

Humans, in contrast with the Elves, experience only limited mentoring under the Valar, and thus narratives of the Second Age, which focus on Humans, position the Valar more conventionally as deities, distant and inaccessible, to be feared more than loved. Yet Humans, too, rebel, first against Eru, and then against the Valar. Several of Tolkien's letters assert that he feels unequal to the challenge of writing a fall of Humans story for his mythology, which did not prevent him from writing such a narrative in his "Tale of Adanel."[46] The Tale reveals that Humans in the First Age experience a direct aural presence of Eru Ilúvatar, rather than interactions with the Valar; yet Humans rebel against the voice of Eru, willingly enslaving themselves to Melkor. When Humans finally encounter the Elves, only the most noble clans perceive the holiness reflected in the faces of the Eldar; some choose to align themselves with the Eldar, learning the teachings the Elves have gained directly from the Valar. At the end of the First Age, the dedication and virtue of these Humans prompt the Valar to grant special blessings, including both long life and a special island home, Númenor.

But the history of the Númenóreans shows that even the most blessed Humans may devolve, under Sauron's influence, to the point of embracing "a Satanist religion"[47] and launching a direct attack against the Valar in Aman. While the Valar have shown willingness to engage in battle with Melkor, their former colleague, they refrain from responding to this incursion by Humans; the Valar recognize the limitation of their authority regarding the second Children of Ilúvatar. Rather than act independently in the face of such insolent power, the Valar appeal to Eru Ilúvatar, who authorizes divine intervention on a catastrophic level. Empowered by Ilúvatar, the Valar finally act; conversely, some manuscripts attribute all the subsequent transformations to Eru, noting that the Valar temporarily give up their authority to govern Arda.[48] A great chasm opens in the sea, swallowing the Númenórean fleet; earthquakes and rockslides bury the Númenórean king and his followers who have encamped on the shore of Aman. The relatively conventional images of the Valar in the later First Age and in the Second Age still allow for very unconventional divine responses to the Children's defiance.

✍ Conclusion

Divine interactions with Elves and Humans reveal the Valar's limitations. Yet in contrast with Greek gods (at least as depicted by Homer), the Valar do not fall prey to their own emotions; they do not experience the anger, jealousy, and lust common among residents of Olympus. And in contrast with Norse gods, the Valar are not themselves subject to abstract fate; while the Music of the Ainur provides a degree of fate to the residents of Middle-earth, the Valar helped to create that Music and produce its fulfillment. Thus, the Valar's actions as caretakers of Arda, labeled incompetence by some readers,[49] stem specifically and almost exclusively from a lack of knowledge.

First, none of the Valar individually grasp all the Music of the Ainur; similarly, each Vala is at best a limited, contextualized interpretation of part of the mind of Eru. While each Vala understands her or his specific area of specialization, none can synthesize the totality of the Music into a coherent whole (the one exception may be Mandos; if he does understand the entirety of the Music, he reveals that understanding in oblique references understood only after the fact). While the Valar can increase their comprehension of both the Music and Eru through sharing knowledge with one another, a Vala or Valier's individual preferences for her or his area of specialization lead to distortions of the whole such that conflicts arise.[50]

Second, the Valar do not comprehend evil, even though it is woven inextricably into the Music of the Ainur. While Tolkien absolves Manwë of foolishness in freeing Melkor (after the latter's long imprisonment) and allowing Melkor to take a position of influence among the Noldor of Aman, Manwë and the other Valar lack awareness of how a rebellious mind such as Melkor's operates; Eru, in contrast, seems to grasp such an understanding, as seen in his words to Melkor after the Singing of the Ainur, and his successful subversion of Melkor's discord.

Third, Elves and Humans, perhaps sentient beings in general, while appearing within the Music of the Ainur, are not themselves composed by the Valar. The "Ainulindalë" indicates that Eru Ilúvatar introduced Elves and Humans into his Third Theme, which the Ainur did not elaborate. In this sense, Elves and Humans rank equal to the Valar, since they both stem directly from the mind of Eru; while Elves and Humans lack the *power* of the Valar, they possess equal *authority* to influence and produce the future.

Fourth, even beyond the existence of sentient beings, the Music of the Ainur does not contain the entire Middle-earth story. Additional elements, events, and beings can be interspersed. While the Valar contribute to the composition of the Music of the Ainur, the ultimate composer, Eru Ilúvatar, retains the prerogative to add further compositional elements at will.

Thus, the Valar lack knowledge because Eru creates them that way and then induces further limitations on their entry into Eä. The "Ainulindalë" claims that only at the end of time will the sentient beings of Arda (including the Valar) completely understand Eru's intention in the Music, as well as grasp the contributions of all its participants.[51] One can infer from the structure Eru creates (distancing himself from Arda and the Valar) and from the ignorance in which Eru placed the Valar in Arda that he values experiential learning, even when such experience causes pain for innocent beings in the Valar's charge. The Valar, Tolkien asserts, are "capable of many degrees of error and failing" that fall between the complete rebellion of Melkor and the apparent inaction sometimes attributed to them.[52]

Ultimately, the responsibility for the Valar's position within Arda lies with the creator of Eru Ilúvatar. One could argue that Tolkien created the Valar with limitations, needing to learn from experience, because humans of planet Earth lack the ability to relate to sentient beings that do not learn through experience. The Valar therefore are gods humanized, as perhaps any depiction of a god by a creature must be. From a narrative standpoint, the Valar and Maiar oscillate between divine and human registers. The closer the Valar appear to Elves or Humans (as in the tales concerning Elves living in Aman), the more Human-like the Valar appear; the greater the distance (as in the tales subsequent to the Noldorin rebellion), the more godlike the Valar appear.

Since the structure of the tales of the First and Second Ages progressively increases the distance between the Valar and the Children of Ilúvatar, tales of the Third Age assume an even greater distance, such that the Valar nearly disappear. The next two chapters, however, will reveal the continued influence of the Valar on the Children late in the Third Age, both through visible representatives and through invisible but direct influence.

Chapter 3

Divine Intervention in the Third Age: Visible Powers

he word *Valar* appears just three times among the half million or so words of *The Lord of the Rings*. Two of the appearances connote no sense of divine intervention (at least not in the Third Age). Just before the Battle of the Pelennor Fields, the narrator compares Théoden upon Snowmane to Oromë in a Valian battle of the First Age (making Oromë the only Vala named in the book, other than Elbereth). Then at the crowning of Aragorn, Gandalf hopes for blessings on the king's reign under the authority of the Valar, a sentiment added only with the book's second edition.[1] Both these utterances refer to the Valar as distant, the first distant in time, the second in space. The third use of the word marks the only instance that could suggest the Valar maintain an active presence in Middle-earth during the Third Age: the exclamation of the Gondoran soldier, Damrod, in Ithilien at the approach of the Oliphaunt, "May the Valar turn him aside!"[2] Admittedly, the words "May the Valar . . ." might have devolved among Gondorans into a meaningless catchphrase used merely to express wishes and hopes, comparable to the English expression "So help me, God"; the first draft suggests such a usage since there Damrod exclaims, "May the gods turn him aside."[3] Yet at heart, the words form a prayer,[4] and as such they connect the world of *The Lord of the Rings* to the cosmological dimensions of *The Silmarillion*.

Outside *The Lord of the Rings* Tolkien asserts continuity between the stories of the first two ages of Middle-earth and those of the late Third Age, beyond simply continuing the material history of the earlier eras. The cosmological structure authorized by Eru at the downfall of Númenor remains unchanged: no longer a flat disk, Arda now forms a sphere with Aman disconnected from Middle-earth. Furthermore, Arda during the Third Age remains monotheistic, and its cultures embrace what Tolkien terms a "'natural theology'" that bears no sense of Christianity.[5] The Númenórean exiles (the Dúnedain and residents of Gondor) see Eru as prime mover, though they devise no formal worship and recognize no holy places during the era of the War of the Ring. While the hallow of Mindolluin may have served as a sacred site, Gondorans neglect it until Aragorn reenters with Gandalf to discover the sapling of the White Tree.[6]

The Númenórean exiles' primary act of religion involves rejecting worship directed toward any creature, in particular no demonic spirit-being; the Númenórean descendants, like the Elves, learn from prior mistakes. While the exiles refrain from formulating prayers of petition to Eru, they foster a general attitude of thankfulness; some, under the influence of Elves, call on the Valar for aid when facing danger (a supposition that leaves unresolved whether Damrod entreated that Valar's aid, since we have no evidence of Damrod's connection to Elves). In short, the Third Age continues the polytheistic monotheism described in the first chapter of this study, though with an increased perceived distance between the Valar and the Children of Eru. The wise during this era, Tolkien asserts, understand Eru's existence, but consider him approachable only by means of the Valar, who are not themselves readily accessible. Tolkien presumes that with the advent of Aragorn, Eru-worship will experience renewal early in the Fourth Age.[7]

Along with his letters, Tolkien's manuscripts imply historical and linguistic connections between the Valar and life in Middle-earth late in the Third Age. Five hundred years prior to the War of the Ring, Cirion, Steward of Gondor, formalizes the bond between Gondor and the northern people who become the Rohirrim by invoking (in Quenya) both the Valar and Eru; Cirion implies divine intervention placed the invocation into his mouth, since it had not been planned. The site's status, as the hidden tomb of Elendil, increases its importance. Another manuscript asserts that the Valar maintain the site, preventing the growth of trees and preserving its peace against the ravages of time and scavengers, even when the Gondorans neglect its upkeep. On a much more mundane level, Hobbit names for days of the week pay tribute to the Valar, whether Hobbits understand that tribute or not. Hobbits translated their name days from those of the Dúnedain, who in turn adapted them from the Eldar. The first three days of the week are dedicated to the stars, the sun, and the moon, the fourth takes its name from the Two Trees of Valinor, while the next two days commemorate heaven (or sky) and sea (and thus, presumably, Manwë and Ulmo); the last is a "High day," dedicated to the Valar in general.[8]

Yet while Tolkien provides evidence that knowledge of the Valar remains late in the Third Age, as well as external assurances that the Wise of Middle-earth retain worshipful respect toward the Valar, moments when the Valar receive credit for reciprocating attention to Elves and Humans remain rare in *The Hobbit* and *The Lord of the Rings,* in part because Tolkien produces stories of a very different nature than *The Silmarillion*. This genre difference can be summarized as between mythology and novel; mythology (*The Silmarillion*) features gods prominently, but novels (*The Hobbit* and *The Lord of the Rings*) focus on the more mundane affairs of Humans (expanded in Tolkien's fantasy world to include all sentient physical beings).

But another Tolkien impulse works against this genre distinction: as a subcreator Tolkien feels compelled to find causes, internally within his fictional world, for effects that arise externally. Thus, Tolkien excuses the apparent lack of divine involvement in *The Lord of the Rings* by asserting that the Valar distance themselves from daily life in Middle-earth, in part because they learned from experience the danger of meddling directly in Elven and Human affairs during the First Age. Yet this distancing does not negate their cosmological functions: while retaining their caretaker roles for Arda and the Children of Ilúvatar,[9] the Valar accomplish some of their work indirectly through representatives.

Detecting the Valar's representatives at work in the Third Age requires information beyond the texts of that era. Often beings with metaphysical origins appear as no more than physical beings in *The Lord of the Rings,* with Eagles and Ents the two most obvious examples. Eagles serve as Tolkien's go-to beings for deus-ex-machina rescues and emergency transportation. As represented in *The Hobbit,* Eagles possess intelligence, rational thought, and speech, but seem merely talking beasts. Eagles, however, originated as spirit-beings in bird-like shape, sent to watch Melkor, bring tidings to Aman, and occasionally interfere in Middle-earth events. By the time of the Third Age, Gwaihir is said to be only a descendant of Thorondor of the First Age, and thus no more (though perhaps no less) a Maia than Lúthien.

Twice in *The Hobbit* and three times again in *The Lord of the Rings* the Eagles come to the rescue. The narrator of *The Hobbit* naturalizes the book's first Eagle appearance by suggesting simple cause-and-effect relationships for it. The Lord of the Eagles hears turmoil in the forest caused by Orcs and Wolves surrounding Bilbo and his friends; being curious, he investigates.

Seeing Gandalf in trouble, the Eagle seizes him, apparently before Gandalf knows of the Eagle's approach. Yet the text leaves space for something more behind the Eagle's actions. The narrator reports an unaccountable level of curiosity on the part of the Lord of the Eagles to understand what is taking place, even though Eagles rarely pay attention to Goblins. Additionally, the narrator reveals these Eagles as special, unlike the common class (which can be cruel and cowardly). Most Eagles of the Third Age represent a significant devolution from the likes of Thorondor, but the Eagles who rescue Bilbo and his friends maintain a sense of nobility, tracing their descent (somewhat like the Númenóreans) from ancient times.[10]

Gandalf's farewell greeting to the Eagles indirectly confirms the link between Eagles and the Valar, hearkening back to the ages when Eagles traveled to Middle-earth by Manwë's decree. "May the wind under your wings bear you where the sun sails and the moon walks," Gandalf says.[11] Given Manwë's association with wind, the expression implies the Eagles' continued allegiance to him, while the reference to the sun and moon suggests an ability to fly even into the deepest heavens; according to *The Silmarillion,* eagle-like spirits can travel to the very Walls of the Night. While an unaccountable level of curiosity and descent from Eagles of the First Age do not prove Manwë's prompting behind the Eagles' rescue of Bilbo and his friends, such factors do make divine intervention a possibility.

Tolkien's insistence on Eucatastrophe as an essential ingredient and the most important purpose of the *Fairy-story* lends particular importance to the appearance of the Eagles at the climax of the Battle of the Five Armies. Tolkien associates Eucatastrophe with "miraculous grace" and "evangelium" stemming from "beyond the walls of the world,"[12] characteristics that connect Eucatastrophic moments to actions of divine will. Since the Battle of the Five Armies tips in favor of the enemy, the Eagles' appearance in the nick of time is miraculous. Just as *The Hobbit* provides naturalistic explanations for the Eagles' rescue of Bilbo and his friends, it equally demystifies the Eagles' appearance at the battle. Long suspicious of the Goblins massing troops, the Eagles congregate in large numbers, perceiving the distant battle by smell. The Eagles seem to initiate their actions without divine command from Manwë; their animal natures, smelling the battle, even contribute to their motivation. Yet the Eagles' watchfulness, particularly given the narrator's assertion that Eagles normally pay little attention to Goblins, leaves open the possibility of an additional motive, since listening for appeals to the Vala is assigned to the Eagles within the Music of the Ainur.[13]

Gandalf's actions at the battle, as the narrator describes them, also open the possibility of outside intervention. First, the narrator observes Gandalf sitting "as if deep in thought"; the narrator guesses that Gandalf prepares "some last blast of magic before the end." Yet the narrator takes pains to indicate the limits of his authorial knowledge; the full quote is "preparing, I suppose, some last blast. . . ."[14] The "I suppose" allows space to interpret Gandalf's actions (or apparent inaction) otherwise; one can equally suppose that Gandalf prays for divine intervention. As *The Silmarillion* shows in Fingon's rescue of Maedhros, praying to the Valar for help can result in Eagles coming to the rescue. In addition, when the Eagles appear at the battle, they do so against a backdrop of the setting sun, suddenly revealed by a burst of wind. The Eagles' appearance from the West, coupled with dramatic wind and light, suggests both Manwë and Varda at work to ensure that good has a fighting chance against evil at the moment when the One Ring has again arisen in Middle-earth. While *The Hobbit* makes no such claims, knowledge of the Eagles' metaphysical origins prompts additional insight into the peculiarities of the book's narrative.

The Ents who appear in *The Lord of the Rings,* in contrast, are much older than Gwaihir. Galadriel and Celeborn call Fangorn "Eldest";[15] to be Eldest, in a continent that houses both Galadriel and Tom Bombadil, is no small claim. *The Silmarillion* implies that the Ents arose in Middle-earth as shepherds of the trees at about the same time as the Elves first appeared at Cuiviénen, though *The Two Towers* suggests Ents arrived prior to Elves (or, technically speaking, prior to the Elves first singing). Appendix F of *The Return of the King* confirms this, describing Ents as the oldest type of people remaining in the Third Age. Since Fangorn bears the name of the primeval forest in which he lives, he may be one of the first generation of Ents. The second "Annals of Aman" suggests the Elves appeared nearly three thousand years prior to the birth of Galadriel; thus, Treebeard may be ten thousand years old.[16]

Ents obviously possess power; they crush rock with bare hands. Yet within *The Lord of the Rings* they seem simply strange creatures, life-forms existing solely within Middle-earth. Even Fangorn lists Ents among the sentient creatures of Middle-earth, along with Elves, Humans, and Dwarves. Adding context from *The Silmarillion* does little to expand an understanding of Ents; their origin stems from a request by Yavanna to Manwë that her beloved trees be protected, motivated in part on learning of her husband's creation of Dwarves, who will use wood to heat metals, in the manner of their creator, Aulë. Manwë communes with Eru and thus recalls a passage of the Music of the Ainur that suggests both Eagles and Ents.

The Silmarillion, associating the appearance of the Ents with the appearance of the Eagles, hints that both are spirit-beings taking on a physical shape for a specific purpose in Middle-earth. In correspondence Tolkien affirms that Ents embody spirit-beings (presumably Maiar) inhabiting tree-like forms. Given their association with trees, it should be no surprise that the Entwives revere Yavanna; the male Ents, in contrast, favor Oromë, who loves trees and the hunt. As Shepherds of the Trees, Ents serve as stewards, much like Gandalf; assuming the trustworthiness of Tolkien's letters, the first generation of Ents are as much Maiar as are Gandalf and Melian. Therefore, moments when Ents, like Eagles, actively oppose evil (the destruction of Orthanc; Beren's battle against the Dwarves who killed Thingol and stole the Nauglamir/Silmaril) serve as examples of divine intervention.[17]

This chapter will examine additional beings who visibly represent the Valar to residents of Middle-earth during the Third Age. The most obvious representatives within *The Lord of the Rings* are the Istari, the Wizards; Gandalf provides the best picture of the Valar in the Third Age (in the same way that, according to Christian theology, Christ forms the most accurate portrait of God in the Bible). Tom Bombadil and his wife, Goldberry, may also trace a lineage back to Aman; Tolkien uncharacteristically obfuscates their origins and cosmological roles, while leaving numerous enigmatic hints. Even the High Elves, while not themselves divine beings, function as representatives of the Valar to accomplish great deeds in the story; Glorfindel and Galadriel, for example, retain in the Third Age some of the aura of Aman that enveloped the newly returned Noldor in the First Age.

The Istari: Servants of the Valar

Gandalf serves as the most obvious means by which the Valar influence the history of the Third Age. Gandalf works to ennoble the Elves during the First Age, though only invisibly prompting fair visions and wisdom in their hearts. But Gandalf assumes the special role of Guardian of the Third Age, Tolkien adds, requiring a visible presence in Middle-earth.[18] Tolkien thus explains away the lack of "Quenta Silmarillion" narratives involving the Maia hero of *The Lord of the Rings.*

Gandalf first enters the Middle-earth legendarium through *The Hobbit,* which identifies him as a Wizard; that story mentions another Wizard, Radagast, whom Gandalf calls a cousin, and who makes a cameo appearance in *The Fellowship of the Ring*. Gandalf there reveals his and Radagast's status as members of an order, headed by a third Wizard, Saruman. Appendix B of *The Return of the King* provides an Elvish name for this order, the Istari, and historicizes the order's emergence, about the year 1100 in the Third Age, simultaneous with the rise of Sauron's shadow over Mirkwood.[19] There may be precisely five Wizards, or there may be more.

The Istari, defined as "those who know," exhibit deep understanding of the history and nature of Arda, a fact that hints at their divine origins, though only a few residents of Middle-earth (including Galadriel, Círdan, and Elrond) understand their true natures. The Istari come from the West as messengers to work against Sauron.[20] As emissaries of the Valar, the Istari are Angels, even "guardian Angels."[21] Rather than opposing the enemy head-to-head, the Istari promote unity and bravery among life forms that possess a power to resist Sauron; in short, they motivate action among Elves, Humans, and so on, instead of accomplishing tasks on their behalf.[22] In Millen's words, they serve as "catalysts, to stir the West into rising against Sauron."[23]

At the same time, the Istari's entry into Middle-earth echoes the entry of the Valar into Eä; they do so only in a reduced or limited form. While neither Elf nor Human, Istari bodies are "real and not feigned"; rather than assuming physical appearances, as the Valar and Maiar choose to do in Aman, the Istari are affixed to bodies that can hunger, grow weary, and even die.[24] This makes the Istari more susceptible to mistakes of judgment and even moral failure, the possibility of falling into sin and evil.[25] Okunishi has defined an Istar as "the structure in which a Maia wanes in power and takes a human form," which makes Gandalf "a limited form of Olorin."[26] Círdan recognizes this change in Gandalf when he welcomes Gandalf to Middle-earth, describing the change as a weariness that Gandalf voluntarily accepts.[27] The Istari's bodies disguise them so that Sauron will not know the Wizards' status as Maiar.

At the same time, though embodied, their virtuous and elevated spirits give the Istari longevity and hardiness. Yet they cannot use their noble spirits to their own advantage; the Valar forbid the Istari from displaying their majesty and from using Sauron's technique of dominating through fear and power; the ends do not justify such means. This strategy stems from the Valar's past mistakes, specifically from their early efforts to protect the Elves. Because the Istari's moral code embraces noncoercion, Sauron considers them weak messengers from the Valar, whom he sees as defeated imperialistic powers seeking to regain lost prestige through colonizing Middle-earth.[28]

On their first arrival in Middle-earth, the Istari travel about as old men, gaining knowledge without revealing their powers. They have no command to travel or work together; instead, the Valar selected them for specific character traits that might benefit their work in Middle-earth. Since the transition from Maia to Istar involves a reduction in power, knowledge, and ability, the Istari need to learn (or relearn) through experience. In fact, while they know their origins from Aman, their memory of the Valar's realm remains a distant vision, a condition that produces a longing to return there; Gandalf reveals this longing when he confesses to Pippin a desire to test his will against the Palantír of Orthanc, in order to view Aman from afar in its glory days, seeing perhaps Fëanor at work and the light of the Two Trees.[29]

The History of the Istari

According to Tolkien's narrative sketch describing the Valar's selection process for the Istari, Manwë, perhaps in consultation with Eru Ilúvatar, summons a council of the Valar to send the Istari as peers, hierarchically equivalent to Sauron, to cultivate influence rather than use direct force. Two Maiar volunteer: Curumo (who becomes Saruman) and Alatar (who becomes Radagast). Aulë supports Curumo's nomination while Oromë supports Alatar. Manwë specifically asks Olórin to go, though Olórin claims fear and weakness should disbar him. Instead Manwë asserts those conditions appropriately qualify him. When Manwë commands Olórin to go as the third member of the Order, Varda ambiguously utters "not as third." Varda's comment makes sense as a prophecy, since Gandalf eventually takes on the position of Chief of his order, a position first assumed by Saruman.[30]

Varda's remark also reveals an element of strife among the Istari from the beginning; Curumo keeps Varda's comment in his thought, the narrator states, implying that his memory produces resentment. Curumo/Saruman thus suffers from pride at the beginning of his assignment as Istar. His later disdain for Radagast (which Gandalf relates to the Council of Elrond) echoes his earlier unwillingness to take Radagast as a companion to Middle-earth; ultimately Curumo feels obligated to accept Radagast to satisfy Yavanna, which essentially places the Valier in the unseemly position of begging Curumo.[31]

Saruman's reputation stems from both his knowledge and his persuasive voice. While the sound of the voice alone can sway some listeners, it over-powers others, as if by a spell that continues to urge through soft whispers. Aragorn sums up Saruman as possessing deep knowledge, subtle thought, and skilled hands, with an ability to control some minds; Aragorn implies a weakness within this latter strength: Saruman successfully persuades the wise but simply intimidates weaker folk (though Tolkien claims Saruman does not use magic or hypnotism, but only disarms his listeners' reasoning). A willingness to intimidate aligns him with the coercive methodologies of Melkor and Sauron, rather than the supportive, empowering work of Gandalf. Saruman's concession that good ends justify evil means forms the central argument in his attempt to convince Gandalf to provide access to the Ring.[32]

Saruman's long-cultivated expertise in the lore of the Rings of Power ultimately contributes to his downfall. His covetousness of Gandalf's ring, Narya, augments hidden antipathy toward Gandalf, who gains some awareness of Saruman's prideful attitude since Gandalf tells Frodo that something prompted him to keep Bilbo's ring secret from Saruman. The White Wizard, in turn, probably perceives the consistent good luck that accompanies Gandalf, luck that Tolkien interprets as divine aid and blessing;[33] in short, Eru and/or the Valar favor Gandalf, which only pushes Saruman to greater resentment.

Saruman's imprisonment of Gandalf shows the White Wizard stronger, or at least more cunning, than his opponent. Saruman's actions reveal that long years of seeking to understand, find, and perhaps even recreate Sauron's Ring has produced acquiescence to Sauron's methods; he even names himself "Ring-maker." Saruman's persuasive attempt reveals that he has already lost sight of the task assigned the Istari by the Valar; his goals of "Knowledge, Rule, Order" prompt him to see the Children of Ilúvatar as a hindrance.[34] His desire for the One Ring illustrates Elrond's observation on the dangers of studying the methods of evil powers.[35]

Treebeard perceives that Saruman plots to position himself as a Power (a word implying a political power in relation to Mordor and Gondor, but also calling to mind, with its capital P, a metonym for the Valar). Saruman, like Melkor long before him, wishes to be more than his Eru-given nature (and his Valar-given mission) allows him to be. Treebeard perceives Saruman's behavior as treachery so evil that no curse in the languages of respectable peoples seems strong enough to condemn it.[36] Besides spying on Hobbits and the Rohirrim, Saruman lies to the White Council. Subsequent to the War of the Ring, the Wise perceive that Saruman had hoped to find the One Ring for himself. Aragorn's reclamation of Orthanc early in the Fourth Age uncovers evidence of Saruman's search: the chain on which Isuldur wore the Ring, locked in a hidden closet.[37]

Saruman's desire to rival Sauron prompts him to lose concern for people and moral causes, which opens him to domination by a superior power such as

Sauron.[38] "Poor Saruman!" Gandalf exclaims in one of Tolkien's drafts; "what a fall for one so wise!"[39] Gandalf, in contrast, succeeds, despite his death; he forms no allegiance in Middle-earth, except to the Valar who sent him, and he reaps the reward of a return journey to Aman. But Saruman's downfall weakens the overall efforts of the Istari, which in turn requires greater effort and sacrifice from Gandalf; Saruman's betrayal, Tolkien implies, necessitates Gandalf's sacrificial death[40] (presumably because Gandalf chooses the route through Moria to avoid straying near Orthanc). Most importantly, Saruman abandons his role as caretaker of the beings of Middle-earth, breaks faith with the Valar who sent him, and ultimately rebels against Eru Ilúvatar.

The other three Wizards remain enigmas in Tolkien's legendarium. Beorn speaks highly of Radagast in *The Hobbit* and Gandalf praises his skill in magic pertaining to shape and color changes.[41] Yet Radagast often leaves a poor impression on observers; Saruman dismisses him as incompetent, and even Gandalf feels compelled to correct his pronunciation of the Hobbits' home country. Birns suggests Tolkien minimizes elaboration of Radagast for practical reasons, finding him "too trivial a riddle to matter in the larger depths" of the story.[42] Radagast's attention to animals prompts some readers to value his work as less important than Gandalf's, who typically focuses on matters of higher beings. Tolkien himself implies that Radagast ultimately fails in his mission,[43] perhaps because, as Rateliff observes, Radagast goes native.

Yet Rateliff also recovers a more admirable Radagast from the traditional view. Radagast boldly approaches his task of opposing Sauron by residing at Rhosgobel near Dol Guldur, one of Sauron's primary abodes. The rapidity with which he leaves Gandalf after delivering Saruman's message may reflect a foreknowledge that Mirkwood may soon be under attack from Sauron's forces, rather than personal fear; furthermore, he faithfully delivers the messages given him, which later contributes to Gandalf's escape from Saruman. Radagast's attention to flora and fauna may in fact reflect faithfulness to a charge given him by Yavanna,[44] which may explain why she promoted him as one of the Istari.

Tolkien provides little information, itself contradictory, regarding the two remaining Wizards. In a 1958 letter he claims ignorance of the colors of the two Wizards that, in a 1954 document, he identifies as blue. In that 1954 document, Tolkien says they have no names except Ithryn Luin or the Blue Wizards. Yet in the narrative of the Valar's selection of the Istari, Tolkien names them Alatar and Pallando. Then in 1972 he names them Morinehtar and Rómestámo, Darkness-slayer and East-helper. Tolkien's diverse statements agree on one point: the Blue Wizards remain irrelevant to the narrative of *The Lord of the Rings* because they disappeared long before into eastern Middle-earth. Saruman, in fact, accompanies them into the East but then returns. Christopher Tolkien suspects Oromë's influence on the Blue Wizards, since hunting expeditions familiarized him with that part of the continent.[45]

Tolkien expresses ambivalent views as to the success of Radagast and the Blue Wizards. A 1954 document claims only one Istar ultimately proved faithful to his commission, presumably Gandalf. The 1958 letter suggests the two Blue Wizards, like Saruman, failed; Tolkien speculates that they founded magic cults that may have endured into the Fourth Age. By 1972 Tolkien declares that the Blue Wizards must have come to Middle-earth much earlier than the other three, sometime during the Second Age; he also expresses a more positive view of their success, suggesting they weakened Eastern forces that might otherwise have overpowered the realms of Western Middle-earth.[46]

Because the War of the Ring marks the end of Sauron's direct influence in Eä, it also marks the end of the Istari as an order.

Gandalf before Death

The Hobbit identifies Gandalf as a mover and shaker of world events. While introducing Gandalf, the narrator reports that adventure stories follow in his wake; shortly after, Bilbo exclaims enthusiastically that Gandalf bears responsibility for young Hobbits leaving the Shire for "mad adventures."[47] *The Lord of the Rings* reveals a larger context for Gandalf's meddling, in which his actions serve an underlying mission, a method behind the madness. He enters alone into Dol Guldur on two separate occasions to discover the Necromancer's presence, and receives credit for persuading the White Council to attack Dol Guldur in Third Age 2941, against the preferences of Saruman. He aids residents of the Shire during The Long Winter of Third Age 2758–59, and befriends Denethor's father, Ecthellion II. Aragorn, cognizant that Gandalf faces severe dangers, declares that dealing with the Ring will likely be his most important task.[48]

To fulfill his mission, Gandalf reveals powers beyond the abilities of Humans and even the most powerful Elves. These abilities illustrate Gandalf and the Istari's metaphysical origins, part of the noble characters they possess even in their reduced condition. Thus, when Pippin, standing on the wall of Minas Tirith, cries out "Gandalf save us!"[49] readers sense Gandalf possesses adequate power to do great things, even against the flying Nazgûl. Indeed, Círdan recognizes Gandalf, when he first embarks from Aman, as the greatest and wisest of all the Istari. Yet most often Gandalf keeps that power cloaked, revealing only glimpses, as when he suddenly grows tall and foreboding at Bilbo's petulance over giving up the Ring.[50]

Gandalf's most noteworthy ability involves fire; in the Shire, this means his fireworks and smoke rings, since most Hobbits only comprehend the simplest aspects of Gandalf's nature.[51] But Gandalf's rescues of Bilbo and the Dwarves in *The Hobbit* rely on fire as a tool. The flash of light Gandalf produces in the high cave of the Misty Mountains kills several Orcs and allows Gandalf to conceal himself. Shortly thereafter in the great hall of the Goblin King, Gandalf extinguishes all the lights and fires simultaneously, with white sparks that burn the Goblins and smoke that blinds them; apparently the sparks do not harm the Dwarves, nor does the smoke prevent Gandalf from seeing and killing the Great Goblin. A few days later Gandalf ignites pinecone firebombs as a defense against Wargs.

In *The Lord of the Rings* Gandalf's prowess with fire (beyond his fireworks at Bilbo's party) first appear on Weathertop, where Gandalf uses flame to ward off Black Riders. At the foot of Caradhras, Gandalf commands fire to save the Company and drive away the marauding werewolves, causing the trees above him to burst into flame.[52] These examples show Gandalf capable of producing fire at will using materials at hand (such as pinecones), but also controlling multiple fires spread out within one large room (the Goblins' Great Hall). He appears capable of making fire using no materials at all except for his staff (on the Goblins' Front Porch), despite his assertion to Legolas on Caradhras that he requires material to work with.

Gandalf uses fire to induce fear in Gollum to ascertain his travels through Mordor; Gandalf admits such uses are harsh but justifies his behavior as necessary to ascertain the truth.[53] Tolkien and Gandalf leave unstated the means by which Gandalf induces such fear; I imagine the mechanism as psychological rather than physical (I assume this in part to avoid seeing Gandalf in the position of administering torture, which Tolkien clearly aligns with Mordor rather than Aman; still, this passage understandably troubles readers).

Gandalf claims such an affinity with fire that to produce it by command equates to announcing his own name. His "word of command, naur an edraith ammen!" spoken to ignite a bundle of sticks on Caradhras, reveals his identity "from Rivendell to the Mouths of Anduin,"[54] acknowledging his reputation for fire abilities extends from the north (Rivendell) to the south (the Mouths of Anduin). But Gandalf's words also suggest a deeper identification with fire, one preceding his use of Narya, the Ring of Fire, and even his incarnation as Gandalf in the Third Age. Gandalf not only uses fire as a tool; he appreciates its beauty[55] as substance or element, much as Ulmo expresses love for the beauty of water in its various forms (snow, ice, cloud). This affinity adds new depth to the otherwise frivolous use of fireworks in the opening chapter of *The Fellowship of the Ring;* Gandalf doesn't merely entertain, but produces temporal works of art.

As noted in chapter 1 of this study, some Maiar exist as fire spirits: the Balrogs who side with Melkor, for example, and Arien, the Maia selected to guide the sun through the heavens. Gandalf may also be one of those spirits of fire; one manuscript describes Gandalf as Sauron's enemy, positioning Gandalf's fire that kindles warmth and goodness against that which consumes and destroys, a description both literal and figurative. Gandalf's nature as a spirit of fire adds a deeper level of meaning to the description of Gandalf at the moment when, offered the Ring by Frodo, Gandalf's face appears lit by an internal fire.[56]

Accompanying his work with fire, Gandalf exhibits other special powers, implemented to assist him with his mission. He speaks a word of command (an action that might justifiably be described as casting a spell) on the beer of the Prancing Pony, making it especially good, according to Barliman Butterbur. Before entering the mines of Moria, he speaks a blessing over Bill the pony.[57] These words comfort Sam, who feels distraught over parting from Bill, but also impart power to the beast.

Gandalf possesses special knowledge, gained through long and wide experience, including languages and lore of various cultural groups of northwest Middle-earth, historical and contemporary. But Gandalf displays other means of acquiring knowledge, besides long experience. While Gandalf lacks omniscience, he shows a heightened awareness of events within the world at large. On a small scale, Bilbo feels that Gandalf possesses inside information about the contents of his Bag End larder (though the Dwarves seem equally informed). On a larger scale, prior to the Battle of Five Armies, Gandalf appears aware that an army of Orcs and Wargs approaches, though the rapidity of their attack surprises him. Gandalf asserts his special knowledge as irrefutable fact, positioning himself as among *the Wise.*[58] Most importantly, Gandalf puts his knowledge to practical use, whether to know with confidence that Bilbo can provision the Wizard and thirteen hungry Dwarves, or to intercede as Elves, Humans, and Dwarves prepare to battle one another in the face of a more serious common foe. As the narrator says when Gandalf retrieves Thorin's sword after killing the Great Goblin, "Gandalf thought of most things."[59]

Gandalf sometimes derives his special knowledge by reading minds. This may result, in part, from Gandalf's long study of Elves, Humans, Dwarves, and Hobbits, and their motivations. In the opening chapter of *The Hobbit* Gandalf readily sees through Bilbo's cordialities intended to dismiss Gandalf from his presence. Then after Bilbo sneaks past Balin by using his magic Ring, Gandalf perceives something new about Bilbo, something invisible to the Dwarves. His facial expression leaves Bilbo thinking that Gandalf has intuited gaps in the narrative (and interestingly enough, the facial expression appears only in later drafts). Even Gandalf's cryptic explanation for his stealthy return to the troll encampment, that he *felt* the group needed him, suggests ability, if not to read minds, then to use the mind to see or hear from afar. What are only hints in *The Hobbit* become blatant statements in *The Fellowship of the Ring.* Gandalf tells Frodo that he has no trouble reading Frodo's mind in Rivendell; he similarly reads Pippin's mind, or at least reads his moral condition, after Pippin rashly looks into the Palantír.[60]

On occasion Gandalf successfully looks into the future, living up to his Valinorean name, Olórin, which means *clear vision* and connects him to the Vala Lórien. Prophecy, however, is not one of Gandalf's major character strengths. Faramir asserts that the Wizard avoids speaking of future events. Primarily minor predictions, Gandalf's rare prophecies invariably come true. In *The Hobbit* he predicts that the Dwarves will ultimately appreciate Bilbo's participation in their adventure,[61] and at their return journey, he predicts Bilbo will need more funds than he anticipates.

Gandalf's accuracy in small predictions continues in *The Lord of the Rings:* his sense that Gollum will play some further role in the history of the Ring; his suggestion that Merry and Pippin will play important roles; his prediction, at the foot of Caradhras, of a later confrontation with Saruman. Some of his predictions may be hunches rather than prophesies; after the fact, he acknowledges his assertion that Gollum might interact with Frodo during the journey to Mordor as a guess.[62] Yet the accuracy of Gandalf's hunches approach the uncanny.

Gandalf himself emphasizes the limitations of his foresight. He admits to Frodo an inability to foresee whether Frodo will take the Ring into Mordor or only to Rivendell. Similarly, while he knows the prophecy of the Nazgûl King's death, the mechanism of its accomplishment remains unknown until

Éowyn and Merry achieve the task. Lack of certainty regarding outcomes means that Gandalf often embraces strategies that appear, according to Aragorn, risky (as Faramir asserts about Gandalf's willingness to send the Ring to Mordor in the company of Hobbits[63]); for those risky decisions to turn out favorably, participants must perform their own roles appropriately. In other words, Gandalf's plans include faith that individuals such as Frodo will perform to the Wizard's level of expectation; as a previous resident of Aman, that faith may include an assumption that the Valar will also do their part.

Gandalf fully grasps his powers and their limitations. Draft notes that Gandalf lacks enough magic to oppose Nazgûl alone later appear directly from Gandalf's mouth.[64] Gandalf compares himself hierarchically with his enemies. "There are many powers in the world, for good or for evil. Some are greater than I am. Against some I have not yet been measured." In the Balrog of Moria, Gandalf acknowledges, he confronts an equal, which almost overpowers him.[65] Judging by appearances, the battle between Gandalf and the Balrog is no fair contest. Gandalf throughout remains unchanged, apparently an old man in a gray cloak. The Balrog, however, reveals itself as man-shaped, encapsulated within a fire that appears as shadow rather than light; a draft of the passage adds that the Balrog feels even larger than it looks.[66] In challenging the Balrog, Gandalf identifies himself as subservient to the Secret Fire, and "wielder of the flame of Anor,"[67] suggesting an allegiance to Eru's Flame Imperishable. Gandalf thus announces to the Balrog which side the Wizard embraces in Melkor's rebellion.[68]

Gandalf's conflict with the Balrog illustrates the Wizard's earlier words to Frodo that he has "not been measured" against some of the world's powers. Since both contestants are Maiar, the battle involves beings created approximately equal. As noted earlier, the Istari accept a reduction of their power as a condition of their appointment. The Balrog, dedicated to evil for at least ten thousand years and awoken from an unconscious state a mere one thousand years before the War of the Ring, may also be a reduced version of its earlier self. Thus, while hierarchically equal on a theoretical level, neither contestant could feel confident of victory; the outcome appears unknowable. Gandalf's ability to prevent the Balrog from passing suggests the Wizard possesses the greater strength, whether innately or because of unseen assistance. Yet the Balrog's ability to include Gandalf in his downfall positions the two as near equals. The hierarchical equivalence of Gandalf and the Balrog, particularly the speculation that both contestants may be fire spirits, lends this battle extra irony and poignancy. Gandalf and the Balrog share a similar Eru-given nature and may have been acquaintances, perhaps even friends, prior to the Singing of the Ainur or even in the earliest era of the formation of Arda.

Interestingly enough, Tolkien considered referencing the Valar directly in the battle of Gandalf and the Balrog. One draft includes a command from Gandalf that the Balrog return to the fires of the deep, adding that Balrogs have been forbidden from showing themselves above ground since the imprisonment of Melkor. Gandalf then contrasts himself, representing white flame, with the Balrog, representing red fire. The Balrog strikes at Gandalf, before whom a sheet of white flame appears; this defensive move causes the Balrog's sword to shatter, but also snaps Gandalf's staff. The Balrog, though blinded, continues its attack on Gandalf, who chops off its right hand as the Balrog's whip (held in its left hand) winds round Gandalf's knees. The draft continues with the Company aghast at Gandalf's fall and apparent death, as in the final publication.[69]

After defeating the Balrog, Gandalf says, darkness descends upon him and he strays "out of thought and time, and . . . wander[s] far on roads" that he leaves undescribed.[70] Readers have long debated whether Gandalf's experience "out of thought and time" equates to death; Tolkien himself contributes to the debate. Appendix B of *The Return of the King* euphemistically states that Gandalf "passes away" on January 25 (Third Age 3019) while his body remains on the mountaintop; then on February 14 he "returns to life," but remains for some time in a trance-like state; three days later, Gwaihir the Eagle carries Gandalf to Lothlórien.[71] Given the structure of Eä's cosmos described in chapter 1 and taking literally Gandalf's statement about exiting time, Gandalf's spirit must exit Eä; had he instead gone to Mandos (as Robert Rorabeck suggests), he would have remained inside time, since Valinor's residents lead a temporal existence. Since the "Ainulindalë" describes just two places outside of Eä, the Void and the presence of Eru Ilúvatar, Gandalf's spirit may have left his Istar body and returned to Eru. Tolkien credits Eru with appropriating the Valar's plan by returning Gandalf to Middle-earth, expanding the plan beyond the Valar's original vision.[72]

Gandalf after Death

Tolkien describes Gandalf's return, or at least the method of its presentation, as *cheating,* a defect he should have fixed.[73] At the same time, he praises Gandalf's death as a meaningful sacrifice in the larger context of the Middle-earth cosmos. By his death Gandalf unselfishly humbles and negates himself, which conforms to Eru's ethical expectations. Because of Gandalf's limitations, he has no knowledge that any other being can guide the war of resistance against Sauron; to die may thus mean that his mission has been in vain. Yet by offering himself in sacrifice to save his friends (and protect the Fellowship's mission), he reinforces his commitment to the ethics, which Tolkien calls "the Rules," that Eru established and the Valar fulfill.[74] In contrast with Saruman, Gandalf chooses ethical behavior over personal success.

Yet Gandalf's death shocks readers, and dismays characters within the story. Faramir laments the demise of the wisdom, power, and lore that Gandalf embodies.[75] Sam complains that everything goes wrong after Gandalf's death.[76] Yet that death enables the secondary Eucatastrophe of his resurrection and return to Middle-earth (which Tolkien anticipated prior to writing the death[77]). Gandalf explains his return to Middle-earth as completing the task first assigned him as an Istar. Yet the Gandalf who appears before Aragorn, Legolas, and Gimli in *The Two Towers* differs from the Gandalf who falls into the abyss of Khazad-dûm. The new Gandalf is enhanced with "superhuman" power and wisdom, "purified" and "turbocharged."[78] Gandalf later claims his "old life [was] burned away."[79] Tolkien anticipated such a change while drafting the scene on the Bridge of Khazad-dûm; notes exploring possible narrative directions query whether the resurrected Gandalf might have more power, as well as a shift from gray to white apparel.[80]

The transformation reveals itself in Gandalf's earliest postresurrection scene, as the Three Hunters each feel a peculiar sense of latent power in Fangorn Forest; expecting Saruman, the three wonder whether the power poses a menace rather than potential assistance. When Gandalf reveals himself, Aragorn's sword bursts into flame, and Legolas shoots an arrow that vanishes in fire; if not before, then the appearance of fire signals Gandalf's presence, but a presence stronger and less guarded than the predeath Gandalf. That new presence, if it so wishes, could command obedience and overpower wills. Tolkien's notes compare Gandalf's new power to the Nazgûl's, but on the side of good.[81]

The new Gandalf, with white hair, white robe, and eyes like the sun's rays, emanates veiled strength. Tolkien's description reveals an advantage of verbal over visual media; while Peter Jackson's film excels at showing postdeath Gandalf as blindingly white, it cannot convey the unspoken perception among the Three Hunters of Gandalf's power. The perception eludes the five senses, as if revealed through intuition. The change from gray to white, however, symbolizes replacing Saruman.[82]

Gandalf's conversation with his three friends reveals aspects of his transformation. He declares himself "more dangerous than anything [Gimli] will ever meet," except for Sauron. Illustrating his beyond-human powers, he looks directly into the sun. He relates words of Gwaihir the Eagle, who assesses the Wizard as amazingly light and even transparent; the Eagle suggests that, if Gandalf falls, he will float like a leaf on the wind. Gwaihir's words and Gandalf's behavior imply that the resurrected Gandalf depends less on his body than previously.[83]

Reading between the lines, Gandalf's return to Eä suggests that Eru's direct intervention[84] rewards Gandalf for his faithfulness by empowering him to face future adversaries with the nature given him when he first entered Eä. The resurrected Gandalf is less Istar and more Maia; one manuscript claims Gandalf becomes "a radiant flame" on his return,[85] adding further evidence that Gandalf's true nature is a spirit of fire. Gimli sums up the change crudely, describing Gandalf's head as sacred.[86]

Yet Gwaihir's words suggest the new Gandalf depends less on his head, on his embodied form, than previously. He possesses limitless energy (until he becomes unaccountably tired while possessing the Palantír) and seems to lack weight, as if he appears to Gwaihir as an avatar, as the spirit-beings of Valinor sometimes assumed. Aragorn perceives this more elegantly than Gimli, asserting that while the four might set out together toward Rohan, Gandalf can arrive sooner than the rest; not content with that assertion, Aragorn poses a rhetorical question, asking whether Gandalf might travel to wherever he wishes more rapidly than Aragorn can. Aragorn expresses a profound and new distinction between them: the postdeath Gandalf can travel disembodied, if he wishes. Maiar (and Valar), Tolkien noted, can transport themselves through willpower, assuming no body hampers them; on arriving, they can assume the body they normally display.[87] For whatever reason, Gandalf does not choose to travel in that way, at least not in any passage of the narrative. He chooses instead to play by the same rules or limitations that had governed him as a body-dependent Istar. Yet, as Kisor observes, "the possibility remains, even if it is never more than suggestion, that Gandalf the White is no longer bound by the physical limitations of time and space."[88]

Or perhaps Kisor (and I) read Gwaihir's statement too literally; Gwaihir might exaggerate (not a typical trait of Tolkien's Eagles). Or the observation of Gandalf's lightness might stem from Gandalf losing weight during his protracted battle with the Balrog. In fact, the resurrected Gandalf soon appears body-dependent. Following his confrontation with Saruman, he experiences such tiredness that he enters a deep sleep, allowing Pippin to steal the Palantír. Tolkien describes Gandalf's healing in Lothlórien as literal rest, since the returned Gandalf is "not discarnate."[89] As noted earlier, Tolkien describes Gandalf's status after battling the Balrog not as death, but as a trance-like state.[90]

Perhaps a reconciliation of these two positions, incarnate versus disincarnate, can be theorized. On Gandalf's death, the connection between his spirit and his body may have been severed, allowing his spirit's exit out of the universe. On being sent back into the universe, he may have resumed embodiment, though perhaps through a slow, rather than instantaneous, process (which would explain Gandalf's assertion on board Gwaihir that he feels life returning, as well as his surprising lethargy after finding the Palantír). In fact, after the War of the Ring, the narrator hints that Gandalf approaches disembodiment once again. As he and his companions set out from Bree on their journey to the Shire, all attract attention, the Hobbits in their gear of war, but especially Gandalf as light shines out of him, his clothing like a cloud over sunshine.[91]

Regardless of whether Gandalf returns to Middle-earth in a body-dependent form, other changes have definitely taken place. Even Merry observes more extremes in Gandalf's personality, including increased joyfulness and seriousness. But while the new Gandalf reveals himself as more than he was, he is also less. After Aragorn speaks the name *Gandalf* to him, the Istar ponders a moment as if just vaguely recollecting that name from long ago.[92] A moment later he reveals that he has forgotten much, but also relearned much he had forgotten. This may confirm the idea that experience outside of Eä, timelessness in the presence of Eru, differs from the linear experience of the unfolding Music of the Ainur inside Eä. If Gandalf exited Eä, he may have experienced the Music once again in its timeless entirety. Thus, Gandalf's assertion that he can see things far away while not perceiving certain things close by may imply that he has regained knowledge of the big picture, while losing some of the details. One such detail is Frodo's journey toward Mordor, with Sam rather than alone. Later Gandalf admits incomprehension as to why Frodo chooses Cirith Ungol as an entryway into Mordor.

Gandalf does not forget the political complexities of Western Middle-earth as he applies his powers to assist in the transformation of Théoden from dotard to robust warrior. In the Hall of Meduseld Gandalf presents an incredible light show, making clear the divine nature of his intervention: thunder rolls and the Hall darkens, leaving Gandalf alone as the room's focus; at Gandalf's command, the sky clears, showing a patch of stars, despite the fact that outside the Hall is broad daylight. Théoden later describes his physical transformation as being shaken by a west wind; Tolkien asserts that the predeath Gandalf could not have accomplished such a transformation.[93]

Yet the physical change itself does not seem to be Gandalf's doing, and here Tolkien's narrative certainly differs from Peter Jackson's film depiction in which Théoden seems to suffer from demon possession (or since he seems controlled by Saruman, Istar possession). The "Synopsis" at the beginning of *The Return of the King* describes Gandalf's work as healing, rescuing Théoden from Wormtongue's spells; another manuscript attributes Théoden's condition to natural causes combined with Wormtongue's power of suggestion and application of mind-altering substances.[94] Rutledge refers to Gandalf's work as "an intervention," analogically similar to confronting an alcoholic.[95]

Thus, Gandalf's work with Théoden does not cast out a power inhabiting the king body-and-soul, but rather removes an external influence. Gandalf himself explains that Wormtongue exerts control over Théoden's will. The key moment, therefore, is the flash of lightning that accompanies Wormtongue's falling on his face dumb. Without Wormtongue's influence of lies and despair (no doubt guided by Saruman), Théoden can harken to Gandalf's words of truth and encouragement. Gandalf does not direct force against Théoden, but only against Wormtongue, the evil influence that prevents Théoden from exercising his own will. Once the evil influence is countermanded, Gandalf relies on reason to influence Théoden. Within two pages Gandalf positions himself subservient at Théoden's feet, recognizing the king's authority within his realm and providing insight so the king can reason independently. Gandalf's strategy will bolster the argument in the next chapter for discerning unseen divine influences at work in *The Lord of the Rings*.

Gandalf provides another display of his power during his visit to Orthanc. *The Return of the King*'s opening "Synopsis" asserts that Gandalf *deposes* Saruman.[96] Saruman's appearance before the diverse victors of the Battle of the Hornburg marks his last attempt to remain a major player in the political affairs of Middle-earth. As such he appears magisterial and condescending, and puts forth all his power of persuasion and eloquence. He appeals to Gandalf's pride, urging a variation of the same reasoning spoken on Gandalf's previous visit. Saruman presumes Gandalf's nature mirrors his own; like other beings who have long entertained evil, Saruman cannot perceive that others think differently than he does. Thus, he makes his appeal, unaware that Gandalf just a few days previously had consciously and genuinely positioned himself subservient to Théoden. Gandalf's dedication to the role assigned him by the Valar has long mastered his pride. As Gandalf tells Saruman, "I am beyond your comprehension."[97]

Gandalf generously offers Saruman an opportunity that parallels Manwë's approach toward Melkor in the First Age; Gandalf will hold the symbols of Saruman's authority (his staff and the keys to Orthanc), and presumably the real power that accompanies those symbols, willing to return them if Saruman's behavior shows reformation. One can only speculate whether Saruman, unlike Melkor, might truly reform, or whether he might only dissemble while maintaining an evil purpose in his heart (approaches embraced by both Melkor and Sauron in earlier ages). Gandalf suggests to Merry that Saruman comes close to accepting the offer for reformation.[98]

Gandalf does not permit Saruman a haughty exit as a statement of his independence from and disdain for others. As Saruman retreats into Orthanc, Gandalf exercises his new authority as chief of the Istari, commanding Saruman's return, declaring him a pitiable fool, casting him from the order and splintering his staff. Gandalf hints that the confrontation involves invisible mental or spiritual struggle. His mind, he says "was bent on Saruman," and afterwards he feels extreme tiredness,[99] an experience that parallels his first skirmish against the Balrog of Moria.

Casting Saruman out of the Istari implies that Saruman has lost the blessing of the higher powers that have initiated his mission. In other words, Gandalf doesn't splinter Saruman's staff as a power struggle between two wizards, but as an action authorized by a hierarchy to which Saruman, in contrast with Gandalf, forgets that he is answerable. Saruman wishes to command, rather than serve, Gandalf says, while Gandalf feels no desire for such mastery over others.[100]

Except for his interaction with Saruman, Gandalf claims to have used no wizardry in events surrounding the Battle of the Hornburg. Instead Gandalf relies again on the power of reason, offering good advice in the face of danger, and the speed of his horse, though his very presence casts fear into Wolves.[101] Perhaps Gandalf continues to veil his powers to preserve the secrecy he has long maintained. He later implies that should his Maian nature be revealed to Sauron, the forces of good will be adversely affected. At some point, he implies, he might need to reveal his true nature, but hiding himself until that time preserves an unspoken advantage.

That time comes in the battles connected with the defense of Minas Tirith, in which Gandalf's power becomes synonymous with white light.

The narrator augments the sense of that power by describing Gandalf on Shadowfax metaphorically: their movement resembles a star surrounded by a halo of light. When Pippin sees Gandalf a few minutes later, he appears pale, as if he has expended great energy, but his eyes retain their smoldering appearance. When Gandalf intervenes to rescue Faramir from his father's self-immolation, Gandalf's appearance seems like white light dispelling darkness. A draft states that white light always surrounds Gandalf, which causes shadows to retreat. And later, before the gates of Barad-dûr, those present see a white light emanating from Gandalf as if it is a sword, which completely confounds the Mouth of Sauron; a draft describes that light as spouting fire.[102]

Along with an increase of power, Gandalf displays greater understanding on his return to Middle-earth. Here again the narrator uses language that implies Gandalf possesses a nature unique among all the participants in the War of the Ring. Standing atop the battlement of Minas Tirith, Gandalf beholds "with the sight that was given to him all that had befallen." The words imply more than just superb eyesight, but the ability to comprehend events and their causes. In the Houses of Healing, Gandalf uses this ability to narrate the deeds of Éowyn and Merry.[103] Perhaps this ability to see from a distance gives Gandalf some degree of knowledge when in parley before the gates of Barad-dûr; at that time, he may sense that Frodo and Sam remain alive and free, or at least that Sauron does not yet possess the One Ring.

If the resurrected Gandalf displays greater understanding and increased divine power after his resurrection, then one can question why he doesn't exercise those powers even more, thus sparing a number of deaths of good beings and perhaps reducing the suffering of Frodo and Sam on their arduous journey through Mordor. One obvious answer applies equally to the parallel question of why the Valar and even Eru Ilúvatar do not interfere more directly: there will be no story of conflict and courage if good powerful beings simply do all the work; Tolkien the writer would have no tale to tell. Ruud asserts, however, that Gandalf could use his powers "more often and more convincingly," but he chooses not to. Ruud speculates: "Had he chosen to manifest his power without restraint, his reliance on that power may have subtly changed his will, until he could end up believing that he must do everything, and distrusting the people he had come to save. In this way he could become more like Saruman, determined that his allies are weak and that he must use his powers to shape things to his own will, to the way they should be." The next step, Ruud observes, would be desire of the Ring itself.[104]

In fact, Gandalf displays a healthy amount of fear regarding the status of his mission, specifically that he might fail, and that beings dear to him might suffer as a result of his counsel and actions. When Faramir describes (to Gandalf and Denethor) Frodo and Sam's intention of traveling through Morgul Vale, Pippin observes Gandalf's hands trembling as he clutches the armrests of his chair. Gandalf worries that Frodo and Sam may have been captured by Sauron, which might explain the darkness newly covering Gondor. Later, in a draft of his remarks during "The Last Debate," Gandalf admits to deep anxiety and continual thinking about the status of Frodo's mission.[105]

Gandalf's actions reveal that he balances an understanding of his strength with an understanding of his limitations, and recognizes that both stem from a higher authority. The word capturing this circumstance is *steward*. The concept of *stewardship* forms "the chief strength of Tolkien's fiction and the chief limitation of his political philosophy," according to Blackburn.[106] Gandalf claims the title of steward in a debate with Denethor, Steward of Gondor, implying that as stewards, both he and Denethor ought to remember whom they serve; stewardship involves recognizing that one possesses only temporary authority, bequeathed by its rightful wielder. Thus, a steward must remain willing to give up authority with the advent or return of the proper authority. This recognition prompts Gandalf, after Pippen foolishly gazes into the Palantír, to offer the stone to Aragorn with a humble bow, much to the surprise of spectators. Additionally, a steward must recognize that he or she remains essentially a servant, no matter how much power allotted that steward and no matter how long the steward has served. Gandalf reveals a willingness to serve over the span of his nineteen-hundred-year mission, and even beyond. On Sam and Frodo's awakening in the Field of Cormallen, he returns to them the gifts of Galadriel, serving as their esquire in the following celebration.[107]

Stewardship also involves a parental role. One responsibility of parenting involves withholding help when children will learn best by functioning on their own. For this reason, Gandalf does not accompany the four Hobbits on their return to the Shire. His explanation implies his function as steward had ended. Additionally, the four Hobbits have achieved a developmental state that should empower them to deal with the Shire's political difficulties on their own.

Gandalf couples his role as steward with a consistent and noble ethic. Pity identifies Gandalf every bit as much as fire, and as Rosebury observes, "the capacity for pity ranks high among the virtues for Tolkien."[108] Crabbe notes that Tolkien here relies on his philological knowledge; until about 1600, *pity* was associated with *piety*,[109] and thus marks Gandalf as holy. His pity for suffering creatures extends even to those enmeshed in evil; to Denethor he expresses pity even for the slaves of Sauron.[110] Similarly he pities Gollum, whom he considers redeemable. Sarti adds that Tolkien's use of the word *pity* "connotes not only the forgiveness of mercy, but also the understanding and sympathy for the situation of the one pitied, as realization of the common humanity which could lead oneself into the situation as well as anyone."[111] Thus pity also breeds humility.

Gandalf's actions reveal pity as a guide for decision making, showing that he learned well from his Valier mentor Nienna. Pity leads him to act cautiously rather than rashly, when passing judgment, offering others the benefit of the doubt without suffering from naïveté. "Many that live deserve death," Gandalf says. "And some that die deserve life. Can you give it to them? Then do not be too eager to deal out death in judgment."[112] This is not just a theoretical statement to Gandalf, who exhibits pity in his response to the antagonists battling over Denethor and Faramir in Rath Dínen; he acknowledges that all participants seek to do what is right. Gandalf recognizes pity in others as an admirable trait that reveals a hidden strength; the pity exhibited by Hobbits in their times of trouble (particularly the Long Winter of 2758–59) cements his original interest in the Shire. Pity is so basic an instinct for Gandalf that he recognizes it can lead to his own downfall; the one motivation that might tempt him to take and use the Ring is pity for the weakness of others, coupled with a desire to do good, as he tells Frodo by the fire at Bag End.[113]

Tolkien couples pity with hope, Gandalf's other ethical imperative. Gandalf's assistance to Théoden is one example of his effort to induce hope in those who oppose the enemy. Yet Gandalf does not reserve his efforts for political leaders only. During the Battle of Minas Tirith, his presence works to remove the mood of despair that the Nazgûl produces among the soldiers of Gondor. Soldiers' hearts lift in his company, just as they despair in the presence of the Nazgûl.[114]

The sum total of Gandalf's powers, knowledge, and dedication to the role assigned him by the Valar make him the ideal opponent of Sauron in the later part of the Third Age, as Aragorn recognizes when he calls for all Sauron's opponents to be ruled by Gandalf in the closing battle of the War of the Ring. Later Aragorn places Gandalf as the central figure in the struggle against the Enemy; the victory, Aragorn asserts, belongs to Gandalf. Treebeard agrees, telling Gandalf that he has proven himself most powerful.

As a mover and shaker within the events of Middle-earth, Gandalf has no equal; he deserves the title given him in one of Tolkien's letters: "Guardian of the Third Age." Yet his success depends on his remaining faithful to the assignment and status given the Istari by the Valar, with the blessing of Eru Ilúvatar; thus, Gandalf also deserves another title bestowed upon him in Tolkien's letters: "the Valar's plenipotentiary."[115]

Tom Bombadil: A Cosmological Mystery

Few Middle-earth-related topics are as hotly debated among Tolkien fans as the identity of Tom Bombadil and his relationship to the legendarium's cosmology (if any).[116] Fans analyze his nature while filmmaker Peter Jackson simply discards him; as Treschow and Duckworth note, Tom Bombadil has been regarded primarily as "either a riddle or an impediment—or both."[117] Yet all see Tom as more than he appears within the narrative.

Tom's exterior may not befit a divine being of Arda. He looks like a small man with a red face creased with hundreds of laugh wrinkles. His blue eyes match his blue jacket and the blue feather stuck into his well-worn hat (an appearance derived from a "colorful Dutch doll owned by the Tolkien children"[118]). He heartily sings nonsense as he tramps about the Old Forest in yellow boots. As with many Tolkien characters, he responds to multiple names: Iarwain Ben-adar among the Elves (Iarwain, Tolkien said, means *old-young*), Forn (a reference to the elder days) among Dwarves, and Orald ("very ancient") among Humans of the North.[119]

Yet Tom's actions bely something greater than his appearance, even from his earliest entrance into the story. The narrator of *The Lord of the Rings* carefully adds a parenthetical "or so they seemed" when describing his song as a string of nonsensical words. More importantly, his song fixates Frodo and Sam who stand under apparent enchantment; when they run toward him, his outstretched hand stops them short, as if they are cursed with immobility.[120] His speech patterns catch readers off guard since Tom relies on unnatural trochaic rhythms (forming a pattern of strong-weak strong-weak), rather than the more natural (for modern English) iambic (weak-strong weak-strong). If those phenomena don't already produce reader suspicion that Tom has special powers, then his ability to open Old Man Willow by singing and smiting it with a branch certainly does. The most surprising of Tom's abilities, at least to the Hobbits, is the Ring's impotence to turn him invisible; he even speaks as if he sees Frodo, to some extent, when Frodo dons the Ring as a test. Flieger suggests Tom is "not less substantial than the waking world but more so. His vivid ultrareality makes the world around him seem pale and insubstantial in comparison."[121]

Inquiring into Bombadil's identity, Frodo receives only enigmatic answers. Tom's wife, Goldberry, says merely "He is,"[122] a phrase reminiscent of Yahweh's self-identification to Moses, "I am"; this phrase leads some readers to conclude that Tom is the creator of Arda, Eru Ilúvatar (or that Tom is the creator of the creator of Arda, J. R. R. Tolkien).[123] When Frodo's expression makes clear he doesn't understand her, she elaborates, describing Tom as master of the surrounding environment, with the word *Master* uttered (in Mathews's view) "in an almost religious sense."[124] Goldberry's words lead some readers to conclude Tom is a nature spirit, the "nature deity par excellence," in the words of Petty, or "the sum total of the power for good in Nature," according to Kaufmann.[125] Hughes asserts that "Tom Bombadil is the Pan of Middle-earth."[126] Tolkien adds credence to these suggestions in a 1937 letter that describes Tom as representing the spirit of the terrain around Berkshire and Oxford, a terrain he laments as disappearing; Tolkien here certainly uses the word *spirit* figuratively, not literally. Similarly, he describes Goldberry as representing seasonal changes and their impact on terrain.[127]

Yet to be master implies at least potential control over the elements; Startzman assumes ability to control carries with it a corollary responsibility, and has identified Tom's position as a "steward like Adam before the Fall perhaps,"[128] or like Gandalf. But if so, Tom exhibits a relatively passive stewardship. Tolkien views Tom as having repudiated control and therefore one who simply delights in seeing and knowing the natural world; it is an innately pacifistic perspective, interested in understanding things and beings because they exist, but unconcerned with applying knowledge. Thus, Tolkien indicates, Tom's mastery is unusual, since it lacks possessiveness and domination.[129]

Not content with Goldberry's answers, Frodo asks Tom directly about his identity. Tom supplies his name as the only possible answer, but he adds another identifier anyway, specifically *Eldest*. He describes himself as present prior to geographical features such as trees and rivers, even prior to fundamental events such as the first drop of rain. He implies that he already resided within his realm when the Elves first came into the West, prior to the First Age. Speaking in third person, he adds, "He knew the dark under the stars when it was fearless—before the Dark Lord came from Outside."[130] These clues are suggestive while still enigmatic.

To be older than the oldest of all living *things* would suggest that Tom Bombadil is *not* a living thing, not a physical being whose creation stems from the prior creation of Eä; instead, Tom must be a spirit being, originally from outside of Eä.[131] This fits Tom's self-identification as present in Middle-earth before the Elves' great migration. But to have known "the dark under stars when it was fearless—before the Dark Lord came from Outside," suggests his presence during the Spring of Arda, the period of growth and peace after the Valar's first war with Melkor and prior to Melkor's destruction of the two great lamps.[132] This is the sole period in Middle-earth's history when it could be described as fearless; even during the three ages in which Melkor is chained, his servants continue to harass the Elves and other life-forms on the continent. In fact, to remember the first raindrop positions Tom as a witness to, or even participant in, the long period of the Valar's creation and shaping of Arda.

If Tom is indeed a spirit being, then he must fit within one of three categories:

1. Vala
2. Maia
3. Other

Intriguing arguments have been made to position Tom as a Vala; one lengthy argument asserts that Tom is Aulë (which makes Goldberry Yavanna), while another finds Tom to be Tulkas (making Goldberry Nessa).[133] At the other end of the spectrum, Tolkien himself uttered words that suggest Tom fits best into no pre-existing category. Tom is an intentional enigma that the author does not wish to explain further;[134] in essence, this explains Tom as inexplicable: "there is always some element that does not fit and opens as it were a window into some other system . . . So Bombadil is 'fatherless,' he has no historical origin in the world described in *The Lord of the Rings*."[135] Shippey thus describes him as "a *lusus naturae*, a one-member category," a position with which Flieger seems to agree.[136] Yet, as many of the writers on Tom Bombadil point out, Tolkien rarely feels content to leave an element in his writing unconnected to the cosmological structure underpinning his legendarium. Furthermore, the authority Tom displays over the Barrow-wight, in essence "remov[ing] the evil spirit from the very structure of the universe,"[137] suggests for Tom both a divine origin and a continuing knowledge of his place within the divine hierarchy.

Yet even Tolkien's assertion of Tom as enigma allows connections to the cosmology Tolkien detailed. Tom has "no historical origin *in* the world *described in The Lord of the Rings*" (emphasis added). A Maia or Vala (or other Ainu) has no historical origin within the novel, having existed prior to time and history; instead, its origin will have been external to, or *out* of the world. And the cosmic elements of Middle-earth are *not described* in *The Lord of the Rings,* which is precisely what makes my book (especially chapter 4) useful. From this perspective, the explanation that makes the most sense (to me) is Foster's, that Tom is a "Maia gone native."[138]

The "Annals of Valinor" suggest several unnamed Maiar entered the continent of Middle-earth along with Melian five hundred years prior to the appearance of the Elves; Tom may have been among them. Gandalf (in an early draft) claims Tom stems from an earlier generation than he, one with different aims and purposes. As a Maia, Tom would exhibit mastery over his surroundings. The difference in the impact of the Ring on Tom and the Istari may stem from the fact noted earlier that the Istari embody a reduced form on their entrance to Middle-earth. While Melian also suffers a reduction in power, hers stems from her persistent embodiment due to marriage with Thingol, an Elf. If Tom marries a fellow Maia, then perhaps no such reduction will result. A Maia of Ulmo might indeed call herself (metaphorically) *daughter of the River,* as Goldberry does;[139] such a connection also explains why she "call[s] up rain with her singing."[140] Like Melian, Tom restricts his authority to a specific proscribed territory (which may be an argument against Tom as the *definitive* spirit of Middle-earth's nature[141]). Flieger notes the vivid dreams Frodo experiences in Tom's house, and even reads the ambiguous sense of time experienced there as a "dreaming wakefulness";[142] the dreams suggest a relationship between Tom and the Vala of dreams, Lórien. Like Gandalf, Tom perceives the Hobbits' mental experiences; he seems aware that they experience nightmares (except for Sam) during their first night under his roof.[143]

Adding further weight to the argument that Tom is a Maia, Gandalf implies parity between himself and Tom: Tom, he asserts, is "a moss gatherer," while Gandalf has been a rolling stone. Since Gandalf's mission as rolling stone ends with the demise of the Ring and Sauron, Gandalf expresses a wish to spend time with Tom.[144] At the kernel of Gandalf's metaphor lies the concept that both he and Tom are rocks, yet with different purposes. One can imagine Tom sent to Middle-earth with a mission, prior to the First

Age, much like the Istari in the Third Age. If like the Valar and Maiar of Aman his appearance is simply an avatar, an appearance not essential to his being, then there need be no surprise that he is not wet when he enters his house during a rainstorm.[145]

Even Tom's limitations suggest his level of power and authority fits best a Maia, rather than a Vala (and certainly not Eru Ilúvatar). Tom expresses knowledge of his own limitations when he reveals that he cannot predict weather. Similarly, he lacks concern for the political dimension of Middle-earth society. Even if he could have assisted in the deliberations of the Council of Elrond, he would not have participated, Gandalf asserts.[146] Instead, he keeps himself within his own boundaries. Yet, as Stanton notes, Tom "needs Good to win in order to survive, whether he acknowledges it or not."[147] Furthermore, he lacks the ability to destroy the Ring and would not be a trusty guardian of it, given his forgetfulness for anything that does not capture his attention; apparently only living things capture his attention, which suggests a similarity between Tom and Radagast.

Yet considering the degree of heat generated from debating this issue, I don't wish to insist that my explanation makes the most sense (even though I think it does). Perhaps the wisest commentators are those who assert the foolishness behind the project of pushing Tom into an identity box in which he doesn't perfectly fit; pursue Tom's identity no further than Goldberry's description: "He is." Treschow and Duckworth, for example, argue that Tom's existence serves primarily a narrative purpose: he provides a narrative digression that allows the Hobbits to realize their limitations while promoting their growth, paralleling the role of Beorn in *The Hobbit;* "attempts to square [Tom's] identity with Tolkien's larger mythology may at times be interesting, but are really beside the point."[148] Brawley, in contrast, finds Tom representative of something, but specifically of that which cannot be defined: Tom is "the experience of the numinous which defies language's ability to express it."[149] Pearce emphasizes and accepts the self-contradictory dimensions of the character; Tom, he says, "is paradox personified."[150] Tolkien himself added that the character neither requires nor benefits from readers' speculations.[151]

More important (for this study) than debating what he *is* is examining what he *does* (and what he *doesn't* do). As master he possesses an intimate knowledge of nature's workings. Tolkien, as much as he dislikes allegory, describes Tom as an allegory or example "of pure (real) natural science."[152] His desire for knowledge about nature is an end in itself, not a means to do something further; Brooks describes Tom as possessing "a clean and pure power . . . which fills the mind with knowledge," rather than exerting itself to control nature or others.[53] Except for making paths and rescuing the Hobbits, Tom exhibits little interest in improving nature within his realm; other than scolding Old Man Willow, Tom takes no apparent action to prevent similar problems in the future. Treebeard comments (in a draft) that Tom understands trees but does not function as a shepherd; he merely watches without interfering. While Tom never influences nature toward evil, he does little to fix or cure the evil within nature.[54]

Tom expresses his wisdom via engrossing stories that give the Hobbits insight into natural life-forms and processes. His storytelling induces a trance-like state in which the Hobbits lose track of time; afterwards, they display ignorance as to whether a few hours or a few days have passed, and more significantly, are unaware that they have missed meals. Tom's stories show him equally conversant with local history, which he expresses back through the First Age down to current events of the Shire. Yet Gandalf observes (in a draft) that few possess the ability to understand his counsels.[55]

Tom provides evidence that he relies on more than his own judgment and knowledge. He claims he did not appear on the path by Old Man Willow as a result of Frodo's calling for help, though in a draft passage Gandalf asserts, when he learns the Hobbits have left the Shire by means of the Old Forest, that Tom will help keep the Hobbits out of harm's way.[56] Tom claims that only *chance* positioned him in the vicinity of Old Man Willow at the very day and hour that the Hobbits need rescuing, though he adds a phrase that casts doubt on the concept of chance: "if chance you call it."[57] As the next chapter will illustrate, passages that attribute events to chance, but then query whether chance is the proper word for what actually takes place, offer the possibility that a larger but invisible power may influence and add purpose to the event.

Perhaps the strongest evidence of Tom's divine nature involves his use of music. When Old Man Willow traps Merry and Pippin, Tom threatens to "sing his roots off."[58] Tom teaches the Hobbits a song that he claims will call him if they should be in need. The song forms an appeal, a prayer, for assistance; an earlier draft of the song included the words "here now we summon you." And indeed, when the Hobbits are trapped within a Barrow, the song works. As Frodo sings, his voice grows in power at the mention of Tom's name. Then, though the narrative positions the Hobbits a half-day's journey from Tom's home, only a "long slow moment" passes before Frodo hears Tom's song of response intertwined with the sound of moving rocks to open the Barrow.[159] Tom then sings Merry, Pippin, and Sam back into consciousness from the spells placed on them by the Barrow-wight; Sabo describes this as "a sort of singing duel."[160]

Tom's apparent ability to transport himself long distance in a short amount of time strengthens the argument that he does not depend on his physical body. He functions as a spirit who simply chooses to appear in an embodied form. His use of song to accomplish action connects him with other characters from the legendarium (such as Lúthien, Finrod, and Aragorn), but the degree of his song's power exceeds any other character except Lúthien, who is a daughter of a Maia. If Tom is a Vala or a Maia (or an Ainur brought separately into Arda), then his use of song to produce an outcome connects him to the Music of the Ainur. Whatever Tom is, his abilities mark him as an example of the metaphysical dimension present in *The Lord of the Rings*. Musk describes Tom as Eru's "representative on Middle-earth, an 'immortal spark' of the omnipotent creator. As Treebeard [i]s Fangorn, so Bombadil [i]s nature."[161] Thus Tom Bombadil joins Gandalf and the Istari as representatives of divinity in Middle-earth during its Third Age.

The High Elves

Elvish influence appears early in *The Lord of the Rings* when Gildor and his colleagues unknowingly drive away the Nazgûl from Frodo and his friends in the oak forest on the path to Woodhall by singing a hymn to Elbereth. Gildor invokes the Valier's name later in his conversation with Frodo in the form of a blessing: "May Elbereth protect you."[162] Later events show greater power wielded by Elves. One brief and understated passage recalls incidents in *The Silmarillion*. After the discovery of a surviving sapling of the White Tree of Gondor, Frodo approaches Aragorn with his request to return to the Shire. At that moment Arwen sings a Valinorean song, while the tree grows and blossoms.[163] Syntactically, the word *while* implies mere simultaneity: the tree thrives at the same time Arwen sings. The context allows a naturalistic cause-and-effect relationship: *because* the tree thrives, Arwen rejoices and sings. Yet similar moments in *The Silmarillion* often assert a reverse, non-naturalistic cause-and-effect relationship: Lúthien's singing, for example, *causes* plants to grow and bloom. The use of simultaneity without assertion of naturalistic cause-and-effect allows the possibility that Arwen, the female Elf who in the Third Age corresponds most symbolically with Lúthien in the First Age, possesses a similar power (or alternatively that the song of Valinor retains its power) late in the Third Age. This possibility allows deeper meaning for the assertion in the Appendices (in the Tale of Arwen and Aragorn) that "from afar [Arwen] watched over [Aragorn] in thought";[164] if similar activities from the First Age serve as guide, Arwen's behavior can be seen as more than just wishful thinking.

While wording describing Arwen's actions suggests the possibility that she applies a special Elvish power, scenes involving the Elf Glorfindel overtly state such a power, particularly his involvement in the events at the Ford of Bruinen. Frodo first perceives Glorfindel as light that shines through the Elf's clothing (a description similar to that of Gandalf as he rides in the company of the Hobbits after the War's end). Glorfindel's touch, while not completely healing Frodo's wound, does reduce the pain. Glorfindel acknowledges himself as one of only a small number of Elves capable of openly opposing the Black Riders. While he cannot prevent all nine Black Riders from attacking Frodo, he appears once again as white light, which Gandalf explains is Glorfindel "as he is upon the other side: one of the mighty of the First-born," a Lord of the Elves displaying a righteous anger.[165] In a draft, Tolkien refers to Glorfindel and other Noldorin Elves as "Elves of power."[166]

That power illustrates one of the differences between Elves and Humans. While Elves such as Gildor and Glorfindel lack the power of the Valar, the Maiar, the Istari, or even Tom Bombadil, they do possess powers and abilities that appear supernatural to other residents of Middle-earth (as evidenced by Sam Gamgee's desire to witness Elf magic). Tolkien describes his Elves in general as most fundamentally representing Humans, but with advanced creative abilities.[167] Thus Kreeft calls Elves "semiangelic beings[;] . . . when we [Humans] look at them we look *in the direction of* the angels."[168] Translating Kreeft's assertion into terms of Tolkien's cosmology, Elves blend Human limitations and Maian/Valian abilities. Petty describes the Elves more conventionally as possessing "natural magic . . . exhaulted [*sic*] above that of the race of men." This magic reveals itself through "heightened senses and the ability to heal the injuries of others through empathy and natural lore," and through "a direct psychic connection with the life of rock and tree and water surrounding them."[169] Whether Kreeft's and Petty's observations represent two different aspects of the High Elves, or whether they are really just two ways of saying the same thing, these dimensions of

Elvish experience, natural magic and angelic qualities, make Elves worthy of examination in a study of divinity in Arda.

To some extent, the heightened abilities of the Elves, when compared with Humans, result from species difference. Elves quickly develop strong wills that give mental power, unknown to humans, over their bodies. This, combined with the fact that Elves' destinies, unlike those of humans, seem tied to the history of Arda, perhaps with no escape from it, produce in Elves a strong relationship between mind and body. Elves' spirits cling tenaciously to the physical bodies in which they house, offering protection from illness and disease, as well as rapid healing from injuries, when compared with Humans. Such abilities indeed appear magical to Humans and Hobbits, as do the Lembas, a food produced from a corn-like grain first devised by Yavanna in Aman. It is prepared and handled only by the Yavannaildi, the maidens of Yavanna, and the recipe is kept secret, since it retains some elements of its origin.[170] Even Tolkien compares Lembas to the Eucharist, which prompts Lynch to call the Elven bread "consecrated nourishment."[171]

While all Elves, or at least all the Eldar, possess some level of special power, some Elves develop that power more than others. Beleg, the renowned bowman, illustrates the power of a Sindarin Elf of the First Age who did not have the benefit of a sojourn in Aman. Beleg uses magic to string his bear-sinew bow that, otherwise, neither Elf nor Human possessed strength enough to bend; he sings magic over his sword to augment the blade's sharpness before using it to cut the chains that bind Turin. The Noldorin Elves, however, develop powers well beyond the level of the Sindar due to their millennia of residence in Aman, learning from the Valar and experiencing directly the light of the Two Trees. At least early in the First Age, the Noldorin Elves appear visibly different, particularly their eyes, compared with Elves who did not journey to Aman.[172] The Noldorin exiles are, in essence, super-Elves.

Gandalf's words to Frodo, that the Noldorin Exiles "live at once in both worlds,"[173] ambiguously references their in-between status. It may mean that the Noldorin Elves live both in the physical realm as represented by Middle-earth and the spiritual/metaphysical realm as represented by Aman; however, since Gandalf discusses Glorfindel's absence of fear in the face of the Black Riders, it may imply that Noldorin Elves live in both the seen world of physical reality and the invisible realm of the undead Nazgûl. In fact, both these possibilities may overlap, being two ways of expressing the same dichotomy. At any rate, Gandalf continues by saying that the Noldorin Elves possess significant ability to confront both the visible and the invisible.

Thus, for many centuries during the Third Age, a period known as the Watchful Peace, Sauron and his followers refrain from activity merely from the threat of the White Council, composed of Elf Lords and Wizards.[174]

By giving the name Glorfindel to the Elf who aids Frodo at the ford of the Bruinen, Tolkien emphasizes the unique and advanced natures of the Noldor, since he creates an intertextual reference to a Noldorin Elf by the same name from the *Silmarillion* tales of the First Age. The first Glorfindel dies battling a Balrog, enabling Tuor and Idril's escape from the destruction of Gondolin. The Glorfindel of *The Lord of the Rings* may be a different Noldorin Elf with the same name, but Tolkien hints that the two are identical, and thus an Elf granted the privilege of leaving Aman to come once again to Middle-earth. Tolkien speculates that Glorfindel may have accompanied Gandalf on his journey to Middle-earth in the Third Age; the author offers a backstory to this scenario: after a period of waiting (a purgatorial experience due to his role in the Noldor's rebellion), he is granted embodiment once again and spends several thousand years in the Blessed Realm among the Valar and Maiar, perhaps even becoming a friend or disciple of Gandalf. Thus, he possesses exceptional power of a nearly divine nature. Alternatively, Tolkien speculates that Glorfindel may have journeyed to Middle-earth in the Second Age to aid Elrond, traveling by means of Númenórean ships.[175]

While Glorfindel accomplishes an important task in aiding Frodo, what really saves the Hobbit from the nine Black Riders is the flood of the Bruinen, which according to Gandalf, comes under Elrond's authority and power, suggesting that Elrond maintains a sphere of influence over a specific geographic region, much as Melian did in the First Age, and as do Galadriel, and perhaps Tom Bombadil, during the Third Age. Elrond founds Imladris, or Rivendell, in 1697 of the Second Age, in the face of Sauron's exhibited power; or he founds it in 750 of the Third Age coincident with Celeborn and Galadriel's founding of Eregion; or in 1697 of the Third Age coincident with the destruction of Eregion, survivors of which form the core of Imladris.[176] Prior to founding Rivendell, he served an apprenticeship under Gil-galad, the last Noldorin king.

Elrond descends from a complex lineage that reflects much of the history of the First Age. His father is Eärendil, who sails through the heavens as the Morning Star throughout the Second and Third Ages of Middle-earth. Elrond's grandparents (on his father's side) are Tuor and Idril. Elrond's great-great grandfather is Fingolfin, Fëanor's half brother, which also means that his great-great-great grandmother is Indis, of the Vanyar. If that's not an illustrious enough ancestry, on his mother's side his great-grandparents are Beren and Lúthien, and thus he descends from the Maia Melian. Elrond thus claims ancestry from the Maiar, from the Noldor and the Vanyar, from the Eldar who did not cross the sea, and from Humans. While he never experiences Aman (until the end of the Third Age, that is) or the light of the Two Trees, his illustrious lineage makes it no surprise that Elrond exhibits special powers.

Galadriel, too, claims a unique background. Born in Aman, her mother is Teleri (and one of her grandmothers a Vanyar), but her father is Finarfin, brother of Fingolfin and half brother of Fëanor; thus, she is considered one of the Noldor. As a Noldo, Galadriel learns from Aulë and Yavanna,[177] though the name of her realm, Lothlórien, suggests an affinity with Lórien, or at least with Lórien's gardens.

Tolkien describes Galadriel as the most important Noldo, second only to Fëanor (and that exception is qualified with a *maybe,* and the assurance that she possesses the greater wisdom). One narrative describes Galadriel and Fëanor as "unfriends." Yet her desire to order dominions without direct oversight by a higher power ensnares her in the Noldorin rebellion, though she continues to revere the Valar. She fights against Fëanor in the Kinslaying, yet accompanies him on his rebellion, in part to oppose him; later in life Tolkien revised Galadriel's story, giving her a desire to travel to Middle-earth separate from and prior to Fëanor's urgings, and involving her in Fëanor's rebellion and the ban of the Valar only by temporal coincidence.[178]

At the end of the First Age, while most exiled Noldorin Elves are permitted a return to Aman, she and a few other instigators of the rebellion are excluded from returning; or contrarily, she refuses the Valar's pardon; or, having already traveled further east than any other Noldo, she only hears of the Valar's summons after the fact.[179] Her husband, Celeborn, is either similarly exiled from Aman (though Teleri) or a Sindar of Doriath. Together they travel east at the end of the First Age and establish realms, first in Eriador, then in Eregion.

Galadriel's songs during the Fellowship's last meal in Lothlórien connect her to the ancient past and the divine beings she knows from Aman, prior to her journey across the Helcaraxë to Middle-earth. Tolkien describes the first as composed, rather than improvised, and created prior to the arrival of the Fellowship. It speaks of geographical features of Aman: Tirion, Eldamar, and the gardens of Lórien. In addition, the song hints at other Valar in its first two lines, which begin "I sang of leaves" and "Of wind I sang";

to a Noldorin Elf, referencing those natural phenomena calls to mind the Powers associated with them, Yavanna and Manwë. The lines also hint at an action of subcreation, that the singing in some way contributes to the production of the leaves and the wind, as if the singing is a prayer to the Valar responsible for the natural phenomena, to which the Valar respond. The song ends with Galadriel's famous query whether a ship yet exists that can transport her back to Valinor.[180]

Her farewell lament, in contrast, Tolkien describes as an improvised expression of personal regret and despair, prompted in part by her experience of refusing Frodo's offer of the Ring. That refusal displays a renunciation of the pride and self-assurance that first prompted Galadriel to leave Aman, as well as antipathy toward any enhancement of her abilities in a way that would violate the moral code of the Valar and Eru; Tolkien's description of Galadriel embracing a moral code echoes his praise of Gandalf's willingness to accept self-sacrifice in confronting the Balrog. Galadriel expresses her lament prior to realizing that the Valar both pardon and honor her. Ultimately, after the War of the Ring, the Valar lift the ban against her return to Aman, rewarding her for opposing Sauron and in particular for refusing the Ring.[181] Frodo's presence aboard a ship leaving Middle-earth in the final chapter of *The Lord of the Rings* signifies the respect extended her by Aman; her lament sung before the Fellowship as it leaves Lothlórien ends with a wish that Frodo might be granted "a purgatorial (but not penal) sojourn in Eressëa," should he successfully finish his quest.[182]

Elven Powers

Neither Elrond nor Galadriel display their powers to the extent Gandalf does. Historical narratives imply that both experience successes as military leaders, which must require as much power as either can muster. Elrond leads forces against the Witch King at Angmar, defeating the Witch King in the middle of the Third Age. Galadriel thwarts three attacks against Lothlórien during the War of the Ring; appendix B of *The Return of the King* claims her realm can be defeated only if Sauron attacks in person. After the war, Celeborn leads troops in a successful assault on Dol Guldur, but Galadriel receives credit for reducing the fortress to rubble and uncovering its dungeon.[183]

Galadriel channels her physical powers, at least during the Third Age, primarily to defensive rather than offensive actions. Even the selection of geographical space for her realm illustrates strategic thinking, as a chess master chooses carefully where each piece will be moved on the board. She establishes Lothlórien, in part, to forestall Sauron's troops from crossing the Anduin. As a political strategy (with cosmic implications) she seeks to diminish the age-old enmities between Elves and Dwarves, because she sees Dwarves as potential warriors against Orcs. While Celeborn mistrusts Dwarves, Galadriel capitalizes upon a cosmological connection: she has been a pupil of Aulë, creator of the Dwarves.[184] Brackmann finds in Galadriel's endorsement of positive relations with Dwarves a confirmation that Dwarves are not merely a cosmological accident; "If the 'far-sighted' Galadriel knew that the dwarves were necessary for the stopping of [Sauron and his followers,] it implies that [Dwarves] were, indeed, part of the Creator-deity's design for Middle-earth from the beginning."[185]

Galadriel's realm seems more clearly defined geographically than Elrond's, and in fact she follows the pattern set by Melian, her friend and mentor, in protecting her borders from intruders. Legolas, after experiencing Lothlórien, asserts that a hidden power prevents evil from impacting the land. Both Frodo and Sam intuitively sense this power, much as Frodo senses the evil power of the Black Riders. When Sam expresses that he feels as if he were "*inside* a song,"[186] Haldir explains that Sam perceives Galadriel's power. The "Lothlórien" chapter of *Fellowship* describes Galadriel's realm as never experiencing blemish, sickness, or deformity. Tolkien's drafts for the chapter go further: the invisible power produces a clean and beautiful domain, evidenced by no aroma of decaying leaves and no broken twigs. Even time functions differently in Lothlórien, though Tolkien debates as to whether Lothlórien operates on an alternative time, or whether no time passes outside Lothlórien while the Fellowship resides there. Some readers, such as Kocher, infer that Galadriel possesses the ability to slow time within her realm.[187]

Both Elrond and Galadriel exhibit prophetic abilities. Elrond foretells the reforging of Narsil, and Gandalf claims Elrond foresaw that the White Council's attack against the Necromancer in Dol Guldur would not destroy Sauron. Frodo assesses his encounter with Faramir as fulfillment of Elrond's prophecy that the Hobbit will find unexpected friends during his journey. Galadriel, while claiming she lacks the power of foresight (even though one draft narrative describes her as "far-sighted"), provides Sam and Frodo, through her Mirror, visions of the future (or possible futures), though mixed with visions of the past and present.[188]

Círdan, even more than Elrond and Galadriel, possesses insight into the future. Círdan, a Teleri who long seeks for Elwë after the Elf leader's disappearance, strongly desires to see Valinor, but his faithfulness to Elwë causes him to miss the island passage granted the majority of the Teleri. He considers building his own boat to cross single-handedly, but a message which he understands to come from Aman warns him against such an attempt. A voice speaking in his mind informs him that later his work at shipbuilding will be of great value to the Elves. "I obey," Círdan replies. He then sees a vision of a shining white boat in the heavens, foreshadowing Eärendil's ship. He continues to experience foresight beyond the ability of any other Middle-earth Elf.[189]

Elves exhibit a sixth sense that provides confidence in knowing about things far off. Legolas knows "in his heart" that the Orcs that hold Merry and Pippen captive did not rest overnight in their journey across Rohan. Elrond and Galadriel exhibit an even more powerful telepathic ability, which Tolkien terms *thought transference*.[190] While resting on their journey toward Rivendell after the War of the Ring, Galadriel, Celeborn, Elrond, and Gandalf recall past events without speaking; rather, they "look from mind to mind"; had there been an onlooker, she or he would see no indication of activity except the light of their eyes responding to the unspoken exchange of thought.[191] Hammond and Scull refer to this moment as a "rare reference" in Tolkien to "extrasensory communication."[192]

Tolkien translates the Elvish name for this ability, *sanwe-latya*, as thought transmission without speaking. He writes at length about the caveats and limitations associated with sanwe-latya: a mind can only perceive another mind when both parties open toward one another. Minds most naturally would be open, in the ideal state, Arda Unmarred. Minds can close themselves to others, but doing so takes an action of will. "Nothing can penetrate the barrier of Unwill."[193] Furthermore, most beings can experience thought transmission with only one other person at a time; greater minds can engage small groups, though only one person at a time can send a thought message,[194] a description that probably applies to Gandalf and the High Elves on their journey toward Rivendell. Transmission of thought is more challenging for Elves than Valar and Maiar, because Elves are mind-body combinations; their bodies form barriers through which the mental messages must pass.

Transmitting thoughts effectively, for Elves, requires training and practice. The ability can be strengthened by affinity (such as kinship), urgency (a desperate need on the part of the sender), or authority (when one has duty to another). Furthermore, using vocal language regularly detracts from the use of thought transmission. Using language becomes habitual to spirit-beings that elect to remain embodied, which likely results in neglecting the practice of thought transmission. Distance between beings, however, does not reduce the ability to transfer thoughts to those accustomed to using the technique; furthermore, thought transmission functions more rapidly than spoken language. Yet despite those advantages, Tolkien speculates, complete revelation of one's mind to another is impossible.[195]

Telepathic ability allows the possibility of reading minds. Gildor seems to see into Frodo's mind when the two meet in the Shire. Galadriel's actions suggest she effectively reads the minds of lesser beings;[196] this apparently includes the ability to place thoughts into those minds. When the Fellowship arrives at the oval chamber where Celeborn and Galadriel sit enthroned, each member is subjected to a test, as Boromir calls it, "offering what she pretend[s] to have the power to give." Sam describes the experience as the Elf Queen examining him from within and questioning his devotion to his mission.[197] The test allows Galadriel to read the character of each member but in a manner that reveals that character to the individual being read.

Beyond mind reading and thought transference, Elven power often associates with objects or devices: mirrors, cloaks, jewels, and of course, rings; as Gee notes, much of what passes as Elf magic, in the eyes of beings such as Hobbits, is simply Elf technology left hidden or unexplained in the narrative.[198] As noted earlier, Galadriel's Mirror allows observers to see events from past, present, and (possible) future. The Mirror shows Sam a vision of forthcoming events in his journey with Frodo, though he only realizes the images are prophetic as they come true in the Pass of Cirith Ungol.[199] Frodo sees a figure that may be Gandalf, an image of the sea and a small ship, and the Eye of Sauron. Here again Galadriel reads Frodo's mind; she adds that she can perceive Sauron's mind, though he is not (yet) capable of seeing hers.

Another magic of the Elves involves the cloaks Galadriel gives the Fellowship. Later events suggest a number of virtues the cloaks possess, including the ability to camouflage the wearer. A draft passage describes this further: the cloaks blend with the natural environment, though they do not, technically, produce invisibility; the draft suggests Galadriel in some way boosts the cloaks' powers. Another draft, after asserting that the cloaks make wearers nearly invisible, suggests that within the borders of Mordor the cloaks function somewhat like Ungoliant's unlight, hiding the wearer in shadow. Elven rope and boats similarly possess special powers, whether intrinsic due to some element of their crafting, or extrinsic as a result of a special blessing given or requested by the Elves; Sam praises the rope from Lothlórien because of its ability to untie itself and come when called.[200]

Two of Galadriel's gifts to the Fellowship reflect her power. To Sam she gives a small box of dirt with her blessing and the promise that it will enable plant growth even amid a barren waste.[201] Galadriel's gift to Frodo connects *The Lord of the Rings* to the overarching history of the First Age: the Phial of Galadriel contains light from Eärendil and water from a fountain of Galadriel. How, precisely, the star's light is encapsulated within the Phial remains a mystery, but its origin links it to the Silmaril recovered by Beren and Lúthien and ultimately to the Two Trees of Aman; the light of the Two Trees further links the Phial to Yavanna, who created the trees. Since Aman is no longer part of the sphere of Arda in the Third Age, the Phial of Galadriel possesses quite literally an otherworldly light. This fact adds an additional layer of irony to Frodo and Sam's use of the Phial to confront Shelob, the last-living child of Ungoliant, who with Melkor killed the Two Trees and consumed their light; as Klinger notes, the Phial's lineage amounts "to an extremely condensed account of the world's history that reaches from the initial radiance of Valinor to the shadow Sauron's renewed threat casts across Middle-earth at the end of the Third Age."[202]

The lack of decay and aging in Galadriel's realm may be attributed to more than her Elven powers. Her Ring of Power and the Elessar, a green jewel designed by a craftsman of Gondolin to encase sunlight, emanate a power of healing and restoration. The craftsman gave the Elessar to Idril, who in turn bequeathed it to Eärendil; the jewel thus traveled to Valinor in Eärendil's great journey during the First Age. With the coming of the Istari in the Third Age, Gandalf returns the jewel to Galadriel at Yavanna's command (an action that counters Galadriel's fear that the Valar have lost interest in Middle-earth). Gandalf adds that Galadriel should eventually bestow it upon the one who bears the same name as the jewel, and thus the Elessar comes to Aragorn. (An alternate story, in the same manuscript, states that Celebrimbor designed a second Elessar specifically for Galadriel, who then passes it on to her daughter Celebrían after Galadriel receives the ring Nenya; Celebrían in turn gives the Elessar to her daughter Arwen who then gives it to Aragorn). One manuscript attributes to the jewel the natural beauty that flourishes around Galadriel.[203]

Tolkien precludes an explanation for how Elven Rings of Power work by providing his characters with an unwritten law that wielders do not speak of their rings. This injunction also bars readers from certainty as to which of the Elven powers discussed above are enabled or enhanced by the wearers' Rings. One manuscript indicates that Sauron touted the Rings as providing Elves of Middle-earth powers and knowledge comparable to those of Aman.

Yet, Tolkien several times changed his mind about Rings; in one draft Gandalf declares that he doesn't know where the Rings are, causing him to presume they have gone over the sea to Valinor. Tolkien initially assumed even the three Elven Rings had been created exclusively by Sauron.[204] Then as the role of the Rings solidified, it intersected the story of the Silmarils: Celebrimbor (a grandson of Fëanor who repudiated the Oath of the Noldor) devised the Rings in the middle of the Second Age.

After Sauron loses the One, the three Elven Rings serve as useful tools for the Elves; they particularly aid defense of Elven kingdoms, though used only secretly. Since they serve defensive purposes, they do not aid wars of conquest, or so Elrond declares; rather, they empower the wearers in knowledge, creativity, and healing, as long as the One Ring is neither recovered by Sauron nor destroyed. The Rings empower the Elves in preservation, maintaining the status quo, reducing the impact of change. As such, the Elven Rings suggest a longing on the part of the wielders for Aman, where change occurs much more slowly than in Middle-earth.[205] Flieger notes that Galadriel uses hers to set apart Lothlórien as "a type of Eden, a world before Evil . . . has stained the air."[206] Given that the Valar had intended Middle-earth as a veritable Eden, Vaccaro observes, the Elven Rings "reinforce support of the Valar's vision for Middle-earth."[207]

Late in drafting *The Lord of the Rings* Tolkien expanded the details of the specific rings, adding names only in the first edition's galley proofs. Narya the Great, bequeathed by Círdan to Gandalf, possesses a ruby that shines red like firelight. Nenya, the Ring of Adamant, wrought of mithril and worn by Galadriel, bears a white gem resembling a cold star. Nenya associates with water, and thus Galadriel's ring connects to the medium through which her Mirror (and perhaps her Phial) operate, and ultimately to Ulmo, the Vala of water. This association opens the possibility that the Ring acquires its abilities by tapping into the power of water in some way, in essence accessing the power of Ulmo, though Stoddard links Nenya to a knowledge of emotions and sympathy. At the same time (and perhaps for the same reason), the Ring increases Galadriel's desire for the sea and for Aman, and thus reduces her joy in Middle-earth. Vilya, given to Elrond by Gil-galad, bears a large blue sapphire on a band of gold. Its special element is air; Bilbo notes the unique qualities of the air of Rivendell. Stoddard connects Vilya to the realm of Manwë, as well as the intellect and the preservation of lore.[208] Of the three Elven Rings, Vilya has the most power; it remains hidden during *The Hobbit* and *The Lord of the Rings,* while Narya and Nenya make at least cameo appearances.

The future of the Three Rings remains uncertain during the last war of the Third Age. Should Sauron recover the One, then the work accomplished through the Three will be undone and their wearers' minds will be revealed to him. If the One Ring were to be destroyed, then the Elves foresee two possible outcomes: either the Three Rings will become free once again to contribute to healing Middle-earth of Sauron's lingering influence, or they will fail and their wearers will fade. For a while Tolkien embraced the first view, but ultimately Galadriel expresses the second, suggesting that Lothlórien will fade with the passage of Time.[209] After the fall of Sauron, Gandalf confirms Galadriel's view as correct; "the power of the Three Rings . . . is ended," he announces, adding that their wearers will either leave Middle-earth or fade away, while Humans will take dominion.[210] Thus the High Elves sacrifice their own power for the greater good, a sacrifice that results inevitably from victory.[211]

The Third Age sees the decline of the Elves, accompanied by a corollary ascendency of Humans, who embrace a more aggressive strategy, one illustrated by the element of their natures permitting them the ability to transform their destinies. Hood associates the Elvish strategy of preservation with the Second Theme of the Music of the Ainur, introduced by Eru to counteract Melkor's discord, noting that the Second Theme ultimately does not succeed. The Third Theme, uninfluenced by the Ainur, surprisingly incorporates the best elements of the Discord to overpower it. Hood identifies the Third Theme with Humans. Thus, Humans do not possess the level of harmony with nature that Elves display. Instead the "dissonance between human beings and their environment is caused in part because of their closeness to the third theme, whose object is to *change* that original pattern of nature into something that can transform the symphony with its distortions into something beautiful. They . . . are in the process of creating, along with Ilúvatar, a new pattern" that will ultimately produce the greater harmony represented by the climactic final chord of the Music of the Ainur.[212] Therefore, not just the Elves' abilities and knowledge, gained in part through the Noldor's millennia in Aman with the Valar, displays cosmic reality; so, too, does the metahistorical pattern of the decline of the Elves.

Conclusion

In *The Lord of the Rings* Gandalf and the other Istari, Tom Bombadil, and even the most powerful Elves function simultaneously as characters and as metaphysical representatives; they operate as proxies for the generally invisible Valar, or to use Gandalf's term, they serve as stewards. As such, they reassure those characters within the story (and reassure those readers outside the story) who possess an understanding of the cosmology portrayed in tales from the First and Second Ages that the same cosmic reality continues to support life events in the Third Age. While readers with no experience of Tolkien's writings other than *The Hobbit* and *The Lord of the Rings* might understandably assume that the magic of the Elves and Gandalf comes from no more personal a power than something akin to the Force of *Star Wars,* readers of *The Silmarillion* and other Tolkien writings must embrace willful ignorance to presume a discontinuity between the divine hierarchy established in the First Age and the magic displayed in the Third Age.

Examining the representatives of the Valar, however, foregrounds a problem of representation raised in the previous chapter (since the Valar themselves represent Eru Ilúvatar). Divine beings become humanized the more distinctly they are represented. Enmeshing divine beings with the affairs of Humans (and other sentient material beings) requires detailed representation. The previous chapter notes that the Valar appear most humanized in the Tales of Aman, when the Valar become enmeshed in Elvish events, such as the rebellion of Fëanor; the Valar's representatives in the Third Age become even more enmeshed in the lives of sentient material beings than do the Valar in the First Age. The genre difference noted earlier, *The Lord of the Rings'* affinity with the novel more than with mythology, necessitates detailed delineation of the Valar's representatives. Thus Gandalf, though associated with mysteries, becomes more clearly depicted in *The Lord of the Rings* than any Vala or Valier in tales of the First Age. *The Lord of the Rings* shows Gandalf's involvement with lesser beings, while *The Silmarillion* tends merely to say that such involvement takes place. The showing makes Gandalf more human, allowing readers to forget, for a time, his divinity.

But enmeshing a character such as Gandalf into the narrative makes problematic depicting his divinity at all. Within *The Lord of the Rings* divine beings appear more human in proximity to Hobbits and Humans and less so in their absence (just as Melian in the First Age appears more Human than other Maiar). Tom Bombadil's greatest display of power can only be inferred from the text: his apparent ability to travel a long distance nearly instantaneously (to rescue the Hobbits from the Barrow). Similarly, Gandalf's most amazing displays of his divine nature (surviving under cold water for an extended period as he battles the Balrog; exiting the flow of time) occur with no witnesses. This suggests an incompatibility between narrative attempts to portray divine beings and the reality (or in this case, fictional reality) of those beings. To narrate the actions of divine beings is to humanize them, and the more humanized divine beings become, the less apparent their divinity.

Increasing the human-ness of divine beings simultaneously increases the possibility that good divine beings might switch sides in the struggle of good versus evil. Tales of the First Age place Melkor's rebellion in the far distant past; while the narratives imply that a good Maia might switch sides as late as the era just prior to Fëanor's rebellion, they make no hint that a Vala or Valier might do so. The Valar appear 100 percent committed to good, just as the Elves appear similarly in the Third Age. The Istari, however, reduced from their Maiar nature (and as a result, more Human) can, and in the case of Saruman do, switch sides. Tolkien's one-time speculation that 80 percent of the Istari fail (and apparently fail *morally,* not just strategically) suggests that, in the author's mind, humanizing the Istari requires failure as more likely than success. Said another way, among the distant Valar-level beings of the First Age, Melkor, as evil, is an anomaly; among the enmeshed and humanized Istari of the Third Age, Gandalf, as good, is the anomaly.

Conversely, maintaining consistent distance between the Valar and residents of Middle-earth in tales of the Third Age eliminates human-like weaknesses attributed to the Valar in documents concerning the First Age. The few fleeting Third Age references to the Valar leaves them unsullied as divine beings, though only for readers familiar with Tolkien's cosmology; readers without that background likely find *The Lord of the Rings'* references to the Valar merely evocatively mysterious. The following chapter will seek to find and interpret even more subtle hints of the Valar's influence on and interference with events in *The Lord of the Rings.*

Chapter 4

Divine Intervention in the Third Age: Invisible Powers

One of the few religious moments in *The Lord of the Rings* occurs when Faramir and his men face west prior to their meal in the cave at Henneth Annûn.[1] "So we always do," explains Faramir to Frodo and Sam; "we look toward Númenor that was, and Elvenhome that is, and to that which is beyond Elvenhome and will ever be."[2] Lobdell observes that such a custom (dubbed "Grace before Meat" in a Tolkien letter[3]) could be explained as "courtesy . . . or a code of behaviour."[4] Yet Faramir's explanation suggests awareness of both history and cosmology. Tolkien's drafts reveal the extent of Faramir's cosmological understanding, adding the phrase "Valinor the Blessed Realm" after "that which is beyond Elvenhome and will ever be."[5] These words position Faramir as a descendant of those Númenóreans who remained faithful to the Valar through the downfall of Númenor and the end of the Second Age. Faramir's blessing exhibits respect for the Powers of Aman and offers evidence that Gondorans continue to recount tales of Númenor, and perhaps still understand those tales as revealing truths of Middle-earth's cosmology; even Tolkien describes Faramir's remark as a glimpse of "divine worship."[6] As Pengoloð says to Ælfwine in a draft of the "Akallabêth" (though a passage explicitly deleted by Tolkien), the tales themselves may preserve among the residents of Middle-earth a sense of the holiness of Aman.[7] Yet moments of worship or reverence rarely appear in the narrative; Richard Purtill, for example, complains that "After creating a rather elaborate pantheon of 'gods', Tolkien in one sense did nothing with it: the Valar play almost no part in the stories in the later part of *The Silmarillion;* much less do they play a part in *The Lord of the Rings.*"[8]

One explanation as to why *The Lord of the Rings* contrasts with *The Silmarillion* in the extent to which divine beings make their presences known can be found in Tolkien's 1954 letter discussing cosmological dimensions of the story with Father Robert Murray. Tolkien remarks that he "purposely kept all allusions to the highest matters down to mere hints, perceptible only by the most attentive, or kept them under unexplained symbolic forms. So God and the 'angelic' gods, the Lords or Powers of the West, only peep through."[9] Tolkien understands this strategy as central to the type of story he wishes to tell. While fantasy should reflect religious truths as understood in reality, it should not do so explicitly.[10]

Faramir's moment of silence is one such example of a passage where Tolkien allows religious truth concerning the Valar to *peep through* as a tradition of the people of Gondor. The Valar do not directly show themselves in the Middle-earth of the Third Age; Gandalf, their representative, suggests they would not do so even if Sauron recovers the One Ring. The Valar formally committed Middle-earth into the keeping of Humans.[11] Furthermore, as Madsen notes (in her intriguingly titled essay, "Eru Erased"), *The Lord of the Rings* encapsulates a primarily Hobbit perspective on events, and "Cosmologically speaking, [Hobbits] do not know very much." This perspective "offers religion obliquely and thus without impediment; it offers religion's effects and not its anxieties."[12]

Judging by those effects, the spirit-beings of Aman do *not* just watch passively from afar, but instead remain actively (though distantly) involved with Middle-earth events. Aragorn, the most important descendant of Elendil at the end of the Third Age, exhibits awareness of divine presences at work in the War of the Ring. At Parth Galen Aragorn asserts that the Fellowship bears no responsibility to persuade Frodo into choosing one road or another; such persuasion is impossible, he adds, since other, stronger powers exert force.[13] Aragorn's words suggest deeper conflict, unseen powers contesting with Sauron in ways beyond the comprehension of the sentient life-forms of Middle-earth. For evidence beyond mere inference, take Gandalf's authoritative assertion to Galadriel: the Valar's "eyes are not dimmed nor their hearts hardened" against the residents of Middle-earth in the Third Age.[14] While the previous chapter examined characters that exhibit divine powers while visibly present within the continent of Middle-earth during the War of the Ring, this chapter will search for the Valar as invisible influences.

To find the Valar at work late in the Third Age, the chapter will follow a four-part structure. First, examining evil powers will establish that spirit-beings present and named within the text use psychic and spiritual power to dominate from a distance. Part two will turn from evil to good characters to examine Gandalf's ability to affect others telepathically. If evil creatures and a Wizard can be shown to exert power from a distance, it stands to reason that more powerful beings can intervene across a larger distance, even across the gap between Valinor and Middle-earth; the last two sections will read between the lines for evidence of such influence. The third section will examine the meaning of *luck* in *The Hobbit,* which reveals the Valar at work even within Tolkien's first Hobbit book. The last section will seek specific Valar in the act of *peeping through* the narrative of *The Lord of the Rings.*

✿ *Evil Powers from Afar*

While Tolkien provides no more than hints of the Valar's influence during the War of the Ring, he displays much less circumspection in revealing the power of evil characters. Curry notes a "lack of symmetry" between the obvious presence of evil in contrast with the invisibility of the Valar.[15] Often evil power makes itself known through a perception of psychic pressure, as when Aragorn feels Saruman's will at work inducing an invisible barrier of weariness during the Three Hunters' pursuit of Merry and Pippin.[16] Shelob produces an even more powerful psychological effect on Frodo and Sam, and even on Orcs. Klinger suggests Shelob induces "a temporal distortion" in the experience of beings who stumble into her lair. In some unexplained manner, she "unsettles the linear progression of time and the logical sequence of causes and effects," which adversely affects the reasoning abilities of sentient beings. Klinger attributes Shelob's effects to her lineage as last descendant of Ungoliant, which thus positions Shelob as an "intrusion of the outer Void on the temporal world ultimately result[ing] in boundless, insensate night, or 'untime.'"[17]

Shelob's psychological effects require proximity, and may not be conscious strategies on her part, but only a natural, constant effect, comparable to an instinct. Sauron, however, can intimidate consciously and at a distance. Dickerson notes Tolkien provides "illustrations of Sauron's power everywhere."[18] Thus evil's power in the Third Age parallels its power in the First (despite Sauron's lower status than his predecessor), when Melkor curses Húrin and his family, and Glaurung the Dragon compels Húrin's son and daughter, Turin and Nienor, by means of a spell; Glaurung overwhelms Nienor such that she experiences total amnesia and temporarily loses the use of her senses and muscles.[19] Sauron exhibits similar powers; as Shippey says, *The Lord of the Rings* "is permeated with the idea of the will of Sauron operating at a distance, stirring up evil forces, literally animating the Ringwraiths, and even the Orcs."[20]

Sauron exerts influence by multiple means. A draft attributes to Sauron the ability to cause sickness in beings that approach him. "Of the Rings of Power and the Third Age" describes a plague that struck Gondor, carried by dark, easterly winds, suggesting Mordor as the source. This, along with the dark cloud cover released as Sauron launched his attack in the War of the Ring, implies that Sauron influences weather. While such efforts have practical strategic value, they qualify primarily as harassment. Sauron shows greater interest in awakening evil beings to more evil, much as Gandalf seeks to encourage good beings to courage and valor. One manuscript, for example, describes a Nazgûl visit to the Barrow Downs that rouses Barrow-wights and other opponents of Elves and Humans; as a result, the text attributes a heightened sense of watchful malice among beings in the Old Forest, such as Old Man Willow. Appendix A of *The Return of the King* suggests Sauron's increased influence in the Third Age may have awoken the Balrog of Moria (and thus when the Dwarves dig too deeply in Third Age 1980, they do not awaken it, but merely release the demon from bondage).[21] Sauron even influences one of the few remaining Dwarf Rings to embrace evil, driving its bearer (Thrór, father of Thráin, father of Thorin Oakenshield) "to folly and destruction."[22] Dwarf Rings are presumed subject to Sauron's influence because he participated in their making, even though some were given by the Elves.[23]

Beyond the general ability to awaken and inspire evil beings and rings, Sauron exerts influence, control even, over sentient beings of Middle-earth, and from a distance. Hood refers to this power as telepathy, while Shippey (describing Sauron's influencing on Frodo atop Amon Hen) uses the words "mental force."[24] Tolkien's phrase is "the machinations of Sauron," as evidenced in the unification of Gondor's enemies.[25] The extent of Sauron's power over living beings becomes obvious when, at the moment Frodo puts on the Ring within Mount Doom, Sauron turns all his attention toward Frodo; the vast army arrayed against Aragorn and his followers suddenly lacks will, like a nest of termites whose queen has died.[26] By leaving undisclosed Sauron's method, his machinations remain mysterious, sometimes connected to Nazgûl, other times to the One Ring, and in the case of Saruman and Denethor, to use of a Palantír.

Frodo feels a psychological impact on his earliest encounter with Black Riders. At first he presumes the attraction is something like curiosity, but almost immediately afterwards he feels an overpowering urge to put on the Ring. Later Frodo feels the same desire more strongly; only the surprise appearance of the Elves (singing a hymn to Varda) rescues him. At the Prancing Pony Frodo again feels the urge to don the Ring, and this time he identifies that source as external, perhaps from the proximity of Black Riders; a few moments later the Ring slips onto his finger, as if the Ring itself responds to the same external pressure. Even Aragorn speculates that the incident is more than accident. Shortly thereafter, Merry, too, feels influenced toward a Black Rider. Meanwhile, back at Crickhollow, Fredegar Bolger experiences increasing levels of fear, rising to terror, when the Black Riders attack and find Frodo gone.[27]

On Weathertop Aragorn credits an inner perception of evil with causing anxiety and fear as he and the Hobbits approach the hill; the unseen presence of the Black Riders disturbs their hearts. As the Black Riders approach the dell below Weathertop, where Aragorn and the Hobbits camp for the night, both Frodo and Sam feel intense dread and fear; Frodo is unable to resist an urge to put on the Ring. After the attack, the Black Riders disappear, and with their physical absence Aragorn no longer *feels* their presence nearby. Then again at the Ford of the Bruinen Frodo perceives in his heart the enemy willing him to stop. After crossing the Bruinen, and facing all nine Black Riders en masse, Frodo's tongue stops and his heart works violently, even after invoking the name of Elbereth.[28]

When the Black Riders, by the midpoint of *The Two Towers* identified as Nazgûl, take wing, Humans, Elves, and Hobbits (and even Gollum) feel intense fear and anguish whenever one flies overhead, even at a great height. Perhaps the height from which the Nazgûl operates increases their ability to induce fear. Or perhaps Sauron permits them to reveal their evil power more clearly as his war with Gondor draws near. The short-term effects of the Nazgûl on Gollum reduce him to a state of paralyzed fear; over time the flights of Nazgûl overhead push Gollum back to his old ways, causing latent treachery to rise nearer the surface.[29]

Even in Minas Tirith a flying Nazgûl affects the hearts and minds of the city's residents. On his first day in the city Pippin finds himself cowering against the wall on hearing the cry of the Nazgûl. Yet even before hearing the sound, he and Beregond feel a sudden sense of terror that Beregond describes as a presentiment of doom. A messenger to Denethor claims that Nazgûl-induced fear has prompted a majority of the Gondoran soldiers to run away; he asserts that the Nazgûl's troops would willingly commit suicide if so commanded. During the attack on Gondor its stoutest soldiers transform into immobile victims of despair at the cries of the Nazgûl. The unseen impact of the Chief Nazgûl appears even more clearly when, on its death, the residents of Gondor feel their hearts lifted in newfound hope. Yet for Aragorn's select group of seven thousand soldiers journeying through Ithilien on their way to confront Sauron, the mere presence of the remaining eight Nazgûl, though silent and out of sight, causes an unshakable dread.[30]

The One Ring is the most referenced mechanism by which Sauron exerts evil power. Isuldur, Tolkien writes, discovers he cannot bend the power of the Ring to his own purposes. Once taken from Sauron, the One Ring retains elements of Sauron's evil, inciting his followers to action; this explains why a band of Orcs attacks and kills Isuldur, causing the Ring to become lost in the river Anduin for centuries. Later, the Ring pulls at Gollum, even though he doesn't possess it.[31] Tolkien describes this as "the terrible call of the Ring."[32] Frodo perceives that call as the Ring grows heavier and more burdensome during the approach to Mordor. Even Sam feels the Ring's power growing more uncontrollable, as he carries it into Mordor.

While Rings of Power and Palantíri will receive more attention in the following chapter (in the section on evil and technology), Sauron's ability to use the Palantír to ensnare both Saruman and Denethor illustrates the unique nature of Sauron's ability to manipulate. Crowe considers Denethor's devolution "the purest case of psychological Unmaking [in *The Lord of the Rings*], since in this case all the damage is done by Sauron at a distance."[33] Denethor's downfall joins Saruman's, as well as Théoden's long period of depression and inaction, as examples of the abilities of evil powers to subvert other wills to their own.

🪶 Gandalf and Power from Afar

Gandalf, in contrast with Saruman and Sauron, does not exert his power to control other people's wills. The previous chapter, however, showed that Gandalf reads the minds of others, and perceives danger from afar. Gandalf himself takes this power a step further, implying some ability to *influence*, if not control, life-forms near him, and even at some distance, telepathically.

His summons of Shadowfax serves as an example; Gandalf says he summoned the horse by bending thought toward him.[34] Shippey suggests the mysterious nighttime appearance of a Wizard-like being to Aragorn, Gimli, and Legolas, on the eaves of Fangorn Forest, "may have been a 'wraith' of Saruman, possibly projected by Gandalf."[35] As the resurrected Gandalf approaches Aragorn, Legolas, and Gimli in Fangorn Forest, Legolas appears partially incapacitated and prevented from taking a proper defensive stance, as if under the influence of a more powerful being. Even early in *The Lord of the Rings*, Gandalf uses a phrase that can be interpreted as telepathic influence; Bilbo, Gandalf asserted, needed *all* Gandalf's help in giving up the Ring.[36] The Ring held Bilbo, as it did all its bearers; it overpowered its wearer's will. Gandalf's assertion may imply that his efforts, verbal and otherwise, worked against the power of the Ring, allowing Bilbo to regain enough of his own will to give it up.

Even if Gandalf's assertion does not imply use of mental influence to help Bilbo, the postdeath Gandalf certainly displays such a power, comparable to Sauron's, and a power not dependent on close proximity to the individual being influenced. The events of Parth Galen in the hours before the breaking of the Fellowship show Frodo in great personal anxiety, wishing for a trusty guide. Frodo exhibits extreme uncertainty, even a lack of will, on leaving the Fellowship to think alone in the woods of Amon Hen.[37] After putting on the Ring to escape Boromir, Frodo sits upon the Seat of Seeing atop Amon Hen. Here Frodo sees a series of images, remote yet distinct. Gazing to the South he sees Minas Tirith, but then feels himself coerced to look past Osgiliath toward Mordor. Ultimately an outside force holds his gaze upon Barad-dûr, the seat of Sauron's power. Frodo perceives two effects of gazing into Mordor from the Seat of Seeing: first, he loses hope; then, he sees Sauron's eye. Somehow Frodo knows that the eye, representing a strong and powerful will, perceives his gaze, though not yet the exact location from which Frodo's gaze emanates. Sauron thus holds Frodo nearly powerless, as Sauron searches for the gaze's source, probing for the Ring bearer.

Events then happen rapidly. First, Frodo throws himself from the Seat. Then he cries out, unsure whether he speaks words of resistance or of submission. But at that moment he experiences an epiphany, a message "from some other point of power," with the words *"Fool, take it off! Take off the Ring!"* Frodo feels the two powers striving within him; at a moment when "perfectly balanced between their piercing points," he comes to his senses, as it were, perceiving an ability to exercise his own will, "free to choose" to take off the Ring.[38] Doing so ends Sauron's ability to pinpoint Frodo's location.

Even a first-time reader sensitive to the diction Tolkien assigns his characters will perceive that the voice "from some other point of power" sounds very much like Gandalf's; Shippey notes its "asperity."[39] The diction resembles Gandalf's famous last words, uttered while clinging to the Bridge of Khazad-dûm, "Fly, you fools!"[40] and indeed both the vocabulary and the use of the imperative mode fit Gandalf's nature when under pressure. More importantly, after reappearing to Aragorn, Legolas, and Gimli in Fangorn Forest, Gandalf implies that the words, or at least the idea, originated directly from him. The Ring was almost revealed to Sauron, Gandalf says, but not quite: "I had some part in that: for I sat in a high place, and I strove with the Dark Tower; and the Shadow passed."[41] Hammond and Scull describe the experience as a moment when Gandalf "struggle[s] with the Eye of Mordor" and fights "to influence Frodo."[42] Kocher may speak hyperbole when he describes this moment as "Sauron and Gandalf . . . contending for Frodo's soul,"[43] but Rutledge concurs, arguing that, without Gandalf's influence, "Frodo would have been finished."[44]

Based solely on the description given in *The Two Towers,* and without carefully coordinating dates within the text, I would presume the "high place" where Gandalf sits is Celebdil or Caradhras, one of the mountains over Moria, to the top of which Gandalf climbs in pursuit of the Balrog. Yet Hammond and Scull quote a "manuscript timescheme" for *The Lord of the Rings,* in the possession of the Tolkien archive at Marquette University, that clearly identifies the "high place" as a hill in Fangorn Forest.[45] In a draft narrating Gandalf's return, Gandalf identified the location as hills close to Methedras,[46] which would position him just southeast of Treebeard's forest. Regardless of his exact location, this story shows Gandalf operating invisibly to Frodo and working from a distance to influence the contents of Frodo's mind.

This is not a one-time-only event; the narrative hints at another such moment when Gandalf influences Frodo from afar, though the influence is more diffuse, less focused than the moment atop Amon Hen. Looking out over the Morannon Frodo ponders whether to enter Mordor's front gate, or to trust Gollum's alternate route. This crucial moment for Frodo, who feels oppressed by the weight of the Ring in such proximity to the land of Sauron, coincides with Gandalf's confrontation with Saruman at Orthanc; yet even at the height of that conflict, Gandalf's "thought was ever upon Frodo and Samwise[;] over the long leagues his mind sought for them in hope and pity."[47]

This quotation offers a rare insight into divine mental powers in Arda. Gandalf's mind appears larger-than-human, godlike, focused on benevolence, and capable of significant multitasking. And the narrative suggests his effort to focus benevolence toward Frodo and Sam produces practical effects, more than simply sending positive thoughts into the universe. "Maybe Frodo felt it," the text says, "not knowing it, as he had upon Amon Hen."[48] Tolkien's "maybe" leaves room for naturalistic explanations but the comparison with the moment of obvious intervention atop the Seat of Seeing implies Gandalf, though distant from Frodo, accomplishes something useful. The words "as he had upon Amon Hen" suggest Gandalf again decreases the unseen oppressive power of Sauron that seeks to subvert other wills to his own. And indeed, after much thinking (and after Sam's comic recitation of the Oliphaunt poem), Frodo feels capable of deciding to follow Gollum. A few miles later, as the group leaves the Morannon and enters Ithilien, they feel a decrease of despondency without the direct gaze of the Eye of Sauron upon them;[49] this illustrates the extent to which Sauron's will has been influencing theirs, and thus the benefit of Gandalf's thoughts of hope and pity directed toward them. Tolkien refers to such moments, when divine beings provide "enhancement of . . . powers as instruments of Providence," as "grace," which he specifically associates with Frodo's ability to resist the power of the One Ring.[50] Such moments contrast with the attack of the Ringwraiths against Frodo at Weathertop, in which, Shippey notes, "Frodo's will has just been overpowered by superior force, . . . using some sort of mental power."[51]

Of course, Gandalf's influence serves the cause of good, in contrast with Sauron's and his Ringwraiths' evil influence, because Gandalf makes no attempt to overthrow Frodo's freedom of choice, but only to overthrow Sauron's influence, which is bent on removing Frodo's ability to choose. Sauron's influence disables, while Gandalf's enables. In these incidents, Gandalf opposes Sauron to achieve an equilibrium in which Frodo can operate under his own power. In essence, Green suggests, he "neutralizes evil beings who, by attacking ordinary [beings] with magic, have themselves broken the rules."[52] Such work fits the stewardship role assigned the Istari when they first entered Middle-earth, to encourage and reinforce the innate powers of good beings to resist Sauron.[53]

Luck: *The Valar and* The Hobbit

While Gandalf reveals an ability to influence others metaphysically, he also provides the key to uncovering evidence of the Valar's direct work in *The Hobbit* and *The Lord of the Rings*. *The Hobbit* lacks the "transcendent dimension" that Rutledge finds "so very present in *The Lord of the Rings*."[54] Yet even here a "transcendent dimension" appears through a close reading of the word *luck* as used in *The Hobbit*. During his riddle game with Gollum, Bilbo is saved in one instance "by pure luck"; nervously begging for more time, he inadvertently answers Gollum's riddle. Later as Gandalf announces he will soon leave Bilbo and the Dwarves to their adventure, he claims their success thus far can be attributed to "good management *and* good luck." The narrator asserts Bilbo was born "with a good share of" luck, when Bilbo guesses the correct direction to find his friends when battling the Mirkwood spiders. Then in the caves of the Wood Elves, as the butler and chief guard grow drowsy from intoxication, the narrator suggests that Bilbo possesses "luck of an unusual kind." As Bilbo clings uncertainly to the barrels that provided the Dwarves' escape, "the luck turn[s] all right" when the barrels wash ashore. Bilbo's ability to extract the Dwarves from apparently hopeless plights motivates Thorin to claim Bilbo possesses "good luck far exceeding the usual allowance"; Bilbo in turn acknowledges that he has "begun to trust [his] luck" more than in the past. When Bilbo's invisibility prevents Smaug from seeing him, he "blesses the luck of his ring." Then when Bilbo awakens and reappears after the Battle of the Five Armies, Gandalf acknowledges that he has "wondered if even [Bilbo's] luck would see [him] through."[55] In the narrative of *The Hobbit,* much depends on luck.

Yet in the ending paragraphs of the narrative, as Bilbo and Gandalf chat by the fireside in Bilbo's (recovered) Hobbit hole, Gandalf implies the involvement of something more than luck. "You don't really suppose, do you, that all your adventures and escapes were managed by mere luck, just for your sole benefit?" Gandalf asks.[56] His rhetorical question, coming after the narrative's insistent reliance on *luck* to explain fortuitous cause-and-effect relationships, raises the possibility that something more than an abstract force operates behind the story, as if a sentient though unseen power has an interest in making events turn out favorably for Bilbo, though for reasons of much greater significance than merely benefiting the Hobbit. Rossi interprets Gandalf's words to suggest that "fate, good fortune, or in its Christian denomination, Providence, is a major actor in the story."[57] Rutledge describes this scene as a moment of "apocalyptic transvision," a metaphysical moment allowing readers to "see through one sphere of reality into the other."[58]

Tolkien perceives within Gandalf's words a central theme of both *The Hobbit* and *The Lord of the Rings:* achievements of individuals granted special grace to succeed against the odds; Tolkien sees such individuals as "ordained,

. . . inspired and guided" toward an objective beyond the individual's abilities.[59] As Dickerson elaborates,

> Gandalf's reference to the events being managed implies the presence of a manager! In other words, there is some hand at work in all of the events of the story, leading the events (and the characters) to their prophesied (and planned or managed) conclusion. This manager, then has both the desire . . . to act, and also the power . . . to bring about his purposes (though to characters within the story who are merely experiencing something beyond their control and their ability to understand, his actions may appear as luck).[60]

Gandalf comments on his rhetorical question in *The Lord of the Rings* when, again before a comfortable fire at Bag End, he informs Frodo that Bilbo's Ring is the One Ring of Sauron. Sauron exerted mental power to find the Ring, yet the Ring itself exerted some separate degree of (sentient?) power to return to him, or at least to leave Gollum; "there was more than one power at work," Gandalf asserts. Yet why should the Ring come specifically to Bilbo? Not because Sauron or the Ring wished for Bilbo to possess it; rather, Gandalf inserts a third power into the equation; "there was something else at work, beyond any design of the Ring-maker." Bilbo, he claims, "was *meant* to find the Ring, and *not* by its maker."[61] This grammatical construction parallels the biblical use of "divine passive," defined by Pederson as "the use in the Bible of the passive voice to indicate that God, who is not named, is the doer of the action."[62] Glover adds that using passive voice "in teleological passages gives a sense of depth and mystery and creates the kind of qualitative difference between the immediate and the transcendent that the devout believer experiences."[63] Gandalf's history among the Powers of Arda places him in a position to know the doer(s) behind the divine passive. He not only knows that "something else at work"; he represents them: the Valar, and beyond them, Eru Ilúvatar. Early in creating his legendarium, Tolkien directly connected the word *luck* with divine intervention; when Beleg searches for Turin, who is held captive by a band of Orcs, "the luck of the Valar" positions him conveniently on the very edge of the Orc encampment. Even in works only tangentially connected to the legendarium, such as *Farmer Giles of Ham,* luck conveys divine intervention; the parson tells Giles that he possesses a luck he can trust, implying a conscious will behind that luck.[64]

Shippey considers luck, in *The Hobbit,* as "a continuous interplay of providence and free will."[65] Yet if luck implies divine intervention, and if finding the One Ring was divinely appointed to Bilbo, then readers might expect to find elements of luck in the one most important narrative event of the Third Age: Bilbo's acquisition of the Ring. As Dickerson notes, the chances of Bilbo finding the Ring accidentally are "astronomically unlikely."[66] Yet examining chapter 5 of *The Hobbit* reveals little evidence of external design. Awakening after being knocked on the head by an Orc attack in tunnels under the Misty Mountains, Bilbo guesses blindly the direction he should travel. Crawling along the tunnel floor, "his hand met"[67] the Ring. Neither Bilbo nor the narrator mentions any impulse or guiding force; finding the Ring seems even less than luck, but a mere accident. Only in a letter does Tolkien describe Bilbo's finding the Ring as a "seeming 'accident'";[68] for such an event to be only "seeming" accidental would require, in Deyo's words, an "inexplicable meshing of divine foresight and mortals' free choice."[69]

Consider how many points of influence will be necessary to ensure that Bilbo finds the One Ring. Elrond and Gandalf must be influenced toward selecting the right path through the Misty Mountains, or the Orcs must be influenced to change the location of their Front Porch. Gandalf might need a special nudge of wariness to ensure he remains alert enough to escape the Orcs when they attack. Then events throughout the Orcs' caverns while the Dwarves and Bilbo are captive will need manipulation. Gandalf might require divine assistance to ensure he takes the proper tunnel. The timing of the silent Orc attack as Gandalf leads his followers will need to be synchronized; events in that attack will need to transpire such that Bilbo will fall and bump his head in a dark, out-of-the-way location,[70] remaining unnoticed by Orcs, Dwarves, or Gandalf. When Bilbo awakens, he will need to be influenced to guess the proper direction to take toward the Ring; he will need to touch the precise square inch of tunnel floor where the Ring lies. And prior to this, Gollum will need to be induced to travel over that same spot, and to lose his Ring (something he has apparently not done in hundreds of years); or if Gandalf is correct that the Ring itself exerts influence on its own behalf to leave Gollum, that influence will need to transpire in a place where Bilbo will find the Ring. In other words, if *chance* is operating, there are many chances available to prevent Bilbo from finding the One Ring; the unlikeliness of finding the Ring is, perhaps, the strongest indication of unseen forces operating with forethought against the odds.

And indeed in an alternative narrative (written by Tolkien many years after *The Hobbit*), Gandalf claims there *has been* forethought: his own. In "The Quest of Erebor" Gandalf explains his concern for the security of Rivendell against an attack by Sauron; at that time (around Third Age 2940) Gandalf has only recently identified the Necromancer of Dol Guldur as a returned Sauron. With the Dragon dominating the Lonely Mountain, the Elves of Rivendell possess few allies in the North. Removing both the Necromancer and Smaug from their seats of power, and restoring a solid Dwarf kingdom in the region, will strengthen the position of Rivendell and its allies. Gandalf, in other words, wishes to see Smaug overthrown, and Bilbo and the Dwarves form a possible means to that end; they are chess pieces that Gandalf can manipulate in his long-term battle against Sauron.[71]

Yet Gandalf readily acknowledges that he, too, is a chess piece, manipulated by a higher and unseen power. "I did no more than follow the lead of 'chance,'" Gandalf admits.[72] The placement of *chance* in single-quotation marks in the text positions it comparable to *luck* at the end of *The Hobbit;* it is only *chance* so-called, and thus operates to suggest "that Providence is at work, or may be at work," even though, Hammond and Scull acknowledge, "Tolkien makes no overt statement."[73] Dubs, while reading Tolkien through Boethius, defines chance as situations in which the rules of cause and effect operate at times when sentient beings are unaware of the causes.[74] Tom Bombadil expresses a similar attitude toward *chance* as "providential 'luck'" in *The Fellowship of the Ring.*[75] When Frodo asks whether Tom's rescue of the Hobbits is a response to Frodo's cry for help or "just chance," Tom replies that his singing prevented his hearing Frodo's call; "Just chance brought me then, if chance you call it. It was no plan of mine."[76] If it is no plan of Tom's, yet still not exactly chance, then it must be the plan of some unseen power (which Shippey attributes to the Valar[77]).

As Gandalf says when he realizes that an old map and key, rescued from an unidentified Dwarf and kept for years with no particular plan of his own, might support his scheme of placing Bilbo with the Dwarves, chance "began . . . to look less like chance."[78] Hood suggests Gandalf's study with the Valier Nienna, whose realm in Aman is symbolically positioned furthest west, and thus with a view away from Middle-earth rather than toward it, inculcated a mode of perceiving hidden outside forces. "Understanding . . . the primal harmonies and having looked out beyond the walls of the world, Gandalf can perceive the providential patterns which show Ilúvatar's specific interventions which correspond to the Third Theme" of the Music of the Ainur. Because of this perspective, Hood concludes, "Gandalf is more sharply aware of Ilúvatar's role in shaping such random things as his own unusual interest in Hobbit-lore . . . and the Ring's decision to leave Gollum just as Bilbo happened by."[79]

Other characters join Gandalf and Tom in using the word *chance* to suggest something more than chance. When the Elves' song to Varda interrupts the Black Rider's attempt to master Frodo's will, Frodo recognizes the unlikelihood of such an occurrence, describing it to Pippin and Sam as "a strange chance." Gildor confirms a few pages later that "there may be more than chance" behind their meeting. Elrond expresses a similar view to the members of the Council, brought together "by chance as it may seem. Yet it is not so." Instead, Elrond asserts, attendees should assume their presence in Rivendell is "so ordered"; rather than assembled by accident, those present are called by a higher power.[80] Because the entity doing the calling remains unspecified, the words leave an impression of "an inscrutable director who is somehow in control," according to Glover.[81] Clearly Tolkien uses *chance* and *luck* as code words to imply a meaning closer to *providence,*[82] a meaning that presumes divine intervention. In a draft of "Concerning Hobbits" Tolkien uses the word *accident* in the same manner: Hobbits become temporarily important in the era of Bilbo and Frodo "by what is called accident."[83]

Appendix A of *The Return of the King* provides details of the chance meeting between Gandalf and Thorin, further emphasizing the event's hidden significance. In or near Bree on March 15, 2941 (Third Age), Gandalf meets Thorin Oakenshield who, to Gandalf's surprise, addresses him. Apparently the two know of one another but have never previously met. In fact, one narrative suggests Gandalf had previously ignored Dwarves. Thorin acknowledges that Gandalf has frequently entered his thoughts lately, as if to suggest that Thorin should speak to the Wizard; Gandalf replies that he in turn has been thinking of Thorin. Both speakers suggest that their thoughts are not simply coincidental, but rather result from external pressure or influence exerted upon their minds.[84]

Gandalf hints that even his interest in Bilbo stems from an external force. He describes himself as drawn toward Bilbo, qualifying the attraction with the word *somehow*. Though Gandalf acknowledges that Bilbo has noteworthy qualities, the adverb *somehow* implies that Bilbo's attraction may not be intrinsic; something (or someone) else may contribute to keeping Bilbo in Gandalf's mind. At the very least, Gandalf's conviction that the

Dwarves must take Bilbo with them, despite the foolish impression Bilbo makes when they first appear at Bag End, suggests an urgency from beyond foresight; Gandalf declares that he "knew in [his] heart" that Bilbo must accompany the Dwarves, otherwise the quest will fail; or rather, he corrects himself, "the far more important events by the way would not come to pass."[85] Gandalf speaks similar words at the Council of Elrond; in the face of Saruman's confident assertion that the Ring is lost forever, Gandalf says his "heart misgave" him, yet his heart also prompts him to recall Saruman's words that the One Ring might possess distinctive markings.[86]

While expressions such as *I know in my heart* are often simple clichés to mean *I firmly believe,* the phrase appears elsewhere in the legendarium, uttered by Manwë to express an understanding derived from Eru Ilúvatar. Gandalf is subordinate to Manwë, just as Manwë is subordinate to Eru. Tolkien in fact speculates on the implications of the Elvish word *Óre,* of which *heart* is an English approximation. While *Óre* means *heart* in the sense of feelings or emotions, Elves also use it to describe thoughts that enter the mind, sometimes from deep reflection, but other times from minds of more powerful beings such as the Valar, and ultimately from Eru. Gandalf's phrase, in other words, though not a definitive reference to a thought planted in the mind by Eru or the Valar, certainly opens the possibility of such influence. Gandalf places heart-knowledge parallel to knowledge acquired prior to entering Middle-earth, and both in contrast with knowledge possessed in his conscious mind; yet Gandalf will not discuss knowledge from beyond Middle-earth except with other beings from beyond Middle-earth.[87]

The concatenation of such expressions by Gandalf suggests awareness that as a faithful representative of the Valar he is subject to leadings and influences from beyond the Great Sea. According to drafts of appendix A from *The Return of the King,* some participants in the War of the Ring presume, after the fact, that Gandalf had a conscious intent in supporting the quest of Thorin and his accomplices, and in bringing them together with Bilbo; yet, the narrator assures otherwise, since Gandalf himself will say only that "he was 'directed', or that he was 'meant' to take this course, or was 'chosen,'" while he consciously perceives only his own politically strategic purposes.[88] By implication, Gandalf is not sent to Middle-earth to operate solely under his own powers. An alternate version of "The Quest of Erebor" implies as much: "I dare say [Bilbo] was 'chosen,'" Gandalf asserted, "and I was only chosen to choose him"[89] The word *only* implies that Gandalf finds being a tool of the Valar a humbling rather than a prideful experience. As he tells

Bilbo at the end of *The Hobbit,* "you are only quite a little fellow in the wide world after all."[90] If Gandalf perceives, after the fact, that he, too, has been influenced from afar for ends he did not envision, then he also is "quite a little fellow in the wide world after all."

So despite a lack of evidence within *The Hobbit* narrative that divine intervention caused Bilbo to find the Ring, documents external to the narrative do make that claim. But does evidence exist of divine intervention elsewhere in the story, apart from references to *luck?* Just a few pages after Bilbo finds the Ring he becomes enmeshed in a life-or-death contest with a creature that desires to kill him. The prologue to *The Fellowship of the Ring* attributes Bilbo's winning the riddle contest and escaping Gollum to luck.[91] Two such moments of luck are Bilbo's guessing the fish and time riddles. With Bilbo baffled by the fish riddle, the pressure mounts as Gollum sizes up Bilbo like a piece of fresh meat, urging him to hurry; just as Gollum enters the water to approach Bilbo, a fish fortuitously jumps out of the water and onto Bilbo's toes. *The Silmarillion* shows Ulmo influencing and appearing to Humans and Elves at bodies of water. Perhaps this fish, jumping at the right time and the right place, signals Ulmo coming to the rescue to ensure events turn out favorably, or at least to ensure that events have the possibility of turning out favorably; the narrator notes, oddly enough, that the fish was "in a fright,"[92] which might suggest a motivation even stronger than Gollum's foot. Of course, the fish jumping at that moment may be mere chance; yet Shippey asks (rhetorically, since it can't be answered definitively from the text) whether chance might be "the way the Valar work."[93]

Gollum's next riddle equally challenges Bilbo and, as noted earlier, the narrative claims he states the correct answer "by pure luck."[94] This, too, may be a moment of divine influence. Concerning the riddle game itself, the narrator describes the game and its associated promises as "sacred"; Tolkien's prologue to *The Fellowship of the Ring* implies that all creatures of Middle-earth (except the most wicked) hold such a view (and a draft adds that even a creature like Gollum would not likely be brazen enough to cheat[95]). Though the word *sacred* has multiple meanings, including *to hold inviolable because of traditional veneration,* it suggests an authority vested in a higher power that can invoke retribution when violated. In short, the only powers in Arda capable of enforcing the sacredness of riddle games are the Valar and Maiar.

More significantly, a short while later Bilbo considers killing Gollum, but he is prevented from doing so because of a sudden insight, "pity mixed with horror," that overwhelms his heart. In *The Lord of the Rings* Gandalf makes much of this moment as a good beginning for Bilbo's possession of the One Ring (despite the fact that Bilbo later lies about the events with Gollum). Gandalf himself practices pity, a quality he learned or strengthened from association with the Valier Nienna. Bilbo's moment of pity, perhaps even his accompanying vision of Gollum's interminable and hopeless life underground, may be a sign of influence from afar, perhaps from Nienna herself; alternatively, perhaps Nienna is responsible for rewarding Bilbo for the pity he exhibits. A moment later, strengthened by his resolution to do no harm, he makes a leap of faith over Gollum to effect his escape.[96]

While the narrative of finding the Ring does not imply divine intervention, events surrounding that moment might hint of such intervention, given the foundational assumption that the cosmology described in Tolkien's other writings remains operational at the end of the Third Age. Cattaneo states this assumption clearly: "In Middle-earth there is no such a thing as 'coincidence.'"[97] What about other moments in *The Hobbit?* Since Ulmo may have played a role in assisting Bilbo during the riddle game with Gollum, passages by bodies of water are worth examining. And indeed by the dark stream of Mirkwood (a body of water that *The Silmarillion* narrator might describe as defiled), the Dwarves and Hobbit successfully find a way across, hooking a boat on the far bank and pulling it loose from its mooring. Nothing except the effort's success suggests divine intervention, though as Rateliff notes, "many traditional tales place a stream as the border between the mortal world and Faerie."[98] The moment may be one in which Ulmo exerts an unseen influence.

Bilbo's dream on the Front Porch of the Orcs' cavern may be another such moment. Of the Valar, Lórien is the one for whom visions and dreams are a specialty, though he remains uncredited as the source or instigator of specific dreams in *The Silmarillion*. But if indeed prophetic dreams and warnings stem from his influence, then perhaps Bilbo's is an example; the dream of a widening crack at the back of the cave awakens him in time to alert Gandalf prior to the Goblin's attack.

Bilbo may grow more susceptible to influence from the Valar as his adventure progresses. If luck is not merely luck, then Bilbo's assertion that he has come to trust his luck more than in the past simultaneously expresses faith in whatever entity causes his luck to be good. Perhaps Bilbo exercises growing metaphysical awareness as he sits in the level niche in the Lonely Mountain where he and the Dwarves hope to find the hidden door. While thinking, he "stare[s] away west . . . to the distances beyond." Those distances are the general location of his Hobbit hole, to which he has turned his thoughts regularly in the course of his adventures; but they are also the direction of the land of Aman and the Valar.[99] Bilbo spends much of the day on which he discovers the mechanism for opening the hidden door staring into the west. On that day, he experiences a strange sensation of expectancy; irrationally, he wonders if perchance Gandalf will reappear. This premonition seems placed into Bilbo's mind, as if an outside force from the west wishes him to be watchful and ready.

While evidence is less explicit, the Valar may be responsible for the "strange lightening of the heart" Bilbo experiences, even though surrounded by despairing Dwarves, when the company becomes locked within the Lonely Mountain. Perhaps the Valar even contribute to the "beginnings of a plan [that] had come into his little head,"[100] which lead to Bilbo's giving the Arkenstone to Bard, an action that Gandalf praises highly; the phrase "come into his little head" both diminishes the probability of Bilbo thinking up a plan using his own "little head," and places agency, whether metaphorically or literally, elsewhere. Contrast the phrase with an alternative Tolkien could have used: *he thought of a plan*. In fact, an early draft shows that Tolkien first wrote "he thought of," then replaced the phrase with words almost identical to those of the final draft.[101]

Even Bilbo's protection during the Battle of Five Armies can be viewed as a moment of divine intercession. As the second time that Bilbo is knocked unconscious, it parallels Bilbo's finding the One Ring. I've described the first occasion as part of a series of events that may show unseen powers manipulating events, both bringing foresight to bear on the situation and reacting to circumstances as they occur, to put the unlikeliest of persons in the position of finding the Ring; foresight or divine intuition seems to grasp that the unlikeliest person is the best possible person. At the end of the story, however, even with the personal growth Bilbo experiences, he is not warrior material. He plays his role in the battle before it starts, by giving the Arkenstone to Bard. Being knocked unconscious can be seen as a gift of divine mercy, sparing Bilbo from probable greater harm. This presumed divine agent can be seen as capitalizing on Bilbo's fear-driven impulse to don the Ring; or if putting on the Ring at that moment is a bad idea, allowing him to be knocked unconscious out of harm's way is a merciful and gracious gift.[102]

In finding some degree of divine influence in these scenes of *The Hobbit,* I embrace an interpretive strategy of reading between the lines, of making inferences from *The Hobbit* based on Tolkien's description of cosmic forces operating in *The Silmarillion*. I feel justified in doing so based on Tolkien's assertion, quoted at the chapter's opening, that he kept "allusions to the highest matters down to mere hints, perceptible only by the most attentive." My strategy, of course, has dangers. First it opens the door to finding in the text that which I already wish to find there; my interest in examining Tolkien's cosmology may lead me to find metaphysical agency where more level heads might not. Furthermore, it may ultimately lead to finding metaphysical presence in almost every word and action of every character, a position that feels ridiculous. Should the glow of Bilbo's sword, Sting, be attributed to Varda? It does, after all, bring Bilbo comfort, and he uses it to see his way through the tunnel. Does a Vala cause the Ring to slip onto Bilbo's finger when he is seen by the Orcs at the tunnel's back door, to counteract "the last trick of the ring" of slipping off his finger?[103] The moment parallels the scene in the Prancing Pony's common room when an evil influence, not a Vala, prompts the Ring to slip onto Frodo's finger. Having suggested that Ulmo assisted the Dwarves and Bilbo as they crossed the stream in Mirkwood, should I also attribute the appearance of deer crossing their path to Nessa, the Valier to whom deer are special, or to Oromë, the Vala of the hunt? The deer's appearance causes Bombur to fall in the water, thus coming under a sleep enchantment. This seems like a bad occurrence (though it led to temporary weight loss for Bombur), an event I hesitate to attribute to the Valar.

Thus, my goal here is only to assert that the moments I've mentioned suggest the possibility of divine intervention; the evidence, based on inference, is admittedly weak. Yet finding such possibilities emphasizes *The Hobbit*'s internal consistency with the world and the cosmology of *The Silmarillion*.

✍ *The Valar and* The Lord of the Rings

Tolkien provides a link between divine presence in *The Hobbit* and *The Lord of the Rings* in the drafts of his prologue to the latter work. In his synopsis of *The Hobbit* Tolkien describes Bilbo finding the Ring "by what seemed like luck."[104] Here again Tolkien implies the opposite of what he says by use of the word *seemed*. Bilbo, too, references luck at the Council of Elrond as part of his concession that he has no further role left in the project of destroying the One Ring, acknowledging he lacks "the strength or luck" to resume his role as Ring bearer.[105] In fact, the quest to destroy the One Ring appears not just unlikely of success, but impossible. Long before the Ring was found Elrond looked into the future and perceived it would likely end in darkness, "unless some strange chance deliver us that my eyes cannot see." Gandalf responded with greater hope, acknowledging that "strange chances" do indeed transpire, and that often the presumed weak will accomplish what the Wise cannot.[106] These words imply that Elrond and Gandalf move forward with their plan to destroy the Ring, not simply hoping that Hobbits (the weak) will succeed when the strong cannot, but out of faith that those Powers whose actions appear as *chance* will support the mission of Ring destruction. Tolkien suggests one theme of his story, that world-changing deeds are often accomplished by the seemingly weak, signifies Eru Ilúvatar's sovereignty as solely responsible for placing Elves and Humans (and Hobbits) in Arda.[107]

The Lord of the Rings incorporates significantly stronger evidence of divine intervention than *The Hobbit*. As Kreeft notes, the story contains "literally hundreds of providential 'coincidences,'"[108] moments when chance is more than chance. Davis asserts that "coincidences . . . are in fact instances of God's will at work."[109] Ryan similarly suggests that "'chance' [in *The Lord of the Rings*] is none other than the divine intention for the world, a cosmic order which is implicit everywhere, and occasionally made explicit."[110] Drury moves a step beyond Ryan to find "a preordained plan" within the book's "incredibly complex events."[111] Rutledge echoes Pederson (quoted in the previous section of this chapter) in finding many passages invoking the divine passive, "a syntactical technique that Tolkien . . . uses repeatedly throughout the epic."[112] These critics agree that Tolkien's story reflects a world in which divine intervention is not only possible, but does indeed take place, implied within the narrative; applying the same interpretive strategies embraced in the earlier discussion of *The Hobbit* will show many moments when the Valar, or perhaps Eru himself, may "peep through" the narrative, to use Tolkien's words.

Yet as English majors learn, literary critics display an amazing power to find that which they wish to find in texts they read. Hammond and Scull, for example, may push the limits of believability when they describe Sam Gamgee's "lor bless you, Mr. Gandalf, sir!" as "not far removed from a Christian invocation of the Lord."[113] In an attempt (weak though it may be) to prevent my reading from overdetermining divine influence during the Third Age, I provide the following disclaimers:

1. I admit that I rely on verbal cues, reading between the lines, seeking metaphysical dimensions beyond a passage's surface meaning.

2. I don't insist that moments when I detect divine influence are definitive, and thus rely on conditional verbs (*may, might*) and vague verb phrases (*could have been*) to express uncertainty.

3. I don't claim that Tolkien intends or agrees with my interpretation.

4. Most important, I confess my desire is to discover possible moments of divine involvement in *The Lord of the Rings* because I find it increases my enjoyment of and appreciation for Tolkien's legendarium (I suspect that if *you* didn't feel similarly, you wouldn't have read this far).

I've kept these disclaimers firmly in my mind as I wrote this portion of the present chapter, hoping that they will serve as safeguards against rash interpretations.

The Valar certainly have motivation for divine intervention late in the Third Age, despite textual assertions that they remain distant and passive. The continued presence of evil in Arda forms a primary motivation. Intervention is within the scope of their responsibilities under Eru Ilúvatar. A completely hands-off approach would hardly be feasible, given the power of Sauron as a disciple of Melkor, who was originally more powerful than most of the individual Valar. If nothing else, the Valar need to protect their own interests. Dismayed at the thought of having lost the Ring, Frodo worries that the sea (and intervening empty space) might not be a barrier to the spread of Sauron's dominion; in a draft of "The Council of Elrond," even Elrond speculates that if Sauron discovers the location of the Elven Rings, he might ultimately extend his influence into Aman.[114] Beyond self-interest, the presence in Middle-earth of descendants from the Faithful of Númenor ought to ensure continued Valian and Maian interest in the Third Age, even if the Valar had ignored Middle-earth during the Second Age (and claims that the Valar ignored Middle-earth during the Second Age may be no more accurate than the similar assertions that the Valar ignored the Noldor during the First Age).

Along with motive, the Valar also have means. Tolkien's manuscripts of the Second Age establish the existence of a *Straight Road* by which residents of Aman might visit Middle-earth even after the change-of-the-world removed Aman from Arda's surface. While establishing the Straight Road, Tolkien shows its use primarily by embodied beings: Elves leaving Middle-earth, occasional Human mariners entering the path inadvertently, and Gandalf and perhaps Glorfindel entering Middle-earth. Yet Tolkien never restricts the Valar to the Straight Road for access to the east. The First Age Legends of Beleriand show the Valar capable of nearly instantaneous intercession across the Great Sea (as exemplified by the response to Fingon's prayer concerning Maedhros), in the same way that Tom Bombadil responds almost instantaneously to Frodo's use of Tom's rhyme. Though Aman is removed from Arda prior to the start of the Third Age, Tolkien does not indicate that the distance between Aman and Middle-earth increased; instead, the portion of Arda that encompasses Middle-earth is transformed into an orb, leaving Aman hanging out in space, somewhat like a moon but apparently not visible from Middle-earth. Similarly, while suggesting a decline in the Valar's power in the Third Age, a fading, Tolkien does not assert that decline prevents the Valar from influencing Middle-earth events. A decreased power does not equate with impotence.

With motive and means established, the search can begin for opportunities when characters might perceive themselves, or the narrator might perceive the characters, as divinely influenced. One such moment occurs as Aragorn, Legolas, and Gimli pursue Orcs across the plains of Rohan. After a night of sleep, Legolas awakens Aragorn and Gimli with the phrase "we are called,"[115] suggesting someone or something doing the calling, an echo of Elrond's assertion that participants in his Council are similarly called. Moments such as this reveal characters, or sometimes the narrator, perceiving a larger purpose, a destiny, behind their own actions; in Tolkien's cosmology, such a sense of destiny implies divine intervention from specific spirit-beings who long ago put destiny into motion, and who remain responsible for producing or influencing destiny. Thus, while character may be destiny, in Tolkien's writings destiny is also characters, beings with names, powers, and personalities, who are simultaneously caught up in and producing the story of Arda. A brief examination of four participants in the War of the Ring who become enmeshed in a larger destiny suggests that something more than blind luck remains in operation late in the Third Age.

Faramir perceives himself, and is perceived by others, as living a life of destiny rather than chance. He speculates that Boromir's journey was doomed from its outset. He urges Sam to consider his mentioning the Ring as fate rather than blunder; Faramir specifically urges Sam to *think* it so, to classify it thusly by faith, since Sam understands more clearly with his heart than with his eyes. Mablung, a soldier of Gondor who associates closely with Faramir, sees Faramir himself as "charmed, or fate spares him."[116] The words of Faramir's associates and the story's narrator combine to suggest purpose for his life and actions, to the extent that those beings who instill that purpose also take special precautions to ensure his safety and survival.

Destiny similarly pervades Aragorn's life and actions, though without erasing or minimizing the dangers he faces. Contemplating the words of lore concerning the Paths of the Dead, he concludes the path is appointed him. Similarly, he sees purpose behind his acquisition of the Palantír of Orthanc. Tolkien's draft of the passage following Aragorn's use of the Palantír shows that Tolkien considered expanding the degree of intention behind the friendship of the Three Hunters; in the draft Aragorn recalls a rhyme describing a journey through the Paths of the Dead by Lords, of the Elves, the Dwarves, and Humans; Aragorn concludes that the rhyme fits their circumstances so clearly that it can't be chance.[117] At the Battle of the Pelennor Fields, the narrator claims Aragorn, along with Éomer and Imrahil, remains unscathed, in part because of native skill, but also because of "their fortune." According to Gandalf, even Aragorn's finding a seedling of Nimloth, the White Tree, occurs at "the appointed hour," as if other powers work to restore the lineage of Elendil in Gondor. At the same time, Gandalf speaks ambiguously of the mechanism by which the lone sapling appears, as if he wishes to preserve the mystery surrounding the means of its appearance.[118] Or perhaps he does not himself know which power bears responsibility for that act of grace.

Merry and Pippin also become enmeshed in destiny, though they seem less aware of their own significance compared with Aragorn. Their capture by Orcs forms a crucial narrative moment when events, to use Galadriel's words, stand on the edge of a knife. If the Hobbits are taken to Saruman, the knowledge extracted from them will inform him (and ultimately Sauron) of the motives of the Fellowship and the approximate location of the Ring; or, if the Hobbits are instead killed, the Ents and Huorns will not likely be roused to wrath against Saruman, which might tip the Battle of the Hornburg against the Rohirrim. From this perspective, the presence of Merry and Pippin on the fields of Rohan, surrounded by Orcs and Rohirrim, takes on international, perhaps even cosmic significance.

And indeed, the narrator hints at divine intervention in Merry and Pippin's escape from Orcs. First, Pippin provides clues for Aragorn by running off perpendicular to the Orc path, leaving footprints and his Elvish brooch. By this action Pippin appears quick-witted, but the narrative opens space for more at stake. Several times, the narrator reveals, an image of Strider the tracker "came into his mind unbidden." While the word *unbidden* allows a material interpretation, that Pippin's unconscious mind produces the image, it allows room for an unseen external influence, much as Gandalf influences the mind of Frodo on the Hill of Seeing. Furthermore, the narrator connects a surprisingly strong word with this scene; rather than just an *image* of Strider, Pippin receives a *vision*.[119] The vision motivates the chain of reasoning that, in order for Strider to find evidence, Hobbit footprints will need to appear on turf not overtrampled by Orcs. While the word *vision* can also be attributed to Pippin's unconscious, it suggests the possibility of intervention by a divine being capable of inducing visions.

Later, when the Rohirrim surround the Orc band, a "thought came suddenly into Pippin's mind." Of course, thoughts *do* come suddenly into people's minds (and, I presume, Hobbits'), and not all such occurrences need be attributed to divine intervention. Yet the subsequent words complicate this sudden thought: "as if [it were] caught direct from the urgent thought of his enemy." The wording suggests more than simple intuition of his enemy's unstated motive; rather it implies insight beyond the level of mere surmise. Yet the enemy has no reason to reveal his motivation to the Hobbits. In fact, Tolkien often uses the words *as if* to suggest one should read between the lines for a deeper significance. Then an arrow, "aimed with skill or guided by fate," strikes Grishnákh's hand, causing him to drop his sword, shriek, and run off, only to be speared by a horseman.[120]

After the Hobbits enter Fangorn, beams of light penetrate the forest ceiling to guide them toward their destined appointment with the Ent, then disappear as they mount Fangorn's stone steps.[121] This change in the weather causes the Hobbits to converse, which in turn predisposes Fangorn positively toward the Hobbits; had he not heard their voices, he reveals, he might have killed them outright, thinking they were Orcs. Later Gandalf confirms the crucial role played by the two Hobbits, enabled by their rapid transport toward Fangorn, and their unlikely escape from the Orcs and Rohirrim.

Merry and Pippin's experience offers evidence that the divine presences active during the First Age remain at work in the Third. But the specific images of the scene just inside Fangorn Forest, guiding light, fortuitous changes in the weather, and the appearance of Ents, call to mind specific Valar: namely, Varda, who authorized placement of the sun in the heavens, Manwë and Ulmo, who control winds and weather, and Yavanna, creator of forests, whose singing in the Music of the Ainur foreshadowed the Ents as guardians of trees. Thus, reading *The Lord of the Rings* with the Valar's specific functions in mind will foreground moments that might be divine intervention in the War of the Ring, whether direct from the Vala herself or himself, or mediated through the efforts of unnamed Maiar associated with the Vala.

"Elbereth! Gilthoniel!": Varda

The one Valier named repeatedly in *The Lord of the Rings* is Varda, whom the Elves invoke as Elbereth. The Elves of Rivendell sing a hymn to Varda in the Hall of Fire. Galadriel, too, sings of Varda, regal and holy, as the Fellowship leaves Lothlórien. On the river Anduin, Legolas utters her name before shooting the winged creature on which a Nazgûl flies. Even earlier in the narrative, when Elves miraculously appear in the woods of the Shire and save Frodo from succumbing to the will of a Black Rider, they sing, appropriately enough, a hymn to Elbereth; a few hours later they part with the Elvish blessing, "May Elbereth protect you."[122] Equally appropriate, at the end of the story, as Frodo and Sam meet Elrond and Galadriel on their way to the Grey Havens, the Elves sing to Elbereth.[123]

Such Elvish invocations suggest the Elves perceive Varda as remaining capable of aiding the Elves in the Third Age; Gandalf, in draft passages of the "Many Meetings" chapter of *The Fellowship of the Ring,* confirms to Frodo that Varda continues to protect them.[124] These Elvish beliefs in turn influence Frodo and Sam. During the attack of the Black Riders below Weathertop, Frodo exclaims "Elbereth! Gilthoniel!"[125] which Tolkien interprets as a hymn or appeal to Varda, and a religious moment in *The Lord of the Rings* often overlooked by readers. The narrator's careful wording of this moment shows that in naming Elbereth, Frodo does more than mimic the Elves; when Hobbits speak her name, it forms an invocation, a defensive gesture, or a shorthand plea for help. Aragorn explains that the name possesses utility when exclaimed before forces of evil; in contrast with Frodo's brave but futile effort to stab his attacker, speaking the name of Elbereth invokes greater power. Tolkien also explains this moment from the perspective of the chief Nazgûl: Frodo, though weak and timid, has dared to use against him a sword forged by enemies of the Nazgûl; since such a sword can only have been acquired in the Barrows, Frodo has shown himself, the Nazgûl assume, stronger than Barrow-wights; worse yet, Frodo's invocation of Elbereth terrifies the Nazgûl.[126] Yet *Elbereth* does not function as a magic word, like *abracadabra,* tapping into some vague inanimate energy; rather, its power stems from the being with whom the name is associated.

At that moment on Weathertop, Frodo needs supernatural help. Falling under the will of the Black Riders, he feels an overpowering urge to put on the Ring, and with the Ring on his finger, he enters the Black Riders' plain of existence. Frodo later considers his own state at the time *madness,* a word that implies an absence of rational self-control. In short, Frodo needs help beyond what Aragorn and the other Hobbits can provide. Perhaps Varda herself intervenes, or another Vala or Valier may act in her name; or perhaps some unknown Maia serves at Varda's behest. While the specific metaphysical being remains unidentified, the text implies that this battle involves more than just one little Hobbit against an ex-Human undead being, himself (formerly) the bearer of a magic Ring (that he knows how to use) and backed by the power and will of the ex-Maia Sauron. Rather, the Powers of Aman show themselves willing to intervene in Human (or Hobbit) affairs when the stakes are high, when evil is overpowering its enemies' wills, and when that enemy of evil possesses a pure heart; Gandalf implies as much when he tells Frodo that "fortune or fate have helped you."[127] And indeed Frodo's will returns to him just enough so that he can remove the Ring, despite being stabbed by a Morgul Blade. The situation parallels the later moment when, atop the Hill of Seeing, Frodo requires Gandalf's intervention to retain the power to exercise his own will.

Furthermore, the narrator implies an outside force not only comes to Frodo's aid, but even anticipates Frodo's need and supplies him with the appropriate supplication. At the moment he attacks the Black Rider's feet, Frodo "hear[s] himself crying aloud" the Valier's name.[128] The passive construction suggests Frodo does not will himself to say those words; he seems, in a sense, surprised to hear himself speak. The first draft is less subtle, stating merely that "he did not know why" he uttered those words; in a later draft (of the passage when Frodo awakens in the house of Elrond) Gandalf expresses surprise that Frodo even knows the name Elbereth.[129] While the words may be current within his memory after his encounter with the Elves in the Shire, the words do not appear to be part of his everyday vocabulary (though he does recognize the name when it is sung by Gildor and his companions). Frodo shows little evidence of religious instruction, and the passage implies simply that he perceives only his great need for help; thus, the Valar not only help but graciously supply an appropriate prayer for Frodo to request that help.

A short time later in the narrative Frodo again calls on the name of Elbereth; this time, beside the Bruinen and confronted with the nine Ringwraiths, Frodo couples her name with that of Lúthien; why Frodo links those two names remains unclear (to me), or to be more accurate, I'm unsure why Tolkien couples those names. Christopher Tolkien implies that the first draft in ink of the narrative clearly uses both names, but that the pencil version on which the ink draft is written joins Lúthien's name to those of Gil-galad and

Elendil. I interpret the change to reflect a conscious desire on Tolkien's part to introduce cosmic dimensions into the narrative. Kreeft goes a step further in asserting this scene as one of two in which Varda directly "saves Frodo."[130]

The second of the two moments noted by Kreeft takes place in Shelob's lair, an event that makes clear Frodo does not simply parrot Elvish phrases taught him by Bilbo. In the darkness of the lair, Galadriel's Phial shines with a brilliant light, as if Eärendil and his Silmaril have come to Arda.[131] Palmer describes this moment as one in which "The very power of heaven, as it were, [i]s held in Frodo's hand,"[132] recalling the lineage of the Phial (discussed in the previous chapter). Frodo once again speaks an Elvish invocation: *"Aiya Eärendil Elenion Ancalima,"* though the narrator reveals that Frodo does not understand his own speech and, in fact, feels as if some other being speaks using Frodo's voice; that the other being's presence remains strong and untroubled by Shelob's stench.[133] Here again Frodo discovers words to speak, supplied by some unseen power; and indeed, this unseen force must be very strong to remain untouched by Shelob. The words given Frodo, "Hail Eärendil brightest of stars,"[134] connect this scene to the end of the First Age, when Eärendil and the Silmaril first appear as a star in the heavens and even come to the aid of the Host of Valinor in its last battle against Melkor. While the words themselves are ineffectual against Shelob, they signify that Frodo and Sam are not alone in battling a being whose history and power far exceed their own. The light itself has a power the words lack, driving Shelob away, for the moment; Milbank notes that the Phial's power seems "to wax and wane in efficacy according to the faith and belief of the holder."[135] The need for such divine interference becomes clearer in the next few pages as both Frodo and Sam experience fear, dread, and menace of the sort that derives from a powerful will exerting mental or spiritual pressure. Just as Lúthien's Maian heritage gives her power beyond that of other Elves, so, too, does Shelob's Maian heritage through Ungoliant give her greater power than that of a mere giant spider-creature.

In this same crucial battle Sam also speaks an unknown tongue, though as one might expect, he takes a more prosaic path to becoming a spokesperson for the divine. Facing Shelob and foreseeing that she intends to kill him, he grasps the Phial and simply utters Galadriel's name, nobly, perhaps, as a knight speaking his lady's name before combat, though more likely simply as the most powerful being he could think of at the moment. But uttering her name stirs voices in his mind of Gildor and his companions walking under starlight in the Shire, and of the Elven music in Rivendell. Recalling their hymns to Elbereth, "his tongue [i]s loosed" and he cries (in Elvish): "O

Elbereth Starkindler from heaven gazing-afar, to thee I cry now in the shadow of (the fear of) death. O look toward me, Everwhite." As Frodo before, Sam is "'inspired' to make this invocation,"[136] and given language proper to its expression. Startzman refers to this moment as "a prayer . . . that suggests the whole world of Galadriel speaking through [Sam],"[137] though Kowalik makes clear the source of the power is not Galadriel but Elbereth.[138] A moment later the divine transport passes, and Sam returns to his normal Hobbit self, desiring simply to protect and avenge his master. Now again the light of Galadriel's Phial does the work of defeating Shelob.

Shortly thereafter, Sam carries the Ring into Mordor in pursuit of his imprisoned master but finds himself stymied by the unseen barrier of the Two Watchers; his will lacks strength to penetrate that barrier, but "a sudden thought . . . came to him" (yet another moment of divine intervention?) to reveal the light of Galadriel's Phial. Once again, divine light overpowers darkness and its magic. Similar invocations, along with the light of Galadriel's Phial, overpowers the Two Watchers as Frodo and Sam leave the Tower of Cirith Ungol.[139]

Use of Galadriel's Phial, the Elvish language, and invocations to the divine, show Sam growing more Elvish as his journey progresses. To the extent that the Elves (or at least the Eldar) possess faith in the Valar, Sam also grows in his faith, though he may be confused as to the source of the assistance he receives. A few pages after the escape from Cirith Ungol, in the midst of Sauron's evil realm, Sam wishes for two things: water and light. Having experienced Elven magic as something deeper, more spiritual, than simple manipulation of matter, he casts his wish toward Galadriel; "If only the Lady could see us or hear us," Sam sighs, in acknowledgment of the distance that lies between himself and the Elf Queen.[140] The ambiguity of the word *Lady,* however, suggests that perhaps another Lady, further away, but significantly more powerful, may receive the prayer directed toward Galadriel. Within the next few pages, Sam finds both wishes granted: winds drive back the darkness to allow a dim light into Mordor, and a trickle of cool though bitter water flows. Two pages later Sam sees one of Varda's stars appear (or perhaps it is Eärendil); its beauty touches deeply the heart of the prosaic Sam Gamgee. Even more, Sam feels hope returning to him along with a fleeting glimpse of his position within the history of Arda. The light of the star impacts not only Sam's eye and his heart, but also his mind; he becomes conscious that beauty and goodness will endure eternally, and that evil is, comparatively, a temporary glitch.[141] Comforted, Sam allows himself to fall asleep beside Frodo, unconcerned for the moment about keeping watch over his master.

The "Valaquenta" says of Varda that she hears voices of those crying for aid on Arda, even from those trapped within Melkor's realm.[142] Events in *The Lord of the Rings* suggest that Varda continues to hear the voices calling her from Middle-earth during the era of Sauron's dominion; but even more than hearing, she may intervene in those events to protect and empower.

"Great Vigor in the Waters": Ulmo

During the First Age Varda is not the Vala most involved in affairs of Middle-earth. Instead, Ulmo, Lord of Waters, focuses his attention on all of Arda, and like Varda, listens to all that transpires in Middle-earth. In the early years, Ulmo typically appears to Elves or Humans near, or calls to them from, bodies of water. Thus, investigating events in *The Lord of the Rings* that occur near water may reveal moments of Ulmo's continued influence. Shippey, for example, raises the possibility that Ulmo may intervene to provide Sam and Frodo with water after Sam's prayer to Galadriel.[143]

An obvious example of Ulmo's influence is Legolas's attraction to the sea, foretold him by Galadriel. While sea-longing forms the psyches of the Noldorin Elves, who crossed the sea (or the Northern ice caps) in their coming to Middle-earth at the beginning of the First Age, even the Grey Elves who have not journeyed to Aman experience an unquenchable awakening of sea-longing once they encounter the ocean. As *The Book of Lost Tales* describes this, any who hear the sound of Ulmo's horn remain affected by it for life.[144] Attributing such power to Ulmo's horn does not resolve the cause-effect relationship: is this a poetic attribution of a natural power to a divine source? Or is the natural power a consequence of the divinity that dwells within the waters of Arda?

Tolkien uses the sea-longing as metonymy; no tales (or poems) describe the Elves of Middle-earth enjoying the sea in-and-of itself (in contrast with the Teleri of Aman, whose preference for the sea positions them as particularly devoted to Ulmo and Ossë). Even the greatest Elven mariner, Eärendil, voyages with the goal of arriving at Aman, with the mission of begging the Valar's intervention on behalf of the Elves and Humans of Middle-earth. Instead, longing for the sea symbolizes the desire for that which is across the sea, toward which the sea serves only as a pathway. Yet Aman, too, is a metonymy; while the Noldorin Elves speak with longing of the beauty and light of Aman, those are ultimately elements of the direct, unmediated presence of the Valar. If Aman draws the Elves simply because of its beauty, then they will not feel conflicted about journeying there; on the occasions when Elves express their reasons for remaining in Middle-earth, they mention its physical beauties: the trees, landscapes, water. The sea-longing shows a desire for Ulmo, and for the Valar, and ultimately for Eru Ilúvatar; the "Ainulindalë" claims the sound of water echoes the Music of the Ainur.[145] Frodo's experience of sea-longing, which overcomes him during his last visit to Rivendell, provides further evidence that such longing stems from desire for the divine; in contrast with Legolas, Frodo has never seen the sea, except in a dream.

Specific scenes within *The Lord of the Rings* near bodies of water suggest moments when Ulmo may be operating. MacArthur suggests Ulmo's influence behind the lucky chance of Déagol and Sméagol finding the Ring; if so, then Ulmo bears indirect responsibility for all events of the War of the Ring. As noted in the previous chapter, Gandalf clearly assigns responsibility for the flood of the Bruinen to Elrond, whom he says commands the river. Neither the narrative of the flood nor Gandalf's comments hint at Ulmo's involvement. In fact, Gandalf implies innate strength of water as a force of nature. Yet such innate power within water suggests Ulmo, whose spirit, according to *The Silmarillion*, resides in all the waters of the world. Perhaps, as Dickerson hints, Ulmo grants Elrond power to command the waters of the Bruinen,[146] much as the Vala delegates certain powers to his Maiar, Ossë, and Uinen. One can even speculate that Ulmo may have called Elrond to found Rivendell, as in the First Age when he called Finrod to Nargothrond and Turgon to Gondolin.

Ulmo may have influenced the Fellowship's ten days on the river Anduin between Lothlórien and Parth Galen. Despite the ever-present possibility of danger, this is one of the safest legs of their journey. Even when once attacked by Orcs, the enemy's arrows cause no harm, which the Company attributes to the darkness and Galadriel's cloaks and boats. More definite evidence of divine interference occurs the next day when the weather changes to a convenient fog, preventing their being seen by the enemy from the opposite shore. Sam admits he normally doesn't care for fog, but finds this incident "a lucky one,"[147] a word noted in an earlier section of this chapter as suggesting influence from a higher power. The gloomy weather continues to aid (though also depress) the Company as they portage around the rapids of Sarn Gebir.

The disposition of Boromir's body following events at Parth Galen demands a supernatural explanation. The laws of science and probability suggest that Boromir's body should be dislodged from the Elven boat by the time it falls to the bottom of the Falls of Rauros. Yet Faramir reports seeing Boromir's body in the boat as it floats many miles downstream in Gondor, minus only Boromir's horn (which washes ashore separately). Tolkien's draft notes for the passage suggest he considered making the image of the boat, surrounded by light, only a vision registering on Faramir's mind, but the final story implies Faramir truly saw Boromir's body. In committing the body to such a burial, Aragorn attributes special power to the river, though saying only that the river will prevent evil creatures from desecrating Boromir's bones. While boats of Lothlórien possess a special blessing to preserve their occupants, it seems unreasonable to grant the boats sentience (unlike the horses of the Elves who consciously keep their riders in the saddle). Thus, the preservation of Boromir's body within the boat suggests Ulmo providing care, perhaps even ensuring that the boat is found by Faramir, who describes himself as compelled to draw close to it. A draft of this passage adds that seabirds mourn Boromir's death when his body finally arrives at the Great Sea.[148]

While some events of *The Lord of the Rings* suggest Ulmo's continuing concern for the Children of Ilúvatar, one aspect of the narrative reveals Ulmo's limitations. At the Council of Elrond, Glorfindel asserts that the Ring will be kept safe if it can be deposited in the depths of the sea. Glorfindel, as a Noldorin Elf, has experienced the Valar firsthand in Aman; if he is the same Glorfindel who resided in Gondolin, he will have known there Ulmo's protective power. Yet Gandalf asserts that the sea will not keep the Ring safely hidden forever, since mysterious beings reside there.[149] Thus Ulmo is not the only power within his waters, as the attack of the Watcher in the Water later reveals. While Oromë and others had hunted Melkor's monsters and Orcs on land, the Valar refrained from killing beings that like themselves came from outside Eä. This mercy extended to spirit-beings, no matter how they may have devolved under the influence of evil, and may have motivated Ulmo to endure evil creatures within his realm. Second, lands might change in cataclysmic events, as in the earliest eras of Arda when Melkor seeks to destroy the work of the Valar; even if Ulmo can prevent the Ring from being found while it is under the sea, some future cataclysm, perhaps induced by a great power in opposition to the Valar, might remove the Ring from Ulmo's realm.

"Wind Is Changing": Manwë

If Eagles connect *The Hobbit* to Manwë, then the same is true in *The Lord of the Rings*. Eagles appear at the final battle against Sauron before the gates of Mordor, though the narrative provides no indication that they might tip the balance of power in favor of Gondor. But their presence suggests Manwë supports the military suicide mission launched to distract Sauron while the Ring travels through Mordor. As Hartley observes, Eagles serve as "spiritual emissaries of Manwë (and therefore of Ilúvatar) [and] interceding Spirits," who support individuals in their resistance to Sauron "especially when the strength of the individual seems at its lowest ebb."[150]

Moments surrounding the earlier Battle of the Pelennor Fields show Manwë's interest there too. Théoden hints at recognition of divine intervention when he explains his own presence among the troops going to battle by saying "a west wind has shaken the boughs."[151] While Théoden's words may be simple metaphor, the specific use of the adjective *west* implies awareness of Powers out of the West at work. He doesn't refer to the immediately preceding location of Gandalf and his three companions, since they come from Fangorn Forest in the East, nor does he refer to the presence of Aragorn, Gimli, and Legolas, whose homelands would be to the North of Rohan.

Winds join the Eagles in representing the will of Manwë. The narrative attributes directly to Sauron the release of foul smoke that casts a depressing darkness over the land and aids his own followers. Although the same darkness unintentionally benefits Sauron's enemies, allowing the Rohirrim to advance toward Minas Tirith undetected, a change in the wind would thwart Sauron's plans. Thus, when Ghân-buri-Ghân announces to Théoden that "wind is changing," and when Wídfara of the Wold of Rohan confirms it, then readers sense a foreshadowing of the turn of the tide against Sauron. As Merry perceives just a few pages later,[152] this weather change comes in the nick of time to assist Rohan and Gondor. Dickerson describes the air movements pushing back Sauron's darkness as "the winds of Manwë."[153] Since the "Ainulindalë" depicts Manwë and Ulmo as allies, it should come as no surprise to find wind and water working together in *The Lord of the Rings;* Wídfara notes a sea scent in the air.[154] As the battle progresses and Éowyn slays the Nazgûl, the sea air brings rain that seems to weep for Théoden, simultaneously extinguishing the fires that burn Minas Tirith. Then a great wind blows the rain northward, revealing the sun for the first time in almost a week.

The same wind enables Aragorn's arrival with the fleet. According to Gimli, Aragorn knows that his troops must arrive at Minas Tirith by the day following the rout of the Corsairs of Umbar; yet the men cannot row the forty-two leagues to Gondor in so short a time. Without wind, Aragorn's expedition will fail. Yet the wind miraculously cooperates and thus Aragorn can be described as carried upon an ocean breeze into Gondor. Following the battle Aragorn reads the sunset as "a sign of the end," foreshadowing many changes in the world. The phrase parallels the recent change in the weather: Sauron's murk and smoke flowing out from Mordor, only to be pushed back in turn by sea winds. Gandalf speaks of "the winds of fortune turning in our favor";[155] whether he implies divine intervention or simply that the momentum of the war has shifted, Gandalf asserts that Sauron *will* read the wind as a sign, connecting it to his vision of Aragorn's remade sword, about which prophecies have foretold. Sauron, as an ex-Maia, well understands the sources of both weather and visions, and if he sees the wind as a sign, so should readers.

Sam and Frodo also benefit from this change in the wind. The darkness hides them as they enter Mordor, but it becomes oppressive as they travel through the barren lands. After Sam wishes he could beg light and water from Galadriel, he observes a change in the wind, which the narrator hints might reveal a larger will as its source. The narrative describes battle in the air, with Mordor's clouds swept back by winds from "the living world";[156] Hartley terms this a "spiritual battle."[157] Later the narrator speaks of Sauron experiencing fear of those winds, which seem to oppose and uncover him.[158]

In case readers feel tempted to attribute these fortuitous winds exclusively to impersonal weather conditions, the narrative provides other moments that suggest a strong power at work through wind. In the Houses of Healing, as Aragorn awakens Éowyn, a wind blows, clean and fresh, resembling a star-filled mountain or sea-side air.[159] Hammond and Scull suggest the reference to mountains and stars "recalls Manwë's home on Taniquetil," while the seashore "brings to mind the shining beaches of Eldamar in the Uttermost West." This atmospheric event thus "seems to hint [that] the peoples arrayed against the evil of Sauron are watched over by powers that occasionally and in small ways intervene."[160]

Along with healing, the wind participates in cleansing the land from Sauron's influence. After the Ring's destruction, an imposing shadow-shape rises into the sky, with lightning at its highest point. This last apparition of Sauron moves threateningly toward the army of Gondor, but its threat proves impotent as wind disperses it. Tolkien indicates that Sauron experiences disintegration.[161] This wind and its impact forms a central element even in the earliest draft notes Tolkien created to speculate about possible plot twists. One note suggests dust and shadows floating into the northeast from a southwesterly wind, though Tolkien changed direction in the final draft to a wind from the North; the draft passage suggests that even Frodo, surrounded by volcanic fumes, thinks he smells and hears the sea. Another draft personifies Sauron's shadow-shape: "cloudwrack out of Barad-dûr [?growing] to shape of a vast black [?man] that stretches out a menacing unavailing arm and is blown away."[162] As Gandalf summarizes to Sam two weeks later, "A great shadow has departed"; while Sauron had been defeated and disembodied at least twice previously, this time he is completely reduced to a mere shadow of evil.[163]

Meanwhile, in Gondor Faramir and Éowyn lack knowledge of the events that Gandalf witnesses, but they do see from afar the dark shadow rising into the sky. Faramir's mind warns him of an imminent evil facing Middle-earth. In contrast, his heart suggests the opposite, the arrival of hope and joy. A moment later he and Éowyn experience the great wind that blows away the ominous cloud, but the narrator here describes the previous moment as utter stillness. The miraculous wind and the dissipation of the shadow-shape impact all the residents of Gondor, who feel joy in their hearts though they can pinpoint no reason for their sensation. Later that day an Eagle arrives (an event Hammond and Scull also connect to the Valar) to announce officially the end of Sauron's realm, but the aura of positivity, seemingly spread by the wind itself, has already provided the emotion to accompany the news.[164]

A similar miraculous wind transpires on the death of Saruman, a scene that parallels the demise of Sauron, though it only came to do so via additions to page proofs for the first edition. By the time the Hobbits confront Saruman at Bag End, his spitefulness has reduced him to the level of attempted murderer. Even then Frodo insists that Saruman's noble origins, and the slim possibility that he might be cured, should prevent the Hobbits from administering the death penalty. Yet Saruman is killed, not by a Hobbit, but by his sniveling beleaguered slave, Wormtongue.[165] Just as Sauron's death results in a shadow-shape ascending into the sky, so, too, around Saruman a mist develops that rises into the sky like a fire's smoke. The mist takes the form of "a pale shrouded figure" that "waver[s], looking to the West";[166] the precise purpose of this gaze into the west remains unexplained, but its direction suggests awareness that Saruman's fate depends on judgment by the Powers of Aman. And indeed, the west provides a chill wind, evaporating the mist with the sound of a sigh.[167] Garbowski asserts that the divine origin of this wind "should be obvious to those familiar with Middle-earth sacred geography."[168] Ryan similarly considers the effect of the wind to show that Saruman's "spirit is rejected eternally by the Realm to which he should have returned."[169] For both Sauron and Saruman, Manwë's wind delivers final judgment—final, at least, within Arda; the wind of Manwë in the Third Age parallels its use in the First Age to drive away the deadly vapor that follows Melkor and Ungoliant's attack on the Two Trees and murder of Finwë.[170] Hartley considers such events moments when Manwë "communicates symbolically through the wind."[171]

Along with wind, air, and clouds, Manwë also loves poetry. Perhaps he influences recitations of poetry in the story; he or his Maiar may function as muses, as when the minstrel of Gondor begs permission to sing a lay on the subject of Frodo's adventures with the Ring. The song deeply moves those listening, producing a state of religious rapture; the narrative uses contradiction to express the effect of the lay, with hearts simultaneously experiencing pain and delight.[172] Sam is especially moved, for he himself has grown more poetic as a result of his journey; perhaps he, too, in his own small way, has been graced by Manwë's muse in his recitations on Trolls and Oliphaunts, and even more in his brief but touching lament of Gandalf.

Visions from Afar: Lórien

One of the coincidences in *The Fellowship of the Ring* that suggests divine intervention surrounds Boromir's arrival at Rivendell, following a 110-day journey, just in time for the Council of Elrond. Boromir describes a dream that prompted his journey, a dream experienced repeatedly by his brother, Faramir, and once by Boromir himself. The dream first comes to Faramir shortly before a sudden attack against Osgiliath by Sauron's forces. Described by Klinger as "almost certainly supernatural" in its source,[173] the dream involves a dark sky in the east contrasted with light from the west; the light itself speaks in verse, urging a search for the broken sword in a land called Imladris, and mentioning Isuldur's Bane and Halflings. Since Rivendell lies north of Gondor, the symbolism of light versus dark, west versus east, obviously does not suggest the dream comes from Elrond; instead, it suggests Gondoran leadership understands that light associates with the West, the land of the Valar.

Flieger notes the summons to Imladris as "the only dream that is both shared and recurrent,"[174] circumstances that prompt Schorr to assert they "cannot be called coincidence; there is some supernatural power at work," the same unnamed power that intends for Frodo to possess the Ring.[175] Scull and Hammond, however, question the shared nature of the dream, wondering whether Boromir tells the truth about his experience, or whether he just imagines or claims he dreamt it after Faramir's repeated tellings. More importantly, Scull and Hammond question the source of Faramir's dream. Their close reading of the circumstances surrounding the dream, as well as the cosmology of *The Silmarillion,* suggests Eru Ilúvatar as the source, since "he was solely responsible for the creation of Elves and Men, and he alone knew the whole history of Arda and could intervene at will."[176] From such a perspective one could infer that the Valar, since they possess little foresight as to the natures of the Children of Ilúvatar, will have little or no prophetic power to induce visions (or at least visions *of the future*) in Elves and Humans.

Yet Tolkien's complex thoughts on prophecy seem both to support and disagree with Scull and Hammond. "No mind knows what is not in it," Tolkien asserts. "No part of the 'future' is there," at least not for a mind situated in time. Such a statement supports the view that the Valar, placed in time, have limited or even no power of prophecy. But Tolkien further theorizes that Eru Ilúvatar is not limited by being placed in time; Eru can know not only what appears to be *the future* to time-bound beings, but also can communicate about it, if he so wills. As Ainur prior to entering time, the Valar receive direct revelation from Eru, and thus can engage in some limited degree of prophecy using that knowledge.[177]

While Tolkien grants only to Eru the ability of completely predicting the future, he allows two dimensions in which the Valar might prophesy: through *insight* or *foresight.* A Vala (or even a wise Elf or Human) might deduce what it deems likely to transpire (insight) and take action to introduce other elements, without having been shown in advance (foresight) those events; Aragorn, for example, sees the black ships of Umbar and deduces where they are going and when they will arrive, without having seen the future. Since Eru Ilúvatar endows the Valar and Maiar with knowledge about the future, at least through the Singing of the Ainur, all might have some ability for prophecy.

Eru bequeathed one Vala, however, with a propensity for conscious and subconscious mental images, including, perhaps, those of the future; *The Silmarillion* describes Lórien as master over dreams and visions.[178] This knowledge has prompted Flieger to see the experiences described in the Lothlórien chapter of *The Fellowship of the Ring* as "a dream sent or dreamed by the God of Dreams." Observing that no member of the Fellowship dreams during the stay in Lothlórien, Flieger suggests "the Company in Lórien is, in one sense at least, inside that dream."[179] While I join Flieger in wishing to see Lórien at work in *The Lord of the Rings,* Tolkien nowhere attributes the source of any specific dream to Lórien, not even in the First Age. By making such an attribution, I seek a logical connection within Tolkien's cosmology that Tolkien himself does little to foster.

Yet the suggestion of Lórien as the source of dreams has some evidence. First, the legendarium positively asserts that dreams might come "of the Valar"[180] and provides examples of that taking place. Second, at least one character within the legendarium experiences dreams in Lórien's realm; the story of the creation of the sun and moon describes Tilion, the Maia given responsibility of guiding the moon, as having often previously visited Lórien's gardens, where Tilion lay dreaming near Estë's pools. Third, the legendarium links Lórien with Melian. *The Silmarillion* reintroduces Melian in the chapter "Of Thingol and Melian" (after mentioning her briefly in the "Valaquenta") as having resided in Lórien's gardens; after her husband's death, she returns to those gardens. While the "Valaquenta" associates Melian primarily with Lórien's wife, Estë, the later narrative emphasizes her link to Lórien (a tenuous association, since it may reference the place rather than the Vala). As chapter 2 notes, Melian has the gift of foresight, and at least one narrative speculates that she may have prompted one of her daughter's dreams (though the dream is also speculatively attributed to the Valar).[181]

Fourth, as noted above, in *The Lord of the Rings* Lórien is associated with Galadriel (who in turn also learns from Melian). Galadriel displays a power (or technology) to induce visions by means of her Mirror. The Mirror, somewhat like a Palantír, allows a viewer to see across both time and distance, though its noncontextualized visions detract from its usefulness as a guide. As Galadriel says, even the wisest viewers of her Mirror cannot accurately discern whether they witness past, present, definite future, or merely possible future. Both Sam and Frodo gaze into Galadriel's Mirror and find it overwhelming.

Yet with only circumstantial evidence that Lórien may prompt dreams in *The Lord of the Rings*, my primary reason for this attribution can best be expressed as a complaint against the book's author: it seems a waste to create a pantheon of powers with one identified as the master of dreams, and then *not* to connect that power with the legendarium's many dream/vision experiences. Since First Age narratives asserted that the Valar do indeed send dreams to Elves and Humans, and since unusual dreams come to Elves and Humans (and Hobbits) in *The Lord of the Rings*, the Vala Lórien seems the most likely source for them (despite the fact that *The Silmarillion* names only one specific Vala, Ulmo, as inducing a dream in the First Age). Given that the name *Lórien* functions metonymically, one can attribute dreams to *Lórien* the concept (representing the vision-inducing power of all Valar and Maiar, and Eru their creator), even if Irmo/Lórien is not the direct source.

Dreams in *The Lord of the Rings,* Grayson points out, serve two primary functions: oracular (prophetic, counsel-giving) and coping (helping characters to deal with traumatic experiences; these also create emotionally complex characters). Frodo experiences a particularly noteworthy series of dreams, the first while yet the master of Bag End; his dreams at that time include images of mountains he does not know, enticing him toward adventure. While developing the story Tolkien considered making dreams the primary motivation behind Frodo's leaving the Shire, an idea that became irrelevant when the need to destroy the Ring arose.

In his one night at Crickhollow, Frodo dreams of the sound of the sea, which he has never before heard (a dream that suggests Ulmo's influence as much as Lórien's; a draft suggests sea sounds return to his consciousness at later moments of danger); on a dark heath he sees a tall white tower on a ridge and feels the desire to climb it to see the ocean.[182] At the same time, he hears a scrabbling and sniffing sound below him, which Hammond and Scull connect with Frodo's experience on the flet in Lothlórien, even though the image appeared in drafts "long before any idea of Lothlórien arose in Tolkien's mind."[183] The following night in the home of Tom Bombadil, he sees another tower, this one suspiciously similar to Orthanc; atop the tower stands a figure who summons an Eagle and flies away on it. His second night at Bombadil's Frodo dreams of a distant green land under a rapid sunrise, a dream that Tolkien's draft notes connect to Frodo's ultimate passage over the sea.[184] Flieger describes this dream as "heaven-sent, an epiphany, a promise of the best that can happen,"[185] despite the hard road before Frodo. At the Prancing Pony Frodo dreams of howling wind and galloping hooves, as well as a wildly blowing horn, which connects with the Black Riders' attack on Crickhollow that very night.

Flieger observes that Frodo, through his dreams, travels "deeper and farther than" other members of the Fellowship.[186] These dreams serve two purposes in Frodo's adventure: first to motivate movement, preventing him from becoming too comfortable, which might cause him to forsake his mission; second, the dreams promote wariness. The "veracity" of these dreams, Amendt-Raduege notes, "suggests divine origins."[187] Lórien, thus, seems a possible source, though Schorr's observation that "almost all" Frodo's dreams include the sound of wind[188] suggests the involvement of Manwë.

Other of Frodo's dreams contribute to a sense of peace and rest, reflecting the realm of Lórien and Estë. Rivendell's Hall of Fire induces in Frodo a dream-like vision, leading ultimately to deep sleep.[189] Much later, as Frodo nears Mordor, Amendt-Raduege observes, "his dreams become increasingly deceptive and dangerous."[190] At the same time, in the desolate lands approaching the gate of Mordor, Frodo experiences a pleasant vision though surrounded by decay and ugliness. He retains no memory of its content, yet it profoundly affects him; the burden of the Ring lessens and his heart feels lighter.[191]

Sam, too, experiences visions of sorts, though an important one takes the structure of a chain of associative thinking; the chain, in part due to its length, seems guided from afar, and thus worth considering as the result of divine influence. Trapped in Shelob's lair with the spider-creature approaching, Sam and Frodo confront physical, mental, and emotional darkness. For Sam, this means despair that produces anger. In the midst of this moment Sam touches his sword, aware that it offers little protection in the dark. Contact with the sword, however, reminds him of the Barrow from which it came. This in turn reminds him of Tom Bombadil; having left the Shire hoping to experience Elven magic, Sam discovered in Tom a more powerful force. The wish for Tom's presence is also futile, but it leads to a vision of light, unbearably bright, which transforms into colors: silver, green, white, and gold.[192] The light then becomes an image of Galadriel bestowing gifts upon the Fellowship. Sam hears Galadriel's voice announcing her gift to Frodo. This series of images prompts Sam to suggest that Frodo use his Phial, which not only provides physical light for their journey through Shelob's lair, but also brings them hope, and ultimately a weapon against Shelob.

Another of Sam's visions provides insight and understanding. On the approach to Mount Doom, after Gollum attacks, Sam sees Frodo and Gollum "with other vision." Gollum he perceives as hardly more substantial than shadow, a being completely overmastered by lust for the Ring. Frodo, in contrast, appears sternly angelic, wearing white, no longer moved by pity.[193] The contrast shows Frodo ennobled through just actions, in opposition to Gollum, depraved and diminished through embracing evil. Sam's vision, combined with his brief experience as a Ring bearer, gives him an understanding of Gollum's perspective, despite Sam's long-standing mistrust and resentment. Pity, of course, suggests Gandalf's influence, but Gandalf's pity and hope evolved from his discipleship with the Valier Nienna, sister of Lórien.

Aragorn displays a trust in dreams as signs and messages, and himself displays prophetic ability. When he hears Boromir's story, Aragorn considers the dream a summons, calling him to Gondor. Yet Gondor (as represented by its steward) has no intention to call Aragorn; in fact, Aragorn's presence threatens the steward's authority, and remains a point of contention between Aragorn and Gandalf on one side, and Denethor and Boromir on the other. Thus, if the dream's message is a summons, it must come from the sender of the dream rather than the receiver. Earlier in the narrative, Aragorn prophesies accurately that entering Moria will be a danger to Gandalf; in fact, in a draft of the "Lothlórien" chapter, Aragorn observes that he does not know the source of his own words of warning. Éomer describes Aragorn as possessing foresight, a family trait, since appendix A of *The Return of the King* similarly describes Gilraen, mother of Aragorn, along with his distant relative, Elrond.[194]

Even Gandalf, in the midst of the Battle for the Gates of Barad-dûr, experiences a rapid vision that causes him to look to the north from where the Eagles suddenly appear.[195] The armies of Mordor consider the Eagles' arrival not merely additional enemy troops, but signs with some decipherable meaning. The narrator emphasizes the lineage of these Eagles, descendants of the famed Thorondor, servant of Manwë in the First Age. As a sign, the arrival of the Eagles suggests that the Valar watch over and contribute to this battle, as they did with the Battle of the Five Armies in Bilbo's adventure. Gandalf's vision may be a notification direct from Aman of the Eagles' imminent arrival.

Past visions and prophecies referenced in *The Lord of the Rings* indicate the significance of the present moment or guidance for the future. Perhaps the best-known prophecy, from Malbeth the Seer,[196] cryptically predicts Aragorn's reliance on the inhabitants of the Paths of the Dead. Elrond first introduces the idea of the Paths by his own cryptic message to Aragorn through Elrohir to remember them. Elrond must perceive the time as propitious for the prophecy to come true, or perhaps he receives divine insight from Aman. An unnamed seer of Rohan supports the logic of Aragorn's apparently suicidal path. Théoden quotes a tale of the Rohirrim implying that the Paths will open at some future time; the Door leading to the Paths is shut and kept by the Dead "until the time comes."[197] This unknown prophet of Rohan provides no details to identify when "the time" will be, but Théoden speculates that perhaps it will be at Aragorn's beckoning.

Past prophecies of the Dwarfs intersect with *The Lord of the Rings*. According to the appendices of *The Return of the King*, after achieving victory against the Orcs of Moria in the Battle of Azanulbizar, Thráin (father of Thorin Oakenshield), wishes to enter Moria but is restrained by the words of Dáin Ironfoot to beware of Durin's Bane; Dáin further prophesies that some important change within Middle-earth will transpire before Dwarves can again reenter Moria. This prophecy comes true when Gandalf leads the Fellowship into Moria and battles Durin's Bane, the Balrog. In a draft of "The Council of Elrond" Gimli mentions an additional Dwarfish prophecy that Moria will be reentered, and even renamed, prior to the end of Arda.[198]

Perhaps the prophecy most important to the narrative of *The Lord of the Rings* comes from Glorfindel, the Elf who aids Aragorn and the Hobbits on their journey to Rivendell. A full millennium prior to the War of the Ring, Glorfindel leads a group of armed Elves to join Círdan and an army from Gondor against the Witch King's fortress at Fornost. Though the evil forces are routed, the Witch King appears at the very end, terrifying the horse of the Gondoran captain, Eärnur (who is later crowned king of Gondor). Glorfindel approaches the enemy, causing the Witch King to run. Forbidding pursuit, Glorfindel prophesies that the Witch King's doom lies far into the future, "and not by the hand of man will he fall." This prophecy forms the background against which Éowyn, with help from Merry, avenges the death of Théoden, announcing to the over-prideful Witch King, "no living man am I."[199]

Neither Lórien, nor the Valar in general, nor above them Eru Ilúvatar, are the sole sources of dreams in *The Lord of the Rings*. Gollum experiences "secret dreams" as he, Frodo, and Sam sleep near Ithilien.[200] Rather than Valar-induced dreams inducing guilt pangs, the context suggests instead that the dreams reflect an ever-increasing desire for the Ring, indirectly strengthened by proximity to Sauron. Additionally, Schorr suggests that the Ring forms an oppositional dream force adversely affecting Frodo; Schorr notes that Frodo's dreams become haunted by fire under its influence.[201] Yet the contexts surrounding the many dreams recounted within the narrative suggest a greater power at work than that of individual unconscious minds.

Hands of Healing: Estë

Elrond and Aragorn both possess skill in healing, a trait associated with the power of Estë, the Vala of healing and rest. Aragorn first reveals such skill while aiding Frodo after the attack of the Black Riders on Weathertop, though much of the comfort he provides arises from the effect of steamed Athelas. Where Aragorn learned of the herb's effects remains unclear: perhaps from lore handed down among the Rangers, or perhaps from Elrond. Aragorn's use of Athelas provides comfort and helps sustain Frodo, though only Elrond can achieve a full healing (and the narrative mentions Elrond's moments of healing only after the fact, never directly narrating such moments).

Aragorn comes into his own as a healer only on his arrival in Gondor, and as Gandalf hears the words of Ioreth. Once again Aragorn puts Athelas to use, but he also displays a newfound ability to work against the physiological, psychological, and spiritual ailments peculiar to his three patients, each of whom comes into close contact with Nazgûl. One of Tolkien's letters states Pippin's spirit leaves him as he falls under dead bodies in the Battle before the Gates of Barad-dûr; such language implies Aragorn calls him back from a near-death experience. When Aragorn commands the three to awaken, they do. Draft notes suggest Aragorn's ministrations are efficacious for more than just the three; Tolkien cryptically notes that Aragorn heals many more after dinner.[202]

The power seems one of authority as much as true physical healing, and Hammond and Scull trace that authority to Aragorn's descent from Lúthien. Yet texts suggest healing involves physical, emotional, or spiritual struggle by Aragorn. After Frodo and Sam awaken in the Field of Cormallen, Gandalf claims Aragorn puts forth his full power to recall them from the edge of death; even so, Aragorn places them (along with Pippin) into a lengthy period of sleep, enabling their bodies to heal themselves.[203] Exactly how Aragorn exerts this power remains unexplained, though an early draft calls it "art or wizardry."[204] The Elessar certainly augments this ability, but Aldrich speculates that an emergent strain of Aragorn's Elvish or Maian ancestry contributed. Or, Aldrich continues, "it ... may be the Valar's gift";[205] within Tolkien's cosmology, such a gift might stem from the Valier Estë.

Pity and Hope: Nienna

Nienna's influence over events in *The Lord of the Rings* appears primarily through Gandalf's ethic of pity and hope, discussed in the previous chapter. As a Maia under Nienna's influence, Gandalf learns patience and takes pity first on the Elves but ultimately on all life-forms of Middle-earth. Characters such as Aragorn and Faramir, in turn, learn wisdom and ethics from Gandalf, showing a trickle-down effect of Nienna's teaching. Faramir grasps the motivations of those around him, as does his father, Denethor; yet while Denethor's special insight leads him to scorn others, Faramir is moved to pity.[206]

Pity prompts a person to work against reason. It suggests making an exception for someone else, to excuse an action that might seem against the rules from a rational perspective. Yet pity might also position a being as more in sync with the rules; it might move one to follow a more fundamental law (or a deeper magic as C. S. Lewis's Aslan might call it). In a draft of the second chapter of *The Lord of the Rings,* Gandalf tells Frodo (then named Bingo) that indeed pity prevented Bilbo from slaying Gollum in the caverns beneath the Misty Mountains, but also that if Bilbo had killed Gollum, he would have broken "the Rules."[207] In essence, Nienna embodies the idea that mercy is every bit as important as, and perhaps even slightly prioritized over, justice.

Galadriel's Gift: Aulë and Yavanna

Even in the First Age, Aulë and Yavanna appear active primarily in Aman, though both spend time in Middle-earth prior to the awakening of the Elves: Yavanna to plant the seeds from which vegetable life spring, Aulë to create the Dwarves. Through the end of the Third Age, Dwarves continue to revere Aulë; appendix F of *The Return of the King* describes the Dwarves picturesquely as beings whose hearts still reflect the fire of the Vala.[208] Thum finds Yavanna's "influence . . . suggested" in the recovery of the White Tree, itself a descendant of Telperion, planted by Yavanna; additionally, "Without the light from her [Two Trees], caught in the phial of Galadriel, neither Sam nor Frodo could have survived the onslaught of Shelob," nor twice pass the Watchers at Minas Morgul.[209] The importance of Ents to the story, and their shepherding of the trees to the Battle of the Hornburg, also reflects Yavanna's wish to see trees protected against wanton destruction.

Aulë and Yavanna's influence may appear most directly through Galadriel's gift to Sam: a box of soil from Lothlórien, blessed by Galadriel. After Sam's unselfish and judicious dissemination of Galadriel's gift, The Shire experiences a higher-than-usual birth rate, with a noticeably unusual number of infants with Galadriel's trademark golden hair. The weather seems in perfect balance, sickness nearly disappears, fruit and pipe-weed grow prodigiously, and beer is superb. Such a bountiful year suggests a special blessing from Aulë and Yavanna. As the Vala with the special provenance of Arda's elements, Aulë would feel particular interest in the contents of Sam's box; Galadriel's blessings over her gift may include an appeal to Aulë. As Palmer appropriately observes, Galadriel's earth functions as "a reminiscence of the earth of Paradise."[210]

Yavanna's role as caretaker of plant and animal life may prompt her to empower the Shire's extreme fertility, but both she and her husband may be further motivated by the fact that the Shire had been afflicted by Maiar at one time associated with Aulë. Sauron, prior to joining with Melkor, had been an attendant of Aulë, but so, too, had Saruman, whom Aulë specifically promoted as a candidate for Wizard. Just as Yavanna instigates the Spring of Arda, prior to the coming of the Children of Ilúvatar, she may foster this Spring of the Shire to overcome the lingering effects of Saruman's wanton destruction. Yavanna's sister, Vána, the Vala of spring and flowers, may assist, as well as Vána's husband Oromë, who has a particular love of trees.[211] The perfect weather suggests Ulmo and even Manwë contribute to this period of blessing.

Higher Powers in Frodo's Quest

Tolkien acknowledges as a theme of *The Lord of the Rings* the potential impact on world affairs of unremarkable beings, overlooked by the wise. As Gandalf says to Elrond as the discovery of the One Ring looms before them, help often comes from weak hands even when the Wise might despair.[212] Such is the case in the First Age when Humans (Beren, Turin, and Tuor, for example) perform great deeds, much to the surprise of the Eldar. In a sense, Hobbits in the late Third Age play the role assigned to Humans in the First Age. But just as Beren and Tuor receive divine aid in achieving their quests, so, too, do Frodo and Sam.

The events of the first half of *The Fellowship of the Ring* seem calculated, or at least put to good use, to increase Frodo's awareness of metaphysical powers. Dubs sites "the 'fortuitous' appearance of Strider at The Prancing Pony and the 'lucky' rescue by Elves who aren't usually seen in those parts but who 'just happen' by" as two early illustrations of "the providential pattern."[213] The dreams (one of which receives confirmation of its validity from Gandalf), the dangers endured and survived, the unbidden utterances of names of powers beyond Middle-earth, function much like Bilbo's experience of luck throughout *The Hobbit*. Just as Bilbo comes to trust his luck, so Frodo's experiences increase his faith. Thus, at the end of the Council of Elrond (a chapter that Drury describes as underpinned by "the presence of providential design"[214]), when Frodo speaks his famous vow to bear the Ring to Mordor, he experiences surprise at hearing his own utterance, "as if some other will used his small voice." Indeed, it may be that another power strengthens him to accept the task that, according to Elrond, has already been appointed him. By the time Frodo and Sam break off from the Fellowship toward Mordor, Frodo believes himself destined, or chosen, to take the Ring to Mount Doom. Later he asserts the task as his doom, though he remains unclear what mechanism, whether good or evil, will bring about its resolution.[215]

Gollum's role in the tale foregrounds divine presence in Frodo's quest. Gandalf's prophecy that Gollum has a task to contribute itself forms, according to Clark, "one of the many hints in the trilogy that an unseen but benevolent providence guides the Ring-bearers and the forces of right despite their errors and imperfections."[216] The unlikely meeting of Gollum and the Fellowship seems surprisingly good luck for Gollum, since he has no food nor any knowledge of an entrance on the West-end of Moria, into which he is driven out of fear of the Nazgûl.[217]

Weeks later, after capturing Gollum, Frodo and Sam debate what should be done with him. Killing him might be justified, given the importance of their quest and the likelihood that Gollum will hinder it: the ends seem to justify the means. As Frodo ponders this, however, far from Gandalf and the rest of the Fellowship, he recalls voices from the past. The voices, Gandalf's and his own, debate Frodo's assertion that he wished Bilbo had killed Gollum: "It was Pity that stayed his hand," says the voice of Gandalf.[218] Filmer reads Frodo's recollection as evidence of "a Divine presence," with the passage's use of capital letters on the words *Pity* and *Mercy,* and use of the passive verb *stayed.*[219] But in contrast with Frodo's dangerous moment atop Amon Hen, this passage gives no clear indication that an outside force brings these memories to Frodo's mind.

Yet Frodo responds to the words *as if* brought to his attention by an outside power. "'Very well,' he answer[s] aloud," to Sam's amazement; Sam clearly perceives that Frodo speaks "to someone who [is] not there."[220] To answer implies Frodo feels challenged or questioned. His response suggests he perceives himself speaking before powerful and commanding witnesses, as if he were Fëanor before the Valar in the Ring of Doom. He utters a response to the unseen powers, a vow that he will not hurt Gollum. Whether the prompting to recall Gandalf's thought comes from a superior power, the ethical imperative clearly does; Frodo's submission to Gandalf's prompting toward pity reflects further submission to the will of the Valar and ultimately Eru Ilúvatar.

Furthermore, the memory of his fireside talk with Gandalf accomplishes more than a reminder of his moral duty; it provides him a specific example of the benefit of practicing mercy on the part of one cursed or destined to bear the One Ring. Gandalf emphasizes that Bilbo benefited from enacting pity toward Gollum, since The Ring gained less power over him than it might otherwise have done. Gandalf implies Bilbo is "divinely rewarded" for showing pity to Gollum, which in turn "would imply a degree of detailed oversight and manipulation of events by Eru or the Valar that is rarely suggested elsewhere," according to Rosebury.[221] In other words, Bilbo receives, in response to his enactment of mercy, a gift of divine grace to counteract the negative effects of the evil Ring; Frodo may have hope of similar grace in response to his mercy toward Gollum.

As this moment suggests, Frodo and Sam perceive themselves as subservient to higher powers as their quest progresses. For Sam this means learning to trust luck, much as Bilbo does in *The Hobbit*. Frodo, in contrast, seems consciously aware that a sentient entity drives him in his quest. As he says to Gollum on their approach to the Morannon, he feels commanded to enter Mordor. While these words simplify Frodo's situation, couching it in terms Gollum can understand, they reveal a growing sense within Frodo that by shepherding the Ring toward Mordor he willingly fulfills the will of another. Neither Gandalf nor Elrond nor Aragorn nor any other person of authority within Middle-earth laid such a command on Frodo; Elrond's words to Frodo instead show Elrond's awareness of higher authorities, who *can* assign the task. Frodo's growing sense of duty extends to his perception of Gollum: he attributes to fate both his need for Gollum's help, and Gollum's ability to bestow it.[222] Given the book's use of *fate* as a code word for divine guidance, Frodo here, too, shows himself subservient to the Valar.

As Frodo, Sam, and Gollum prepare to take the road toward Minas Morgul, they experience a moment of divine confirmation, if not divine intervention. At the crossroads from Osgiliath, Frodo looks into the west and his mind considers the lands that lie before him, covered at that moment by Sauron's dark fumes. For some reason, his mind takes him further than the continent of Middle-earth to the Great Sea, which he considers unsullied. Frodo here recognizes an impassable boundary for Sauron's potential domination (despite concerns previously noted that Sauron, if he possesses the Ring, might threaten even Aman). The light from the setting sun then highlights an ancient decapitated statue, covered in Orc scrawls. A beam of the sun focuses on the head of the statue, lying by the side of the road, with a gold and silver crown formed by flowers growing naturally. The moment brings this thought to Frodo's lips: "They cannot conquer forever."[223]

They here seems to reference all the combined forces of evil, of which Sauron is only the currently most powerful representative. Given the structure of the Middle-earth cosmos, *they* cannot conquer forever because evil remains ultimately weaker than good. Or more accurately, evil beings cannot ultimately overpower all good beings, since underpinning good is the life-force, the Flame Imperishable, of Eru Ilúvatar. It may be coincidence that flowers of Yavanna have grown to form a crown on the statue's head, and that a beam from the sun, a collaborative creation by the Valar, shines just at that moment; or it may be the Valar's method of confirming their own stewardship role in protecting and preserving the social structures of the Children of Ilúvatar. Rutledge considers this moment "an *apocalypsis,* a revelation—an inbreaking of the divine presence as a signal for faith." At the very least, the experience suggests to Frodo the confidence of the Powers of the West in the face of evil, a confidence that whether his mission succeeds or fails, the ultimate battle between good and evil remains a foregone conclusion. A page later, Frodo "reluctantly . . . turns his back on the West" to face his task within the darkness of Mordor.[224]

This passage, I suggest, shows the divine beings of Aman extending grace to residents of Middle-earth. Sarti explains that Tolkien's characters sometimes received grace in order to complete tasks set before them.

> Yet grace is only a supplement to natural strength, and it is the inclination of the character and his choice by free will to follow the right path—[to] recognize his own small part in the Plan and to surrender to the only Will that deserves humble surrender—which is essential. Often . . . only the well-meant and selfless decisions and actions of the characters allow the Plan to move forward. Immediate success is not pre-ordained in the plan. The Quest could have failed if the characters had failed, and the eventual deliverance of the free peoples delayed for ages, for such failure is then taken up and made part of the plan.[225]

The most important such failure is Frodo's ultimate inability to drop the Ring into the fires of Mount Doom and, worse yet, his decision to place it on his finger. The Hobbits feel rejuvenated as the end of their quest nears. When Sam carries Frodo, he finds Frodo especially light, perhaps because of their short rations, but also perhaps due to "some gift of final strength . . . given to him." In their final approach both Frodo and Sam experience "a sense of urgency which [they] did not understand," as if some outside power calls them. Even Gollum's attack proves beneficial, since nothing less would have roused Frodo to action.[226]

On entering Mount Doom, however, Frodo and Sam are bereft of external divine assistance. In "the heart of the realm of Sauron, . . . all other powers were here subdued,"[227] as illustrated physically by the impotence of Galadriel's Phial. Taking the narrator's assertion literally, that is, to include the Powers of Aman among those subdued in the heart of Sauron's realm, then it comes as no surprise that Frodo fails to destroy the Ring by his own will; his own Hobbit will, though strengthened through trial during his quest, is no match for the dominating Maia-strength force that remains in the air, as it were, in the very place where Sauron forged the One Ring thousands of years earlier. Rorabeck suggests Frodo at this moment "suffers a loss of will,"[228] while Milbank adds that Frodo's experience of "psychic disintegration" and dehumanization on the last stages of his journey further erodes his strength.[229]

Unlike Gandalf against the Balrog of Khazad-dûm, this is not an evenly matched contest. And unlike earlier moments, such as Sauron's attack against Frodo atop the Seat of Seeing, neither Gandalf nor Vala can contest Sauron's will to an extent that would leave Frodo's will free to choose. Not just Frodo's long possession of the Ring nor its powerful hold on him,[230] but the power of Sauron now has the advantage in its struggle to dominate Frodo's will because no divine interference from Aman or its representatives counterbalances evil force. Frodo's "freedom is utterly flattened. He is completely overwhelmed,"[231] Woods asserts. Abbott sees this moment as particularly important for Tolkien, a "Christian author," given its echoes of Ephesians 6:12: "For our struggle is not against flesh and blood, but against the rulers, against the authorities, against the powers of this dark world and against the spiritual forces of evil in the heavenly realms."[232]

On this moment hangs the destiny of Middle-earth, possibly of all Arda. While Frodo wears the One Ring, Sauron realizes his earlier folly and perceives one last hope: that Frodo will *retain* the Ring until Sauron can confront him. Frodo has grown since his Weathertop experience, and thus might use the Ring to prevent Sauron's eight remaining Nazgûl from attacking. Though dominated by Sauron, who possesses their Rings, the Nazgûl would at least feign obedience to Frodo while he bears the One Ring. The situation compares, Tolkien suggests, to one small but brave Human in possession of an overwhelming weapon, faced by strong and agile savages wielding poisoned swords. Frodo's many weaknesses include lack of experience in using the Ring; the Nazgûl's chief weakness in this situation is their fear of the Ring, which they cultishly revere. Yet can they but tempt him to leave Mount Doom, then close up the entrance, they will buy time for Sauron to arrive; against him, Frodo, even with the Ring, possesses no hope.[233]

Tolkien's draft notes reveal elements of Frodo's inward struggle only hinted at in the final draft. As Frodo enters the tunnel leading to the Crack of Doom, he perceives a strongly persuasive voice bequeathing peace, power, and reward, if only he submits to Sauron (a scene echoing Christ's temptations in the wilderness). Frodo, mentally pinioned between yielding and resisting, suddenly thinks to keep and use the Ring, as master of Middle-earth. Frodo imagines himself ruling Hobbits, who in turn rule the world, with great songs and poems, and all life a bountiful feast. Tolkien attributes the thought to Sauron. At that moment Frodo hears the cries of Nazgûl and discovers he lacks the will to remove the Ring. Gollum inadvertently comes to the rescue.[234]

Yet Gollum's presence at Mount Doom suggests supernatural powers at work. While Blackburn finds "Tolkien's tidy disposal of temptation at the moment of crisis somewhat too providential to be reassuring,"[235] Hibbs sees Gollum serving as "an unwitting instrument of divine providence."[236] MacArthur suggests "Gollum was specifically chosen by the Valar to provide the means by which the Ring can destroy itself."[237] Gollum's inadvertent contribution to the quest provides, in Urang's view, "vindication both of [Gollum's] freedom to pursue his own evil will and of an overruling Providence which exercises its freedom in his willful act. . . . Frodo here seems not to be free to do either good or evil. Tolkien has chosen to emphasize one side of the paradox of grace and freedom, giving the last word to an overriding grace."[238] Clark attributes even more to divine involvement, implying that the spiritual power behind "benevolent fate or providence" not only rescues Frodo, but "trips Gollum up by the heels at the edge of the abyss."[239]

Tolkien refers to Frodo's paradox as "an apparently complete trap," one that requires sacrifice. The good of Arda depends on enduring suffering beyond which a normal individual could endure. Thus, Frodo is "in a sense doomed to failure, doomed to fall to temptation or to be broken by pressure against his 'will.'" But the power of the temptation is not the overriding force; events inside Mount Doom might have transpired otherwise had Frodo not been "under the duress." Ironically, a powerful person would not have resisted the Ring so long; a weak person could not resist the Ring's call at the moment of truth. Therefore, the quest to destroy the Ring "was bound to fail," both as a strategy for protecting Middle-earth, and for Frodo's individual ennoblement, or sanctification. Careful readers, Tolkien asserts, should understand that "it is *quite impossible* for [Frodo] to surrender the Ring," and that the narrative foreshadows such a failure. In short, Frodo's failure forms an essential component of the "'theory' of true nobility and heroism" at the foundation of *The Lord of the Rings*.[240]

But, Tolkien emphasizes, Frodo's failure is *not* moral. A failure can be judged *moral* only when a person's endurance falls short of what one can be expected to endure; in fact, moral blame decreases the closer one approaches that limit. Frodo experiences demonic torture that breaks his mind and overpowers his will; donning the Ring is no more a failure of morals than if his body, rather than his mind, were being broken.[241] The situation supports Petty's assertion of a primary theme in Tolkien: that "the will of evil is stronger than that of mortals."[242]

Frodo's motive in accepting the burden of the Ring counters his failure. Love for others, a desire to save the Shire, even at his own expense, prompts Frodo, who humbly acknowledges his own inadequacy. Furthermore, he embraces Gandalf's ethic of pity and mercy. To pity Gollum, an apparent foolishness, relies on the ethical value of pity. Thus, Gollum's act of evil against Frodo (Tolkien describes it as robbery) displays grace: it provides Frodo with the best help anyone could have offered at that moment. Frodo's pity toward Gollum provides Frodo's salvation from a force too strong for him. Tolkien cites Aragorn's honoring Frodo as evidence that Frodo voluntarily did all that he could; the extent to which Gollum saves the day illustrates the importance of mercy, the value and effectiveness of forgiveness.[243]

Yet it is not merely Frodo's prior mercy that produces the outcome of the destruction of the Ring. At the moment when Frodo fails, "The Other Power then took over: the Writer of the Story (by which I do not mean myself), 'that one ever-present Person who is never absent and never named.'" Frodo's task, in other words, that which he can (by means of his own sacrifice) achieve, involves transporting the Ring to "the destined point, and no further." Grace, Tolkien adds, "is not infinite," and is normally limited to that required to accomplish the appointed task.[244] Neither Frodo nor the Wise can expect more.

🖋 Conclusion

This reading of *The Lord of the Rings* finds the Valar central to its events. Of course, to find hints of divine intervention in Frodo's quest begs another question: Why isn't there more divine involvement? Consider the possible further intervention that could be provided by just one Valier: Does Yavanna provide for Frodo and Sam the thornbush on which they land after their jump from the bridge below the Tower of Cirith Ungol? If so, couldn't she provide something less painful? Couldn't Yavanna do something about the Neekerbreekers that so trouble the Hobbits in the Midgewater Marshes? Mightn't she rouse the Ents and Huorns without necessitating Merry and Pippin's tortuous forced march across Rohan?

Hood sums up this problem:

The real question . . . is why Providence waited so long to help Frodo, or gave him so little aid, when he clearly relied from the outset on the Providential pattern, or 'luck' as he and Sam call it at various points. . . . Surely, had it so desired, this 'luck' could have arranged for Frodo to have had an easier journey, to be less starved, less exhausted, less tormented, to have more supplies and in short to be better prepared for the final assault of the Eye on Mount Doom.

Hood answers her question a few pages later: "In allowing Frodo to succumb before rescuing him, Providence . . . challenges its interpreters (and Tolkien . . . challenges his readers) to look beyond superficial triumphs and appreciate the deeper and more important realities of love and freedom."[245] What's important, in other words, is not merely the triumph of good over evil, but the implementation of those values that emanate from the character of Eru Ilúvatar.

As Cattaneo asserts, "Providence is the most striking [theme] in *The Lord of the Rings*. . . . Divine intervention is woven inside every big or little event."[246] Hutton similarly claims Tolkien's narrative expresses a constant sense of "providentialism, of an unseen and benevolent hand guiding events," a sensibility that may stem from pagan sources as much as Tolkien's Christianity.[247] The frequency with which such references occur in the text must imply providence, Mills argues; the only alternative is to dismiss *The Lord of the Rings* as "a horribly contrived plot."[248] According to Tolkien, even Sauron notices the extent to which fortune prefers his enemies, especially at moments when he perceives himself poised to achieve a great victory.[249]

Whatever the source, moments when good overcomes evil, when the Eagles arrive in the nick of time, when five Nazgûl fail to overcome Frodo on Weathertop, when Ents and Huorns rouse to destroy an empire; these are not deus-ex-machina moments, but moments of *Deus*, "grace earned through mercy from the Powers that be."[250] As Foster has observed, the Valar, the Gods of the West, and their Maiar helpers, serve as unnamed characters representing "the existence of a higher Order which arranges coincidences (and meaningfully employs the laws of causality and nature) so as to provide significant alternatives."[251] They serve as the agents through which Eru Ilúvatar produces eucatastrophe. Without them, the quest to destroy the One Ring would be doomed.

Chapter 5

The Problem of Evil in Arda

ne of the most thoroughly satisfying things about *The Lord of the Rings*," according to Ellwood, "is the fact that, with few exceptions, the good guys are very very good and the bad guys are horrid."[1] And indeed, good and evil often seem clearly differentiated in Tolkien's writings, at least to the reader, if not always to characters inside the stories. Some early critics saw this as an unfortunate oversimplification on Tolkien's part; one early anonymous review suggested, as far as bad guys go, "we are never told exactly in what their wickedness consists."[2] Other early readers perceived a clear indication of why evil characters deserved their label; an early review in the *Times Literary Supplement* asserted "the contrast in the story is absolute: it is that between love and hatred."[3]

Some readers, noting the novel's focus on war, wish to see greater complexity and ambiguity regarding good versus evil, or at least an acknowledgment that in war both parties see their *own* sides as good. Tolkien himself notes that those who choose to read about war ought not complain when one side dislikes the other.[4] Shippey contextualizes Tolkien as part of the generation shaped by experiences in two world wars, and thus having "come into contact with something irrevocably evil." From this perspective, Tolkien shares common ground with modernist authors, such as T. S. Eliot, with whom he is often contrasted. The significant difference, Shippey adds, between Tolkien and many of his postwar writer colleagues is that "he also provides answers and solutions" to the problem of evil.[5]

The Lord of the Rings thus offered a corrective to those affected by modernist despair following World War Two. Flieger asserts that one of the primary reasons to read Tolkien remains gaining "a deeper understanding of the ambiguities of good and evil and of ethical and moral dilemmas of a world constantly embroiled in wars with itself."[6] Tolkien's depiction of a firm and unmistakable line between good and evil asserts that some evils, or some levels of evil, are inarguably wrong, or "irrevocably evil," to use Shippey's phrase. Rutledge has praised "Tolkien's capacity for imagining radical evil—the sheer banality of its lesser ministers and its genius for devising impersonal, industrial methods of implementing mass murder without compunction from a safe distance."[7]

Yet in Tolkien's cosmology determining right from wrong ultimately requires recognizing one's existence as a creature, and thus acknowledging the authority and sovereignty of a creator; the Elves express a simple ethic: created beings "should not 'think to overpass the bounds that Ilúvatar hath set.'" That ethic explains why Melkor's intervention into Arda should be considered unambiguously bad and the Valar's efforts to sustain Arda and aid its residents should be considered good: Melkor wishes to abolish Ilúvatar's boundaries, while the Valar seek to uphold them. Admittedly, Tolkien's work began with a less clear-cut ethical division between right and wrong; *The Book of Lost Tales* posits a significant gray zone between good and evil, for example, when its narrator suggests that Beren's blatant lie when Melkor captures him "must have been inspired" by the Valar or Melian, noting that the lie preserves his life. Similarly, Lúthien lies before the Sauron figure of *The Book of Lost Tales,* despite the narrative's assertion that Elf maidens typically avoid falsehoods.[8]

Christopher Tolkien describes transformations over time in his father's writings as becoming progressively more preoccupied with theological concerns,[9] a preoccupation that critics have found consonant with Tolkien's Catholic theology. Tolkien's efforts reveal the author elaborating greater consistency in examining the implications of his own theory of evil. This chapter will examine that theory, which is largely consonant with Catholic theology: evil originates through the intervention of one rebellious divine being; it spreads as other divine beings join the rebellion; and it requires corresponding counterinterventions from the creator-god and divine beings who remain faithful to him.

At the same time, Tolkien pursues implications of his theory of evil that evolve from his own subcreation, which, while not necessarily divergent from Catholic theology, are not typically discussed by critics interested in foregrounding Tolkien's Catholicism. Tolkien's legendarium, for example, posits a moral space between good and evil in which beings with limited knowledge and experience, even divine beings, make mistakes and learn; those mistakes include the possibility of stepping in the direction of rebellion against Eru. Divine intervention, even by good beings, might do as much harm as good. Additional issues Tolkien raises regarding evil include its complicated relationship to rationality, the assumption within the narrative that some apparently sentient evil beings possess, due to Melkor's interference, no hope of redemption, and the association of technology with evil.

✍ Tolkien's Theory of Evil in Middle-earth

Examining the conflict of good versus evil requires positing some degree of dualism. Some dualists posit good and evil as equals, coexisting eternally and interdependently. Kocher approaches such a dualism when he asserts that the creator of Middle-earth "needs evil in order to bring on times of peril that test his creatures to the uttermost, morally and physically";[10] while Kocher may use the word *need* euphemistically to mean *relied on* or *chose to utilize,* an Eru with a *need* for evil would be a less-than-all-powerful deity caught up in a structure with some other independent force not under Eru's control.

Croft, however, distinguishes two forms of dualism: rather than radical dualism ("two opposing fundamental principles [that] are co-equal and co-eternal"), Tolkien embraces "moderate" dualism, which assumes "one primordial principle [that] through some moderating event" comes into conflict with a "second principle in some way . . . derived from the first."[11] From this perspective, the story of evil in Arda (discussed in chapter 1) can be summed up as: Melkor's freedom, in itself good and derived from Eru, comes through Melkor's own choice into conflict with Eru's primordial principles of perfection and goodness.

Tolkien's "moderate" dualism connects Middle-earth to its author's Catholic worldview. Houghton and Keesee describe Tolkien's theory of evil as Augustinian; rather than a complete opposite of good, evil is perversion of good that inevitably remains dependent upon it.[12] Glover calls evil "a corruption" while Tolkien terms it "a tendency to aberration from the design."[13] Pearce describes evil in Tolkien's legendarium as "parasitic": "it is counter-creative and can only destroy[; thus,] it often destroys itself in the blindness of its malice."[14] Since evil is derivative, choosing evil is not choosing an alternative path, but instead a path toward nonexistence. Thus, Rosebury adds, "[E]vil is conceived in terms of freely-chosen negation, of a willful abdication from the original state of created perfection."[15] Seeing evil as "privation of perfection or corruption of perfection," according to Treloar, connects Tolkien to medieval metaphysics.[16] Thus, Shippey asserts, Boethius may be as good a source for Tolkien's view of evil as is Augustine;[17] Milbank seeks a synthesis of these views, finding Augustine's influence on Tolkien's "attitude to evil as a privation . . . and a Thomist understanding of evil [a]s a deficiency in being."[18]

Some readers have interpreted Tolkien's depiction of evil through a lens colored more by John Calvin than by Thomas Aquinas. This perspective sees evil as an element of Eru's plan; "Ilúvatar gave Being to something in which evil already had been introduced," according to Vink.[19] Tolkien discusses evil in ways that support Vink's assertion, as when he describes "the essential mode of the process of 'history' of Arda that evil should constantly arise, and that out of it new good should constantly come."[20] Yet Tolkien's statement, and perhaps Vink's, applies only to the *history* of Arda; within that history, Eru can be said to use evil as a tool for furthering his agenda. As chapter 1 showed, however, the narrative of evil begins *prior to* the history of Arda, and that narrative positions evil *outside* Eru's plan. Tolkien focuses on evil as rebellion against pre-existing order. Melkor repudiates all rules given by Eru, and seeks also to abolish the laws of nature, though he finds he cannot. The laws of nature remain unchangeable and thus constantly remind Melkor of Eru's ultimate invincibility, and that Melkor has peers with the same lineage as himself; these truths only multiply his rage.[21] The story of evil as rebellion parallels, in its essence, the story of Milton's *Paradise Lost.*

Yet *Paradise Lost* posits a perfect, righteous, unmarred Earth into which Satan (himself already fallen) introduces evil through temptation to produce the Fall of Humans, which then induces corollary negative effects into all of nature. In Middle-earth, in contrast, evil enters the substance of the world long before sentient life-forms arise. From this perspective, Middle-earth is doomed to suffer the presence of evil, since evil has been foreshown in the Music of the Ainur. Nothing in Arda remains, or even begins, pure or unaffected by evil. Even further, Tolkien presumes that much of Eä has been similarly marred by Melkor. Because evil has infected all of Eä, evil has become essential to the universe; this is not because there can be no universe or sentient existence without evil, nor because Eru depends on evil, but rather Eru elects to use evil as "the essential mode of the process of 'history.'"[22] In other words, history will be a continuous reminder and repetition of Eru's announcement to Melkor subsequent to the Singing of the Ainur, that any being attempting to arrest history away from Eru's plan will instead find himself or herself Eru's tool for creating something more marvelous than that created being can conceive.[23]

The role Eru assigns evil can be described as the opposite of, or a parody of, eucatastrophe. In setting forth the theory underpinning the story of Númenor, Tolkien notes that evil's ability to reemerge after defeat perpetually echoes the Fall,[24] the original entrance of evil forming a barrier between Eru and the fallen being. Just as happy endings to stories foreshadow the final eucatastrophe that will bring the history of Arda to a close, the perpetual reemergence of evil will remind Arda's inhabitants that they reside in a fallen world.

Thus, evil is "subcreatively introduced," as Tolkien describes it, making corruption of all things possible, though not necessarily inevitable.[25] Melkor takes on incarnate form in an effort to correlate himself with physical matter, in essence to make the whole world his body (in the same way that Sauron, on a much smaller scale, places much of his power into the One Ring). Thus "all 'matter' is likely to have a 'Melkor ingredient,'" though Melkor invests more of himself into some elements (gold, for example) than others (such as water, which is Ulmo's). Because of his influence everything in Middle-earth possesses "an inclination to evil." Sentient beings whose origins stem from the matter of Arda, whose existence depends on the conjunction of spirit and matter, are already affected by evil such that they are likely to do wrong and suffer the consequences.[26]

With this in mind, the Valar's decision to bring the Elves to Aman, in an effort to protect them from Melkor, cannot possibly cure or remove the evil latent within their beings. Even if Melkor sincerely repents from his rebellion, the impact of his earlier revolt cannot be undone, since the power exerted against Eru and the Valar will continue to produce evil effects. This realization fosters a growth moment for the guardians of Arda, producing a sense of foreboding, a premonition of sorrows that will stem from the Children of Ilúvatar. Christopher Tolkien, commenting on this aspect of Arda's history, points out the irony that only the death of Míriel in Aman teaches the Valar the extent of evil's infiltration of Middle-earth. That realization, though late in coming, may be another instance, along with the unchaining of Melkor, illustrating the innate inability of righteous creatures to grasp the nature and impact of evil, at least not until having learned through painful experience; perhaps, Christopher Tolkien speculates, "the Valar had been deluded" as to evil's nature and power.[27]

The Valar use the term "Arda Hastaina," or "Arda Marred," to describe the condition of the world inhabited by evil; this phrase contrasts with "Arda Alahasta," or "Arda Unmarred," the world they can imagine, to some extent, had Melkor not intruded rebellion. At the same time, the presence of latent evil within matter does not make matter evil; the Elves consider matter completely good, at least originally.[28] In fact, matter can be self-healing, as long as sentient life-forms refrain from rousing its latent evil. Yet Hood notes that physical environments slowly degrade unless counteracted by a power for good,[29] such as the power exuded by the Valar or the Elves (or perhaps even the unrecognized power of the Hobbits).

Powerful evil beings possess three main goals within Tolkien's legendarium: domination, corruption, and destruction. The three goals form an uncomfortable conceptual spectrum, with domination (which includes some desire to preserve and sustain) in opposition to destruction, and with corruption in between. Domination reflects Melkor's desire to promote himself as an authority, to overthrow the Valar, and to put himself in the place of Eru; since he lacks authority, validity, and creative power as god, he substitutes force at the expense of sentient beings' free wills. Early manuscripts describe a Spell of Bottomless Dread, an exercise of metaphysical power that binds his slaves.[30] Bullock considers Melkor's reliance on force as "the greatest of all evils" in Tolkien's writings, which explains why Melkor's torture of Húrin (making him passively witness two decades of inevitable misfortune for his wife, son, and daughter) qualify as one of the cruelest experiences Melkor devises.[31]

That which Melkor dominates he corrupts; that which he cannot dominate, he attempts to corrupt, since corruption suggests divergence from Eru's design. When dominated agents no longer provide service, or when agents with free wills oppose him, he seeks to destroy. In fact, he pursues domination in order to increase the power he can apply toward destruction. While building a hierarchic mass of subordinate servants, Melkor apes Eru's appointment of the Valar and Maiar, and relies on Eru to maintain the laws of nature that support his followers' abilities to act. Ultimately, the two poles of Melkor's motivation—domination and destruction—reveal a contradiction; rebellion against Eru remains tenable only as long as Eru cooperates.

While Tolkien's depiction of evil positions it as dependent on good, Shippey notes that *The Lord of the Rings* gives equal time to the idea that evil is a force rather than an absence.[32] Good beings have the responsibility of resisting evil, though evil, as embodied in Melkor and Sauron, can overpower incarnate beings and defy the efforts of created spirit beings such as the Ainur.[33] As Shippey says, within Tolkien's legendarium "good is attained only at vast expense while evil recuperates almost at will."[34] Yet Tolkien insists that evil will not be permanent; ultimately, good will conquer. As Gandalf suggests in a *Lord of the Rings* manuscript, the Wise express confidence that Sauron ultimately faces certain failure and destruction.[35]

🖋 *Evil versus Folly*

Tolkien understands evil and free will to mean "that God permits what God does not intend," according to Rutledge.[36] Evil certainly fits into the category of *that which God permits but does not intend,* but it doesn't necessarily follow that all items in the category are evil. God might not intend that Humans think of pink elephants, for example, but for Humans to think of pink elephants is not necessarily bad. Whether such an in-between conceptual space is true in the Christian understanding of reality, it appears true in Tolkien's cosmology, as Melkor's fall into evil shows when compared with Aulë's creation of the Dwarves. Dickerson, writing in the authoritative *J. R. R. Tolkien Encyclopedia,* describes Aulë's action as "a moral error";[37] Evans finds no "real difference between Aulë's independent creation of the Dwarves and Melkor's solitary composition of musical themes at variance with Ilúvatar's."[38] The following reading, in contrast, identifies significant differences between the two stories.

The Silmarillion declares that Melkor embraces evil and becomes the enemy of Eru Ilúvatar and the Valar. Melkor's full commitment to evil implies no hope of transformation or redemption (at least not within the bounds of Eä and the flow of time). Yet as Elrond asserts in *The Fellowship of the Ring,* "Nothing is evil in the beginning."[39] A major subplot of the "Ainulindalë" narrates Melkor's journey from good to evil, though it indicates no precise moment when Melkor turns the corner, as it were, consciously and irretrievably dedicating himself to evil.

In fact, eleven specific factors contribute to Melkor's downfall, listed below in more or less sequential order:

1. Extreme curiosity (regarding the Imperishable Flame, the substance of Eru Ilúvatar's creative force)
2. Self-induced solitude (within the Void)
3. Impatience (unwillingness to wait on Ilúvatar's timing)
4. Desire to create "things of his own"[40]
5. Intruding discord into the Music of the Ainur (*The Silmarillion* defines Melkor's discord as thoughts of his own imagination that do not fit with Eru's themes[41])
6. Covetousness of Ilúvatar's creation
7. Desire to increase his own power and glory
8. Lying to himself[42]
9. Pursuing discord in the face of Ilúvatar's correction

10. Allowing shame (in the face of Ilúvatar's rebuke) to evolve into secret anger
11. Eschewing the virtues embraced by the Valar, such as pity and steward-ship

Each of these issues contributes to Melkor's downfall, to his devolution into a state of complete dedication to evil. Yet many of these factors are not intrinsically evil. All may be potentially dangerous, some simply unwise; the "Ainulindalë" does not indicate which one factor, added to the others, is the straw that breaks the proverbial camel's back. But together the individual actions form steps along a path, a trajectory; as Rosebury notes, "Melkor begins as an impatient creative spirit; as the myth proceeds, his activity becomes progressively more destructive."[43]

Insight into Melkor's downfall comes from comparing his story with another *Silmarillion* tale of a powerful spirit being who does wrong but does *not* turn to evil, the tale of the creation of the Dwarves as narrated in the *Silmarillion* chapter "Of Aulë and Yavanna." This second chapter of the "Quenta Silmarillion" comes after the introductory history of the Valar's initial work in Arda: shaping its substances into continents, the Spring of Arda under the two great lamps, the establishment of Aman as the Valar's place of residence, the creation of the Two Trees and the Bliss of Valinor, and the Sleep of Yavanna over the continent of Middle-earth. Yet internal evidence within chapter 2 suggests it should be contextualized within the events of chapter 1, perhaps early in the Bliss of Valinor.

As Aulë works in secret to devise the Dwarves, Ilúvatar speaks to him, angry yet pitying.[44] The text conceals the means by which Ilúvatar speaks, whether from afar or within Arda; in fact, simply introducing this as a problem may reveal a false dichotomy resulting from Eru Ilúvatar's apparent success in distancing himself from his creation. The Valar's decision to enter Eä requires them to leave Eru's direct presence in some way; yet the reliance here on a spatial metaphor may produce the (possibly incorrect) conclusion that Eru is in some way *not* in Arda. Yet nothing about the legendarium demands Eru's absence, only his invisibility, even to the Valar, unless he wishes otherwise. This chapter of *The Silmarillion* suggests Eru's relationship to all of Eä parallels that of the Valar to Middle-earth during the Third Age (see chapter 4); his influence is present within the Valar's work, though not in a manner that overrides their own wills.

Functioning outside of Eru's will, however, is the issue Eru Ilúvatar raises when he confronts Aulë. Because Aulë possesses only *being* within himself, not the power of imparting it to others, the Dwarves appear sentient, but they move and speak only when Aulë wills it; when Aulë focuses his attention elsewhere, his Dwarves only stand idle, as puppets. "Is that thy desire?" Ilúvatar asks rhetorically.[45]

Or at least I presume the question is rhetorical. In Ilúvatar's interactions with Melkor and the other Valar, he appears to comprehend the thoughts and motivations of his created beings. If so, then the question's intent must be to help Aulë comprehend his own intentions. Ilúvatar appears interested in Aulë's attitude as much as his actions. As Seeman notes, Tolkien's legendarium illustrates that power can be used in two ways: for subcreation or for domination. The first impulse is good, the second evil.[46] Aulë's desire to subcreate life-forms inadvertently positions him as dictator over his creation.

Aulë's response to Eru displays no desire for lordship. Instead, he desires beings to teach and love, who can enjoy the beauties of Ilúvatar's creation. In confessing his impatience, Aulë suggests that Eru himself has placed the desire to create within his heart. "The child of little understanding that makes a play of the deeds of his father may do so without thought of mockery, but because he is the son of his father. . . . As a child to his father, I offer to thee these things."[47]

Aulë's metaphor is remarkable in several ways. First, Aulë apparently expresses it prior to the appearance of Elves and Humans, and thus prior to any tangible examples of biological father-son relationships. Either the Vision of the Ainur clearly depicted patrilineal relations, or the Valar apply the metaphor later to explain the otherwise inexpressible to the Elves. Second, Aulë echoes Tolkien's own theory of subcreation.[48] Since Humans are made in the image of a creative God, mimicking him by imaginatively creating our own worlds (as Tolkien does) honors God. Third, and most important, the metaphor shifts some degree of responsibility, for the impulse if not the actions, to Aulë's creator.

Then follows one of the most moving incidents in the history of Arda. Asking whether it might be best to "destroy the work of [his] presumption," Aulë picks up a hammer to smash his creation, tears flowing from his eyes[49] (a scene, Flieger notes, reminiscent of the biblical Abraham's willingness to sacrifice his son, Isaac[50]). Ilúvatar compassionately intercedes, accepting Aulë's offer to submit the Dwarves to his will and granting Aulë's wish that the Dwarves be sentient beings, even while Aulë renounces them.[51]

Yet though Ilúvatar ultimately accepts Aulë's creation, Aulë's actions still bear consequences. First, Ilúvatar insists the Dwarves be placed at rest, hidden under mountain stone, until some unspecified time after the appearance of Eru's Firstborn, the Elves.[52] Eru will not permit Aulë to upstage the Third Theme in the Singing of the Ainur. Second, Eru refuses to improve the Dwarves, beyond granting them sentience, despite Aulë's request that Ilúvatar fix his work; the Dwarves remain, in Milbank's words, a "somewhat botched creation."[53] Just as importantly, the creation of the Dwarves introduces further discord into Arda. Eru himself predicts strife between his own Children and the Dwarves, a division that Eru characterizes as between Children of choice and those of adoption[54] (a characterization that provides an additional parallel with the biblical Abraham, as God blesses both Ishmael and Isaac, but predicts strife between the two). Eru's prediction prefigures the long history of conflict between Elf and Dwarf, beginning in the First Age and achieving just a hint of reconciliation late in the Third Age, as Gimli befriends Legolas and enacts chivalry toward Galadriel. As Whitt suggests, the "thousands of years of strife [between Elves and Dwarves] are the consequence of Aulë's single act of disobedience."[55]

Aulë's choice to maintain his silence among the Valar, even to his own wife, produces yet more discord. When he finally reveals to Yavanna his own actions and Eru's resulting mercy, she foretells that his secrecy will result in the Dwarves having no innate love for growing things. She rebukes her husband, prophesying that the Dwarves will develop a natural love for Aulë's preferences; since those preferences included smithery, she expresses fear for the fate of her favorites, the trees. Aulë's creation, in other words, threatens Yavanna's. When Aulë responds that the Children of Ilúvatar will also threaten Yavanna's creation, Yavanna does not feel comfort.[56]

In this story, Aulë pursues an action that he should not pursue, much as Melkor before him; like Melkor's discord during the Singing of the Ainur, Aulë's creation of the Dwarves is wrong, outside the boundaries Eru Ilúvatar has set, and it receives Eru's rebuke. In fact, comparing Aulë's actions with those of Melkor reveals many of the same issues at stake:

1. Extreme curiosity (regarding the creation of sentient life)
2. Self-induced solitude (under the mountains of Middle-earth)
3. Impatience (unwillingness to wait on Ilúvatar's timing)
4. Desire to create things of his own
5. Intruding discord into Middle-earth and Aman
6. Covetousness of Ilúvatar's creation (though Aulë's actions when rebuked by Ilúvatar show contrition)

These actions are not innately evil, though progressing through the list grows increasingly dangerous, moving a Vala steadily closer to the point of committing evil. All the Valar exhibit some degree of curiosity about the Children of Eru, as well as impatience for the Children's appearance. Some, Ulmo in particular, embrace solitude, or at least separate themselves from the other Valar (the extent to which Ulmo interacts with the Maiar Ossë and Uinen is unclear). Several show a creative impulse, Varda with her stars and Yavanna with plant life in general and the Two Trees in particular; of course, those creations, in contrast with both Melkor and Aulë's desires, are foreseen in the Singing of the Ainur. More serious yet are intruding discord and covetousness; those impulses display a mind already at variance with that of Eru and the Singing of the Ainur, though Yavanna can be seen as exhibiting near-covetousness toward her creations (as exhibited in her reluctance that Dwarves or Children of Eru should harm her beloved trees).

Yet the remaining items on the list of Melkor's progression to evil do not appear in Aulë's story:

1. Desiring to increase his own power and glory; Aulë wants beings to exist so he can serve rather than control them
2. Pursuing discord in the face of Ilúvatar's correction; Aulë's immediate confession and contrition moves Ilúvatar to compassion
3. Lying to himself
4. Allowing shame (in the face of Ilúvatar's rebuke) to evolve into secret anger; instead, Aulë moves from contrition to joy in the experience of Ilúvatar's mercy
5. Eschewing the virtues embraced by the Valar, such as pity and stewardship; instead, Aulë desires stewardship and his tears show his pity for the fate of the Dwarves he has brought into existence

The differences between the two can be summed up in Ilúvatar's motivation for showing Aulë mercy: "I have seen thy humility, and taken pity on your impatience."[57] The virtue of humility underpins Aulë's reaction to Ilúvatar, and even those secret actions that Ilúvatar declares beyond Aulë's power and authority. Aulë's humble attitude outweighs his potentially rebellious actions. *The Silmarillion* declares that Aulë does not swerve from faithfulness to Eru and ultimately submits his actions to his creator's will.[58] Elsewhere the legendarium states that Eru finds Aulë guilty of "impatient love."[59] In contrast, Melkor's lack of humility, his pride (coupled with envy[60]), confirms his actions as rebellion, opposition to love. As Rateliff has observed, "pride is the cardinal sin in Tolkien's ethos," as seen in *The Lord of the Rings,* for example, in Saruman's inability to pity lesser life-forms.[61] Similarly, Barajas-Garrido attributes evil to Sauron "because he loves himself but not Eru. If he loved Eru he would accept his goodness and respect the free will of others."[62] In this regard, Middle-earth is, like Tolkien himself, fully compatible with Christianity, Catholicism in particular. Evil reveals itself as much in the relationship between creator and creature as it does in a creature's actions.

At the same time Ilúvatar indicates that Aulë's stepping outside the range of his delegated authority is stepping in the wrong direction. One manuscript compares the creation of the Dwarves to that of the Orcs; both stem from Valian willfulness, though creation of the Dwarves lacks Melkor's evil mockery in creating Orcs.[63] If Aulë were to persist in his willfulness, it might lead him to a fall similar to Melkor's. Tolkien has commented that Aulë "in a sense 'fell,'"[64] though his use of the qualifying phrase and the quotation marks suggest it is not quite that. Aulë, in fact, offers a word to express his mistake, saying "I have fallen into *folly.*"[65] This word appears in the wisdom literature of the King James Version of the Bible, especially Proverbs. In the Judeo-Christian tradition it means the opposite, or lack, of wisdom. Tolkien's use of the word implies a similar meaning, which suggests that the Valar, though inherently good and unfallen, lack some knowledge, and this in turn leads them to make mistakes from which they learn and suffer the consequences (and because of the Valar's vast responsibilities, a Vala's mistake may reap consequences for millions of life-forms). "Even the 'good' Valar . . . could at least err," Tolkien acknowledges.[66]

Aulë's example of a child mimicking its parent suggests folly as a wayward-ness from which the child learns to obey, and evil as a waywardness from which the child grows to desire more waywardness. Any finite being will have a weakness, Tolkien asserts in a commentary on Manwë's naive trust that Melkor has reformed after long imprisonment; Tolkien defines weakness as "inadequacy to deal with some situations," adding that such a weakness is not sinful if it is not willed, and when a created being does the best it can.[67]

Tolkien's perspective suggests consequentialism, an ethic that judges whether an action is evil or good based on its effects. At the same time, the story of Aulë suggests virtue ethics, which judges actions by the character of the actor; from this perspective, Aulë's actions are acceptable because of his humble character, while Melkor's similar actions display his pride. Asking which ethical system most accurately fits the story places an interpreter into a chicken-or-the-egg dilemma: it depends on which is cause and which is effect; did Melkor's pride drive him into solitude and produce the desire to create things on his own, or did those two actions produce his pride? The story does not resolve that debate.

What is definitely missing, however, is a clearly announced deontological ethics, a system of right and wrong based on rules. Tolkien does not provide, for Valar, Elves, or Humans, a Sinai moment itemizing Eru's law, though perhaps ethics form such an integral part of Eru's nature that it enters into the history of Arda through the Singing of the Ainur. At most, Tolkien's characters suggest an inner, natural law, though one that presumes a minimal quantity of guidelines, so ingrained that violating them seems to break nature rather than break a law outside nature. Tolkien's "Notes on *Orë*" describes the Elves' sense of natural law as inner counsel stemming ultimately from Eru, though the one example of natural law in Tolkien's writings is the law against bigamy.[68] Elves seem to understand without being told that killing other Elves is wrong, an understanding that precedes the Kinslaying at Alqualondë, though that event certainly ingrains the natural law even deeper into Elvish nature.

The space occupied by *folly* further impacts Tolkien's view of *the Fall*. The Judeo-Christian story of the Fall of Adam and Eve suggests a one-time event: a single impulsive decision by one or two individuals, changing history forever. Tolkien's mythology posits a fall as a gradual experience, a series of events, a trend over time. Flieger sees Fëanor's devolution as "a series of smaller falls" (compared to the biblical Fall of Adam and Eve), each "in some way a fall into self-will and selfishness."[69] She similarly notes that the "Tale of Adanel," which describes the first Human fall under the influence of Melkor, foregrounds "a decline, ... a more gradual event," rather than "the traditional Judeo-Christian watershed moment of choice in which all is lost."[70]

Additionally, Tolkien's understanding of evil reflects a specifically Catholic worldview, which ranks sins based on their severity. Mortal sins break a human's relationship with God; venial sins harm the relationship, but not to the breaking point. Mortal sins imply actions with serious consequences performed with full knowledge that the action is both serious and wrong, and with full consent of the actor's will. Venial sins, in contrast, imply limited culpability. From this perspective, items 1–6 (of the list of Aulë's errors) may be venial, while 7–11 can be considered mortal. Tolkien applies a sense of ranked sin in his own literary criticism. Speaking of Gawain, hero of the medieval "Sir Gawain and the Green Knight," Tolkien asserts that one should not merely ask whether Gawain fails in his duty in not reporting to the lord of the house the gift of the lady's garment; rather, one must think about how and to what extent he fails. Tolkien asserts three planes within Gawain's story, all ethical (in Gawain's case, these are the promise made to the lord, courtesy that pertains to his relationship with the lady, and "real morals, virtues and sins"[71]). As Gawain's story illustrates, these differing ethical claims on Gawain lead to conflict. The same is true in Aulë's case. To be created in the image of a creative god implies not just a desire to subcreate, but a duty to do so. Aulë's later service to the Elves of Aman shows that he is intended to teach and guide; his impulse to create the Dwarves can be seen as one divine impulse overriding a competing divine impulse.

Tolkien does not consistently use the terms *folly* and *evil* in the manner outlined here; Faramir, for example, describes the post-Númenóreans using both words: they "fell into evils and follies."[72] Sometimes, however, the distinction helps comprehend Tolkien's purpose. Pippin is an "honest fool" after gazing into the Palantír of Orthanc and confessing his actions to Gandalf;[73] while Pippin does something he should not do, he does not commit evil and does not need forgiveness. In contrast, Frodo at Parth Galen perceives that Boromir has "fallen into evil" (described in draft notes as evil entering the heart)[74] when he tries to take the Ring by force. This puts Boromir beyond mere folly and transforms his later defense of Merry and Pippin, coupled with his regret for violating his vow to support Frodo, into an act of redemption, as Aragorn recognizes. Hammond and Scull suggest Boromir dies "in a spiritual 'state of grace', having at last fought off the spell of the Ring."[75]

Saruman, in contrast, is called a fool, to his face, by Gandalf at Orthanc when Gandalf takes Saruman's place as head of the Istari. To be a fool implies that Saruman is not yet so deep in evil that he cannot repent and return to good, if only his pride does not impede him. Saruman's decision to preserve his sense of pride rather than pursue humility is the turning point causing his complete removal from the holy Order, and a rapid decrease in his powers, devolving to a level Tolkien elsewhere describes as "mere Magician."[76] It turns him, in other words, from a mixture of folly and evil into a state in which folly no longer mitigates evil. In another context, Gandalf uses the term *folly* to reveal self-doubt regarding the plan of the Wise to send the Ring into Mordor in the possession of Hobbits; such a strategy, he admits, might represent wisdom, but might instead be folly.[77]

Tolkien's innovation, in the face of biblical applications of the term *folly* to fallen beings, is to propose *folly* as a category into which unfallen beings might enter, without their yielding to evil. As chapter 2 of this study emphasizes, divinity, as perceived by residents of Middle-earth, lacks perfection of both knowledge and action. Lack of knowledge leads the Valar to imperfect actions (with *imperfect* defined as *not producing uniformly positive outcomes*). The Valar make mistakes (such as summoning the Elves to Aman, or withholding the light of the Two Trees from Middle-earth[78]) from which they learn and grow, and by which the Elves suffer; and while those mistakes are wrong, they remain folly, not evil, because the perpetrators retain humility. Perhaps Celeborn uses the term in this technical sense when he speculates that Gandalf has fallen "from wisdom into folly" when he leads the Fellowship into Moria, thus encountering the Balrog.[79] Galadriel, in contrast, defends Gandalf, suggesting that Celeborn's assertion is itself folly. One manuscript describes Gandalf as verbally rebuking folly,[80] suggesting that those he rebukes drift, perhaps unwittingly, toward evil.

Folly is a danger zone, a moral space in which a being might do wrong without doing evil. Said another way, it's as close to evil as good creatures can go without experiencing a fall from which they need redemption. It coincides with, and thus expands, the definition of evil sometimes distilled from Tolkien's work as *good pursued badly*. From a narrative standpoint, folly allows Tolkien to create morally perfect beings that perform imperfectly without changing their moral status. Thus, folly illustrates the Catholic principle that both sinners and saints need God's grace, and that God extends grace prior to its need.

The space folly occupies on the moral continuum may even be necessary for good to function effectively in its battle with evil. Croft has evaluated moments in *The Hobbit* and *The Lord of the Rings* when disobedience leads to good ends. In a question heavily laden with moral dilemmas, she asks: "How . . . can the right kind of disobedience lead to eucatastrophe, where obedience in the same situation could lead to disaster?"[81] Croft traces moments of disobedience in *The Hobbit,* ranging from Bilbo's initial incivility to Gandalf to his ultimate disobedience of Thorin's command to bring him the Arkenstone. Bilbo's deception of Thorin, coupled with appeasing Thorin's enemies, has "the eucatastrophic effect of holding off the battle between the Dwarves and their opponents until exactly the moment of the Goblin and Warg attack." In fact, she suggests, such disobedience to social and moral conventions is precisely what Gandalf finds potentially useful in aligning Bilbo with the Dwarves.

Croft examines similar moments in *The Lord of the Rings* when disobedience leads to good outcomes, ranging from Frodo's friends' conspiracy to spy on him in the Shire, to Pippin's use of the Palantír; from Éowyn and Merry's disobedience of Théoden to Gollum's attack on his "master" inside Mount Doom. The carefully constructed plot of Tolkien's story makes it "difficult to *not* see any particular act of disobedience contributing in some way to a later moment of eucatastrophe."[82] The weakness in Croft's perspective is taking the reductive view that an incident such as Boromir's attempt to take the Ring from Frodo *causes* Frodo's resolution to leave the Fellowship and strike out alone toward Mordor; when examined from the perspective of divine intervention, such moments may be interpreted as hidden divine wills reacting to and using human behaviors such as Boromir's attack (while not necessarily *causing* that attack) to accomplish ends not anticipated by Boromir. Still, Croft's acknowledgment of disobedience's central role in the story's plot suggests the narrative requires the moral space of folly to allow fallen beings to work with divine beings in the battle against evil.

🖋 Organized Evil versus Unaligned Evil

Blackburn argues that Tolkien's major villains (specifically in *The Hobbit*) act in groups, or at least represent groups, while "heroes are strongly individual," deeply committed to their personal integrities.[83] This only partially applies to the legendarium at large, since some evil beings—Shelob, for example—function as loners. The distinction may in fact be that evil beings who function in groups find greater success, or at least survive longer, than evil loners. Melkor, and Sauron after him, embraces a hierarchically organized approach toward consolidating power through domination. Some of their followers appear completely dedicated to them, such as the nine Nazgûl, who Stratyner has compared to an evil version of the medieval *comitatus,* or band of thanes dedicated to the service of their lord (who often formalize their commitment to him by giving rings).[84] Yet, as Auden notes, "all alliances of Evil with Evil are necessarily unstable."[85]

Thus, Melkor and Sauron, as evil masterminds, face four categories of threats to their domination:

1. Opposition from the Valar and forces aligned with them (such as Gandalf and the Vanyar) or at least not in rebellion against them
2. Opposition from forces in rebellion against the Valar that are, up to a point, potentially redeemable (such as the Noldorin Elves during the First Age, and Saruman for at least some of his career during the Third)
3. Dissatisfaction from within the ranks, or forces (such as the Orcs Shagrat and Gorbag) that wish to break away from submission to Melkor or

Sauron, to function independently (which, if achieved, will, place them
into category 4)

4. Opposition from "unaligned evil(s),"[86] forces that oppose the Valar but
also resist Melkor or Sauron (Shelob during the Third Age, for example)

The successful defeats of Melkor's forces shortly after the awakening of the
Elves and again at the end of the First Age illustrate the first category of opposition to organized evil. Eönwë's leadership of the Host of the Valar and
Tulkas's chaining of Melkor foreshow the inexorable ultimate victory of good
over evil. These victories are marred, of course, by the Valar's folly, first in
releasing Melkor after spending thousands of years in Mandos's dungeons,
and second in allowing Sauron and Balrogs to endure in hiding after Melkor's
final defeat. In the Third Age Gandalf remains consistently dedicated to the
objectives and values of the Valar, and thus in opposition to Sauron, though
Gandalf, too, as Celeborn suggests, may on occasion have yielded to folly.

Much of the primary narrative arc of *The Silmarillion* illustrates the second category of opposition to organized evil. The Noldor under Fëanor rebel
against the Valar, yet the Valar maintain hope for reconciliation. The Noldor
prove formidable foes of Melkor during the First Age; while only foolish pride
suggests an ultimate victory in their war against Melkor, they do achieve some
stunning victories in battle, and even their defeats are noble. Whether Fëanor
and his sons are forgiven remains open to speculation. If they embrace evil
to the point of no return, then their dedication and continued commitment
to rebellion moves them from category 2 to category 4; this seems the position of the last remaining sons of Fëanor, Maedhros and Maglor, who steal
the two recovered Silmarils from the Host of the Valar following the War of
Wrath. Among characters in *The Lord of the Rings,* Tom Bombadil might
be considered, if not actively opposing the Valar, at least unsupportive due to
his policy of uninvolvement in the political affairs of Middle-earth; Rateliff
refers to Bombadil as "an unaligned good."[87]

Category 3 represents internal threats within organized evil: exertion of
its members' wills against the organization. While Sauron might control
creatures such as Orcs through direct threat, they in turn can remain aligned
with evil while rebelling against their master. Thus, as Sam listens to Gorbag
and Shagrat talk in the passageway leading from Shelob's lair, he overhears
their desire to pursue evil out from under the domination of Sauron. Gorbag
weaves for Shagrat a fantasy vision of Orc Shangri-La: communal living with
a few trusted peers, near conveniently accessible loot, and with no powerful

overseers. Later Sam and Frodo overhear two Orcs, different varieties as Sam speculates, accusing one another of lack of fidelity to the powers that be; they fight and one kills the other, a tendency Frodo says Orcs always exhibit.[88]

Squabbling among different groups of Orcs, common Orc behavior according to Aragorn, illustrates lack of commitment toward the cause of evil as exemplified by Melkor and Sauron. Aragorn adds that one can hardly discern whether evil creatures are in league with one another or are cheating one another. The slaughter of Orcs in the Tower of Cirith Ungol derives from the enmity of one type of Orc against another. Yet instability of Orc alliances does not arise only in the Third Age; even in the First Age, Orcs secretly laugh at Melkor's humiliation by Beren and Lúthien.[89] As Rosebury points out, Tolkien's tales display "only one form of political order, . . . a military despotism which terrorizes its own soldiery as well as its enemies."[90] Yet Orcs laughing in secret at Melkor and expressing a wish to be out from under Sauron suggest that despotism breeds contempt.

Category 4 of opposition to organized evil illustrates evil's nonmonolithic nature. While all evil contributes to rebellion against Eru Ilúvatar, evil beings do not always unite in their efforts, and not all evil beings can be cowed into serving Melkor or Sauron. Good beings also do not always unite, but moments of decisive victory tend to occur when good beings forge alliances despite conflict. Rebellion, in contrast, breeds further rebellion, sometimes even against the original rebels; Rogers describes evil within *The Lord of the Rings* as "in its essence distributed."[91] Tolkien expresses frustration with readers who presume a character that opposes the Hobbits, such as Old Man Willow, must be under the command of Sauron; readers should allow for entities hostile to Hobbits and Humans who are not subservient to the primary exponent of evil.[92] Furthermore, evil derives from and depends on good, while the reverse is not true. Evil ultimately divides while good leads toward unity, a truth revealed in the story of Melkor's worst attack on the Valar, killing the Two Trees of Valinor, by forming an alliance with Ungoliant, a fellow rebel that does not accept the values of organized evil.

The narrator of the "Quenta Silmarillion" describes Ungoliant as having joined Melkor, but then disowning him, pursuing instead her own evil desires. In Freudian terms, she devolves into pure Id. Feeding on light while simultaneously hating it, she produces darkness, not as an absence of light, but as a substance of evil, shadow, and fear; this last tendency earns her the epithet "Gloomweaver."[93] Crowe describes her as "an ambulatory black hole"[94] since she produces nearly palpable darkness. Yet her single-minded focus on selfish consumption leaves her separated from that on which she feeds; her strength and will have diminished such that she is nearly incapacitated.

Melkor's attempt to seduce her to his aid includes his infamous promise to give her "with both hands" whatever she desires.[95] When Melkor stabs his spear into each of the Two Trees, Ungoliant drinks the sap;[96] Petty interprets this attack as "literally defil[ing] the greater indwelling spirit of Ilúvatar."[97] Flieger, in her study of the significance of light within Tolkien's legendarium, notes that the creation of the Two Trees (and the later creation of the sun and moon) shows that "light is not to be the property of any person"; as Flieger notes, tongue in cheek, "those who seek to possess it exclusively have lost sight of it altogether."[98] The sudden consumption of light causes Ungoliant to grow at a rate that induces fear in Melkor. The two flee within a cloud of darkness that distresses and blinds even the Valar; along the way Melkor kills Finwë and steals the Silmarils (along with a large quantity of Fëanor's lesser jewels).

As the two approach Melkor's former seat of power, Melkor finds he cannot escape Ungoliant; he has inadvertently created a monster, who once again rebels against him.[99] After consuming the lesser jewels of Fëanor, she demands the Silmarils, which he withholds in one hand. She has increased in power, while he has expended much of his. As Ungoliant seeks to strangle Melkor, Melkor then cries out the loudest and most terrible cry ever uttered in the north of Middle-earth.[100] Earthquakes and landslides ensue, but Melkor's cry calls to the Balrogs and other evil creatures (possibly including Orcs and Sauron[101]) in hiding since Melkor has been chained, several ages previously. Coming to Melkor's rescue, the Balrogs' flame whips tear apart Ungoliant's webs, causing her to flee in fear.

Melkor's battle with Ungoliant reveals the self-contradictory nature of evil, since it embraces two opposing impulses:

1. the desire to dominate, to control the life-forms and forces within the universe
2. the desire to destroy, to consume the universe into oneself

Ungoliant illustrates the second of these desires. Her hate and lust motivate her to consume light, which represents all good in Arda. Her desire to consume drives her to the extent that ultimately, some tales suggest, she consumes herself. Her drive, therefore, is a death drive, a suicide lust. Given Eä's finite nature, the project of consuming it (were it feasible) would ultimately lead to the point where nothing remains to consume except oneself. Ungoliant embraces an innately irrational and self-contradictory form of evil.[102]

Melkor's desire contrasts and compares with Ungoliant's. The chief difference between the two, the essential ingredient that gives Melkor victory over Ungoliant, stems from his retention of a semblance of virtue. He achieves victory, not because of greater power (at that moment), but because he retains rationality; a rational being, Tolkien asserts, cannot be completely evil. In Freudian terms, while Ungoliant represents pure Id, Melkor still possesses Ego. Rather than merely consuming all that he encounters, Melkor wishes to control and dominate; it pushes him to organize, to devise a hierarchy with himself at the top and others firmly in place beneath him. He does this so effectively that his great cry calls to his side Balrogs, who remain faithful through Melkor's three ages of imprisonment. Faithfulness is a virtue; Tolkien speaks of residual good within evil creatures as reflecting the goodness into which those beings were created.[103] Faithfulness's value as a virtue diminishes, of course, because Melkor induces faithfulness through fear more than love. Yet his reliance on the faithfulness of his underlings illustrates that Melkor's form of evil depends upon his continued ability to exercise his Eru-given powers; his evil rebellion requires access to the continued presence of good in the universe.

Yet to pursue evil while wishing to retain elements of virtue is contradictory; Hood notes that in Tolkien's work evil "hat[es] what it desires and reject[s] what it wants."[104] While retaining rationality provides a crucial difference at the moment when Ungoliant nearly overpowers Melkor, it proves to be a superficial or short-term difference. Melkor's impulse to implement rebellion while retaining a hierarchically organized power structure is delusional. Rebellion is opposition to Eru; organizing power hierarchically mimics him. Seeman notes that evil deviates from norms "embedded in the created order, [and thus] deviance is inherently ambivalent and contradictory. Its ambivalence stems from the fact that it is self-defeating."[105] Hood adds that "Evil is simultaneously self-impelled and self-destructive."[106] Crowe observes that Melkor's acts of rebellion and destruction have the motive of increasing his own power, but to an observer appear as foolishly destructive as Ungoliant's. An early manuscript describes Melkor, just prior to his downfall at the end of the First Age, as a blind fool, desiring only to destroy.[107]

In the long run, should Melkor gain the upper hand against the Valar and Eru Ilúvatar, Melkor, too, would succumb to the suicidal death wish to which Ungoliant falls prey. In fact, when Melkor first hears Tulkas's laughter in pursuit of him, Melkor swears he will break apart Arda so that it can belong to no one; he soon discovers he lacks the power. As one version of the "Ainulindalë" notes, "the Earth may not be wholly destroyed against its fate"; in other words, Melkor's ability to mar the work of Eru Ilúvatar has limits. While Melkor desires destruction, at least of incarnate life-forms, whose very existence enrages him,[108] his dedication to evil causes his devolution into an incarnate, bound to his embodied form.

Two ages after Melkor's defeat of Ungoliant, Sauron exhibits within *The Lord of the Rings* a death drive similar to Melkor's. While Sauron possesses more wisdom than Melkor, understanding the value of sustaining a power hierarchy of dominated incarnate beings, he originally possessed a measure of love for those beings; Tolkien asserts that Sauron never reaches the stage of "nihilistic madness" exhibited by Melkor, though Sauron approaches more closely to pure evil.[109] Sméagol (admittedly not the wisest teacher of cosmological truths) asserted Sauron's ultimate goal as consuming the world and everything in it. Faramir (a student of Gandalf and thus a more reliable cosmologist) confirms Sméagol's assertion; Sauron ultimately wishes to destroy and devour everything.[110] Thus Lense interprets Sauron's Great Eye as "a 'window into nothing,' the opening into the abyss, an emblem of ultimate despair."[111]

In the long run, Melkor's and Sauron's ambitions hold out no more hope for the continued existence of the universe than do Ungoliant's. As a strategy within Arda, rebellion only succeeds in the face of some more powerful force against which one can rebel; rebellion, in other words, depends on a more powerful force to maintain order against which the rebellion can focus. The moment in which Melkor or Sauron "wins" in his war of rebellion will be the moment when nothing remains. Nagy says it this way: "a mythological subject trying to usurp the place of the metaphysical center runs into the paradox of being the alternative to totality, and therefore of being empty, erased."[112]

Also like his predecessor, Sauron works with both organized and un-aligned practitioners of evil, from a position every bit as self-contradictory as Melkor's. Levitin identifies three inherent weaknesses in Sauron:

1. His "lust for domination . . . drives him to extremes of cruelty far beyond the point of usefulness."
2. His "craving to hurt others drives him to illogical actions."
3. His "inability to command solidarity in [his] forces. An evil being only loves himself, and will not willingly help another for his own sake."[113]

At the top of Sauron's power structure sit the Nazgûl, who remain faithful to their master's wishes because Sauron completely dominates their wills.

Éowyn, in a draft document, references this in her confrontation with the Chief Nazgûl, claiming she does not fear him, nor the more powerful being that has consumed him. In draft notes Tolkien considers Sauron returning to the Nazgûl their Rings of power, since their wills have been completely enslaved.[114] Because Sauron, like Melkor before him, uses others to accomplish his deeds while he remains behind protective walls, the Nazgûl king, rather than Sauron, serves as Gandalf's primary antagonist, making the confrontation between those two at the gates of Minas Tirith the most critical moment in the War of the Ring, outside of Frodo's wrestling match with Gollum on the brink of the Crack of Doom.

Sauron from his beginning appreciated order and efficiency; Tolkien, in fact, finds Sauron similar to Saruman in this regard. Melkor attracts Sauron because he seems effective at accomplishing his goals. And while Sauron has fallen under the influence of Melkor's desire for destruction, and his hatred of Eru, Sauron cannot be a "'sincere' atheist" because of his personal knowledge of Eru prior to the creation of Eä. Yet Sauron teaches atheism because it effectively reduces resistance to his own will. Sauron presumes Eru has lost interest in Eä following the change in Arda's structure with the downfall of Númenor.[115]

Just as Melkor forms an alliance with Ungoliant, Sauron late in the Third Age associates himself with an unaligned rebel, Shelob, who not only parallels Ungoliant, but descends from her. Like Ungoliant, Shelob houses herself in darkness, of a form more palpable than the absence of light; on entering her lair the Hobbits encounter a black fog that blinds both eyes and minds. But rather than consuming light, Shelob drinks blood; this suggests she has devolved further than her mother toward an animalistic state, while her mother was, most likely, an evil spirit taking on physical form. At the same time, Shelob remains something more than animal; the narrator of *The Two Towers* describes her as evil in a spider's shape, and a draft describes her eyes as both animalistic and revealing a self-conscious sense of purpose.[116]

Like her mother, though, Shelob serves only herself, a narcissist. Also like her mother, she holds an irrational drive toward destruction, desiring death, in both body and mind, for all living creatures; Shelob wishes to consume all of Arda.[117] Her desire is an "indulgence that consumes, . . . nothing more than possessiveness, the extreme of isolating, self-indulgence,"[118] according to Burns. Thus, her presence on the border of Mordor places her into apparent conflict with Sauron; she does not serve him, and her indiscriminate desire to destroy aims as much at him as at his enemies. Yet Sauron considers her no threat, recognizing that her hunger decreases her power. As Melkor uses Ungoliant to his own advantage, Sauron uses Shelob as an unwitting guard against intruders into his realm. He even feeds her occasional Orcs and prisoners, as a homeowner might offer a tidbit to a favorite cat.[119]

Tolkien's greatest examples of unaligned evils, Shelob and Ungoliant function outside the hierarchically organized structures of Melkor and Sauron. While contributing indirectly to the rebellion against Eru and the Valar, Shelob and Ungoliant potentially rival Melkor and Sauron. Rational evils presume they can control irrational evils, a safe assumption as long as the irrational evil remains relatively weak. Shelob, because of her isolation and perpetual hunger, cannot compete with Sauron. Ungoliant, in contrast, for a brief moment could compete with Melkor, given the circumstances to which he contributed.

The existence of unaligned evil within Middle-earth supports the earlier assertion that its underlying cosmological structure is not rigidly dualistic. Good and evil do not balance one another, nor are they eternally coexistent. Evil depends on good, while the reverse is not true. Furthermore, the stories of Ungoliant, Shelob, and other unaligned evils (such as the Watcher in the Water) provide more insight into the nature of evil: the opposite of good is not evil, Tolkien's work suggests, but nonexistence. Evil is ultimately movement toward a nonexistent state.

🖋 Redeemable and Irredeemable Evil

The four categories of opposition to evil leaders, listed in the previous section, suggest a possible trajectory of moral devolution or progress for sentient beings. Elrond's metaphysical observation, quoted earlier, deserves repeating here: "Nothing is evil in the beginning."[120] Thus every evil being must have begun good (or at least every evil species; whether life-forms such as Humans suffer from original sin in Tolkien's legendarium remains unclear). An earlier section of this chapter examined eleven specific steps detailed in the fall of Melkor. Most such falls are not depicted at that level of detail, but many display a more general trajectory:

1. Alliance with, or at least tacit adherence to, the values embodied by the Valar and Eru Ilúvatar
2. Initial rebellion against one or more of those values (the space identified earlier as *folly*)

3. A fall due to continued adherence to rebellion or incremental increase in moral severity of that rebellion
4. Complete dedication to evil, apparently irreversible (at least within the bounds of the space-time continuum)

This schema can also be conceived as a spectrum graphing a being's moral state.

1. Good	2. Folly	3. Fallen	4. Evil

Tolkien's narratives show some fluidity among the distinct points of this spectrum; some residents of Arda transition from one to another, while others do not or cannot. Some characters begin their narrative arc in category 1 yet descend as far as category 4; Melkor, for example, begins with the same innate righteousness as the other Ainur but becomes the chief rebel, fancying himself in opposition to his creator. The kings of Númenor form a more extended example. The first king of Númenor, appointed by the Valar, remains respectful and reverent toward them. The subsequent three thousand–year history of the island shows steady turning away from that reverence until the final king launches a military attack against the Valar, despite repeated warnings to desist.

Redeemable Evil: Boromir, Galadriel, and Gollum

While the legendarium clearly shows that beings may experience a downward trajectory from category 1 to category 4, it also implies the possibility of a return journey, at least from category 2 and 3 back up to a higher level. Bilbo's exchange with Thorin, and Gandalf's words about the Dwarf king after the Battle of Five Armies, implies that Thorin achieves, or is granted, a redemption.[121] Gandalf's final confrontations with Saruman, and even Frodo's injunction that the Hobbits not kill Saruman/Sharkey, suggest redemption for Saruman remains possible, even if unlikely. Ryan observes that "not all who practice cruelty, cynicism, irreverence, pessimism or pride are beyond redemption" in Tolkien's work.[122] Such redemption forms a central motif in the portrayal of several important characters in *The Lord of the Rings*.

Boromir's narrative arc defines a fall and subsequent repentance over the few months' journey of the Fellowship to Parth Galen. Entranced by the Ring, Boromir obsesses over its power and desires it for himself. As often transpires when a good being willfully embraces folly, Boromir shows mixed motives: simple lust for power and glory merge with an honest desire to benefit his people. Tolkien at first considered making Boromir a character beyond redemption. Notes composed shortly after drafting the death of Gandalf propose that Boromir will completely succumb to evil. A moment later Tolkien queries himself as to whether Boromir might not repent, a query followed with an additional note answering the query in the negative and suggesting that Boromir will be killed by Aragorn. Obviously, Tolkien changed his mind. In a later draft Aragorn (then named Trotter) tells Legolas and Gimli that Boromir sought to take the Ring from Frodo, but adds that he repented and suffered the consequences.[123] A note penciled in the draft questions whether Trotter should keep that information to himself. In the published text, Aragorn's words to Boromir subsequent to his self-sacrificial defense of Merry and Pippin assert that Boromir satisfactorily atoned for the fall he experienced through his attempt to take the Ring by force.

One of the back stories Tolkien devised for Galadriel also shows a successful repentance, though over a much more extended time span of nearly seven thousand years.[124] As observed earlier, Tolkien experienced a change of heart as to the degree of guilt Galadriel warrants from aligning herself with Fëanor's rebellion, specifically regarding her involvement with the Kinslaying. In terms of the four-part scheme outlined above, Tolkien's change of heart can be characterized as first placing her fall at category 3 (outright rebellion), but then wishing to reposition her as never passing beyond category 2 (mere willfulness); said another way, Tolkien ultimately saw Galadriel guilty of no more than folly. Even so, Galadriel's choices lead to consequences that seem (to her) eternal: being denied passage to Aman could mean that she might never die (since death for Elves, as a subsequent chapter will show, involves such a passage), or that her death will lead to a singularity, a fate outside the normal parameters of Elven experience, unforeseeable and perhaps cut off from all Eä. Thus, the invitation to exit Middle-earth subsequent to her renunciation of the One Ring implies that her eternal destiny as an Elf has been restored.

Even Gollum, though lacking the powers and advantages of the Noldorin Elves, illustrates the trajectory from evil to repentance, but a failed trajectory. Gollum (as Sméagol) starts off very badly, committing the evil of murdering his close companion, Déagol. In terms of the four-part schema outlined earlier, Gollum jumps to category 3 in a very short time. Yet Gollum's narrative shows him subject to greed and resentment prior to killing his friend (who, Tolkien notes, is also likely a relative). Prior to discovering the One Ring, Déagol gives Sméagol his expected birthday present; Déagol, self-centered and small-minded, begrudges providing the gift; Sméagol, even more greedy and small-minded, uses his birthday to guilt Déagol into giving him the Ring, while also belittling Déagol's original gift.[125]

Sméagol kills Déagol around Third Age 1100, just a hundred years after Sauron insinuates himself into Mirkwood as the Necromancer. Gollum's use of the Ring leads to antisocial behavior that eventually causes his community to shun him. He then embraces isolation, and over time develops a hatred of light, the element most associated with good in Tolkien's legendarium.[126] To hate light is to hate all it stands for, including the Valar and Eru Ilúvatar; arguably, Gollum by this point has devolved to category 4, complete dedication to evil.

Yet Gollum, in his journey with the Hobbits, experiences an unexpected transformation, largely due to mercy extended by Frodo. Crabbe describes mercy within *The Lord of the Rings* functioning as "the refusal to accept any being's less than perfect state as his essential nature. Justice would pay each according to what he has done; mercy pays him according to what he might do—according to the ideal." Crabbe describes such mercy as "an essentially creative act—it leaves the possibilities for a recreation of the self open as does any healing process."[127]

Discussing mercy calls to mind Gandalf's ethic of pity and mercy. And indeed Gandalf, as an idealist, remains hopeful of Gollum's repentance though, tempering his idealism with realism, he acknowledges such a fate as unlikely. Gandalf urges continued hope for Gollum's cure during the time the Elves of Mirkwood hold him prisoner. A draft of the Council of Elrond records a different response to Gollum's escape, in which Gandalf concludes Gollum does not desire healing. Since an outcome such as healing from evil cannot be foreknown with certainty, Gandalf's ethic requires hoping for repentance, no matter how faint that hope appears. Frodo, at the Forbidden Pool of Henneth Annûn, acknowledges that Gollum is not completely wicked, though Faramir perceives evil eating away at Gollum.[128]

With the impact of mercy in mind, the most critical moment of Gollum's life (apart from his murder of Déagol) occurs on the Stairs of Cirith Ungol, a moment from which readers, in Burke's view, "find the utmost pity for Gollum."[129] After conspiring with Shelob, Gollum finds Frodo sleeping with his head in Sam's lap; this vision of love and companionship almost overpowers Gollum's lust for the Ring until Sam awakens and accuses Gollum of sneaking. Tolkien's letters indicate that Gollum develops love for Frodo as a caring master, and that Gollum comes close to repenting, an assertion reiterated in appendix B of *The Return of the King,* but with a sentence structure suggesting he merely regrets his plan to take Frodo and Sam to Shelob, and thus does not necessarily repent his desire for the Ring. The opening "Synopsis" of *The Return of the King* expands the time span in which Gollum wrestles against his own evil impulses to include the entire period of his journey with Frodo.[130] That journey, the passage implies, forms a probationary period during which he vacillates between embracing good and evil.

Though Gollum, gazing at the loving care of Sam toward Frodo, stands on the cusp,[131] Sam's unfortunate though understandable reaction to Gollum's pawing at master "'aborted' [in Purtill's words] Gollum's incipient repentance."[132] Tolkien emphasizes the realism of Sam's action; sometimes good people inadvertently prompt a return to evil in others, rather than a change of heart.[133] At the same time, Gollum's verbalized internal debate as he leads Frodo and Sam toward what he hopes will be their deaths emphasizes his ambivalence toward self-reformation. Abbott absolves Sam of guilt in his action toward Gollum, insisting that Gollum's decisions "destroyed any small hope of his potential redemption, resulting in his *damnation* and separating him forever from Frodo." Structurally, then, Gollum parallels Sam, whose decisions lead to his own redemption.[134]

As noted in the cases of Boromir and Galadriel, an individual's repentance changes the future. Tolkien speculates as to the story's outcome had Gollum repented, which could have transpired if Sam exhibited greater pity. The entry into Mordor would of necessity have been different, as would the quest of Mount Doom. The focus of the tale would have become Gollum and his inner conflict over his love for Frodo and his love for the Ring. While practice would have increased his devotion to Frodo over time, it would not have overpowered the Ring's influence. Gollum would have sought to satisfy both the claims, but eventually he would have stolen the Ring by trickery or force. Putting on the Ring a final time, Tolkien speculated, would have given Gollum insight that he could not possibly withstand Sauron, and that his own sacrificial death would be the best service he could perform for Frodo; as a result, he would voluntarily leap into the fiery chasm.[135]

Irredeemable Evil: Orcs as Thinking Automatons

Like Gollum, the various peoples of Middle-earth possess free wills; even the Dwarves, Tolkien points out, are "not evil by nature."[136] Thus when such creatures choose evil, redemption remains a possibility until their wills become permanently overpowered by their past choices. Yet as Auden notes, some wicked creatures in Middle-earth, in fact entire species, appear irredeemable: Trolls and Dragons, for example, but especially Orcs, who play highly visible roles as bad guys in the legendarium.

Tally notes that Orcs have the deck stacked against them. Tolkien's readers, he observes, are "definitively positioned as already anti-Orc before the stories even begin."[137] Part of the reason is Orcs' ugliness. Evil coincides with ugliness in Tolkien's legendarium, and thus Orcs appear consistently unpleasant to the lovelier Elves and Humans: deformed bodies, foul faces, and laughter like the clash of metal against metal. Tolkien provides real-Earth comparisons for Orcs' appearance, though perhaps in questionable taste by twenty-first-century standards: Orcs resemble the "least lovely Mongol-types." Apparently multiple races of Orcs evolved, though here again Tolkien's depiction feels uncomfortable to contemporary Western sensibilities: powerful black Orcs first appear in Third Age 2475;[138] there are no white Orcs.

Orc behavior contributes to reader antagonism, as well as the antagonism of all good beings in the legendarium. Orcs delight in destroying life-forms, according to Legolas. They receive pleasure from torturing other beings and practice cannibalism. Orcs are additionally cursed with an ugly language, as Gandalf notes. Melkor taught Orcs Orquin, a perversion of the Valarin language known to Melkor. Sauron then devised the Black Speech referenced in *The Lord of the Rings*. Orcs' hatred of one another contributes to development of multiple Orc dialects, dubbed *jargons* by Tolkien. The author even indicates he sanitized his representations of Orc speech into English to protect the sensibilities of readers; providing a more accurate translation would disgust the few readers who would understand it.[139]

In short, Tally observes, Orcs are "presented with surprising uniformity as loathsome, ugly, cruel, feared, and especially terminable." Tally quotes Ellmann's 1968 *New American Review* article on *The Lord of the Rings:* "the only good Orc is a dead Orc."[140] Herein lies the dilemma: how can an entire race or species of beings be so evil that killing a member of that race or species is innately good?

One solution is to see Orcs as automatons, in Harvey's words, "slaves of evil [having] no minds of their own" and incapable of choosing good. Colebatch observes that Orcs' apparent irredeemableness does not stem solely from their being under the power of Melkor or Sauron; "Apparently even after the destruction of Sauron and the Ring no Orc has a chance of being 'saved'."[141] From this perspective, Harvey suggests Orcs lack wills, free or otherwise; instead, they are "mindless and committed to an evil course through no choice of their own."[142] Barajas-Garrido concurs, finding Orcs' lack of free will prevents their choosing between right or wrong.[143] Chism explains Orcs' inability to choose by suggesting they are "genetically evil."[144]

This perspective seems borne out through the entire legendarium, in which no character ever suggests that pity and mercy should be extended to Orcs or Goblins, in contrast with evil Humans (though Gandalf does once express pity for all of Sauron's slaves, which may include Orcs). Even the Drúedain hold a pitiless hatred for Orcs. Good (and even neutral) beings uniformly assume that Orcs deserve instant death; a description of one battle indicates they die like straw consumed by fire.[145] Mathews notes that Orcs are "killed off practically by the dozen and they seem to be totally expendable."[146] Even after death, Orcs deserve no shred of respect or dignity; subsequent to the Battle of the Hornburg, dead Orcs are left to be eaten by Wolves, while enemy Human bodies receive proper burial.[147] Shippey pragmatically sees Orcs as a narrative necessity: the Silmarillion tales "needed a continual supply of enemies over whom one need feel no compunction."[148] And certainly, Tolkien never hints that an Orc could develop into anything other than fully evil, a perspective Tolkien acknowledges as purely fictional, not based on his own understanding of Earth reality: in real life, Tolkien acknowledges, we find no people formed to be exclusively evil by their creator, nor corrupted to the point of being irredeemable.[149]

If Orcs, like the One Ring, are completely evil,[150] then they probably lack an eternal destiny, a thought some readers find "theologically intolerable,"[151] and unsupported by the legendarium; Orcs have a sense of life after death, according to Gorbag's assertion that the Nazgûl can "skin the body off you . . . and leave you all cold in the dark on the other side."[152] Auden sums up the problem thus: existence of wholly evil beings "seems to imply that it is possible for a species that can speak, and, therefore, make moral choices, to be evil by nature." The problem compounds when considered theologically; "if evil can not only seduce the good but also create beings who are evil from the beginning, then one cannot, as Tolkien does, call God 'The One'; there must, in that case be Two, a good One and an evil One,"[153] the radical dualism that Tolkien's theory of evil seems otherwise to oppose.

Other readers, such as Birzer, presume that Orcs are at least theoretically redeemable,[154] agreeing with Eggington that, as with all living things, "their life-force is originally part of The Flame Imperishable."[155] Kocher acknowledges that "Never in Tolkien's tale are any Orcs redeemed, but it would go against the grain of the whole to dismiss them as ultimately irredeemable."[156]

Tolkien has added weight to this interpretation, as he has to the idea that Orcs are automatons. In one letter the author catches himself in the act of nearly asserting Orcs *are* irredeemable. As corruptions by Melkor, Orcs are "creatures begotten of Sin, and naturally bad. (I nearly wrote 'irredeemably bad'; but that would be going too far . . .)."[157] The apparent contradiction of irredeemable Orcs in a cosmos that doesn't allow for such creatures means that, as Tolkien acknowledges in the late 1950s, Orcs are "not easy to work into the theory and system" he hopes to have woven as an underlying unity to his tales.[158]

Rosebury, a critic who has thought at length about the problem of Orcs, assures readers that "the legitimacy of killing Orcs" is a "moral dilemma" that Tolkien "reflected anxiously about." Elves, Rosebury notes, do not capture Orcs, which would have produced the moral predicament of either killing Orcs as helpless captives, or of attempting to reform them; to kill Orcs instantly (and as a duty rather than a joy), rather than capture them, is a means of extending mercy, Rosebury implies. Rosebury then distinguishes Elves, who develop a degree of moral judgment that reflects the Eldar's contact with the Valar, from "virtuous pagans" such as Beorn and Helm, who joyfully destroy Orcs. In the case of Beorn, Tolkien hints at past wrongs suffered, which positions Beorn's killing of Orcs as revenge. Revenge is "always wrong" in Tolkien's work, but there are "gradations of judgment on particular acts of revenge, ranging from outright condemnation to what one might call non-approving respect." Three factors allow revenge in Tolkien's characters:

1. "being in general a person of good will"
2. "having grounds proportionate to the revenge"
3. "having deliberated . . . long and responsibly before acting"[159]

These factors, Rosebury implies, provide an understanding of characters such as Beorn, who might be respected, if not condoned, even by enlightened Elves, for unreserved elimination of Orcs.

Yet Shippey remains unconvinced that Tolkien's carte blanche extension to good characters of a license to kill can be so easily justified. "[O]rcs are moral beings,"[160] he bluntly asserts. "The episode of Shagrat and Gorbag reveals . . . an underlying morality much the same as ours." The two Orcs' dialogue, Colebatch adds, implies "a standard of good behavior that *should* be observed, and both [Shagrat] and the other Orc to whom he speaks recognizes and acknowledges this however hypocritically."[161] Shippey and Colebatch point to Gorbag's assertion that leaving a wounded comrade behind to fall into enemy hands is a "regular Elvish trick."[162] This and other scenes involving Orcs show that they understand "the idea of goodness, . . . humor, . . . loyalty, trust, group cohesion, and the ideal of a higher cause than themselves," and as Gorbag's words imply, they "condemn failings from these ideals in others." Yet, Shippey observes, the Orcs' sense of morality apparently has "no effect at all on actual behavior."[163]

The apparent lack of interest among other life-forms as to whether Orcs are redeemable is surprising considering that, as Shippey says, "Tolkien's presentation of the Orcs is . . . a quite deliberate realism. Orcish behavior is human behavior."[164] Tneh follows Shippey's lead, seeing in Orcs "the universal condition of Man," though specifically Humans at their worst.[165] Several readers emphasize the human-like natures of Orcs, to the point that those readers exhibit Gandalf-like pity toward them. Tally, for example, notes that Shagrat and Gorbag in their conversation appear "as worried employees, not sure if their superiors are as competent as claimed, but absolutely certain that the decisions made by their bosses will directly affect them, likely for the worse. These are reasonable, and altogether human concerns." Their desire to be independent of dictatorial overseers "might well be the American Dream."[166] Hammond and Scull suggest Grishnákh and Uglúk "show considerable loyalty to their masters"[167] and Tally reads Bolg's Goblin attack on the Dwarves and Elves in *The Hobbit* as showing that Orcs value "familial honor," since Bolg seeks vengeance for the death of his father at the hands of Dáin Ironfoot's father killing Azog, Bolg's father.[168]

Colebatch suggests Orcs exhibit aesthetic appreciation, given Shagrat's description of Frodo's mithril vest as a "pretty shirt."[169] A reference in *The Hobbit* to a "small goblin imp" implies Orcs possess some sort of family life.[170] Tneh finds in Orc dialogue "a glimpse of the [O]rcs as comfort-seeking creatures that wish that the war would be over so that things would be better for their own kind."[171] In *The Lost Tales* Orcs reveal a human-like sense of fear as they tremble at rumors of Turin's prowess. Most troubling, Tally observes with irony that Orcs show greater kindness to Merry and Pippin as captives than the good side shows to Orcs (though the Orcs' somewhat kind actions do not stem from kind personalities). Even Frodo presumes Orcs would likely enjoy good food every bit as much as himself.[172]

Yet Tolkien insists upon a fundamental difference between Orcs and the Children of Eru: Humans and Elves do evil on occasion and can even become enslaved by Melkor. Orcs, in contrast, commit evil continuously and experience pleasure in causing harm. Their sole restraint from committing more evil is the limitations of their own power, not a sense of mercy or prudence.[173] In short, Tolkien remains consistently inconsistent in his portrayal of Orcs. Seen from a distance, as they appear most commonly in the legendarium, their sole purpose is to be destroyed by good beings who possess the power to do so. Yet up close, as they occasionally appear in *The Lord of the Rings,* Tolkien invariably humanizes them.

As a result, Tolkien's depictions of Orcs present two irreconcilable views, exemplified in several essays from the late 1950s (published in the "Myths Transformed" section of *Morgoth's Ring*). One essay asserts the Elvish belief that Orcs are completely corrupt, lacking pity, and committed only to evil; as such they are irredeemable (at least as far as Elvish and Human efforts are concerned); Orcs function like ants, unable to resist domination by a more powerful evil force. Yet, the same document asserts their corruption is "of independent wills"; thus, they possess the power to ignore Melkor's commands (when they are distant from him) and can act against Melkor's plans.[174] They are indeed automatons, Tolkien implies, but automatons that can think for themselves.

The origin of Orcs further complicates theorizing their place within the Middle-earth cosmos. That origin remains murky, except for one important and consistent fact: Melkor clearly intervened. The tale of Aulë and the creation of the Dwarves shows that only Eru Ilúvatar can create beings with reasoning ability and functioning wills; since Orcs (seemingly) possess both, they must have been corrupted from an earlier state of goodness.[175] Tolkien's most common speculations about Orcs' origins suggest an Elvish background. Tally considers this the "canonical view": that Orcs are perverted from Elves, specifically from among the Avari, those Elves who resisted the summons of the Valar to Aman, or possibly earlier, during the 350 years after the Elves' awakening and prior to their first interaction with the Valar.[176] *The Silmarillion* supports this view, one of the reasons the view can be considered canonical, by describing Melkor's capture of the Elves and their subsequent torture to the point of corruption and enslavement.[177]

Tolkien provides much additional evidence for such an origin. He glosses one Sindarin name for Orcs, *Glamhoth,* as *folk of dreadful hate.*[178] The word *folk,* like *peoples,* normally indicates sentient beings. Treebeard, in his rhyme about life-forms of Middle-earth, lists just four *free peoples:* Elves, Dwarves, Ents, and Humans (Merry and Pippin, of course, suggest a fifth category for Hobbits). Tolkien's letters more clearly narrow the field of possible Orc origins to Elves (though one manuscript hints of a human origin). As corruptions of Elves,

Orcs lost the serial longevity native to Elves (and tales of Orc immortality or reincarnation stem from confusing Orcs with their Maiar leaders, who often embody themselves into an Orc form).[179]

Luling, in an attempt to explain Orcish nature (and to exonerate Elves and others from their blatant destruction of Orcs), speculates about Melkor's method for corrupting Elves. After Elves (or Humans) in Melkor's capture die, their spirits leave their bodies, but Melkor "revives their corpses"; he then makes these "zombies" breed. He places some of his power into them (as Sauron does with the One Ring), so they possess independence. As such, Orcs are only a mockery of speaking creatures, and have no individual moral choice. "They [a]re not in the full sense alive," and thus, in Luling's view, there is "no objection to killing them."[180]

If *Orcs as corrupted Elves* forms the canonical view of Orc origins, then a variant view, also endorsed by Tolkien, presumes that Melkor *devised* Orcs (along with demons, Dragons, and monsters) in a manner comparable, presumably, to Aulë's creation of the Dwarves; this variant view, in fact, precedes the canonical view in the development of the legendarium. In this view, Orcs resemble Dwarves, since both develop from a willful act of a very powerful spirit-being; in contrast, however, the creation of the Dwarves has no evil at its source.[181]

Tolkien provides ample evidence for this variant view, as he does for the canonical view. One version of the "Ainulindalë" describes Orcs and Demons as "companions . . . of [Melkor's] own making," leaving unaddressed precisely what Melkor did to make them; elsewhere Tolkien indicates the Orcs originated from stone.[182] Sturch, in contrast, speculates that Melkor "began with non-rational but living material of some kind . . . and gave it, not only malice and misery, but such intelligence as it had," somewhat like Trolls, Melkor's parody of Ents.[183] In the variant view, Melkor forms Orcs after he has seen Elves, and in an attempt to mock them. While the canonical view suggests corruption of the Elves may have occurred prior to their meeting the Valar, the variant view suggests Melkor might have devised Orcs as late as after his escape from Aman with the Silmarils. While the variant view emerged first, Christopher Tolkien observes that his father sometimes embraces both the canonical and variant views within the pages of a single document.[184]

As Tolkien contemplated Orcs in the late 1950s, he speculated on another possible source: the Maiar. If the first two back stories can be considered the canonical view and a variant, this might be the heretical view (since it ultimately requires that creatures from a lower, embodied order routinely kill those from a higher and, at least originally, disembodied order). According to this view, some of the spirit-beings Melkor corrupted, both in the Singing of the Ainur and after the Valar entered Arda, may have formed the first Orcs, taking on permanent embodiment, much as Melian became permanently affixed to her body. As a result, these Orcs cannot return to spirit form until death releases them from their bodies, at which time they will be damned "like Sauron," incapable of acting physically while still full of hatred.[185]

Of course, Tolkien immediately perceives the weak link in this explanation: "would Eru provide *fëar* [souls] for such creatures?" Thus, Tolkien's reasoning turns from one extreme of the chain of being to the other: rather than spirit beings, Orcs are animals. Talking, he concludes, does not definitively indicate that a being possesses a soul, and thus Orcs are human-looking beasts, no more independent than domesticated dogs. Tolkien cites parrots as examples of speech without self-aware consciousness.[186] Another gloss of *Glamhoth* supports this view: "din, uproar, the confused yelling and bellowing of beasts,"[187] a definition suggesting Orcs as monstrous perversions of wild animals, which explains the lack of free will posited by critics such as Harvey and Barajas-Garrido. Tolkien provides evidence for this view in his assertion that Sauron's Orcs have "little or no *will*" except when Sauron's mind actively focuses on them.[188]

Yet this solution leaves Tolkien unsatisfied. Thus, he returns, at least in part, to the canonical view: "It remains therefore terribly possible there was an Elvish strain in the Orcs."[189] If Tolkien cannot resolve the origin of the Orcs, perhaps readers should not speculate where the author fails. Petty, perhaps wisely, avoids the issue of the Orcs' origin, stating only that "Melkor somehow fashioned creatures called Orcs."[190] Colebatch takes a parallel but more sophisticated approach by metacritically examining the tendency of Tolkien fans to expend energy on the problem of Orcs:

> It is a tribute to the power of the whole tale that [the nature of Orcs] does seems a problem worth considering. Tolkien's creation is so strong and vivid for those it speaks to that we can forget, at some level, that it is a fantasy and ask more of it than any work of fiction can reasonably be expected to answer. From the literary or story-telling point of view Orcs were necessary as enemies expressing certain facts about the nature of evil. It is obvious from the general thrust of the work and from his other writings . . . that Tolkien emphatically did not, in the real world, think of the real enemy forces (e.g. Germans in World War II) as sub-humans beneath the claims of Mercy and fit only for extermination.[191]

The fact that the nature of Orcs disturbs readers shows that Tolkien has produced a form of realism through fantasy; the best response, Colebatch implies, is for readers to remind themselves that it's just make-believe.

One final dimension of Orcish natures might also be worth leaving exclusively as a fictional unknown: Orc sexuality. All theories of Orc origins posit a biological method of Orc reproduction. According to the heretical view, the evil Maiar developed into always-embodied Orcs "by practicing[,] when embodied[,] procreation." In the canonical view, Tolkien describes the corruption of Elves into Orcs as the method by which Melkor "did . . . breed the hideous race"; in case readers wonder whether Tolkien uses *breed* metaphorically, Tolkien adds an explanatory note: "For the [Orcs] ha[ve] life and multipl[y] after the manner of the Children of Ilúvatar," though they discretely do their multiplying underground "in the bowels of the earth."[192] This from an author sometimes seen as avoiding sexuality to the point that one critic titled her essay "No Sex Please—We're Hobbits."[193]

Elsewhere Orcs are named the "broodlings of Melkor."[194] Tolkien speculates at various times that Orcs, after they had been devised, created, or perverted, were further cross-bred with Trolls, Elves, Humans, animals, and (coming full circle to the heretical view once again) Maiar. All this cross-species mating contributes to fashioning Orcs as a mongrel composite. Sauron may have contributed to the process during Melkor's imprisonment. Saruman then refines it further, performing secret breeding experiments on Orcs, resulting in the Uruk-hai, labeled *half-orcs* by Gamling of Rohan, combining elements of Orcs and Humans.[195]

Orc sexuality takes on relevancy in Tolkien's cosmology given that the irredeemability of the Orcs seems to function hereditarily. While Tolkien posits that Melkor could and did completely corrupt an individual, he doubts Melkor's ability to completely corrupt *groups* of people, particularly such that the corruption is passed down, generation to generation. In one of his musings on Orcs, Tolkien suggests Eru must have acted to make evil hereditary (which would put Eru in the awkward position of creating an apparently irredeemable evil race).[196] Clearly Orc sexuality is no more resolved in Tolkien's legendarium than the origin of Orcs as a species.

Croft speculates that the ultimate goal of Melkor's, Sauron's, and Saruman's Orc breeding, regardless of which view of Orc origination one embraces, may well have been to create soulless beings, which would have lacked free wills.[197] If so, the project seems to have failed, since Tolkien asserts Orcs (as corrupted Elves) on death are imprisoned in Mandos;[198] as this study's chapter on death will show, death for embodied beings involves separating the soul from the body, with the body remaining in Middle-earth to return to its elements and only the soul going to Mandos. The end of Orcs is as unclear as their beginning.

Technology and Evil

Melkor and Sauron accomplish their evil interventions in Middle-earth by exerting power, which, Tolkien notes, makes power "an ominous and sinister word" in his writings, except in regard to the Valar.[199] As Shippey notes, the notion that *absolute power corrupts absolutely* "is the core" of the *The Lord of the Rings*.[200] The "relentless renunciation of power" required of the good and wise of Middle-earth, Harris observes, makes *The Lord of the Rings* "a paradox in the genre of heroic romance."[201] Since technology extends and focuses power, it comes as no surprise that Tolkien displays an antitechnological stance in his writing, particularly given the increase in technological power for making war that Tolkien witnessed in the first half of the twentieth century. Many readers sense a bias in Tolkien's writings against technology, or *machinery* as Tolkien refers to it, an implication that, if not inherently evil, technology is at least evil by association. Sauron, and evil beings like him, show a natural inclination for machinery.[202]

The Lord of the Ring's presumed antitechnology stance has been a central element of its reception since its earliest days. During the book's American rise in popularity in the 1960s and 1970s, readers naturally associated the threatening power of the One Ring with the atom bomb, an allegorical reading that Tolkien discouraged, even while acknowledging the complete folly of humans giving themselves so much power (comparing it to dispersing firearms to prisoners in hope of creating peace). *The Lord of the Ring*'s contrast between the nature-compatible culture of the Shire,[203] and the environmentally destructive practices of Sauron and Saruman with their "Massive industrial complex[es]," [204] positions the book as eco-friendly by first-wave eco-critics, and as offering a complex and provocative "environmental philosophy" by second-wave eco-critics. Readers sense the author's love for nature and his opposition to development without regard for environmental impact. A draft note shows Tolkien associating images of destruction in the story with the effects of modern industrialism, finding chemical pollution, observable in early twentieth-century England, suitable imagery for describing the terrain around Mordor. Pools of industrial waste symbolize evil in general for Tolkien, who sees nature inevitably thrust into a victim role in the struggle of evil against good.[205]

Veldman notes an "antitechnological stance"[206] in Tolkien's personal life. Tolkien writes, for example, of the "'infernal combustion' engine," and bemoans that labor-saving devices only create more work. Even while supporting Britain's war effort, Tolkien remained aware of the destructive power of war technology; in a letter to his son (then at the front) he describes a sky-wide armada of planes, as a result of which, by the time his son receives the letter, "somewhere will have ceased to exist." A few letters later he confesses that he considers warplanes particularly horrible, though such horror may be no more reasonable than a meat-eater complaining about slaughterhouses. While Christopher Tolkien served in the Royal Air Force, his father compared modern warplanes with ill-advised Hobbits riding Nazgûl to free the Shire.[207]

Tolkien couples his antitechnology views with a love of nature; the author confesses particularly high regard for trees. Tolkien's attitude toward nature might be labeled Christian stewardship, which in turn complicates his views of technology. Christian stewardship suggests that humans, as children of God, exist in a caretaker relationship to the Earth, having the right to use it but not abuse it. As one of Tolkien's characters in an abandoned sequel to *The Lord of the Rings* expresses, such use should be accompanied with reverence.[208] To *use* nature, however, implies some level of tools to manipulate and control it; despite his presumed antitechnology views, Tolkien makes no complaint about the simple agricultural and culinary tools used by the Hobbits, and the author himself relied on contemporary technology, as Scull and Hammond argue. Furthermore, chapter 3's discussion of the High Elves residing in Middle-earth in the Third Age reviewed several technologies that contribute positively to life in Middle-earth; the Three Elven Rings, Galadriel's Mirror and Phial, and the Elessar impact environments for the better.

So while Tolkien's view should not be oversimplified as a knee-jerk reaction against technology, the connection between technology and evil in the legendarium deserves examination. Created objects cause much trouble in Middle-earth, and even simple items, such as rings, possess an efficacy, perhaps even agency, to do evil. Though resisting, in general, allegorical readings of his work, Tolkien also reserves for himself the right to state the most accurate allegorical reading: *The Lord of the Rings*, Tolkien asserts, illustrates the foolishness of using evil power to defeat evil, the unjustified assumption that technological progress is good (or even inevitable), and the problems that arise from the general love of technology. In today's world, Tolkien asserts, technology takes the role that might have been assigned to evil magic in past ages.[209]

The legendarium's attitude toward technology might best be termed *pessimistic ambivalence*. While acknowledging technology's positives along with its negatives, the negatives take greater prominence than the positives. Fëanor's Silmarils illustrate this, even though the Elves treat the Silmarils as art objects rather than devices. The Silmarils, created pure and hallowed by Varda, exert power over Elves, Dwarves, and even Vala, producing evil effects. Finrod speculates to Beren that Fëanor's oath causes the jewels to be cursed, such that anyone who expresses desire for them awakens their inherent power.[210] Even the best creations of the Children of Ilúvatar seem cursed, destined to cause more harm than good.

Rings of Power

Readings of Tolkien as antitechnology often focus on the One Ring, which evolved as a plot device to provide conflict for Tolkien's proposed sequel to *The Hobbit*. Early manuscripts of *The Lord of the Rings* show Tolkien struggling through four drafts of chapter 1, seeking some reason for Bilbo or one of his relatives to leave the Shire for adventures; finally, Tolkien realizes that Bilbo's Ring can provide a motive. This discovery leads Tolkien to speculate further about the Ring, its origin, and its impact.[211]

Most importantly, Tolkien realizes the Ring's parasitical claim on its bearer's psyche. After long contact with the Ring, the bearer becomes dependent upon it, not for what it can do, but for its presence. The bearer becomes so symbiotically attached to the Ring that she or he cannot bear its absence, like Gollum after possessing the Ring for hundreds of years (2,400 years in one manuscript, changed to 1,900 in another, about 940 in a third, and 478 in yet another). Bilbo, Tolkien suggests, after a mere 60 or so years could not give up the Ring. In one rejected draft passage Gandalf asserts that the Ring prevented Bilbo from parting with it. Here, perhaps, is the One Ring's symbolism for postindustrial humanity's dependence on technology; it has greater explanatory power for smart phones than it has for atom bombs. From this perspective, Bilbo's giving away his Ring becomes a Thoreau-like repudiation of property's power over its supposed owner. In a draft of *The Fellowship of the Ring* Gandalf explains that Bilbo, by surrendering his Ring, saves himself from inevitable destruction.[212]

The Ring ultimately evolves into a character, possessing some degree of will and sentience. Neither Isuldur nor Gollum lose the Ring; the Ring leaves them, seeking to return to Sauron even prior to its master's reembodiment. Petty speculates that the Ring's near-sentience allows it to perceive Déagol's vulnerability, pulling him downward toward the bottom of the river, and even drawing his hand into the riverbed to find the Ring.[213] But if the Ring possesses some degree of will, it is not free will; like Orcs, the One Ring appears solely evil, always and only corrupting. Even if a strong-willed good character uses the Ring for some good purpose, the use itself will ultimately backfire against the wielder, causing more harm than good.

The Ring strengthens Sauron beyond Maia level, as if he crosses over the Eru-established division between Maiar and Valar. On the other hand (or to be more anatomically correct, on the hand with the missing ring finger), Sauron without his Ring is weakened. When Isuldur cuts the Ring from Sauron's hand, Tolkien writes, Sauron's power leaves him and he hides as a mere spirit in the shadows. Without the Ring, Sauron depends more on servants and remains blind to the purposes of bearers of Elven Rings. Thus, when Aragorn reveals himself to Sauron via the Palantír, Sauron assumes Aragorn possesses the Ring and wishes to challenge Sauron's might, to place himself as the Lord of Mordor.[214]

Tolkien speculates what would occur were Sauron to recover the Ring. A draft implies all Middle-earth would be doomed. Gandalf says the sign of Sauron's recovery of the Ring would be darkness beyond anything previously perceived, affecting both hearts and minds.[215] Birzer observes that "the sole purpose of the One Ring is to re-order the world in Sauron's image, to mock, to corrupt, and to pervert Ilúvatar's creation."[216] Since the Valar have apparently vowed to refrain from direct interference, Sauron's recovery of the Ring could only be counteracted by direct intervention from Eru Ilúvatar.

Tolkien also speculates as to what would happen if a powerful good being, perhaps Gandalf or Aragorn, were to use the Ring. Any new Ring lord would grow more powerful while simultaneously desiring even more power. She or he would ultimately yield to the desire to dominate followers, absorbing Sauron's power and thought, so that Sauron's followers would become adherents of the new Ring lord. The bearer would even allow others to worship her or him as a god. The Ring would inevitably corrupt its bearer with increasing selfishness.[217] Shippey describes the One Ring's power as "addictive."[218]

Yet as long as the One Ring remains unused, the positive work of the Three Elven Rings continues. Those Three complicate the simple *technology is evil* stance often attributed to Tolkien. Created by good beings (though Noldorin Elves and thus under the Doom of Mandos) for good purposes, the Three are made with special knowledge acquired from Sauron, but without any of Sauron's direct power. Yet the Three work against change and decay in the world, as well as the Elves' world-weariness; therefore, Tolkien notes, even the motive for creating the Three Rings includes a delusion from Sauron that obliquely attacks the Valar: an effort to transform Middle-earth into a realm as beautiful as Aman.[219] Still, Gandalf, Galadriel, and Elrond use their Rings to good ends, to assist them in achieving objectives suited to their natures.

While the Three Elven Rings preserve good within Middle-earth, the use of the One Ring would turn them instead against the Elves as a means to control them. Fortunately, the Elves perceive Sauron's design the moment he first dons the One Ring; thus they take off their Rings, preventing Sauron from controlling them. As long as Sauron possesses the One, the Three are impotent; while the One is lost, the Three promote peace, happiness, and preservation.[220] The Three Elven Rings thus pose a contradiction; while not evil and while capable of great good, they are controlled (or at least control-lable) by a greater evil. One can only speculate that Elves could have turned their Three into tools of evil, had their wills and natures been so inclined. This further implies that the Three are not themselves good; rather, their users are good.

The lesser Rings display primarily evil power. Sauron perverts and curses the Rings he gives to Humans, initiating their decline into Ringwraiths late in the Second Age. The Rings betray their wearers and reduce them to the level of machines. The bearers lack wills of their own and serve their Rings, which Sauron keeps. In essence, the Rings allow Sauron to accomplish within a single lifetime the same automaton state achieved by Melkor through his multigenerational Orc breeding program. Human holders of Rings transform into zombie-like beings, possessing unending but unendurable life. Yet one manuscript reveals that the Nazgûls' wills had shortcomings, even when entirely under Sauron's will; all except the Witch King, their leader, are aquaphobes and prone to wander off when alone during the day. Furthermore, Sauron does not always behave as if he has the Ringwraiths fully under control, relying on threats to motivate behavior.[221]

Rings versus Stones

The centrality of the One Ring to the narrative of *The Lord of the Rings*, combined with the author's disparaging words for advanced technologies of the modern era, position Tolkien as opposed to the instrumental view of technology (which sees technology as ethically neutral until used for either right or wrong).[222] Yet Hood notes that evil beings are "not made evil by the use of technology but rather by . . . ruthless pursuit of . . . conquest."[223] The evilness of the One Ring stems from the evil of its maker, not from its status as a technological device. Tolkien does in fact narrate a story in which technology becomes laden with power, much like the One Ring, but a power for good, rather than evil. Just as Sauron transfers some of his power into the One Ring, the Drúedain place some of their power into physical objects, which in turn protect them from evil, and indeed one Tolkien draft overtly compares the two, noting that the Drúedain activity parallels, though in a lesser form, the transfer of Sauron's power into the foundation of his fortress and into the One Ring.[224]

The narrative, "The Faithful Stone" in *Unfinished Tales*, tells of the Drûg Aghan who stands watch at night over the household of his friend, Barach, during a time when Orcs harass the Drúedain. On receiving a message that his own family needs him, Aghan brings a *watch-stone*, a rock statue carved in his own likeness, which the Drúedain believe can possess some of the fierceness of the being it represents. Aghan explains that he infused the stone with some of his own powers. A few nights later Barach awakens to discover Orcs preparing to burn his house (with an evil fiery substance like brimstone, reminiscent of Saruman's blasting powder[225]). As Barach prepares his bow, he witnesses an unknown Drûg fell one of the Orcs with his fist, sending the others fleeing into the forest, then trampling the flames barefoot. The next day, after Aghan's return, the two men discover the watch-stone sitting atop one of the fleeing Orcs, with the statue's legs cracked and blackened. Aghan declares it is better for the watch-stone's feet to become burned than his. Then he reveals that he awoke that morning with blistered legs, implying that his own power possessed the watch-stone, motivating it to aid in Barach's defense.

While this seems a good use of technology (and of magic), it also reveals technology as a double-edged sword. By putting some of his strength into the watch-stone, Aghan not only empowers it to increase the safety of his friend's family; he inadvertently allows that technology to harm him. As Aghan expresses, if a being transfers power into a created object, then that being must be willing to receive some of the hurt it receives.[226] This in essence sums up the pessimistic ambivalence of Tolkien's attitude toward technology; it's not that technology used for good purposes *might* have negative consequences, but rather that it *will* have such consequences. Technology's use will always harm the user, even while it helps.

The Palantíri

The Seeing Stones of Númenor, the Palantíri, like Rings of Power, forcefully illustrate Tolkien's pessimistic ambivalence toward technology. At first glance, Palantíri might seem ideal illustrations of the instrumental view of technology; a Palantír can do much good, but also allows for evil influence. Tolkien describes the Palantíri, much like the One Ring, as possessing some degree of sentience, or in Walker's words, "implicit life."[227] Yet in contrast with the One Ring, Tolkien absolves the Palantíri of inherent evil, finding them created innocent, for good purposes, until Sauron perverts them as tools to dominate and deceive.

Yet the Palantíri reveal a latent tendency to induce unhealthy desire to use them, a desire that may be augmented by an outside power. After merely picking up the Palantír outside Orthanc, Pippin feels irresistibly drawn toward it to such an extent that he steals from Gandalf; the narrative describes Pippin unable to sleep and incapable of placing the Stone out of his mind. Gandalf, on learning of Pippin's desire, speaks of it as an illness or addiction that can be cured. Even Gandalf confesses that he wishes to look into the Palantír, to forcibly turn the Stone away from Sauron's use in order to see across time and distance to the glory days of Aman.[228] The narrative remains unclear as to whether Pippin and Gandalf feel drawn to the Stone due to some inherent aspect of the technology itself, or whether Sauron in some sense cast a spell on the entire system of Stones that draws people to them.

Gandalf ultimately hints at further intentionality behind Pippin's use of the Palantír. Since it prompts Gandalf to refrain from using the device, he and his companions have been "strangely fortunate," saved from a serious misstep; Gandalf's words imply that, rather than an evil yearning placed into Pippin's mind by an evil, or evil-influenced, Palantír, some unnamed force for good may have prompted Pippin's restlessness as a mechanism for preventing Gandalf from revealing himself to Sauron. Or more complicated still, perhaps the force prompting Pippin's action is evil, but is unwittingly co-opted by a higher power to produce a good outcome from Pippin's folly. As Gandalf later speculates, perhaps Pippin's foolishness aids the cause, since the identification of the Stone as a Palantír provides Aragorn with a tool to prompt Sauron to misstep.[229] Tolkien connects the discovery of the Palantír to *chance* as Gandalf uses the word, to imply something more than chance.

The connection between technology and evil appears primarily when technology makes a huge leap, as with Rings of Power, devices of mass warfare, and even the new mill at Hobbiton (a development that at least one Hobbit considered positive). The term *Luddite* might apply appropriately to Tolkien, given the Luddites' opposition to new technologies because they displaced people (who used less advanced technologies). One could write off Tolkien as displaying a merely reactionary opposition to development (the *knee-jerk* view described earlier in this section), were it not for the knowledge of Tolkien's firsthand observation of and victimization by advanced war technologies of World War One, and his thoughtful anxiety over developments in World War Two. Pessimistic ambivalence seems an appropriate stance toward technological developments, and in many ways parallels the overall gist of eco-criticism.

🍃 Conclusion

While the elimination of Melkor or Sauron as evil powers in Middle-earth marks the ends of eras, they do not mark the end of evil. As the Singing and Vision of the Ainur show, evil forms such an integral element of Arda that removing the original cause of evil does not eliminate evil's effects. As a result, moments in the history of Middle-earth when evil experiences defeat are never ultimate. Evil lives on in the hearts and minds of those beings whom Melkor and Sauron corrupts, as the evil men of the East illustrate after the first defeat of Sauron. Isuldur speaks of Sauron's vengeance enduring, even after Isuldur defeats Sauron by cutting off his Ring. In fact, Tolkien leaves open the possibility that Melkor and Sauron may still exert influence after their defeats and disembodiment. In one note Tolkien surmises that Sauron can no longer act as a person in Arda, yet may continue to operate through Humans.[230] While the statement can mean simply that Sauron's indirect influence lingers after he no longer exists, readers may also infer that Sauron might exert direct influence, though only in a disembodied manner.

Dedication to evil, coupled with the innate power wielded by beings such as Melkor and Sauron, suggests Tolkien views evil in Middle-earth ultimately functioning as sociopathy. Melkor registers high on all six of the diagnostic measures of dissocial personality disorder (when having just three of the measures qualifies the diagnosis):

- Callous unconcern for the feelings of others.
- Gross and persistent attitude of irresponsibility and disregard for social norms, rules, and obligations.

- Incapacity to maintain enduring relationships, though having no difficulty to establish them.
- Very low tolerance to frustration and a low threshold for discharge of aggression, including violence.
- Incapacity to experience guilt, or to profit from adverse experience, particularly punishment.
- Marked proneness to blame others, or to offer plausible rationalizations for the behaviour bringing the subject into conflict with society.[231]

Such an understanding foregrounds the selfishness exhibited by evil beings, but also cloaks in mystery the causes of evil. While psychologists suggest both congenital and environmental triggers for sociopathic behavior, precise and treatable causes remain unknown. In the case of Melkor, however, his creation and his environment are, theoretically, completely under the control of Eru Ilúvatar. In Middle-earth, as in Earth's monotheistic religions, one is hard-pressed to avoid implicating the god of the universe as ultimately responsible for allowing the emergence of evil.

Chapter 6

Death

he real theme" of *The Lord of the Rings,* Tolkien explains to correspondents, is "Death and Immortality." One letter clarifies Tolkien's assertion: Elves and Humans "represent the problem of Death as seen by a finite but willing and self-conscious person."[1] I suspect few readers identify "Death and Immortality" as *the real theme* of the story (none of my students have done so). Perhaps *a significant undercurrent,* or a *noteworthy subtheme,* but hardly the story's *real theme.* In fact, only as one reads *The Silmarillion,* the section on Númenor in particular, or the Dialogue of Finrod and Andreth ("Athrabeth Finrod ah Andreth"), does the tension emerge between Elves and Humans on the matter of death as an inescapable experience of divine will.

Elves and Humans obviously differ in Tolkien's legendarium. Elves, generally speaking, feel content with their existence, never tiring of the cyclical phenomena of nature; Humans soon tire of repetition, seeming to live in perpetual unrest. More importantly, Humans experience relatively short lives, while Elves live immortally. This distinction, however, has exceptions; at least one Human (Tuor) does *not* die, while many Elves *do* die. A more useful distinction is that Humans experience either *natural* death (through old age or disease) or *unnatural* death (through murder, death in battle, suicide, or lack of will to live), and in fact are destined by Eru to experience at least one of the two; Elves, in contrast, have no requirement to experience death, or if so, only *unnatural* death. Christopher Tolkien identifies Elf death as *potential* rather than *inevitable.*[2]

Equally important to understanding death in Elves and Humans is the distinction between the Children of Ilúvatar, on the one hand, and the Valar and Maiar, on the other hand. As noted earlier, Valar and Maiar sometimes adapt bodies for themselves, but they do not depend on those bodies (except in cases when they remain embodied, or rely on their bodies, to the point that they become fixed in that form). Elves and Humans, in contrast, are body-dependent; their existence within Middle-earth, at least in the way that Eru intends that existence, requires a body. While Valar and Maiar are pure spirits, Elves and Humans conjoin spirit with matter, which the Elves term *Fëa* and *Hröa*. Fëa, Tolkien clarifies, corresponds to soul, mind, and self-awareness, and is based on the concept *radiance,* since light best symbolizes the spirit that dwells inside the body. Tolkien devises a term, *mirröanwi,* for incarnate beings whose spirits dwell in flesh.[3]

For Elves and Humans, Fëa do not simply reside in Hröa; instead, the two are each designed for the other, intended to form a continuing harmony. Because of the interdependence of Fëa and Hröa, separation of one from the other causes the being to cease to exist in the form intended by Eru Ilúvatar (a concept Agøy notes is "sound Catholic doctrine"[4]). At the same time, Fëa cannot be destroyed within Eä, and thus the Fëa of an Elf or Human exists even after its Hröa is destroyed. In fact, an Elvish Fëa retains the memories and experiences from its period of embodiment. Yet transformation from Fëa/Hröa to just Fëa is not an improvement, not simply to have "shuffled off this mortall coile," as Hamlet conjectures about death. Existing only as Fëa is a reduction for an Elf or Human, a disability comparable to an embodied person losing a major appendage, or perhaps losing all major appendages. Thus, Tolkien describes a disembodied Fëa as exiled, without a home.[5]

Finrod, in his philosophical dialogue with the Human wise woman Andreth, notes that the combination of Fëar and Hröar (Tolkien's plurals for Fëa and Hröa) produces between Elves and Humans a kinship that separates both from lesser and greater life-forms. At the same time, the Fëar of Elves and Humans closely resembles those of Valar and Maiar, while the Hröar of Elves and Humans closely resembles those of the embodied lower life forms devised in the Singing of the Ainur, creatures that supposedly lack Fëar. Thus, the new aspect of Eru's Third Theme in the Singing of the Ainur is the combination of Fëa and Hröa. While the substance of Arda that forms Hröar comes under the dominion of the Valar, the Fëar of Elves and Humans come into existence directly and solely from Eru.[6] This unique nature of Elves and Humans is somewhat diluted by the presence of other beings that seem to possess both Fëa and Hröa (Hobbits, Ents, and Dwarves, for example), by the presence of lower beings displaying consciousness that might imply the presence of Fëar (a fox that expresses surprise at seeing Hobbits wandering at night in the Shire, and Old Man Willow, who appears capable of murder motivated by revenge), and by the presence of humanoid beings who, at least at first glance, don't fit the Fëa and Hröa model (such as Wizards and Nazgûl).

Despite the complications that arise from the legendarium regarding which classes of beings have Fëar and Hröar, understanding the concepts makes comprehensible Tolkien's depictions of death in the legendarium. For Tolkien, death within his imaginary world has one primary, precise meaning: the separation of Fëa from Hröa.[7] Since this definition applies equally to both Elves and Humans, the important differences between Elf and Human deaths lie in the perceived inequity regarding death's inevitability for Humans, and the fates of Fëar after death.

An additional possible meaning of the word *death* deserves brief consideration: complete annihilation of a Fëa. Finrod raises this meaning as a theoretical possibility in his conversation with Andreth; while Elves, he says, use the word *death* to mean the separation of Fëa and Hröa, the spirit leaving the body, Finrod imagines the possibility that a being might "perish utterly," the discontinuation of *both* Fëa and Hröa. Yet no being in Eä appears to possess the power of eliminating Fëar, except perhaps Eru Ilúvatar, who shows no inclination to exercise such power; Tolkien hints, in fact, that perhaps even Eru cannot destroy Fëar once he has created them.[8]

This chapter will examine death as the separation of Fëa and Hröa, the complications surrounding that separation, and the involvement of Eru and the Valar in Elf and Human postdeath experiences. One of the most important complications is the nonfinality of death for Elves; while only one Human, Beren, returns from the dead in Tolkien's mythology (with the express permission of Mandos, Manwë, and Eru), dead Elves face the possibility of divinely sanctioned reincarnation, a possibility that requires divine involvement in Elven postdeath experience. For Humans, the narrative insistence that death be considered a gift from Ilúvatar forms a complication. Equally troubling are the half- and unbeings, Half Elves and Halflings, and Nazgûl and the undead; these groups require special handling by the divine overseers of Middle-earth.

🖋 *Elf Death*

A central experience of the Eldar in Middle-earth following the First Age is a death metaphor: passage over sea. Even after the transformation of the world at the downfall of Númenor, Eldar travel the Straight Road to Valinor, a passage that signals the end of their lives in Middle-earth. The alternative is to stay in Middle-earth but experience fading, the perception of change over time that marginalizes Elves and their presence in Arda.[9] Fornet-Ponse describes fading as "The dominance of *fëar* over *hröar* [that] increases by time, thus 'consuming' the bodies and leading to the 'fading' of Elves because the body becomes at last only a memory held by the spirit."[10] As Elves experience fading, their work becomes less about creating and shaping than about preserving that which has been and forestalling that which is to come, an effort that Tolkien describes as one of the most dire effects of Melkor's rebellion. The Eldar, in fact, presume that by the end of Arda, they, perhaps even all Elves, will have transformed toward invisibility, unless the Elves will to make themselves known within the minds of Humans.[11]

Like death, crossing the Great Sea often leads to partings. Galadriel's return to Aman, for example, means her parting from her husband, Celeborn. Though her songs in the "Farewell to Lórien" chapter of *The Fellowship of the Ring* imply she has long wished a return to Aman, her renunciation of the One Ring prompts the Valar to renew their offer of pardon, and she joins Gandalf, Elrond, Bilbo, and Frodo on their journey along the Straight Road. This leaves Celeborn despondent, according to Sam in the planned but abandoned epilogue to *The Lord of the Rings,* with the land and trees as consolation. Yet, Sam asserts, when Celeborn tires of Middle-earth, he, too, will likely travel the Straight Road to Aman, which implies the possibility of reunion between himself and Galadriel. Similarly, Celebrian, wife of Elrond, chooses to leave Middle-earth (after torture by Orcs) almost seven hundred years prior to the War of the Ring. The narrator emphasizes the finality of the journey; Celebrian will never return to Middle-earth.[12] Yet, because the Straight Road remains, Elrond might also hope to reunite with Celebrian in Aman.

While fading mimics the declining health of older Humans, and while traveling the Straight Road seems an obvious metaphor of death, passage over sea is *not* death for Elves.[13] Instead, Noldor such as Galadriel return to a land they know well from the millennia dwelt there prior to the First Age; for the remaining Eldar, passage over sea is a final though delayed acceptance of the summons of the Valar. Those Elves who travel the Straight Road remain Fëar conjoined with Hröar, and thus alive as immortals.

Yet Tolkien limits the immortality he grants the Elves by calling it "longevity or counterfeit 'immortality'"; genuine immortality would extend beyond the temporal boundaries of Eä (which means the ultimate destiny of Elves deserves further attention in the following chapter on the End of the World). Tolkien speaks of the Elves as immortal only *within* the world; their immortality, therefore, is in fact "serial longevity," which may last only until Arda's end.[14] Guaranteeing Elvish immortality only through Arda's life span opens the possibility that death may ultimately be inevitable for Elves, as well as Humans (and might even involve "perish[ing] utterly," to use Finrod's words).

Furthermore, because an Elf's Hröa incorporates the matter of Arda, it can be damaged to the point that it no longer remains joined to its Fëa, which results in an unnatural death. Fëar, however, remain indestructible, incapable of being subsumed into material elements. When an Elf experiences unnatural death, the Fëa becomes houseless and the Hröa returns to the matter of Arda. Such an experience, however, is outside Eru Ilúvatar's will for the Elves, and thus highlights another effect of Melkor's marring.[15] While unnatural deaths of Elves occur primarily in Middle-earth, the deaths of Fëanor's parents illustrate that unnatural deaths can occur even in Aman.

When Fëar become separated from Hröar, the Valar immediately summon the Fëar to the Halls of Mandos. What happens next depends on two factors: the will of the Fëa and the will of Mandos. Standard operating procedure involves a period of waiting. This period resembles the Catholic concept of purgatory, and thus involves correction, instruction, strengthening, and comfort, as the individual needs or deserves, though only if the Fëar cooperate; Tolkien's description resembles human psychotherapy. During this period of waiting, Fëar observe in some undisclosed manner the developments of Arda's history, though they cannot act within that history or communicate with others; a disembodied Fëa, in fact, is naturally solitary.[16]

The Silmarillion describes the Halls of Mandos as a place where the dead sit in shadowy contemplation. Tolkien's earlier conception, however, is bleaker and more Norse. A passage apparently intended as an interpolation into the ending of "The Lay of Leithian" describes Mandos's realm as further west than Valinor and the place where the dead wait while loved ones in Middle-earth forget them. A deathly quiet reigns, though with the passing of each age, a profound sigh is heard. *The Lost Tales* provides more details about the Halls of Mandos, caverns dug below the earth, gloomy and full of echoes. Mandos designates one large, black cavern as the primary site of judgment for Elves. A single lamp in the center of the cavern lights the space; all the furnishings and draperies are black. Elves spend their time in this hall, recalling their lives' events and actions.[17]

While the Valar summon, in fact command, disembodied Elvish Fëar to the Halls of Mandos, they do not force such a journey. The Fëar of Elves remain free to refuse the summons (an idea that only enters Tolkien's writing in 1958), just as many living Elves refuse the original summons to Aman. Such Fëar wander about, unwilling to leave Middle-earth yet not alive within it; Tolkien describes such Fëar as ghosts, haunting locations they once knew. But to refuse the summons also shows Melkor's influence. Some Elf Fëar refuse because Melkor has enslaved them; others, tainted by *the Shadow,* wander, some regretful and self-pitying, others bitter, angry, and envious. Such disembodied Fëar are physically invisible, though one Fëa can directly perceive another. The Valar, for example, communicate directly to disembodied Fëar, though those that refused the summons are obdurate, remaining imprisoned in their memories of former purposes, particularly if those purposes are evil.[18] Tolkien speculates that this happens often in the early history of the Elves among the Avari, who refuse the original summons to Aman.

Living Elves are warned against communicating with disembodied Fëar. For one thing, having been tainted by Melkor, such Fëar lie. Furthermore, some disembodied Fëar seek a return to embodiment, either by forcibly expelling a Fëa from its Hröa, or by enslaving both Fëa and Hröa, as Sauron the Necromancer does. "The Passage of the Marshes" chapter of *The Two Towers* hints at the possibility of Elf Fëar being thwarted from taking their expected journey. Gollum calls the ghost-like images in the Dead Marshes corpse candles. The images have no substance, as Gollum confesses with disappointment.[19] Thus, the experience must be either a devilish trick, merely an image of the dead beings recorded and projected as in a hologram, or an even more devilish trick of confining the Fëar of the dead beings, still connected to an image of their Hröar, preventing the spirits from traversing the Straight Road to the Halls of Mandos.

After their long period of rest and rehabilitation in the Halls of Mandos, Elvish Fëar can choose from two main futures. The first option retains the status of disembodied Fëar; Elves making this choice simply remain as-is within Mandos. Tolkien briefly considered allowing such unbodied Elves to leave Mandos, either permanently or temporarily. Such Fëar would have been free from longing to act within the world, but still interested in observation and reflection. They could have communed with minds of living Elves, if those Elves remembered the departed Fëar or allowed them access. As he developed this option, Tolkien concluded that more and more Fëar choose it as the history of Arda progresses; then Tolkien apparently changed his mind, crossed out the passage, and reverted to the more straightforward injunction against live Elves communing with disembodied Fëar.[20]

Tolkien developed a second option at much greater length, though it has proven uncomfortable for readers who wish to see Tolkien's metaphysics as fully Christian-compatible. Even Tolkien felt uncomfortable enough with the idea to consider a full-scale revision of his work late in life. Tolkien's second option is a limited, precise, and idiosyncratic form of Elvish reincarnation.

The Problem of Reincarnation

While an Elf's Fëa could be separated from its Hröa if severely wounded, at least one manuscript referred to this as "seeming death."[21] In contrast with death for most Humans (Beren being the obvious exception), Elf death is not necessarily permanent. Some can return, their Fëar reconnected to Hröar via reincarnation. Tolkien developed this concept at length, while apparently feeling antipathy for the term. As Flieger points out, "for a practicing Catholic like Tolkien, the idea of reincarnation would have been theologically problematic."[22] Yet Tolkien vigorously defends the idea both as an appropriate theme for fiction, and as a possible mode of creation that God in His freedom can utilize if He wishes. While reincarnation may be heresy if applied to Humans in the real world, it may reveal truth as a component of mythology. Theologians and philosophers, he asserts, would be foolhardy to discount the idea that God might weave reincarnation into the life cycle of rational beings in some other world.[23]

And thus, Tolkien felt free, more or less, to build reincarnation into the lives of Elves. Tolkien's concept of reincarnation, however, might be described as conservative. It did not involve the possibility of one life-form reentering existence as a different life-form, nor did the social status of a reincarnated being depend on the degree of goodness displayed in a previous existence. Instead, reincarnation involves a Fëa reentering Hröa as a direct result of divine intervention. Tolkien contemplated two primary methods of accomplishing reincarnation: embodiment through rebirth or reconstitution of a Hröa by an act of the Valar. Tolkien wrote at greatest length about rebirth and only proposed the alternate method late in developing his legendarium.

Rebirth for Elves involves being reborn through their offspring, or even to the same parents as their previous embodiment; Tolkien does not depict childbirth for Elves, let alone conception (which seems problematic for reincarnation by rebirth). A reborn Elf reexperiences the childhood discovery of the world, though eventually its memory of earlier life will awaken. When the reborn Elf grows to maturity, it comprehends both its earlier and more recent embodiment as a continuity of identity and experience, possessing the knowledge gained from both life spans.[24]

Since Elf death involves becoming unbodied, rebirth constitutes reembodiment. In the combination of Fëa and Hröa that produces Elves, "Fëa is the master"; therefore, reincarnated Fëa will impact the development of the Hröa more than vice versa, producing an identity consistent with the past. Elves cannot change even their names, let alone their genders or other aspects of identity. Reborn Elves physically resemble their former selves, such that former friends will recognize them, a fact that makes things interesting for those who married prior to death and whose former spouses remain alive. In such cases, willingness to remarry the former spouse becomes a consideration as to whether an Elf will be permitted to reincarnate. A healthy Elf, or properly cured one, will naturally wish to remarry his or her former spouse. This impacts where and to whom the Elf can be reborn. While Elves traditionally experience rebirth among their own relatives, the tradition may be ignored to ensure that the reborn Elf will meet her or his former spouse.[25]

Reincarnation by rebirth is ultimately Eru's domain; while the Valar can authorize a rebirth, they need to surrender Fëar to Eru, who then considers their cases, possibly arranging for rebirth. "The Converse of Manwë and Eru" suggests that Tolkien apparently wished to change this aspect of his mythology in the 1960s; the "Converse" records a dialogue in which Eru informs Manwë that he and the other Valar possess the power to rehouse Elvish Fëar directly into Hröar, without the need for rebirth. Tolkien speculates that the concept of reincarnation may have entered into Elvish mythology when it came under the influence of Human scribes, who may have contaminated it with Human legends.[26] Reembodiment by the Valar, without the mediation of rebirth, appears to be Tolkien's proposed solution. In Rateliff's explanation, "The original (adult) body was either re-created by the memory of the spirit or created by the Valar, under dispensation from Ilúvatar."[27] A thorough revision of the tales to match these new metaphysical concepts never materialized.[28] Christopher Tolkien guesses that his father wished to eliminate the idea of reincarnation within his stories, but found himself unable to do so without damaging them.

An Elf's prior life impacts the length of time spent in the Halls of Mandos prior to its rebirth. Early manuscripts associate a millennium with the period of waiting in the Halls of Mandos, though Mandos himself wields final authority. Finrod, who sacrifices his life for Beren, receives an early release from Mandos. A disembodied Elf guilty of evil acts, and then refusing to repent, might receive limitations and conditions on reincarnation, or even be refused reembodiment altogether. An early version of the Doom of the Noldor implies that slain Noldor will desire their bodies, but cannot expect to be returned to them. In the most grave cases, decisions on whether an Elf should be permitted rebirth are referred to Eru; such is the case with Fëanor. Others will not consent to the correction and instruction offered during the time of waiting in the Halls of Mandos. The Valar will not force an Elf to accept reincarnation, and thus an Elf Fëa can refuse reembodiment.[29]

Glorfindel is, perhaps, the most obvious example of Elf reembodiment. The *perhaps* in the previous sentence results from Tolkien's discomfort in connecting the Glorfindel of *The Silmarillion* with the Glorfindel of *The Fellowship of the Ring*. If the two are indeed one and the same, then the narrative of his life and death and life can be summarized as follows: The Glorfindel of *The Silmarillion* dies in noble battle with a Balrog while defending Tuor and Idril in their escape from the destruction of Gondolin. Glorfindel's Fëa then goes to Mandos, remaining there until Manwë grants permission for its release. While there, Glorfindel obtains forgiveness for his role in the Noldorin rebellion, and then resumes embodied life via reincarnation; he chooses to stay in Aman since Gondolin has been destroyed. In Aman he becomes both comrade and disciple of Olórin, and ultimately chooses to return to Middle-earth with him when Gandalf accepts the role of Istari. Glorfindel's greater power than most Elves late in the Third Age, his ability to face the Nazgûl, stems from his reincarnation; through rebirth Glorfindel has reverted to his prerebellion innocence, and has then learned from Maiar throughout the Second Age.[30]

At the same time, Glorfindel's return to Middle-earth is the exception rather than the rule. Tolkien apparently discounts the ability of reincarnation taking place in Middle-earth. Instead, most reincarnated Elves remain in Aman, for the simple practical reason that no convenient mode of transportation exists, particularly after the fall of Númenor, that allows an embodied being to travel East along the Straight Road. Ships leaving Middle-earth to transport Elves to Aman take a one-way route. Tolkien does not preclude such a journey, but says simply that return to Middle-earth is exceedingly dangerous.[31]

If conjoined Fëa and Hröa can be separated once, it stands to reason that rejoined Fëa and Hröa can also be separated, suggesting the possibility of third and fourth embodiments for Elves. The tradition views second rebirths as rare, though Tolkien notes that the Elves can only speculate as to the cause: perhaps such is the will of Eru; or perhaps a reborn Elf is stronger and wiser, and thus less likely to experience a second death; or perhaps Elves who do experience a second death have no wish for a third life.[32] Such is the case with Míriel, who doesn't even wish to prolong her first life.

The Problem of Míriel

One of the most troubling of Elf deaths is that of Míriel, first wife of Finwë and resident of Valinor. After giving birth to Fëanor, Míriel feels her energies consumed; thus, she desires relief from the burden of living. She lies down to sleep in Lórien on a bed of flowers, where her body remains uncorrupted, attended by Estës's maidens, though her Fëa goes to the Halls of Mandos.[33] This situation places Finwë and the Valar in considerable distress, and significantly occupies Tolkien's mind in the late 1950s.

Much of the distress stems from the shocking realization that the Elves can experience unnatural death, even in the near-ideal setting of Aman. A dialogue between Manwë and Eru begins with Manwë's expression of dismay that an unexpected evil has appeared in Arda. Many such separations occurred in Middle-earth (apparently either during the Eldar's march to the western shore of Beleriand, or among Dark Elves).[34] But this first Aman death forms a painful growth experience for the Valar, realizing that the layers of protection they devised for the safekeeping of the Elves in Aman are themselves permeated from the beginning by Melkor's willful, destructive impulse.

Additional distress arises because Míriel's death effectively terminates her marriage to Finwë, who wishes to have more children; therefore, Finwë seeks to remarry, also a first such scenario among the Elves. The Valar's decree allowing Finwë to remarry, "The Statute of Finwë and Míriel," also requires that Míriel express a desire to stay dead (that is, for her Fëa to remain permanently separated from her Hröa) and that Mandos confirm her desire after a waiting period of ten years. Mandos further determines that Míriel should be deemed innocent, since her death results from a need for rest that she can't overpower.[35]

Documents associated with Tolkien's "Silmarillion"-related work of the late 1950s record a debate among the Valar concerning Míriel's status.[36] The debate provides useful insight into Elf death (as well as a unique look at interactions among the Valar). Manwë begins the debate by reminding his fellow Valar that the Elves stem from *Arda Marred;* that is, unlike traditional interpretations of the first few chapters of Genesis (in which humans are created unflawed but become flawed through the exercise of their free wills), the cosmic history of Arda presumes Elves are fashioned from its substance *after* it has become flawed through Melkor's insertion of evil. Aulë in response argues that Míriel's situation arises not because she is formed from Arda Marred, but because the birth of Fëanor, stemming directly from the will of Eru, has overwhelmed Míriel. Ulmo responds that since Míriel died, and since death is unnatural in *Arda Unmarred,* it must proceed from Arda Marred; phenomena that arise direct from Eru's intervention, Ulmo reminds his peers, will not cause grief or uncertainty. Thus, while agreeing with Aulë that Fëanor's birth stems from Eru's will, Míriel's death in contrast stems from evil.

As the debate continues, Yavanna sides with Ulmo, rather than her husband, so far as to assert "My Lord Aulë errs"; anything produced from the substance of Arda, such as the Hröar of Elves, cannot exist completely free, but rather reveals the influence of Melkor, who has vigorously contaminated Arda's substance. Nienna, no surprise, argues that Míriel and other Elves must be pitied because they combine the extremes of strength and weakness. Each Elf Fëa has an impregnable will, equal to the strength of the Valar themselves; that is, the Valar have no ability to overpower Elf wills. Yet Elves are weak in terms of power and comprehension. Míriel, Nienna suggests, lacks power to resist the weariness resulting from giving birth to Fëanor. Yet, Ulmo argues, her Fëa has failed to retain hope, presuming her condition cannot be healed; then Finwë allows himself to despair, which in turn deserves blame. Vairë argues last, asserting in essence that the Valar should judge neither Míriel nor Finwë until they have experienced a similar loss.[37]

Ultimately the Valar permit Míriel to embrace the separation of her Fëa from her Hröa. Míriel's body, however, remains in perfect condition, causing Nienna to appear before Mandos some time later asking him to reconsider the decree that her Fëa and Hröa must remain separated. She argues that Míriel should be permitted to enjoy her body and its skills once again, rather than be trapped in a memory of life as weariness. Mandos, however, remains unmoved.[38] To reunite her Fëa and Hröa means she would technically return to life, giving Finwë two living wives, which would disturb Elvish nature and custom, as well as injure Finwë's second wife, Indis.

When Melkor slays Finwë, however, the Elf's Fëa reunites with that of his dead first wife. Finwë then pleads before Melkor that Míriel's Fëa be reunited with her Hröa. It will be good for Míriel, Finwë argues, and will not harm Indis (since she has the comfort of living sons). Furthermore, Finwë promises to stay dead which, he feels, should void the Doom that says Míriel will need to stay dead if Finwë remarries. Mandos sees Finwë's offer as providing hope for healing since unselfishness and self-abnegation prompt it. Míriel's Fëa thus reunites with her Hröa, with Manwë's blessing; on entering her body she reawakens "as one that cometh out of a deep sleep," despite the fact that she has been conscious as a houseless Fëa.[39]

Míriel's return to life, however, does not produce long-term happiness. After regaining her past memories and learning of events that transpired since her death (an observation that seems to contradict Tolkien's assertion that Elven Fëa in Mandos remain aware of the world's events), she remains disconsolate, and wishes for no Elven companionship. So, she returns to the service of Vairë, who places her in charge of weaving the lives of the Noldor into tapestry-like images; sometimes Finwë observes her work. Ultimately Míriel assumes a new name: Fíriel, which means both *she that sighs* and *she that dies,* based on the root word *fire,* to expire, as in a breath exhaled.[40]

✍ Human Death

As noted in the introduction to this chapter, the inability to escape death forms a major distinction between Humans and Elves. Aldrich notes that the first three lines of the "Ring Rhyme" associate death with Humans as an essential element of their natures; while Elves are associated with the sky and Dwarves with stone caverns, humans are "mortal . . . doomed to die," a phrase that reiterates human mortality (*mortal, doomed, die*). For humans, the sole escape from death is "*through* death," according to Aldrich.[41] Elves find the fates of Humans strange and mysterious.[42]

Yet having established the immortality of *all* Fëar, both Elvish and Human, it follows that Human death must parallel Elvish death, as a transformation rather than a complete cessation of existence. Human destiny postdeath ultimately involves leaving Eä altogether, and thus as Williams observes, the issue "is not just that [humans] die; it is that [they] die *and leave the world.*"[43] Setting aside for the moment the transformation from embodiment to disembodiment, death for most Elves is primarily a change of geography (or, following the downfall of Númenor, cosmography): from Middle-earth to Aman; Human death is a change from *within* geography to *without* it: from Middle-earth to an existence outside the space-time continuum.

A draft of the "Ainulindalë" sums up the Human condition this way: Humans live only a short time in Eä; though not bound to the world as the Elves, they will not "perish utterly forever."[44] Since Tolkien describes only two locations outside Eä, Human destiny may take them either to the Void, a location that seems unlikely, given Melkor's disposal there, or to the presence of Eru. Thus, some Elves speculate that Humans, on death, may enter the direct presence of Eru Ilúvatar, for some purpose that the Elves cannot guess.[45]

The possibility of entering the presence of Eru justifies the Elf euphemism for Human death as the gift of Ilúvatar. Elvish serial longevity guarantees the existence of Elvish Fëar solely within Eä's finite history. While the Elves hope for a future beyond the end of the world, they view Humans somewhat wistfully, even enviously, as being guaranteed some mode of existence even after the end. Additionally, Tolkien describes serial longevity as a burden. Death, therefore, should be a release from that burden, Finrod argues.[46] Garbowski thus contrasts Elf immortality with human mortality by identifying the former as "an endless extension of the known" and the latter an "unknown becoming."[47]

Finrod claims Elves plainly perceive this difference of destiny, as if it can be known to one of the senses. Humans fear death, Finrod asserts, solely because it has accumulated negative associations due to Melkor's lies; if death were untainted by those lies, Humans would not dread it. The "Ainulindalë," in fact, suggests that before the history of Arda will end, not just the Elves but even the Valar will grow to envy Eru's gift to Humans.[48] Here, as Flieger points out, lies the relevance of the subtitle of "The Lay of Leithian," "Release from Bondage": Elvish deathlessness equates to "bondage to life."[49]

Humans, in contrast, do not grasp that big-picture distinction, arguing that they are expected to accept Eru's gift blindly, in faith. From an experiential standpoint within Arda, death appears to be the end. Humans have no Valar to teach cosmology; they have no Human Noldor returned from Aman with firsthand knowledge of the Powers of Eä (with one exception: Beren, who returns from death but apparently leaves no description of his death experience and interacts with no other Humans). Because Elves do not die by nature, and because their accidental deaths hold the potential of reversal via reincarnation, Humans feel Elf death bears no similarity to their own. In fact, some Humans believe the race should have possessed a longevity similar to that of the Elves. Andreth considers death imposed upon Humans through the evil impact of Melkor. Rather than a gift from Ilúvatar, death feels abominable, a final verdict imposed with no appeal. Though Finrod asserts death as Eru's gift, thus justifying the Elves' envy, Andreth insists on the opposite: that Humans, at the very beginning of self-awareness, knew confidently that they possessed immortality without end.[50]

Finrod reveals the illogic of Andreth's argument. Andreth claims immortality as an embodied being, implying that Human bodies are imperishable. Yet that body takes its substance from the matter of Arda, which is bounded both spatially and temporally. Finrod implies that physical reality will someday end, so that bodies constructed from physical reality will also inevitably end. An imperishable body is a contradiction in terms. Furthermore, Finrod infers that Andreth views Human Hröa and Fëa as misaligned from the moment of their creation. Yet harmony of Hröa and Fëa is an essential element of incarnate existence, if unmarred by Melkor's evil. Therefore, Finrod implies, if Human Fëa and Hröa experience discord, then Humans have been impacted by evil. Tolkien expresses another rationale for seeing death positively. Even if death were foisted upon Humans as a punishment by Eru, punishment by a divine being, intended as a blessing to the recipient, should be seen as a gift from the divine.[51]

The Elves find other evidence to presume that Human destiny lies outside Eä, such as Human discontent with reality as they experience it. Elves gain a satisfaction from mere existence in the world, a feeling of contentment largely foreign to Humans. Humans appear driven to seek something, and thus find themselves incapable of contented relaxation, of being *in the moment*. Tolkien describes Human decay and death as introduced into Human experience, accompanied by a sense of haste.[52] "No rest in this world," according to Garbowksi, "indicates a hunger for the transcendent." At the same time, Human "inability to accept death" suggests "a lack of trust in God."[53]

Yet conflicting with the Human sense of "no rest in this world," Humans also experience a deep love of Arda, which, one Elf observer asserts, enables humans to fulfill the destiny given them. Such a love makes leaving Arda painful, even if Humans feel certain of their postdeath fate. The lack of enthusiasm exhibited among the Elves on the topic of leaving Middle-earth for Aman illustrates the psychic trauma that accompanies such a transition. Elves speculate that the worst part for Humans must be that the place and time of Human death is outside Human control.[54]

While Elves aver confidence that Human death leads to a destiny outside Eä, they can only speculate as to the procedure by which Human Fëar get to wherever they go postdeath. *The Book of Lost Tales* describes a hall in Mandos's realm that houses, at least temporarily, Human Fëar. It resembles the one allotted Elves: all black, with a single light (this a brazier with a single coal, rather than a lamp), pillars of basalt, and a roof of bat's wings; Mandos's wife presides over this chamber on a black throne, pronouncing judgment on Humans. Tolkien's earliest Silmarillion manuscript, in contrast, asserts that Humans do not go to Mandos on their demise, but later manuscripts (and even a revision written on the earlier one) reasserts the Elvish belief that Human Fëar experience a sojourn in the Halls, though in a section inaccessible from that allotted Elves. A Hall of Waiting for Human Fëar seems a narrative necessity in the case of Beren, since Lúthien sings before Mandos to beg that he be reembodied; Mandos would not likely possess the authority to recall Beren from beyond the Walls of Night had Beren already exited Eä. Prophecies of Turin's involvement in the battle at the end of Arda's history suggest that, at least in Turin's case, Humans can reside in the Halls of Mandos for millennia, though the earliest version of Turin's tale suggests he and his sister are permitted to enter Mandos only after prayers from their parents and a period of fiery cleansing from their sorrows and blemishes.[55]

What lies in store for Humans after their experience in Mandos's Halls remains a mystery. Some Elves speculate that only Mandos, Manwë, and Eru Ilúvatar know where Humans go after their time in Mandos, though other manuscripts cast doubts as to whether even Manwë knows. The Elves speculate that Human destiny is not within the authority of the Valar, and perhaps not even an element of the Music of the Ainur. While the Valar can return Elves to embodiment under their own authority, they lack authority to "withdraw the gift of death" from Humans, since it comes direct from Eru.[56] As *The Silmarillion* says, "One alone[, Eru,] can change" the Doom of the World (meaning, in context, the fate of Humans).[57]

Some Humans who benefit from significant contact with the Elves, such as Aragorn, develop faith that Human souls are immortal. Hammond and Scull paraphrase an unpublished Tolkien letter in which he expresses Aragorn's trust that divine intentions for Humans postdeath are good, and that he and Arwen can expect to meet again, since they give themselves in trust and obedience. Yet moments when Humans exhibit confidence regarding their postdeath experiences remain rare. One such moment emphasizes irony. After the death of Niniel, Brandir recites to Turin the dying words of Glaurung the Dragon that reveals Niniel as Turin's sister and drives her to suicide. When Brandir perceives Turin's intention of killing him, he says he has no fear of death because it might permit him to seek his beloved across the Great Sea.[58] Perhaps Brandir's last words referenced the sea as a metaphor, or they may suggest he believes he would interact with other recently arrived Human Fëar in the Halls of Mandos.

Uncertainty of what follows death induces in Humans a morose attitude toward it, either depression or grim resignation, more often than hope. Such is the scene when the young Turin learns from Sador the difference between Elves and Humans, and learns that his dead sister, Lalaith, will not return to life. Sador asserts that no Human can ascertain where Turin's sister has gone. Even the Elves grow sorrowful when they first apprehend Human death after a relatively short life span.[59]

Human uncertainty regarding death is compounded by the apparent certainty of an accessible Elvish paradise on Aman. For Humans Aman (outside of Mandos's Halls) is theoretically accessible but practically inaccessible. Transportation is readily available for Elves, but Humans are forbidden from traveling there by the Valar, perhaps at the command of Eru. *The Silmarillion* hints of tales of seafaring Humans, lost at sea and permitted to enter the Straight Road; such Humans, however, see only a glimpse of Elvish paradise prior to dying themselves. If Humans were allowed into Aman, the Valar could not change the speed at which aging occurs, so Human lifetimes would be less than a year of Aman's time. Growing to age while everything around one (including Elves and Valar) experience no change or lessening of joy would be a burden that would ruin Human experience of Aman. Furthermore, in Aman Human Fëa would come into opposition to Human Hröa; while Hröa would flourish and delight in its existence, Human Fëa would feel imprisoned and grow weary of perpetual pleasure. Ultimately, either the Fëa would wither, leaving the Hröa as a witless animal, or the Fëa would forcibly part from the Hröa, which might produce sudden death, or leave the Hröa alone in a less-than-animalistic state; it would become, in fact, monstrous, a working out of Melkor's will that would prompt the Valar to destroy it.[60]

Humans are discouraged from willfully inducing death prior to the death experience decreed by fate or prompted by circumstance, regardless of whether Humans contemplate suicide due to despair, or to experience Eru's promised future. Suicide is never commendable in Tolkien's legendarium. Denethor chooses the heathen path of self-immolation rather than face death passively but nobly, an action compounded in its evil in that he proposes simultaneous murder of his own son. Gandalf makes clear, in fact, that the heathen kings Denethor references were prompted by allegiance to Melkor and/or Sauron.[61] Turin's death seems the exception to the rule against suicide, as if readers ought to perceive his death as self-inflicted mercy killing, given the unconquerable evil fate that enmeshes him. Prophecies suggest an ultimate forgiveness for Turin's action, since Turin will come to be ennobled in Arda's Last Battle.

At the same time, the opposite of suicide, resisting death, is equally unwise. A lust for eternal life becomes the downfall of the Númenóreans. *The Silmarillion* describes them as falling under a shadow, a phenomenon demonstrating the will of Melkor at work in Arda, even after Melkor's demise. Because the Númenóreans associate immortality with the Elves, they grow jealous of the Elves and their home, Eressëa, an island closer to Aman to which Humans are not permitted to sail. At first the Shadow exhibits itself as unquiet, but it grows to murmurings against the fate of Humans, which is death. While envious of the Elves, the Númenóreans show themselves ignorant of Elvish experience of life. Faramir explains to Frodo and Sam that the Númenóreans (and their Middle-earth descendants) desire unchanging eternal life.[62] But such is not the experience of the Elves, who see the world changing and experience it as grief.

The earliest kings and queens of Númenor do not fear death. Instead, they die, like Aragorn, of their own free wills while possessing clear minds. Later monarchs, however, resist death; for Númenórean kings, a long, robust manhood of perhaps four hundred years might still decay at the same rate as normal Humans. Christopher Tolkien describes world-weariness as the first sign of impending death, part of their Eru-given natures that differentiates them from Elves; apparently Eru intends for world-weariness to prompt Humans to accept the transition from within the space-time continuum to without. Tolkien identifies the effort of Númenórean kings to resist death as both wicked and foolish; the wickedness stems from disobedience to Eru, while the foolishness results from resisting the transformation to something better. The massive tombs devised by kings of Númenor and by the post-Númenórean exiles exemplifies both cultures' preoccupation with death.[63]

The Problem of Beren and Lúthien

Beren and Lúthien introduce two complications in the distinction between Elf and Human death in Arda. Lúthien reveals a permeability in the division between Elvish and Human death; she exchanges her Elvish fate for a Human one, dying as a Human and apparently leaving Eä. Beren shows a permeability in the division between Human life and Human death; like the biblical Lazarus, he dies, returns to life, and dies again.

Even before achieving its apotheosis, the story of Beren and Lúthien complicates Human death by inserting ghost images into the tale. Gorlim, one of the outlaw followers of Beren's father, Barahir, sees a ghost image of his deceased wife, then appears as a ghost himself. *The Silmarillion* and "The Lay of Leithian" frame this ghostly appearance within a dream, which might suggest divine intervention in the mind of Beren, rather than an actual visitation by a postdeath Human Fëa. The dream-state ghost appearance of Gorlim thus matches and opposes the apparition of his wife that Gorlim witnesses; the narrator of "The Lay" notes that Humans presume Melkor somehow creates the devilish phantom that tricks Gorlim.[64]

A ghost is just one of Beren's unusual experiences, for whom death is an ever-present danger. Narratives of Beren and Lúthien illustrate Humans' lack of confidence about their destinies. A plot synopsis Tolkien devised while composing "The Lay of Leithian" gives Lúthien the words "But life perchance lies after death" as she expresses her resolve to follow Beren anywhere; the *perchance* works against confidence. In fact, after Carcharoth bites off Beren's hand, Lúthien bursts into tears from the prospect of separation from Beren.[65]

Yet Lúthien appears more confident of an afterlife as death looms for Beren. She asks that he "await her beyond the Western Sea"; *The Silmarillion* narrator asserts that Beren's spirit purposely protracts his stay in Mandos's Halls in order to await Lúthien. Lúthien predicts a final farewell on the shore of the Outer Sea (to the west of Aman), suggesting that as the site from which Human Fëar leave Arda.[66] Lúthien's prediction implies some means of transportation devised by divine beings, for a journey parallel to the Elves crossing the inland sea from Middle-earth to Aman; or more accurately, since Humans journey one-way from Aman and presumably leave Arda, this journey parallels the Elves' use of the Straight Road following the downfall of Númenor.

Lúthien, too, dies, though of grief. One version suggests she wills the separation of her Fëa and Hröa. *The Silmarillion* describes her (first) death similar to the death of Míriel: after her Fëa leaves her Hröa, her body remains unwithered. Her Fëa arrives in the Halls of Mandos, where both her loveliness and her sorrow surpass that of other residents. Boldly, she sings to Mandos, kneeling before him. The narrator describes her song in terms that echoes the Music of the Ainur, interweaving two themes of Elvish sorrow and Human grief. The narrator further asserts that the song is the most sad and most beautiful ever sung. Combined with Lúthien's tears of grief, the song uncharacteristically moves Mandos to pity. Elves of Aman treasure the song and perform it subsequently (though the narrator does not say who performs it, or how the song comes to be known outside the Halls of Mandos).[67]

Being moved by pity creates a predicament for Mandos. While he can permit a meeting of the two lovers (and thus Lúthien's prediction of a final farewell on the western shore of Aman comes true), Mandos lacks authority over the ultimate fate of Human Fëar, or to interfere with the destinies of Elves. Thus, Mandos consults Manwë, who communes with Eru.[68] Manwë gives Lúthien two choices; Beren, in contrast, is given no choice, though his destiny will be greatly affected by Lúthien's.

Lúthien's first option is to remain Elf. *The Silmarillion* implies that in choosing this option she could immediately leave the Halls of Mandos, apparently in a reembodied state. This option would allow her to dwell among the Elves of Aman and ultimately forget all her unhappiness; at the same time, it would require eternal separation from Beren. Option two involves a return to Middle-earth, with Beren as companion, to live together with no promise of happiness or extended life. This second choice can be offered only with Eru's explicit permission (exercising his right to introduce elements not found in the Music of the Ainur).[69] Lúthien chooses option two.

Of their brief postdeath life together, little is known. One draft refers to this second life as "a time of respite which Lúthien had won, ere both should die,"[70] a respite that the "Annals of Beleriand" measures at about thirty-eight years (some manuscripts speak of the two being granted long lives; others insist the "doom of mortality" arrives rapidly).[71] Option two, however, requires that Lúthien be transformed from an immortal Elf into a mortal Human, ultimately to exit Arda permanently.[72] One manuscript describes this transformation as payment required for the opportunity of living with Beren. Beren, too, will be required to face death a second time. As Flieger points out, theirs is "a qualified and limited resurrection."[73] In fact, after the recovery of the Silmaril, Beren and Lúthien's close proximity to the jewel induces death at a more rapid pace, an assumption the narrative attributes to the Wise. While the cause of this effect remains unspoken, the narrative offers as explanation the simple assertion that the jewel is "too bright for mortal lands,"[74] a reminder that Lúthien is Elf no more.

To emphasize the finality of this second death, to forestall any further singing at the feet of Mandos, the narrative adds an intensifier: Beren and Lúthien "died *indeed*."[75] The "Annals of Beleriand" connect their deaths with a doom of Mandos.[76] Yet another version, the narrative of Trotter (the character who eventually evolves into Aragorn) to the Hobbits below Weathertop, emphasizes the experience as transformative travel, not a complete cessation; together the two long ago left "the confines of the world."[77] Appendix A of *The Return of the King* emphasizes the separate destinies of Elves and Humans simply by noting that Lúthien takes on mortality and therefore is no longer numbered among the Elves.[78] This means Lúthien becomes separated from both her father (who must have gone to the Halls of Mandos on his death) and her mother (who returns to Aman following the death of her husband). Shippey describes Lúthien's death as "escap[ing] from deathlessness,"[79] but Melian perceives Lúthien's destiny as "a parting beyond the end of the world," which induces in Melian a grief that surpasses the experience of any other resident of Arda.[80]

Yet the narrative implies that Lúthien chooses more than a few decades of love with Beren, followed by a death that will separate her from him; rather, in accepting Human form and destiny, she aligns herself with Beren in his ultimate destiny beyond Arda. Aragorn's retelling emphasizes this Human-centric version of the narrative; Lúthien, he says, chooses Human destiny in order to experience the afterlife with Beren.[81] While the narrator records no promise by Mandos, Manwë, or Eru, Lúthien appears confident that her acceptance of Human death involves the probability that her Fëa will eternally unite with Beren's outside the space-time continuum.

Half-Elves, Halflings, and the Half-Dead

The distinction between Elven and Human death becomes more complicated with the appearance of the Half-Elven and the Halflings. Two patriarchs of the Half-Elven, Tuor and Eärendil, join Lúthien in illustrating the permeability of the distinction between Elf and Human death. Tuor, son of the human Huor and cousin of the very human Turin, might be described as the contrary of Lúthien. Just as she abjures her Elvish heritage to embrace the fate of Humans (out of love for Beren), Tuor gives up his Human heritage to embrace the fate of the Elves (out of love for Idril). *The Silmarillion* identifies Tuor as the sole human to be "numbered among" the Elves and separated from Human destiny. Since Tuor's son, Eärendil, possesses both Human and Elven ancestry, the Valar judge him to be among the Elves, though they prohibit him from returning to Middle-earth after his successful journey to Aman.[82]

Eärendil's marriage to Elwing, who as a descendant of Beren and Lúthien also possesses mixed Elvish-Human genetics, produces the Half-Elves.

While Eru denies the Valar authority to counteract Human death, he allows them judgment in regard to the destinies of Half-Elves. The Valar give the Half-Elves a choice: align themselves with the Elves, thus assuming Elvish serial longevity followed by an uncertain destiny at the end of Arda; or choose Humanity, granting them a much shorter life span, but guaranteeing an unknown form of existence after death. Elrond famously chooses Elven existence, though a draft document suggests he could choose mortality even after living for several thousand years as an Elf.[83] His brother, Elros, chooses human existence and becomes the first king of Númenor.

While Elros's offspring apparently have no choice but to accept Human destiny, the situation grows still more complex for Elrond's children. They, too, are Half-Elven, though also described as "three parts of Elven-race." A prophecy uttered at their birth asserts (through an unidentified prophet) that they can live as Elves as long as Elrond remains in Middle-earth; if he takes the Straight Road to Aman, however, they must choose their destinies, with the following restriction: if they leave Middle-earth with their father, they will remain Elves; if they stay in Middle-earth, they will transform into mortals. Tolkien later amended the geographical basis of the decision to suggest they could either follow their father (and be Elves) or *marry* (and become) Human.[84]

For Elrond, the end of the Third Age means that he must face one or more painful losses, since he has two sons, a daughter, and a surrogate son/potential son-in-law in Aragorn.[85] If Aragorn does not fulfill his destiny and dies without being crowned king, Elrond will be separated from him forever, even if his three children chose the destiny of Elves; Arwen, too, will be separated from Aragorn. However, since Aragorn does achieve his quest, and thus fulfills the condition Elrond set for marriage with Arwen, Elrond, if he remains an Elf, will be separated from both his daughter and Aragorn. Because of the doom placed on the children of Elrond, Arwen's separation from Elrond will be permanent, "beyond the ends of the world"; the use of plural for *ends* might imply geographical boundaries, but a draft uses singular to imply temporality.[86] The separation of Elrond from his daughter thus parallels that of Thingol and Melian from Lúthien.

Appendix A of *The Return of the King* narrates the bittersweet story of Arwen's realization of her choice. The narrator notes her fate includes dying only after losing whatever she has gained from choosing humanity. While

Aragorn suggests the possibility that Arwen might repent her choice and follow her father to Aman, Arwen asserts that no ship will bear her west, and that she has no choice but to accept the fate of Humans. Only then does she grasp the meaning of death in relation to Human existence; her realization produces pity for Humans, observing that if death is indeed a gift from Eru, it is a bitter gift to receive. Hammond and Scull reference an unpublished Tolkien letter that indicates Arwen could choose to die along with her husband, but her Elvish-influenced (though now mortal) nature prevents her.[87]

The appendix also describes Arwen's life subsequent to the passage of her father and the death of her husband: her eyes no longer emanate the light associated with High Elves, and she appears gray and cold, like a winter night with no stars. Both the direct description (light of the eyes quenched) and the figurative language (night with no stars) suggest a physiological transformation from Elf to Human. To emphasize the finality of her choice, the narrator notes that her grave lies in Lothlórien, and will remain there until she is forgotten by Humans.[88]

Elrond may experience a similar separation from his two sons. Celeborn reportedly moves to Imladris to live with the sons of Elrond after Galadriel journeys to Aman; since Galadriel leaves Middle-earth on the same boat as Elrond, his sons apparently do not travel with him to Aman, which implies they have accepted the doom uttered at their birth. Even Aragorn, when he first broaches to Elrond his desire to marry Arwen, hints with prophetic foresight that Elrond's children will soon be forced to choose either parting from their father, or parting from Middle-earth.[89] Thus while Elrond's journey to Aman may reunite him with his wife, it may separate both from their children.

While Arwen's self-sacrifice results, as her father predicted, in unhappiness after the death of Aragorn,[90] it also eases Frodo's suffering over loss of the One Ring. Arwen first recognizes Frodo's disquiet, which Tolkien describes using a word associated with Elvish reaction to the changes of the world: "Slowly [Frodo] *fades* 'out of the picture.'"[91] Frodo's own words reveal the lingering impact of the evil Ring he bore so long; his melancholy observation that the Shire cannot, after all, offer him the consolation of home reveals, Tolkien asserts, that he remains subject to the temptation of pride, a desire to be a hero in the Shire, rather than finding contentment in having served as an instrument of good. Mixed up with this is a milder form of the regret, exhibited more strongly by Bilbo and Gollum, that the beloved Ring has been lost.[92]

Though Arwen does not indicate by whose authority she speaks, she bestows upon Frodo the right to take ship into the West by the Straight Road.

Frodo, however, experiences no Tuor-like transformation of Hobbit into Elf. Even Arwen's words suggest a finite visit to the West, until Frodo experiences healing from his labors and wounds. Tolkien likens Frodo's experience to the Catholic experience of purgatory, but one conjoined with reward. Tolkien's words echo the experience of Elven Fëa postdeath: Frodo will experience a time of peaceful reflection, inculcating deeper insight into his own nature and position in Arda, spent among Elves across the sea. Yet ultimately Frodo will need to embrace his fate as a mortal, since not even the Valar can bestow upon Frodo or Bilbo the same fate as Tuor; ultimately the two Hobbits willingly die, much like Aragorn. Tolkien refers to this rare example of mortals accepted into the West as a "special grace" that allows the recipients an experience closer to the original intentions of Eru Ilúvatar. Tolkien does not describe Hobbit death. Nelson very reasonably assumes that Hobbit death and afterlife parallel those of Humans.[93]

The Lord of the Rings, of course, only hints at Frodo's post–Middle-earth experience, in a remarkable passage noteworthy because the narrator temporarily leaves the shore of Middle-earth to follow Frodo along the Straight Road before turning back to remain in Middle-earth with Sam. The narrator describes Frodo passing into the West, finally smelling a sweet fragrance and hearing the singing from a shore, framed by a sunrise over a green countryside. How the narrator gains knowledge of Frodo's precise experience remains unexplained, but Tolkien interprets the passage as suggesting that Frodo and his companions travel no further west than Eressëa. In addition to Frodo and Bilbo, a similar allowance is granted Sam and even Gimli, prior to their deaths.[94]

The Problem of the Half-Dead and the Undead

While Half-Elves and Halflings complicate the presumed differences between Human and Elven deaths, half-dead Humans add a darker complication. The Chief Nazgûl implies to Éowyn that Sauron possesses the power to rob a Human of its body while maintaining power over its soul (though the Nazgûl call it *mind*);[95] while readers should not take metaphysical assertions of Nazgûl as gospel truth, the assertion suggests the possibility of houseless Human Fëa, just as with the Elves. Other references to houseless Human Fëar, however, reveal a unique problem associated with them: large groups of not fully dead beings, capable of concerted corporate action. In contrast, the few references to houseless Elven Fëar suggest that such beings remain isolated problems in Middle-earth; no tales report armies of dead Elves.

Humans sometimes experience partial death en masse. The Númenórean troops that set foot on Aman, for example, receive special treatment due to the insolence shown by attacking the Valar. When Eru Ilúvatar empowers the Valar to change the shape of Arda, the Númenórean king and his warriors fall victim to a landslide; instead of traveling to the Halls of Mandos, their Fëar become trapped in the *Caves of the Forgotten* until the Last Battle at the end of Arda.[96] The description suggests those Humans do not experience conventional Human death, that they have not (yet) received the Gift of Ilúvatar. While those Humans are technically dead (their Fëar, presumably, separated from their Hröar), they are left entombed, in stasis or limbo (in the conventional sense, not the Dantean or Catholic sense), rather than being called to Mandos. They are the Human equivalent of Elvish houseless Fëar, except that houseless Fëar of Elves intentionally resisted the summons to Mandos, while the dead Númenórean troops are apparently denied a summons.

The dead Númenóreans parallel the wraiths Aragorn calls to aid his companions in battling the Corsairs of Umbar. They, too, appear to be disembodied Fëar that have not traveled to Mandos. Aragorn refers to them as the "Sleepless Dead," though the prophecy spoken of them by Malbeth the Seer describes them as if asleep in some sense: "The Dead [will] awaken," the prophecy said, when the destined hour of the Oathbreakers arrives. That prophecy places them into an in-between state, a dim twilight, where they are a "forgotten people."[97] Isuldur's curse denies them rest until they fulfill the oath of fealty sworn to him. Amendt-Raduege interprets the houseless status of such Fëar as indicating the Humans are "guilty of some sin."[98]

The narrative of the Paths of the Dead incorporates elements of mystery: Halbarad, Aragorn's kin, prophesies his own impending death; Legolas sings unknown words to comfort his horse; Gimli feels unaccountably afraid in an otherwise ideal Dwarf setting; and everyone feels an unseen terror. Legolas perceives a visual image of the dead, both Humans and horses; while they remain invisible to Humans and Dwarves, other modes of perception, such as sound, reveal them: Gimli notes a continuous murmuring of voices in an unrecognizable tongue. Then as the Dead begin to follow the Company, Gimli hears a shadowy sound of trampling feet. The movement and murmuring suggest sentience on the part of the dead; even more so does the voice of their leader when it responds to Aragorn's question as to why the Oathbreakers follow after him. The response, to keep the promise earlier broken and ultimately find peace,[99] implies that residing in Middle-earth as houseless Fëar is unsatisfying, both to the Sleepless Dead and to living Humans in their vicinity.

The situation of the half-dead seems to differ from that of *the undead,* the Nazgûl, though Tolkien queried himself in a draft as to whether the Nazgûl might in fact be Barrow-wights on horses.[100] The Barrow-wight that Frodo and his companions encounter, however, appears significantly different from the Nazgûl, since it apparently possesses a physical arm that Frodo can dismember with a sword. At the same time, its incantation, paying homage to "the dark lord"[101] (which I presume to be Sauron) and his goal of earthly destruction, suggests a spirit-being aligned with evil. Tolkien refers to Barrow-wights as evil beings from Angmar and Rhudaur;[102] as noted in chapter 1, spirit-beings that reside at length in bodies often become fixed within those bodies, especially if they decline in powers through dedication to evil. Perry agrees that Barrow-wights are "evil spirits," but differs in regard to their means of embodiment; rather than devising their own bodies, Perry suggests the Wights "animate the bodies of the dead,"[103] while Amendt-Raduege describes them as comparable to the undead: "ghostlike but not a ghost, living but not alive, haunting but also haunted."[104] Bombadil's extermination of the Wight, and his description of the Hobbits having returned from deep water, does little to clarify the Wight's nature.

The use of *un* as a prefix for the word *dead* suggests an opposition, as in *free* versus *unfree.* Stratyner sees *undead* as implying "a state of being which of all others in Middle-earth is least desirable."[105] Yet the undead can be comprehended in at least two ways: as houseless Fëar, or as invisible but embodied beings. Rawls embraces the first view, describing the Nazgûl as "a spectral existence," having "lost their corporeal forms." This explains why they lack the sense of sight and instead possess only "the uncanny extra senses bestowed by the rings,"[106] though descriptions of the Sleepless Dead do not imply any lack of sight. Faramir's description supports Rawls's view: the Nazgûl are Humans that fall into evil and are then consumed by Sauron's rings; as a result they exist simultaneously as ghosts and living beings.[107] Both the Sleepless Dead and the undead are wraiths, with the primary difference between the two external: the undead have Rings of Power (though kept by Sauron), enhancing certain abilities of the Nazgûl, and fixing their wills under the domination of Sauron; in contrast, the dead, while apparently prevented from journeying to Mandos, retain their free wills, such that they can choose to follow Aragorn (or presumably choose not to).

The alternate interpretation asserts that the undead remain embodied, but that their bodies become invisible. "Of the Rings of Power and the Third Age" describes the Humans on whom Sauron bestowed Rings as experiencing never-ending life, but claims their dependent immortality becomes insufferable for them. Davis explains that "*not* dying is a curse. . . . [T]he undead *cannot* die, and that is part of their punishment for their greed." Davis notes that Tolkien follows Aristotle in accepting that to exist in an "unnatural" state "is worse than death."[108] At first the Nazgûl retain their own wills, but ultimately each comes under the authority of Sauron's Ring. They then become permanently invisible to everyone but Sauron; more accurately, they dwell within the shadow realm. While the passage adds that Nazgûl wail with voices sounding like death,[109] it carefully avoids saying that the undead actually died. Thus Kocher asserts that they "inhabit their original bodies, but these have faded and thinned in their component matter until they can no longer be said to exist in the dimension of the living."[110] Kisor agrees: "the fading wrought by the Ring refers to invisibility, not insubstantiality. It is a question of appearance, not being."[111] Shippey concurs, though he reduces the Nazgûls' physicality to the minimum possible, comparing them to smoke, "physical . . . but at the same time effectively intangible."[112]

Whether the undead are most appropriately described as somewhat alive (that is, Fëar retaining Hröar) or mostly dead (that is, Fëar separated from Hröar), the Chief Nazgûl apparently experiences full death at the hands and weapons of Éowyn and Merry. At least one passage suggests a separation of the Chief Nazgûl's Fëa from Hröa; Merry's sword "cleaves the undead flesh," thus ending the spell that allows its mind to operate its unseen body. Other passages speak more vaguely, such as the line in *The Return of the King* describing only the Nazgûl's voice as thin and bodiless, drifting away with the wind; the sound of the voice dies, the narrator adding that it is never again heard.[113]

Equally uncertain is where the Chief Nazgûl (and, presumably, the remaining eight several weeks later) go following the transition from undead to dead. "Of the Rings of Power" describes the Chief Nazgûl entering into darkness. It earlier describes the Nazgûl as carrying darkness with them, so entering darkness pictures the Chief Nazgûl consumed by its own weapon. Earlier still, however, Gandalf's words to the Witch King imply a more or less spatial fate, *the abyss*, prepared especially for the Nazgûl; Gandalf follows this description with another even more ambiguous, to enter into nothingness, prepared not only for the Nazgûl, but for Sauron as well.[114]

Gandalf's use of *nothingness* and *the abyss* calls to mind the concept of *the Void*, which Melkor explored prior to the creation of Eä, an activity associated with his rebellion against Eru; the Void may also be the place where Melkor was sent, perhaps even imprisoned, at the end of the First Age. Garabowski, however, sees in Gandalf's injunctions "an impression of hell without the common ontological metaphor of flames." Specifically, the image "approach[es] one modern theological view of hell as ultimately a kind of annihilation, or non-being."[115]

While the focus of this section is the complications that arise from hybrid creatures such as Half Elves and Nazgûl, those complications in turn impact understanding of the Elves, since Tolkien asserts that the High Elves live in both the seen and unseen worlds, the latter of which he associates with the Nazgûl. Notes from Tolkien's manuscripts suggest even he remained unsure what the assertion meant.[116] Kocher speculates: "Elves have learned to penetrate also into that ambiguous region where life verges upon death. The Valar have taught them how."[117] Frodo the Halfling enters at least briefly this "ambiguous region" as he begins to fade after being stabbed with a Morgul blade at Weathertop. By the time of his arrival at the Ford of Bruinen, Frodo has lost some of his ability to perceive the real world around him, but gained an ability to perceive the otherwise invisible Nazgûl as realities (as well as an enhanced sense of Glorfindel). Flieger notes that Frodo, after being healed by Elrond, appears to Gandalf's eye as transforming "into translucency rather than darkness."[118] Thus Frodo's experience parallels, rather than directly follows, the decline of the Nazgûl into undeath.

Death for an Ainu

Death as a transition state from one mode of existence to another forms a universal aspect of the sentient material life-forms of Middle-earth. Thorin the Dwarf describes his own imminent death as entering chambers of waiting, where he will join his forefathers until the end of Arda; his words suggest a period of conscious rest, much like the Elves experience in the Halls of Mandos. A later manuscript suggests the Dwarves spend their time in the chambers improving their crafts and expanding their knowledge.[119] Even Gorbag's words to Shagrat, overheard by Sam, suggest Orc death as a transition from one state into another, rather than annihilation; the Nazgûl, Gorbag asserts, were inclined to "skin the body off" underlings with whom they are displeased, apparently separating the underling's Fëa from Hröa; such an action leaves the being "all cold in the dark on the other side."[120] *The Book of Lost Tales* narrates the death of Carcharoth, the wolf-monster bred by Sauron (and thus seemingly purely animal in nature), as a spirit leaving a body and rushing (while "howling faintly") to Mandos.[121]

Because death involves separation of Fëa from Hröa, it primarily concerns beings with bodies: Elves, Humans, Hobbits, and the other sentient beings of Middle-earth. And since *The Lord of the Rings, The Hobbit,* and *The Silmarillion* all depict primarily Elf, Human, and Hobbit perspectives on reality, death as a subtheme of Tolkien's narratives comes as no surprise. Also no surprise is ignorance of what death might mean for nonembodied beings. Yet in the few scenes depicting death for an Ainu or Maia, it, too, is described as separation of spirit from body (as with Gandalf's death, discussed in chapter 3).

Lúthien, herself half Maia, imagines or prophesies death as applied to Sauron, threatening him with the jaws of Huan if Sauron does not betray Melkor and surrender the keys of his fortress. Sauron's death, Lúthien asserts, would involve his spirit returning in fear to endure Melkor's contempt and anger; she implies that Melkor would imprison Sauron's naked soul, which would babble and cry eternally. In an alternate passage, Lúthien imagines Sauron in death "languish[ing] in the dark bosom of the world."[122]

To "languish" and to babble and cry suggest Sauron's death, had it occurred, would not have involved a complete cessation of being, but rather a transformation from one state to another. Lúthien's surmises describe simple disembodiment, without loss of consciousness. Loss of embodiment has major ramifications for a being such as Sauron. Like Melkor, Sauron has become more and more dependent on his embodiment to exert power. Thus, death as applied to a Maia-level Ainur in Middle-earth, particularly one who has been dedicated to evil, results in loss of effectiveness, not complete loss of existence. Of course, to exist without power to effect one's desire is a severe frustration.

Sauron does indeed yield to Lúthien (thank goodness! One can hardly imagine *The Lord of the Rings* without him), and over the subsequent two ages he experiences some of what Lúthien prophesied on at least three separate occasions. At the drowning of Númenor, Sauron is reduced to mere spirit, losing the embodied form through which he has exerted evil power. That spirit returns to Mordor where it dwells in darkness and silence, until Sauron consolidates his power to reembody. Then at his battle with the Last Alliance, as Isuldur cuts the One Ring from Sauron's hand, Sauron abandons his body, his spirit hiding in a deserted region of Middle-earth. He remains disembodied for a long time, but eventually reforms himself into the Eye of Sauron. Perhaps the Eye serves as metonym for an entire body; or perhaps the eye *is* the entirety of Sauron's body. When Frodo, with Gollum, destroys the One Ring, Sauron is completely vanquished,[123] a permanent defeat, the narrative implies. Yet other language suggests that Sauron, as a sentient being, is not destroyed. Appendix B of *The Return of the King* uses the word *passing* to explain Sauron's death, which suggests a transition into a disembodied state.

Similar language describes the deaths of both Melkor and Saruman. Melkor is forcibly disembodied and imprisoned within the Timeless Void. Two important aspects characterize the Void. First, it is outside Eä (or so the word *Timeless* implies); second, it is outside the presence of Eru Ilúvatar. The situation resembles Napoleon living in exile on Saint Helena, though a science fiction trope of becoming trapped in an alternate dimension, inaccessible to the space-time continuum, might be more appropriate. Saruman's death parallels Melkor's. *Unfinished Tales* describes him as thrown down, thoroughly humbled, and completely dead, phrases implying finality. The follow-up phrase, however, clarifies the nature of that finality, indicating that Saruman's spirit goes to the place appointed as its doom, with a location specified only as not in Middle-earth.[124] Shippey sees Saruman becoming, in essence, a wraith, "hoping for some forgiveness from the Valar,"[125] but not receiving it.

✐ Conclusion

Death for a being that begins its existence as an Ainur suggests several truths about death in Tolkien's legendarium. First it emphasizes the Augustinian worldview. Being relegated to the Timeless Void sounds less horrible, perhaps, than being consigned to hell, but it must be less pleasant than the presence of Eru Ilúvatar, or the physical world of Middle-earth where one can exert one's powers according to one's Eru-given nature. Second, it clarifies a limitation placed on the Valar as rulers of Arda that shapes their ethics. While the Valar serve as authorities, they lack the power to terminate a soul. That right belongs exclusively to Eru Ilúvatar, though Tolkien's stories never show Eru exercising such authority, and his continued tolerance of Melkor's existence, even in the Timeless Void, suggests he is loath to exercise it. Respect for Fëar forms a bedrock principal of Eru's dealings with his own creation, and seems to have prompted the extreme tolerance and patience exhibited toward Melkor's and Sauron's insistence on incorporating evil into Arda; of course, that tolerance allows Melkor and Sauron to disrespect Fëar, and Fëar/Hröar combinations, that are lower in the metaphysical hierarchy.

The existence of the half-dead and the undead reveals the ambiguity surrounding the concept of death. Typically, the term implies, within Tolkien's writings, a temporary and sometimes reversible condition; Elves can be reincarnated, Humans have a certain destiny beyond Arda, and even Melkor may still indirectly influence phenomena in Eä. Yet at the same time death implies an irrevocable finality. While Humans have a certain destiny beyond Arda, they have no guarantee that their destiny will take the shape of life as they know it, or even that it will involve consciousness, let alone embodiment. Similarly, the Elves' immortality is contingent upon the existence of Arda; while Elves may hope in an afterlife (and while Eru's dedication to what Christians refer to as *the immortality of the soul* seems to make that hope a safe one), Elves have no promise of life after Arda. They may face eternal nothingness.

Ultimately the fates of Humans, Elves, and rebellious Ainur may be beyond Human comprehension. Said another way, Tolkien may have perceived himself writing about a subject he could not settle satisfactorily about his own creation. Thus, perhaps the only answer one can provide in response to questions of ultimate destiny is: Eru knows.

Chapter 7

Eucatastrophe, *Estel,* and the End of Arda

olkien's manuscript of *The Lost Road* includes a "Song of Fíriel," sung by a young woman in the household of Elendil in the last days of Númenor. The Song summarizes Arda's cosmology, attributing the creation of the world to The Father, who destined it for Elves and Humans, under the authority of the Valar. The Valar, it continues, are beloved by Elves and Humans (no longer uniformly true at that stage of Númenor's history), blessed and holy, and residing in the West, except for the fallen Melkor, who no longer exists in Arda. Fíriel's song, however, does not address merely the beginning of time to the then-present; instead, it reminds listeners that the cosmos, as understood in Middle-earth, has two temporal boundaries: a beginning, but also an end. As this study has examined, life, death, and the presence of evil, all can be traced to the Singing of the Ainur and Eru's creation of the world. Yet the Singing of the Ainur came to a definite conclusion, based on the divine will of Eru, just as the cosmic structures of Arda will conclude.

The end of Arda, and even the end of Eä, does not necessarily mean an end for its sentient beings. Just as the Valar preceded Eä as Ainur, they may be permitted an exit at Arda's end, perhaps resuming their earlier status. The unique nature of Humans, the desire implanted in them by Eru for something beyond Arda, along with statements about Humans by the Valar and speculation about them by the Elves, testifies to Human destiny beyond Eä. If the Valar represent the metaphysical dimension of Arda, that which is beyond the world's physical reality, then Human destiny beyond Eä, as well as the existence of Eru and the Ainur outside Eä, might be described as meta-metaphysical, that which is beyond both the physical and spiritual dimensions of Arda. Fíriel's song concludes with an acknowledgment of the end of Arda and the Human desire for something more, beyond that end: "But my heart resteth not here for ever [*sic*]; for here is ending, and there will be an end and the Fading, when all is counted, and all numbered at last, but yet it will not be enough, not enough. What will the Father, O Father, give me in that day beyond the end when my sun faileth?"[1]

Tolkien recognizes Fíriel's desire for meaning and existence beyond the temporal-spatial bounds of physical reality as a fundamental element of Human life on Earth; he considers it the most primal Human desire, which he labels "the Great Escape" from death.[2] That desire parallels, Tolkien notes, the desire within readers for a happy ending to a faerie story.

Tolkien coined the term *eucatastrophe* to describe "the sudden happy turn in a story which pierces you with a joy that brings tears."[3] Happy endings, he theorizes, form essential structural elements in stories, in part, because they prefigure the happy ending Christianity asserts for Earth: the elimination of death and evil, ushering in an eternity of peace and joy. Such an ending for Earth can hardly be imagined without divine intervention. Tolkien insists, however, that even smaller eucatastrophic moments offer evidence of divine intervention, as when Bilbo proclaims the coming of the Eagles in the climactic battle of *The Hobbit*.[4] Eucatastrophe, literally *good catastrophe,* reveals "a sudden and miraculous grace: never to be counted on to recur."[5]

Understanding eucatastrophe is crucial to grasping Tolkien and his work. As a structural element, it shapes many of his narratives. As Drury notes, "small eucatastrophes contribute to [the story's] developing pattern," suggesting an ultimate happy ending, while implying divine involvement in events such as "close escapes."[6] Thus a eucatastrophic moment such as the flooding of the Bruinen that (temporarily) washes away the Ringwraiths, masterminded by Elrond and aided by Gandalf, prefigures the moment when the One Ring, beyond all hope, falls into the fires of Mount Doom. Tolkien himself identifies the reunion of the surviving members of the Fellowship, and the glorification of Frodo and Sam, as *The Lord of the Ring*'s eucatastrophe.[7]

On a deeper level, the concept of eucatastrophe shapes the history of Middle-earth. Mende suggests *The Lord of the Rings* provides resolution for *The Silmarillion* in part because *The Lord of the Rings* emphasizes eucatastrophe. Even beyond the two books, eucatastrophe structures the full history of Eä. The final, climactic chord that ends the Singing of the Ainur is accomplished by Eru Ilúvatar himself. It is unforeseen yet provides a fit conclusion. Thus, hints regarding a similarly fit but unforeseen end of all things, or at least of all Arda, arises at various moments in Tolkien's writings. Andreth, in her debate with Finrod, mentions a prophecy of future, ultimate eucatastrophe, that Eru himself will one day enter Arda, providing healing for Humans and overcoming Melkor's marring.[8]

As a tool for coping with the obvious evil one encounters in the everyday world, eucatastrophe fosters hope, *estel* in Elvish. In the face of defeat, pain, and suffering, recognizing eucatastrophe inoculates one against despair. Drury notes that "a pattern of hope" permeates *The Lord of the Rings,* a fact that causes Hyles to assert that the book "vehemently declares that hope is a viable alternative in the face of evil."[9] Assertions of estel appear within all hierarchical levels of creatures in Tolkien's mythology. The Valar desire eucatastrophe; *The Book of Lost Tales* describes the Valar foreseeing, at the regularization of the sun and moon (and thus the regularization of time), a slow waning of their powers until the end when Eru Ilúvatar will return them to their former states. In fact, even evil creatures hope for eucatastrophe; Hammond and Scull interpret the song of the Barrow-wight (from the "Fog on the Barrow-Downs" chapter of *The Fellowship of the Ring*) as a hopeful prophecy, or wishful thinking, of a dead land conquered by Melkor.[10]

While eucatastrophe for a Barrow-wight would be plain catastrophe for the good beings of Middle-earth, Hammond and Scull's interpretation suggests that even the most corrupt beings cling to a hope for eucatastrophe (though the desired eucatastrophe of evil beings is itself a corruption). Tolkien's practice of championing eucatastrophe in his writing, every bit as much as his embrace of fantasy, separates his work from the literary naturalism of other writers of his era, who often embrace a bleak, hopeless view of Humans as victims in the face of capriciously overwhelming but impersonal forces. Yet eucatastrophe implies more than mere hope, but rather faith in a powerful divinity's ability and desire to produce ultimate happy endings. Eucatastrophic moments, therefore, are *evangelium,* showing the possibility of a divinely induced joy outside of both Arda and Earth.[11]

Glimpses of eucatastrophic evangelium, however, remain fleeting in Tolkien's work. Garbowski sees eucatastrophes as counterbalanced by death; since "Tolkien did not wish to offer any easy consolation in his treatment of death,"[12] he refrains from the *happily ever after* convention. Tolkien acknowledges that the long ending following the defeat of Sauron in *The Return of the King* shows that such victories come with costs; at least until the final, barely imaginable, ultimate healing of Arda, not even earth-shaking victories can be considered final.[13] Yet eucatastrophe, without an ultimate victory of good over evil, is merely a tease, a prolonging of the inevitable bad end and the offering of a false hope.

This chapter will examine the ultimate eucatastrophe of the history of Arda, the final Armageddon-like battle bringing an end both to Arda and to Melkor's rebellion, and the subsequent establishment of Arda Healed. The narratives of this event provide a fitting bookend to the "Ainulindalë" story of creation. They also suffer from the same logical impossibilities of the creation narrative; if the end of Arda is the end of time, then it makes no more sense to speak of events *after* the end of the world than it does to speak of events *prior to* the creation of time. Nonetheless, the Elves embrace both logical impossibilities, presumably with the assumption that neither is impossible for Eru Ilúvatar. And as will be shown, divine intervention of the highest magnitude will be required to achieve the ultimate eucatastrophe of Arda.

✸ *The End of Arda*

The "Music of the Ainur" section of *The Book of Lost Tales* refers to Arda's ultimate eucatastrophe as *the Great End* (elsewhere calling it *the Great Wrack*), an event prophesied in *The Lost Tales* even prior to the narrative of the origin of evil,[14] the phenomenon making eucatastrophe necessary. In the famous letter to Milton Waldman in which the author overviews his mythology, Tolkien admits a basis for Middle-earth's Last Battle in Ragnorök, the end of the world in Norse mythology, which Shippey calls "the Norse Armageddon."[15] While acknowledging his debt, Tolkien also declares that the end of Middle-earth differs significantly from the Norse myth. Birzer suggests an additional source beyond Norse legends, and much closer to Tolkien's personal religious views: descriptions of the Apocalypse in the biblical book of Revelation.[16]

The manuscript labeled by Christopher Tolkien "The Earliest 'Silmarillion'" provides a full description of the apocalyptic end of Arda. After much time, the Valar will grow weary. Melkor will return, perhaps in embodied form, for the final battle, named Dagor Dagorath. The two chief proponents of this battle will be the Maia Eönwë and Turin, or rather, Turin's spirit. The location of this great Armageddon will be central Aman, where Turin will kill Melkor using his treasured black sword, thus providing an ultimate vengeance for Húrin, Húrin's family, and the rest of humanity. Christopher Tolkien spoke of this moment as the deification of Turin, whose involvement may fulfill Ulmo's prophecy that Arda can only be restored with help from Humans, or the somewhat vague impression among the Wise of the Elves that Humans are destined to play a central role in the transition from Arda Marred to Arda Healed. The Elves view the constellation Menelmakar, the Swordsman of the Sky, as prophetic of Turin's involvement in the Last Battle. Eärendil, too, will descend from the heavens for the battle. Yet the combined forces of Valar, Elves, Turin, and Eärendil will not be enough to conquer Melkor; Finrod reasons that Eru must participate directly, otherwise Melkor will gain the mastery.[17] Eru's intervention in the drowning of Númenor thus foreshadows similar intervention in the Last Battle.

Subsequent to the battle, the two missing Silmarils will be recovered (in some unspecified manner) and their composition finally made known. Maedhros, the son of Fëanor, will crack open all three and Yavanna will use their light to restore life to the Two Trees. The mountains the Valar raised to protect Aman from attack will be leveled, allowing the light of the Two Trees to spread across the sea to Middle-earth; "Gods and Elves and Men shall grow young again, and all their dead awake," the manuscript asserts, though Tolkien later crosses out the words "and Men," adding instead that the prophecy says nothing of Humans, other than the role of Turin.[18] How the dead will awaken (given that dead Elves remain conscious in the Halls of Mandos) remains unexplained.

Tolkien provides several variant end-time prophecies. In one Manwë will remain atop his mountain in Aman until the last days, which will witness various cataclysmic events. Treebeard's prophecy on his parting from Celeborn and Galadriel suggests lands covered in water at the end of the First Age will reemerge. Another prophecy foretells the destruction of the sun and moon; Eönwë, out of his love for the sun, will then destroy the world, in turn destroying Melkor; after the rekindling of the Two Trees has spread their light across the world, the sun and moon will reappear. In yet another version, Melkor will destroy the sun and moon, and Eärendil will descend as a bright flame to attack him, forcing Melkor out of the heavens and onto earth, where Tulkas will fight him, joined by Eönwë on his right and Turin on his left; Yavanna will break open the Silmarils, and as the Gods grow young and the dead Elves awaken, Eru's purposes concerning his Children will be fulfilled.[19] Humans have no role in this version either, except for Turin, who is "name[d] among the Gods," changed to "among the sons of the Gods," and later still "among the sons of the Valar."[20]

Ultimately, the Ainur, joined, perhaps, by the Children of Ilúvatar, or perhaps only by Humans, will sing a music even greater than the original Music of the Ainur. In this Second Music, Eru's themes will be performed as they should have been the first time, since the performers will fully understand his intentions and their role in producing them. Eru will be completely pleased by the rendition and will implant within it the Secret Fire.[21] While the passage is cast as summative, as bringing the history of Arda to a grand finale, a coming full circle for the story of the world, it leaves the possibility of something more. If the first Music of the Ainur was generative, then so, too, might be the last; while the Ainur contributed to the first Singing in ignorance, their full understanding in the Second Music implies complete harmony. And Eru's contributing the Secret Fire to the thought expressed in the Singing may be the mechanism for producing Arda Healed, a new physical/temporal reality, which may form a habitation for Humans, perhaps the Elves, maybe even Valar and Maiar.

Arda Healed may or may not be the Arda intended by Eru when he propounded themes for the Great Music of the Ainur. Davis interprets Middle-earth's end-time prophecies to suggest that the "Ainulindalë" will take on its original, intended form at the end of days: "when the Ainur are completely merged in the consciousness of the divine, in tune, then their music creates instantaneously."[22] However, Elves speculate that Arda Healed will not be the same as Arda Unmarred, the world that Elves could imagine, had it come into existence untainted by Melkor's rebellion. Rather, according to the words of Manwë himself, Arda Healed will possess added beauty as a result of Melkor's marring, a result that only Eru Ilúvatar can produce by direct intervention: a eucatastrophe.[23]

Andreth refers to this as "the Great Hope" and speculates that Arda Healed will be a third thing, neither Arda Marred nor Arda Unmarred; instead, Arda Healed will incorporate the history of Arda Marred. She questions even whether the triumphant final chord of the First Music of the Ainur is truly final; perhaps the Valar are so overwhelmed by the Music's apparent end that they remain unaware of that which continues. Alternatively, she suggests, since Eru is not himself bound and restricted by the Music, perhaps he envisions more than he shares with the Ainur; perhaps the Music, and the subsequent vision, foretell the future only to a limited extent, beyond which will be unknowable until it arrives. Here Andreth enacts in her dialogue with Finrod the distinction that Elves often note in regard to Humans; while Elves are bound by the Music of the Ainur as if it is fate, Humans possess an Eru-given power to redirect their lives, a power the Elves consider strange since it gives Humans the ability to counteract and work against the goals of the Valar.[24] On the intellectual level, Andreth shows that the strange ability involves *thinking outside the box* of the Music of the Ainur.

Arda Healed may allow for continued Elvish-Human interaction. Some Eldar postulate that Elves and Humans might merge into one group, or that some Humans, if they don't live in the New Arda, might at least visit occasionally. Finrod, for example, in his debate with Andreth, recalls a vision of a refashioned Arda in which the Elves, "completed but not ended," sing songs to Humans, in inexpressible joy. Perhaps Human and Elf existence within Arda Healed might still require physical reality, or if not required, physical embodiment may remain occasionally enjoyable for the Children of Ilúvatar. Some Elves speculate that, after the end of Arda, they will dwell in Arda Healed but will not be restricted to that world. Thus, Elves and Humans might be transformed into pure spirits, yet still permitted to reenter time at will, though only during the era of Arda Healed. Finrod describes the concept as "abid[ing] in the present forever."[25]

Elsewhere Tolkien theorizes two differing understandings of Arda Healed as either existing outside time such that Arda's history can be perceived all at once, or yet within time but without the marring instigated by Melkor. The Elves, he notes, often accept both options. Not to be left out, Dwarves assert (despite the Noldorin Elves' assumption that on death Dwarves return to stone, and Tolkien's statement that Elves and Humans know nothing about Dwarves' eternal destiny) that Aulë will provide them a position among the Children of Eru; specifically, they assume their craft skills will play a prominent role in re-making Arda. Even Ents may have a place in the afterlife, perhaps finally becoming reunited with the Entwives.[26] Hobbits, in contrast, do not speculate about the end of the world; instead, as Shippey notes, they practice a coping strategy of refusing "ever to look into the future at all."[27]

Tempering these visions of future bliss, manuscripts emphasize that speculation, even prophecy, about the end should not be considered revelation; while one manuscript quotes Manwë predicting a healing for Arda, another leaves only the possibility that Manwë and Varda *might* possess such knowledge, but suggests neither they nor Mandos reveal specific details. This uncertainty is of greatest concern for the Elves. As noted in the previous chapter, Elves assert confidently that Human death involves leaving Arda, and apparently leaving the temporal-spatial limitations of Eä; Humans, in other words, have an exit from the finite history of Middle-earth. Elves do not hold the same confidence about their own destinies; though given immortality, their lives and fates are intricately connected with the history of Arda. Despite speculation and prophecy, the Elves, and perhaps even the Valar, have no definite knowledge of their fates after the end of Arda. Tolkien's earliest expression of this thought claims that the Elves know that Humans will sing in the Second Music of the Ainur, though Eru's plans for the Eldar remain unknown.[28]

Yet lack of complete certainty about the future does not necessarily work against estel. Eru Ilúvatar's dedication to the immortality of the souls he creates forms one reason to hope that he has some plan for the Elves, even if Eä is no more. Words spoken by Elves to the people of Númenor, when those people grow mistrustful of Eru's postdeath intention for them, speak with equal force to the Elves: Ilúvatar will not allow created beings who love him and his creation to perish utterly; thus Elves (and Humans) must trust, and trust, if given to Eru, "will not be despised."[29] Furthermore, Elven Fëar come from outside of Eä, direct from Eru; their origin outside Eä suggests their ultimate destiny also lies there.

Yet Tolkien provides the Elves with nothing more than estel. Tolkien (taking the role of commentator on an established tradition, a position he often espouses about his own writing) speculates Eru provides no further details on the end because Eru insists that his Children exhibit belief in his existence and goodness, and from that to assume hope for the future,[30] which positions estel as a central theme of Tolkien's Middle-earth writings. Ultimately this hope is faith in eucatastrophe and the divine beings that enact it: no matter how messy, convoluted, and inhabited by evil the events of Arda may become, Eru Ilúvatar will ultimately transform them into beauty and good.

🖋 Conclusion

Still, for the Elves, the poignancy of Fíriel's song, quoted at the beginning of this chapter, remains: *what will Eru provide on that day beyond the end?* While Tolkien hints at various possibilities, he does not resolve the question. Perhaps Tolkien's concept of eucatastrophe provides some explanation as to why Eru, as the ultimate creator of Arda, and Tolkien as the creator of Eru, does not provide a more definitive vision of eternal bliss: why, in other words, neither creator embraces the clichéd ending, *and they lived happily ever after.* Ultimate eucatastrophe, putting an end to evil and suffering, would also mean an end to eucatastrophe. Arda Healed will have no further need for divine intervention providing glimpses of evangelium; instead, evangelium will have been achieved.

Ultimate eucatastrophe means an end of hope: not a hopeless world, but one in which hope is no longer necessary. The hoped-for will have arrived. Yet, as Tolkien shows, eucatastrophe forms such an integral element of the lived experience of the Children of Eru (as well as the humans of Earth) that living in a world no longer needing eucatastrophe seems unfathomable. Ultimate eucatastrophe, like story itself and philosophical examinations of cosmology, is an attempt to express the inexpressible, or as Tolkien says in a letter to Rhona Beare, an attempt "to express, in the only way I can, some of my (dim) apprehensions of the world."[31]

Notes

🖋 Introduction

1. Tolkien, *The Letters,* 220.
2. Flieger, *Interrupted Music,* 36–37.
3. Tolkien, *The Letters,* 193.
4. Moorman, "'Now Entertain Conjecture of a Time,'" 62.
5. Caldecott, *Secret Fire,* 117.
6. Ellwood, "The Good Guys," 11.
7. Pearce, "The Hidden Evangelism," 32.
8. Urang, *Shadows of Heaven,* 120.
9. Brawley, *Nature and the Numinous,* 94; emphasis in the original.
10. Madsen, "Light from an Invisible Lamp," 43.
11. Bossert. "'Surely You Don't Disbelieve,'" 74.
12. Tolkien, *The Letters,* 275, 288, 355.
13. Ring, "Ad Valar Defendendi," 18.
14. Tolkien, *The Letters,* 243, 283, 220.
15. Dickerson, *Following Gandalf,* 93.
16. *Tolkien on Fairy-stories,* 65.
17. *Tolkien on Fairy-stories,* 66.
18. Tolkien, *The Lost Road,* 388.
19. Tolkien, *Mr. Baggins,* 48.
20. Moseley, *J. R. R. Tolkien,* 37.
21. *Tolkien on Fairy-stories,* 253; Tolkien, *The Letters,* 271.
22. Scull and Hammond, *The J. R. R. Tolkien Companion and Guide: Reader's Guide,* 331.
23. A recollection of Anthony Curtis, qtd. in Scull and Hammond, *The J. R. R. Tolkien Companion and Guide: Chronology,* 611.
24. Tolkien, *The Letters,* 145, 210.
25. Apeland, "On Entering the Same River Twice," 44.
26. Tolkien, *The Letters,* 260.

27. *Tolkien on Fairy-stories,* 226.
28. Tolkien, *The Book of Lost Tales,* 1:44.
29. Tolkien, *The Silmarillion,* xii.
30. Purdy, Letter to the Editor, 34.
31. Flieger, *Splintered Light,* xiii.
32. Shippey, *The Road to Middle-earth,* 169.
33. Tolkien, *Morgoth's Ring,* 370.
34. Krueger, "The Shaping of 'Reality,'" 251.
35. Lobdell, *The World of the Rings,* 49.
36. Fuller, "The Lord of the Hobbits," 18.
37. Wright, "The Vision of Cosmic Order," 263.
38. Purtill, *The Lord of the Elves and Eldils,* 104.
39. Grotta, *J. R. R. Tolkien,* 96.
40. Qtd. in Larsen, "[V]Arda Marred," 31.
41. Kane, *Arda Reconstructed,* 252.
42. Tolkien, *The Lost Road,* 333; Tolkien, *Morgoth's Ring,* x; see also Tolkien, *The Book of Lost Tales,* 1:xiv–xv.
43. Tolkien, *Morgoth's Ring,* 205; Tolkien, *The War of the Jewels,* 298; Tolkien, *Unfinished Tales,* 3.

🖋 *1. Tolkien's Cosmogony and Pantheon*

1. Tolkien, *The Letters,* 146.
2. Kosyfi, "Ancient Greek Gods," 47.
3. Burns, "Norse and Christian Gods," 166, 168.
4. Tolkien, *The Letters,* 205.
5. Tolkien, *The Book of Lost Tales,* 1:45, 293; McIntosh, *The Flame Imperishable,* 50–51.
6. Flieger, *Splintered Light,* 50.
7. Tolkien, *Morgoth's Ring,* 345, 322, 329.
8. Upstone, "Applicability and Truth," 60.
9. Tolkien, *The Letters,* 204; Tolkien, *The Book of Lost Tales,* 1:283.
10. Williams, "The Everlasting Hobbit."
11. Veldhoen, "J. R. R. Tolkien," 1–14.
12. Eden, "The 'Music of the Spheres,'" 192; Flieger, *Splintered Light,* 59.
13. Tolkien, *The Silmarillion,* 3.
14. Tolkien, *The Letters,* 284, 345.
15. Tolkien, *The Silmarillion,* 3.
16. Tolkien, *The Silmarillion,* 3.
17. Tolkien, *The Silmarillion,* 3; Tolkien, *The Lost Road,* 174.
18. Tolkien, *The Silmarillion,* 3.
19. Hart, "Tolkien, Creation and Creativity," 44.
20. Knight, "*The Magical World of the Inklings,*" 113.

21. Tolkien, *The Lost Road,* 171.
22. Naveh, "Tonality, Atonality, and the 'Ainulindalë,'" 31.
23. Nagy, "Saving the Myths," 93.
24. Lewis, *The Discarded Image,* 92.
25. Eden, "Music in Middle-earth," 444–45.
26. Tolkien, *The Silmarillion,* 6.
27. McIntosh, "Ainulindalë," 60; Eden, "Elves," 151; Sammons, *War of the Fantasy Worlds,* 47; McIntosh, *The Flame Imperishable,* 140–41.
28. Tolkien, *The Silmarillion,* 7.
29. Klinger, "Hidden Paths of Time," 175.
30. Flieger, *Interrupted Music,* xii.
31. Tolkien, "Fate and Free Will," 187. Here I dare to disagree with my esteemed colleague, Flieger, who reads the "Ainulindalë" to infer that the Singing of the Ainur was left incomplete (*Interrupted Music,* xii).
32. Tolkien, *The Letters,* 284; Tolkien, *The Book of Lost Tales,* 1:50.
33. Tolkien, *The Silmarillion,* 4; Tolkien, *The Lost Road,* 180, 70.
34. Tolkien, *The Silmarillion,* 4.
35. Tolkien, *The War of the Jewels,* 341; Tolkien, *The Silmarillion,* 4; Tolkien, *The Lost Road,* 172.
36. Naveh, "Tonality, Atonality, and the 'Ainulindalë,'" 39.
37. Tolkien, *The Silmarillion,* 4; Tolkien, *The Lost Road,* 173; Tolkien, *Morgoth's Ring,* 9.
38. Tolkien, "Ósanwe-kenta," 30n3.
39. Naveh, "Tonality, Atonality, and the 'Ainulindalë,'" 31–32. My student, Kayla Wilson, has argued that Eru's amiable reaction to Melkor's discord implies that Eru is not upset with Melkor, and offers as explanation a Calvinist reading of the text that sees Melkor's actions as predestined by Eru.
40. Tolkien, *The Lost Road,* 173.
41. Tolkien, *The Lost Road,* 173; Tolkien, *The Silmarillion,* 5; Tolkien, *The Book of Lost Tales,* 1:51.
42. Tolkien, *Morgoth's Ring,* 10.
43. Elam, "The Ainulindalë," 61.
44. Tolkien, *The Silmarillion,* 6.
45. Tolkien, *The Lost Road,* 174.
46. Hood, "Nature and Technology," 7.
47. Tolkien, *The Letters,* 287.
48. Tolkien, *The Book of Lost Tales,* 1:52.
49. Tolkien, *The Book of Lost Tales,* 1:52.
50. Crabbe, *J. R. R. Tolkien* (rev. ed.).
51. Tolkien, *The Letters,* 284.
52. McIntosh, "Ainulindalë," 70.
53. Tolkien, *The Silmarillion,* 9.
54. Tolkien, "From 'Quendi and Eldar,'" 20n20 (the bracketed word indicates the editor's best guess based on a barely legible manuscript); Tolkien, *The Letters,* 259.

55. After publication of *The Lord of the Rings*, Tolkien began to use the word *Arda* to mean the solar system, rather than Earth, and *Imbar*, defined as *The Habitation*, for the Earth (Tolkien, *Morgoth's Ring*, 337, 349).

56. Tolkien, *The Book of Lost Tales*, 1:246–47; Tolkien, *The Silmarillion*, 82; Tolkien, *Morgoth's Ring*, 336; Tolkien, *The Letters*, 284.

57. Shippey, *J. R. R. Tolkien*, 237.

58. Tolkien, *The Lost Road*, 176; Tolkien, *The Silmarillion*, 9; Tolkien, "Ósanwe-kenta," 24; Tolkien, *Morgoth's Ring*, 425; Klinger, "Hidden Paths of Time," 176.

59. Tolkien, *Morgoth's Ring*, 350; Tolkien, "Ósanwe-kenta," 24.

60. Birzer, "Eru," 171; Garbowski, *Recovery and Transcendence*, 84.

61. I am indebted to my student, Isaac Carreon, for suggesting the parallel between Eru's distance from his creation and Deism.

62. Tolkien, *The Book of Lost Tales*, 1:45.

63. Tolkien, *The Letters*, 204; Flieger, *Splintered Light*, 53.

64. Rosebury, *Tolkien: A Cultural Phenomenon*, 189.

65. McIntosh, *The Flame Imperishable*, 61.

66. Tolkien, *The Lost Road*, 53.

67. Hutton, "The Pagan Tolkien," 66.

68. Shippey, "Mythology, Germanic," 450.

69. Burns, "Norse and Christian Gods," 176.

70. Hart, "Tolkien, Creation and Creativity," 43.

71. Rosebury, *Tolkien: A Cultural Phenomenon*, 107.

72. Tolkien, *The Letters*, 284.

73. Burns, "All in One," 2–11.

74. Agøy, "The Fall and Man's Mortality," 26.

75. Tolkien, *The Letters*, 146.

76. Tolkien, *The Silmarillion*, 15.

77. Tolkien, *The Letters*, 146.

78. Tolkien, *The Letters*, 368.

79. Flieger, *Splintered Light*, 54.

80. Pearce, *Tolkien: Man and Myth*, 91.

81. Tolkien, *Morgoth's Ring*, 16.

82. I am grateful to my student, Katie Huffman, for pointing out the significance of Valian personality.

83. Whittingham, *The Evolution of Tolkien's Mythology*, 82.

84. Burns, "All in One," 11.

85. Bruce, "The Fall of Gondolin," 112.

86. Wood, "The Silmarillion," 12.

87. Masson, "Mythology and the Silmarillion," 5–6.

88. Glover, "The Christian Character," 5.

89. Tolkien, *The Lays*, 218.

90. Tolkien, *Morgoth's Ring*, 69; Tolkien, *The Silmarillion*, 11.

91. Tolkien, *Morgoth's Ring*, 15.

92. Coombs and Read, "Valaquenta," 31–32.

93. Tolkien, "Ósanwe-kenta," 25.
94. Tolkien, "Ósanwe-kenta," 25; Tolkien, *The War of the Jewels,* 406.
95. Tolkien, "Ósanwe-kenta," 25, 30.
96. Tolkien, *The Silmarillion,* 11.
97. *Oxford English Dictionary,* 3254.
98. Tolkien, *The Letters,* 285.
99. Watkins, "Satan and The Silmarillion."
100. Sly, "Weaving Nets of Gloom," 115.
101. Vincent, *Culture, Communion and Recovery,* 30.
102. Purtill, *The Lord of the Elves,* 126.
103. Lewis, *Perelandra,* 200.
104. Tolkien, *Morgoth's Ring,* 201, 380.
105. Burns, "Norse and Christian Gods," 174.
106. Tolkien, *Morgoth's Ring,* 69.
107. Burns, *Perilous Realms,* 153.
108. Tolkien, *Morgoth,'s Ring* 49, 244.
109. Tolkien, *The Shaping,* 327; Tolkien, *The Letters,* 283.
110. Tolkien, *The Silmarillion,* 20.
111. Tolkien, "Ósanwe-kenta," 25; Tolkien, *The Lost Road,* 183; Tolkien, *The Letters,* 282.
112. Tolkien, *The War of the Jewels,* 397, 406–7.
113. Tolkien, *The Silmarillion,* 21; Tolkien, *Unfinished Tales,* 37.
114. Flieger, *Splintered Light,* 55.
115. Burns, "Norse and Christian Gods," 168, 175.
116. Tolkien, *The Letters,* 282.
117. Tolkien, *Morgoth's Ring,* 66.
118. Flieger, *Splintered Light,* 56.
119. Tolkien, *Morgoth's Ring,* 412n4.
120. Tolkien, *The Silmarillion,* 16, 35–36.
121. Tolkien, *Morgoth's Ring,* 349; Tolkien, "Ósanwe-kenta," 30n4; Tolkien, *The Book of Lost Tales,* 1:204; Tolkien, *The Lost Road,* 334; Tolkien, *Morgoth's Ring,* 138, 361–62, 206, 129; Tolkien, *The Silmarillion,* 18.
122. Tolkien, *The War of the Jewels,* 399; Tolkien, *The Silmarillion,* 16, 36; Tolkien, *The Lost Road,* 178; Tolkien, *The Book of Lost Tales,* 1:56; Tolkien, *The Book of Lost Tales,* 2:292; Tolkien, *The Book of Lost Tales,* 1:107.
123. Tolkien, *The Peoples,* 396.
124. Larsen, "[V]Arda Marred," 32.
125. Tolkien, *The Silmarillion,* 16.
126. Tolkien, *Morgoth's Ring,* 399.
127. Tolkien, *The Silmarillion,* 16, 17; Tolkien, *Morgoth's Ring,* 201.
128. Tolkien, *Unfinished Tales,* 412.
129. Tolkien, *The Silmarillion,* 21; Tolkien, *The War of the Jewels,* 246.
130. Tolkien, *The Silmarillion,* 19; Tolkien, *The Lost Road,* 422; Tolkien, *The War of the Jewels,* 400; Tolkien, *The Silmarillion,* 17; Tolkien, *The Shaping,* 267.

131. Tolkien, *The Silmarillion,* 17.
132. Tolkien, *Unfinished Tales,* 31.
133. Tolkien, *The Lays,* 72, 156; Tolkien, *The Book of Lost Tales,* 2:156–57.
134. Tolkien, *The Silmarillion,* 36, 17.
135. Tolkien, *Morgoth's Ring,* 35; Tolkien, *The War of the Jewels,* 400; Tolkien, *The Silmarillion,* 36, 21; Tolkien, *Unfinished Tales,* 32; Tolkien, *The Shaping,* 95; Tolkien, *The Book of Lost Tales,* 1:126; Tolkien, *The Shaping,* 113; Tolkien, *The Lost Road,* 246–47; Tolkien, *The Book of Lost Tales,* 1:168; Tolkien, *Morgoth's Ring,* 145.
136. Tolkien, *The War of the Jewels,* 341.
137. Tolkien, *The Silmarillion,* 44.
138. Tolkien, *The Book of Lost Tales,* 1:66; Tolkien, *The Shaping,* 95; Tolkien, *The Lost Road,* 225; Tolkien, *Morgoth's Ring,* 350, 150.
139. Tolkien, *Morgoth's Ring,* 235.
140. Tolkien, *Morgoth's Ring,* 278; Tolkien, *The Silmarillion,* 19.
141. Tolkien, *Unfinished Tales,* 32; Tolkien, *Morgoth's Ring,* 246–47n; Tolkien, *The Silmarillion,* 21.
142. Tolkien, *The Shaping,* 95; Tolkien, *The Silmarillion,* 21; Tolkien, *The Lost Road,* 225; Tolkien, *Morgoth's Ring,* 150.
143. Tolkien, *The Book of Lost Tales,* 1:8, 19; Tolkien, *The Lost Road,* 396, 430; Tolkien, *Morgoth's Ring,* 49.
144. Tolkien, *Morgoth's Ring,* 172; Tolkien, *The Silmarillion,* 57; Tolkien, *The Book of Lost Tales,* 2:7, 41; Tolkien, *The Shaping,* 103, 14; Tolkien, *The Lays,* 38; Tolkien, *The Lost Road,* 435.
145. Tolkien, *The Two Towers,* 313. A brief discussion of the evolution of Gandalf's names appears in Tolkien, *The War of the Ring,* 153.
146. Tolkien, *Unfinished Tales,* 405–10; Tolkien, *The Letters,* 411.
147. Shippey, *J. R. R. Tolkien,* 259.
148. Tolkien, *The Silmarillion,* 22, 25; Tolkien, *The Lost Road,* 226; Tolkien, *Morgoth's Ring,* 68; Tolkien, *The Silmarillion,* 19.
149. Tolkien, *The Silmarillion,* 20; Tolkien, *Morgoth's Ring,* 52, 392; Tolkien, *The Silmarillion,* 20; Tolkien, *Morgoth's Ring,* 146; Tolkien, *The Shaping,* 95; Tolkien, *The War of the Jewels,* 399; Tolkien, *The Book of the Lost Tales,* 2:295, 8.
150. Tolkien, *The Lost Road,* 419; Tolkien, *The War of the Jewels,* 416.
151. Burns, *Perilous Realms,* 153.
152. Tolkien, *The Book of Lost Tales,* 1:301–2.
153. Tolkien, *The Silmarillion,* 22; Tolkien, *The Lays,* 282; Tolkien, *Morgoth's Ring,* 149; Tolkien, *The Return of the King,* 431, 395; Tolkien, *The Lays,* 225, 239; Tolkien, *The Shaping,* 96; Tolkien, *The Lost Road,* 429; Tolkien, *The Shaping,* 95.
154. Tolkien, *The Silmarillion,* 23, 16, 411.
155. Tolkien, *Morgoth's Ring,* 16, 40.
156. Tolkien, *The Silmarillion,* 23; Tolkien, *The Shaping,* 96; Tolkien, *The Lost Road,* 226, 399, 414, 416; Tolkien, *Sauron,* 314; Tolkien, *The Lays,* 5–6; Tolkien, *The*

Shaping, 96; Tolkien, *The Lost Road*, 81; Tolkien, *The Shaping*, 96; Tolkien, *The Silmarillion*, 184, 18; Tolkien, *Morgoth's Ring*, viii.

157. Tolkien, "Ósanwe-kenta," 31; Tolkien, *The Shaping*, 128–29; Tolkien, *The Lost Road*, 312; Tolkien, *The Silmarillion*, 25; Tolkien, *The Lays*, 340.

158. Tolkien, *Morgoth's Ring*, 405; Tolkien, *The Book of Lost Tales*, 1:296; Tolkien, *Morgoth's Ring*, 391.

159. Tolkien, *Morgoth's Ring*, 79; Tolkien, "Ósanwe-kenta," 26–27.

160. Tolkien, *Morgoth's Ring*, 15, 17, 53, 66, 18; Tolkien, *The Book of Lost Tales*, 1:157, 162.

161. Tolkien, *Morgoth's Ring*, 52; Tolkien, *The Lays*, 272; Tolkien, *Morgoth's Ring*, 394–95; emphasis in the original.

162. Tolkien, *The Book of Lost Tales*, 2:13, 28, 14; Tolkien, *Sauron*, 284n17; Tolkien, *The Book of Lost Tales*, 1:262; Tolkien, *The Lays*, 31, 273; Tolkien, *The Lost Road*, 147; Tolkien, *Sauron*, 54; Tolkien, *Unfinished Tales*, 266; Tolkien, *Morgoth's Ring*, 395; Tolkien, *The Lost Road*, 311; Tolkien, *The Letters*, 259.

163. Abbott, "Tolkien's Monsters (Part 2)," 41; Sookoo, "Animals in Tolkien's Works," 20.

164. Tolkien, *Morgoth's Ring*, 98.

165. Bridoux, "Of the Ainur," 6–7; Apeland, "The Forces of Evil," 24–25.

166. Tolkien, *The Shaping*, 13; Tolkien, *The Lost Road*, 232; Tolkien, *The Book of Lost Tales*, 1:98; Tolkien, *The Letters*, 180; Tolkien, *The Shaping*, 362; Tolkien, *The Lost Road*, 151; Tolkien, *The War of the Jewels*, 74; Tolkien, *The Book of Lost Tales*, 2:185; Tolkien, *Morgoth's Ring*, 80.

167. Tolkien, *The Fellowship of the Ring*, 428–29.

168. Shippey, *J. R. R. Tolkien*, 239.

169. Tolkien, *The Book of Lost Tales*, 2:175, 74.

170. Tolkien, *The Silmarillion*, 23.

171. Tolkien, *The Book of Lost Tales*, 1:299.

172. Tolkien, *The Silmarillion*, 111.

173. Tolkien, *The Fellowship of the Ring*, 370.

174. Tolkien, *The Silmarillion*, 21.

175. Tolkien, *The Silmarillion*, 7, 10.

176. Kreeft, "Afterward," 170.

177. Tolkien, *The Silmarillion*, 44.

2. The Valar in the World

1. A portion of this section has been published in Brotton's *Ecotheology in the Humanities*, though with additional conclusions pertinent to the study of ecotheological criticism (McBride, "Stewards of Arda"). That portion is published with permission: *Ecotheology in the Humanities: An Interdisciplinary Approach to Understanding the Divine and Nature*, edited by Melissa J. Brotton (Lexington Books), Copyright © 2016 by Lexington Books. All rights reserved.

2. Tolkien, *The Book of Lost Tales*, 1:65–68.

3. Tolkien, *The Silmarillion*, 10.

4. Tolkien, *The Legend*, 59.

5. Tolkien, *The Silmarillion*, 10; Tolkien, *Morgoth's Ring*, 14.

6. Garbowski, "Middle-earth," 423.

7. Tolkien, *The Lost Road*, 159.

8. Kane, *Arda Reconstructed*, 33.

9. Tolkien, *The Lost Road*, 123–24; Tolkien, *Morgoth's Ring*, 50–60, 330. Yet another estimate suggests nearly thirty thousand years between the Valar's entry into Eä and the start of the First Age, which begins with the first sunrise (Tolkien, *The Shaping*, 319).

10. Tolkien, *The Silmarillion*, 12.

11. Crowe, "Making and Unmaking," 62.

12. Tolkien, *The Silmarillion*, 12; Tolkien, *The Lost Road*, 123.

13. Tolkien, *The Silmarillion*, 13; emphasis added.

14. Tolkien, *Tolkien on Fairy-stories*, 28–29.

15. Tolkien, *The Silmarillion*, 6.

16. Goñi, "Reflections from the White Tower," 14.

17. Tolkien, *Morgoth's Ring*, 99, 401, 404.

18. Tolkien, *The Silmarillion*, 13; emphasis added.

19. Tolkien, *The Silmarillion*, 12, 316; Tolkien, *Morgoth's Ring*, ix.

20. Tolkien, *Morgoth's Ring*, 15, 406.

21. Tolkien, *Morgoth's Ring*, 14; Tolkien, *The Silmarillion*, 29; Tolkien, *Unfinished Tales*, 49; Tolkien, *The Silmarillion*, 55.

22. Tolkien, *The Silmarillion*, 29; Tolkien, *Morgoth's Ring*, 32, 153.

23. Tolkien, *The Lays*, 6.

24. Tolkien, *The Shaping*, 312; Tolkien, *The Silmarillion*, 31; Tolkien, *The Book of Lost Tales*, 1:106; Tolkien, *The Silmarillion*, 31–32.

25. Tolkien, *The Silmarillion*, 32; Tolkien, *The Lost Road*, 226, 229.

26. Tolkien, *The Book of Lost Tales*, 1:243.

27. Tolkien, *The Book of Lost Tales*, 241; Tolkien, *The Silmarillion*, 345.

28. *Oxford English Dictionary*, quoted in Hammond and Scull, *The Lord of the Rings: A Reader's Companion*, 10.

29. Tolkien, *Morgoth's Ring*, 338, 375; emphasis in the original.

30. Tolkien, *Morgoth's Ring*, 401.

31. Tolkien, *Morgoth's Ring*, 67; Tolkien, *The Silmarillion*, 33.

32. Tolkien, *The Lays*, 133; Tolkien, *Morgoth's Ring*, 98; Tolkien, *The Lost Road*, 247; Tolkien, *The Book of Lost Tales*, 1:76; Tolkien, *Morgoth's Ring*, 54.

33. Tolkien, *The Shaping*, 312; Tolkien, *The Silmarillion*, 33; Tolkien, *The Shaping*, 99; Tolkien, *The Lost Road*, 123.

34. Tolkien, *The Silmarillion*, 82–83.

35. Tolkien, *Morgoth's Ring*, 244, 425.

36. Tolkien, *The Silmarillion*, 37.

37. Tolkien, *The Silmarillion*, 49; Tolkien, *The Book of Lost Tales*, 1:126.

38. Flieger, *Splintered Light,* 77.
39. Tolkien, *Unfinished Tales,* 272.
40. Tolkien, *The War of the Jewels,* 421.
41. Tolkien, *The Book of Lost Tales,* 1:260, 44, 49, 159.
42. Tolkien, *The Lost Road,* 246; Tolkien, *The Shaping,* 15; Tolkien, *The Peoples,* 366; Tolkien, *The Shaping,* 181.
43. Tolkien, *The Letters,* 148.
44. Tolkien, *The Silmarillion,* 312; Tolkien, *The Lost Road,* 158.
45. Tolkien, "Ósanwe-kenta," 29.
46. Tolkien, *The Letters,* 147; Tolkien, *Morgoth's Ring,* 345, 346.
47. Tolkien, *The Letters,* 205.
48. Dickerson and Evans, *Ents, Elves, and Eriador,* 60; Tolkien, *Sauron,* 336; Tolkien, *The Letters,* 206; Tolkien, *Sauron,* 372; Tolkien, *The Silmarillion,* 344.
49. Randolph, "The Singular Incompetence," 11–13.
50. McIntosh, *The Flame Imperishable,* 84–86.
51. Tolkien, *The Silmarillion,* 4.
52. Tolkien, *The Letters,* 202.

🦋 *3. Divine Intervention in the Third Age: Visible Powers*

1. Tolkien, *The Return of the King,* 138, 304; Hammond and Scull, *The Lord of the Rings: A Reader's Companion,* 633.
2. Tolkien, *The Two Towers,* 341. Beyond the three direct references to the Valar, a few indirect references appear in the text, as when Elrond speaks reverentially of beings who dwell across the sea (Tolkien, *The Fellowship of the Ring,* 349). The word *Valar* appears often in the Appendices, and 342 times in *The Silmarillion.*
3. Tolkien, *The War of the Ring,* 136.
4. Hammond and Scull, *The Lord of the Rings: A Reader's Companion,* 467.
5. Tolkien, *The Letters,* 220.
6. Tolkien, *The Letters,* 206.
7. Tolkien, *The Letters,* 387, 206–7.
8. Tolkien, *Unfinished Tales,* 319, 313–21, 323; Tolkien, *The Peoples,* 123.
9. Tolkien, *Unfinished Tales,* 406.
10. Tolkien, *The Hobbit,* 108.
11. Tolkien, *The Hobbit,* 116.
12. Tolkien, *Tolkien on Fairy-stories,* 68.
13. Tolkien, *The Hobbit,* 273; Tolkien, *The Silmarillion,* 44.
14. Tolkien, *The Hobbit,* 270.
15. Tolkien, *The Return of the King,* 321.
16. Tolkien, *The Two Towers,* 189; Tolkien, *The Return of the King,* 510; Tolkien, *Morgoth's Ring,* 71, 93.
17. Tolkien, *The Letters,* 335; Tolkien, *The Silmarillion,* 45; Tolkien, *The War of the Jewels,* 353.

18. Tolkien, *The Silmarillion,* 25; Tolkien, qtd. in Hammond and Scull, *The Lord of the Rings: A Reader's Companion,* 749.

19. Tolkien, *The Hobbit,* 121; Tolkien, *The Fellowship of the Ring,* 78; Tolkien, *The Return of the King,* 455; Tolkien, *The Silmarillion,* 372.

20. Tolkien, *The Peoples,* 360; Tolkien, *The Return of the King,* 403.

21. Tolkien, *Unfinished Tales,* 406; Tolkien, *The Treason,* 422; Tolkien, *The Letters,* 159.

22. Tolkien, *The Return of the King,* 403; Tolkien, *The Silmarillion,* 372; Tolkien, *The Letters,* 201.

23. Millen, "The Istari," 9–10.

24. Tolkien, *Unfinished Tales,* 405–6.

25. Tolkien, *The Letters,* 202, 237.

26. Okunishi, "Olórin," 37.

27. Tolkien, *The Return of the King,* 456.

28. Tolkien, *Unfinished Tales,* 405–6; Tolkien, *The Return of the King,* 455; Petty, *Tolkien in the Land of Heroes,* 269; Tolkien, *Morgoth's Ring,* 397.

29. Tolkien, *The Two Towers,* 260.

30. Tolkien, *Unfinished Tales,* 410.

31. Tolkien, *Unfinished Tales,* 410; Tolkien, *Mr. Baggins,* 273; Tolkien, *The Silmarillion,* 360; Tolkien, *The Peoples,* 384.

32. Tolkien, *The Return of the King,* 455; Tolkien, *The Two Towers,* 2012, 219; Tolkien, *The Letters,* 277.

33. Tolkien, *Unfinished Tales,* 407; Hammond and Scull, *The Lord of the Rings: A Reader's Companion,* 251.

34. Tolkien, *The Fellowship of the Ring,* 449, 340.

35. Tolkien, *The Treason,* 150; Tolkien, *The Fellowship of the Ring,* 347.

36. Tolkien, *The Two Towers,* 113.

37. Tolkien, *The Two Towers,* 289.

38. Tolkien, *The Two Towers,* 48; Tolkien, *Unfinished Tales,* 407, 432n14.

39. Tolkien, *The Treason,* 427.

40. Tolkien, *The Silmarillion,* 361; Tolkien, *The Letters,* 237.

41. Tolkien, *The Fellowship of the Ring,* 288.

42. Birns, "The Enigma of Radagast," 123.

43. Tolkien, *Unfinished Tales,* 390.

44. Tolkien, *Mr. Baggins,* 272–74.

45. Tolkien, *Unfinished Tales,* 407, 410; Tolkien, *The Peoples,* 384–85; Tolkien, *Unfinished Tales,* 411.

46. Tolkien, *The Unfinished Tales,* 407; Tolkien, *The Letters,* 280; Tolkien, *The Peoples,* 385.

47. Tolkien, *The Hobbit,* 17, 19.

48. Tolkien, *The Peoples,* 234, 237; Tolkien, *The Return of the King,* 460, 448, 460; Tolkien, *The Peoples,* 206; Tolkien, *The Fellowship of the Ring,* 234; Tolkien, *The Return of the King,* 192.

49. Tolkien, *The Return of the King,* 99.

50. Tolkien, *Unfinished Tales,* 406; Tolkien, *The Fellowship of the Ring,* 42.
51. Tolkien, *The Letters,* 390; Tolkien, *The Fellowship of the Ring,* 48.
52. Tolkien, *The Fellowship of the Ring,* 346, 251, 390. For this translation, I am indebted to Hammond and Scull, *The Lord of the Rings: A Reader's Companion,* 276.
53. Tolkien, *The Fellowship of the Ring,* 89.
54. Tolkien, *The Fellowship of the Ring,* 380.
55. Tolkien, *Unfinished Tales,* 408.
56. Tolkien, *The Fellowship of the Ring,* 67.
57. Tolkien, *The Return of the King,* 337; Tolkien, *The Fellowship of the Ring,* 396.
58. Tolkien, *The Fellowship of the Ring,* 77.
59. Tolkien, *The Hobbit,* 73.
60. Tolkien, *The Treason,* 26; Tolkien, *The Hobbit,* 99; Tolkien, *Mr. Baggins,* 200; Tolkien, *The Fellowship of the Ring,* 290; Tolkien, *The Two Towers,* 220.
61. Tolkien, *Unfinished Tales,* 414; Tolkien, *The Two Towers,* 353; Tolkien, *Unfinished Tales,* 339.
62. Tolkien, *The Return of the King,* 165; Tolkien, *Unfinished Tales,* 416; Tolkien, *The Return of the King,* 107.
63. Tolkien, *The Fellowship of the Ring,* 100; Tolkien, *The War of the Ring,* 391, 54, 163.
64. Tolkien, *The Treason,* 9, 82, 132.
65. Tolkien, *The Fellowship of the Ring,* 290–91, 424, 370; emphasis added, 425.
66. Tolkien, *The Treason,* 199; Tolkien, *The Fellowship of the Ring,* 428.
67. Tolkien, *The Fellowship of the Ring,* 429.
68. Tolkien, *Morgoth's Ring,* 44; Tolkien, *The Letters,* 148.
69. Tolkien, *The Treason,* 198.
70. Tolkien, *The Two Towers,* 135.
71. Tolkien, *The Return of the King,* 465.
72. Rorabeck, *Tolkien's Heroic Quest,* 59; Tolkien, *The Letters,* 203.
73. Tolkien, *The Letters,* 201.
74. Tolkien, *The Letters,* 201, 202.
75. Tolkien, *The Two Towers,* 353.
76. Tolkien, *The Return of the King,* 259.
77. Tolkien, *The Return of the Shadow,* 462.
78. Tolkien, *The Letters,* 202; Hammond and Scull, *The Lord of the Rings: A Reader's Companion,* 746; Green, "The Ring at the Centre," 17; Percival, "Of the Maiar," 7.
79. Tolkien, *The Return of the King,* 280.
80. Tolkien, *The Treason,* 211.
81. Tolkien, *The Two Towers,* 122, 124; Tolkien, *The Treason,* 422.
82. Tolkien, *The Two Towers,* 125.
83. Tolkien, *The Two Towers,* 131, 132, 135.
84. Hammond and Scull, *The Lord of the Rings: A Reader's Companion,* 395.
85. Tolkien, *Unfinished Tales,* 408.

86. Tolkien, *The Two Towers,* 137.
87. Roberts, *The Riddles,* 132; Walter, "The Grey Pilgrim," 204; Tolkien, *The Two Towers,* 133; Tolkien, *The Peoples,* 388.
88. Kisor, "Incorporeality and Transformation," 26.
89. Tolkien, *The Letters,* 203.
90. Tolkien, "Scheme," qtd. in Hammond and Scull, *The Lord of the Rings: A Reader's Companion,* 396.
91. Tolkien, *The Return of the King,* 339.
92. Tolkien, *The Two Towers,* 216, 125.
93. Tolkien, *The Two Towers,* 168; Tolkien, *The Letters,* 202.
94. Tolkien, *The Return of the King,* x; Tolkien, *Unfinished Tales,* 371.
95. Rutledge, *The Battle for Middle-earth,* 168.
96. Tolkien, *The Return of the King,* xi.
97. Tolkien, *The Two Towers,* 238, 239.
98. Tolkien, *The Two Towers,* 208, 240, 209.
99. Tolkien, *The Two Towers,* 221.
100. Ruud, *Critical Companion,* 244; Tolkien, *The Two Towers,* 242–43.
101. Tolkien, *The Two Towers,* 180, 189, 199.
102. Tolkien, *The Return of the King,* 100, 101, 114, 155; Tolkien, *The War of the Ring,* 229; Tolkien, *The Return of the King,* 205; Tolkien, *The War of the Ring,* 230.
103. Tolkien, *The Return of the King,* 161, 170.
104. Ruud, "The Voice of Saruman," 150.
105. Tolkien, *The Letters,* 272; Tolkien, *The War of the Ring,* 403.
106. Blackburn, "'Dangerous as a Guide to Deeds,'" 64.
107. *Romenna Meeting Report,* qtd. in Hammond and Scull, *The Lord of the Rings: A Reader's Companion,* 520; Tolkien, *The Return of the King,* 158; Tolkien, *The Two Towers,* 255; Tolkien, *The Return of the King,* 287.
108. Rosebury, "Revenge and Moral Judgment," 15.
109. Crabbe, *J. R. R. Tolkien* (rev. ed.), 81.
110. Tolkien, *The Return of the King,* 105.
111. Sarti, "Man in a Mortal World," 111.
112. Tolkien, *The Fellowship of the Ring,* 93.
113. Tolkien, *The War of the Ring,* 377; Tolkien, *Unfinished Tales,* 345; Tolkien, *The Fellowship of the Ring,* 95.
114. Tolkien, *The Return of the King,* 119.
115. Tolkien, *The Return of the King,* 169, 303, 317; Tolkien, *Sauron,* 132; Tolkien, *The Letters,* 327.
116. Hammond and Scull, *The Lord of the Rings: A Reader's Guide,* 24.
117. Treschow and Duckworth, "Bombadil's Role," 177.
118. Hammond and Scull, *The Lord of the Rings: A Reader's Companion,* 124.
119. Hammond and Scull, *The Lord of the Rings: A Reader's Companion,* 128, 761.
120. Tolkien, *The Fellowship of the Ring,* 168.
121. Flieger, *A Question of Time,* 201.
122. Tolkien, *The Fellowship of the Ring,* 173.

123. For a discussion of Tom Bombadil as Eru, see Vanhecke, "Old Tom Bombadil Was a . . . ," 6–7). Yet Tom Bombadil's limitations should be evidence enough that Tom is not the Almighty of Eä. If not, then surely the wise Elrond's assertion that Tom is "a strange creature" should be; to call the creator a creature would be blasphemy from one who had witnessed the Host of the Valar victorious over Melkor (Tolkien, *The Fellowship of the Ring*, 319). Furthermore, Tolkien's authority may be invoked against this theory: no embodiment of Arda's creator ever appears within the legendarium, Tolkien asserts (*The Letters*, 237).

  For a discussion of Tom Bombadil as J.R.R. Tolkien, see Nance, "A Solution to the Tom Bombadil Problem," 10–13.

124. Tolkien, *The Fellowship of the Ring*, 174; Mathews, *Lightning from a Clear Sky*, 22.

125. Petty, *One Ring to Bind Them All*, 38; Kaufmann, "Aspects of the Paradisiacal," 166.

126. Hughes, "Pieties and Giant Forms," 88.

127. Tolkien, *The Letters*, 26, 272.

128. Startzman, "Goldberry and Galadriel," 6.

129. Tolkien, *The Letters*, 179, 192.

130. Tolkien, *The Fellowship of the Ring*, 182.

131. Stevenson, "T.B. or not T.B.," 16–21.

132. Tolkien, *The Return of the Shadow*, 122.

133. See Hargrove's "Tom Bombadil" and "Who Is Tom Bombadil?"

  Ruud refutes Hargrove's arguments with rhetorical questions: "why, if [Tom] were Aulë, would he take so little interest in the affairs of dwarves, for instance? And why would Goldberry, as the powerful Yavanna, seem to take so little part in the affairs of the forest beyond making dinner and making it rain?" (Ruud, *Critical Companion*, 262).

134. Tolkien, *The Letters*, 174, 192.

135. Qtd. in Hammond and Scull, *The Lord of the Rings: A Reader's Companion*, 134.

136. Shippey, *The Road to Middle-earth*, 105. Flieger, "Tolkien and the Philosophy of Language," 789.

137. Startzman, "Goldberry and Galadriel," 7.

138. Foster, *The Complete Guide*, 496. While offering Foster as support for my argument, I wish to take responsibility for its strengths and weaknesses. Others, such as Hammond and Scull (*The Lord of the Rings: A Reader's Companion*, 138) and Duriez (*Tolkien and* The Lord of the Rings, 79), at least recognize the assertion as a strong possibility. Williamson similarly argues that it is "not . . . unreasonable to speculate that" Goldberry is a Maia ("Emblematic Bodies," 136).

139. Tolkien, *The Lost Road*, 123–24; Tolkien, *The Return of the Shadow*, 214; Tolkien, *The Fellowship of the Ring*, 172.

140. Hammond and Scull, *The Lord of the Rings: A Reader's Companion*, 136.

141. Glover, "The Christian Character," 3–8.

142. Flieger, *A Question of Time*, 202–3.

143. Tolkien, *The Fellowship of the Ring*, 179.

144. Tolkien, *The Return of the King*, 340.

145. Tolkien, *The Fellowship of the Ring,* 180.
146. Tolkien, *The Fellowship of the Ring,* 347.
147. Stanton, *Hobbits, Elves, and Wizards,* 30.
148. Treschow and Duckworth, "Bombadil's Role," 191.
149. Brawley, *Nature and the Numinous,* 105.
150. Pearce, *Tolkien,* 165.
151. Tolkien, *The Letters,* 192.
152. Tolkien, *The Letters,* 193; emphasis in the original.
153. Brooks, "Tom Bombadil," 13.
154. Tolkien, *The Treason,* 416.
155. Tolkien, *The Return of the Shadow,* 401.
156. Tolkien, *The Return of the Shadow,* 351.
157. Tolkien, *The Fellowship of the Ring,* 175.
158. Tolkien, *The Fellowship of the Ring,* 169.
159. Tolkien, *The Return of the Shadow,* 123.
160. Sabo, "Archaeology and the Sense of History," 99.
161. Musk, "Tom Bombadil," 13.
162. Tolkien, *The Fellowship of the Ring,* 83.
163. Tolkien, *The Return of the King,* 311.
164. Tolkien, *The Return of the King,* 425.
165. Tolkien, *The Fellowship of the Ring,* 279, 280, 286, 294, 295.
166. Tolkien, *The Treason,* 14.
167. Tolkien, *The Letters,* 176.
168. Kreeft, *The Philosophy of Tolkien,* 78.
169. Petty, *Tolkien in the Land of Heroes,* 143–44.
170. Tolkien, *Morgoth's Ring,* 209, 270; Tolkien, *The Peoples,* 403–4.
171. Lynch, "The Literary Banquet," 16.
172. Tolkien, *The Lays,* 48, 51; Tolkien, *Unfinished Tales,* 23.
173. Tolkien, *The Fellowship of the Ring,* 295.
174. Tolkien, *The Fellowship of the Ring,* 294; Tolkien, *The Return of the King,* 414.
175. Tolkien, *The Peoples,* 377–78, 378–79.
176. Tolkien, *The Fellowship of the Ring,* 296; Tolkien, *Unfinished Tales,* 250; Tolkien, *The Peoples,* 168, 169, 179.
177. Tolkien, *Unfinished Tales,* 235.
178. Tolkien, *Unfinished Tales,* 241; Tolkien, *The Peoples,* 337; Tolkien, *Morgoth's Ring,* 128; Tolkien, *The Peoples,* 338; Tolkien, *The Letters,* 431.
179. Tolkien, *The Peoples,* 338, 185.
180. Tolkien, *The Fellowship of the Ring,* 418–19.
181. Tolkien, *The Peoples,* 321, 338; Tolkien, *The Road Goes Ever On,* 68.
182. Tolkien, *The Letters,* 386.
183. Tolkien, *The Peoples,* 195; Tolkien, *The Return of the King,* 468.
184. Tolkien, *Unfinished Tales,* 412, 354, 256–57, 246–47.
185. Brackmann, "'Dwarves Are Not Heroes,'" 101.
186. Tolkien, *The Fellowship of the Ring,* 438, 455; emphasis in the original.

187. Tolkien, *The Treason*, 241; Kocher, *Master of Middle-earth*, 92; Tolkien, *The Fellowship of the Ring*, 371.
188. Tolkien, *The Silmarillion*, 367; Tolkien, *The Fellowship of the Ring*, 328; Tolkien, *The Two Towers*, 385; Tolkien, *Unfinished Tales*, 246.
189. Tolkien, *The Peoples*, 385–86.
190. Tolkien, *The Two Towers*, 34; Tolkien, *Morgoth's Ring*, 398.
191. Tolkien, *The Return of the King*, 325–26.
192. Hammond and Scull, *The Lord of the Rings: A Reader's Companion*, 650.
193. Tolkien, "Ósanwe-kenta," 23.
194. Tolkien, "Ósanwe-kenta," 30n2.
195. Tolkien, "Ósanwe-kenta," 24–25; Tolkien, *Morgoth's Ring*, 399.
196. Tolkien, *The Fellowship of the Ring*, 122; Tolkien, *The Peoples*, 338.
197. Tolkien, *The Fellowship of the Ring*, 464.
198. Gee, *The Science*, 185.
199. Tolkien, *The Treason*, 251; Tolkien, *The Two Towers*, 432.
200. Tolkien, *The Treason*, 343; Tolkien, *The War of the Ring*, 398, 163.
201. Hammond and Scull, *The Lord of the Rings: A Reader's Companion*, 666.
202. Klinger, "Hidden Paths of Time," 159.
203. Tolkien, *Unfinished Tales*, 261–63.
204. Tolkien, *The Treason*, 259; Tolkien, *The Return of the Shadow*, 320; Tolkien, *The Treason*, 254–55.
205. Tolkien, *The Peoples*, 33; Tolkien, *The Fellowship of the Ring*, 352; Tolkien, *The Peoples*, 305.
206. Flieger, *A Question of Time*, 91.
207. Vaccaro, "Rings," 572.
208. Tolkien, *Sauron*, 111–12; Tolkien, *The Return of the King*, 383, 381; Fisher, "Three Rings for—Whom Exactly?," 99–108; Stoddard, "Symbelmynë," 155; Tolkien, *Unfinished Tales*, 249.
209. Tolkien, *The Fellowship of the Ring*, 352; Tolkien, *The Treason*, 286; Tolkien, *The Fellowship of the Ring*, 472.
210. Tolkien, *The Return of the King*, 308.
211. Tolkien, *The Letters*, 241.
212. Tolkien, *The Letters*, 241.

4. Divine Intervention in the Third Age: Invisible Powers

1. Hammond and Scull, *The Lord of the Rings: A Reader's Companion*, 474.
2. Tolkien, *The Two Towers*, 361.
3. Tolkien, *The Letters*, 281.
4. Lobdell, "Ymagynatyf and J. R. R. Tolkien's Roman Catholicism," 28.
5. Tolkien, *The War of the Ring*, 164.
6. Tolkien, *The Letters*, 194.
7. Tolkien, *The Peoples*, 159, 4.

8. Purtill, *J. R. R. Tolkien*, 125.
9. Tolkien, *The Letters*, 201.
10. Tolkien, *The Letters*, 144.
11. Tolkien, *The War of the Ring*, 401.
12. Madsen, "Eru Erased," 155, 164.
13. Tolkien, *The Fellowship of the Ring*, 522.
14. Tolkien, *Unfinished Tales*, 262.
15. Curry, *Defending Middle-earth*, 94.
16. Tolkien, *The Two Towers*, 36.
17. Klinger, "Hidden Paths of Time," 172, 182.
18. Dickerson, *Following Gandalf*, 100.
19. Tolkien, *Sauron*, 87, 94.
20. Shippey, *J. R. R. Tolkien*, 136.
21. Tolkien, *The Return of the Shadow*, 216; Tolkien, *The Silmarillion*, 368; Tolkien, *Unfinished Tales*, 364; Tolkien, *The Return of the King*, 439.
22. Tolkien, *The Return of the King*, 441.
23. Tolkien, *The Return of the King*, 445.
24. Hood, "The Lidless Eye," 132–33; Shippey, *J. R. R. Tolkien*, 138.
25. Tolkien, *Unfinished Tales*, 304.
26. Hammond and Scull, *The Lord of the Rings: A Reader's Companion*, 747.
27. Tolkien, *The Fellowship of the Ring*, 111–12, 116; Hammond and Scull, *The Lord of the Rings: A Reader's Companion*, 156; Tolkien, *The Fellowship of the Ring*, 216, 219, 224, 235, 238.
28. Tolkien, *The Fellowship of the Ring*, 256, 264, 286.
29. Tolkien, *The Two Towers*, 300.
30. Tolkien, *The Return of the King*, 43, 111, 118, 160, 199.
31. Tolkien, *Unfinished Tales*, 286, 285; Tolkien, *The Fellowship of the Ring*, 333.
32. Tolkien, *The Two Towers*, 305.
33. Crowe, "Making and Unmaking," 66.
34. Hood, "The Lidless Eye," 132–33; Tolkien, *The Two Towers*, 114.
35. Shippey, *J. R. R. Tolkien*, 108.
36. Tolkien, *The Two Towers*, 122; Tolkien, *The Fellowship of the Ring*, 87.
37. Tolkien, *The Fellowship of the Ring*, 513.
38. Tolkien, *The Fellowship of the Ring*, 519.
39. Shippey, *J. R. R. Tolkien*, 109.
40. Tolkien, *The Fellowship of the Ring*, 430.
41. Tolkien, *The Two Towers*, 126.
42. Hammond and Scull, *The Lord of the Rings: A Reader's Companion*, 392.
43. Kocher, *Master of Middle-earth*, 138.
44. Rutledge, *The Battle for Middle-earth*, 144.
45. Hammond and Scull, *The Lord of the Rings: A Reader's Companion*, 396.
46. Tolkien, *The Treason*, 426.
47. Tolkien, *The Two Towers*, 318–19.
48. Tolkien, *The Two Towers*, 319.

49. Tolkien, *The Two Towers*, 319, 324.
50. Tolkien, *The Letters*, 326.
51. Shippey, *J. R. R. Tolkien*, 137.
52. Green, "The Ring at the Centre," 19.
53. Tolkien, *The Letters*, 180, 202.
54. Rutledge, *The Battle for Middle-earth*, 21.
55. Tolkien, *The Hobbit*, 85, 116; emphasis in the original, 155, 173, 180, 203, 212, 272.
56. Tolkien, *The Hobbit*, 286.
57. Rossi, *The Politics of Fantasy*, 102.
58. Rutledge, *The Battle for Middle-earth*, 42.
59. Tolkien, *The Letters*, 365.
60. Dickerson, *Following Gandalf*, 180.
61. Tolkien, *The Fellowship of the Ring*, 88; emphasis in the original.
62. Pedersen, "The 'Divine Passive,'" 23–27.
63. Glover, "The Christian Character," 3–8.
64. Tolkien, *The Book of Lost Tales*, 2:80; Tolkien, *Farmer Giles*, 126.
65. Shippey, qtd. in Hammond and Scull, *The Lord of the Rings: A Reader's Companion*, 234.
66. Dickerson, *Following Gandalf*, 187.
67. Tolkien, *The Hobbit*, 76.
68. Tolkien, *The Letters*, 159.
69. Deyo, "Wyrd and Will," 61.
70. Tolkien, *The Hobbit*, 76.
71. Tolkien, *Unfinished Tales*, 335–40; Tolkien, *The Letters*, 158.
72. Tolkien, *Unfinished Tales*, 336.
73. Hammond and Scull, *The Lord of the Rings: A Reader's Companion*, 109.
74. Dubs, "Providence, Fate, and Chance," 136.
75. Treschow and Duckworth, "Bombadil's Role," 181.
76. Tolkien, *The Fellowship of the Ring*, 175.
77. Shippey, *The Road to Middle-earth*, 114.
78. Tolkien, *Unfinished Tales*, 338.
79. Hood, "Nature and Technology," 10.
80. Tolkien, *The Fellowship of the Ring*, 118, 124, 318.
81. Glover, "The Christian Character of Tolkien's Invented Worlds," 3–8.
82. Wheeler, "Providence and Choice," n.p.
83. Tolkien, *The Return of the Shadow*, 311.
84. Tolkien, *The Peoples*, 281; Tolkien, *The Return of the King*, 448.
85. Tolkien, *Unfinished Tales*, 337, 339.
86. Tolkien, *The Fellowship of the Ring*, 329, 282.
87. Tolkien, "Notes on Óre," 13; Tolkien, *Unfinished Tales*, 344.
88. Tolkien, *The Peoples*, 282–83.
89. Tolkien, *Unfinished Tales*, 345.
90. Tolkien, *The Hobbit*, 287.
91. Tolkien, *The Fellowship of the Ring*, 33, 34.

92. Tolkien, *The Hobbit,* 83, 84.
93. Shippey, *J. R. R. Tolkien,* 145.
94. Tolkien, *The Hobbit,* 85.
95. Tolkien, *The Return of the Shadow,* 262.
96. Tolkien, *The Hobbit,* 93.
97. Cattaneo, "Divine Presence and Providence," 12–14.
98. Tolkien, *Mr. Baggins,* 399.
99. Tolkien, *The Hobbit,* 199. I am indebted to my colleague, Tony Zbarachuk, for the trenchant observation that Tolkien often uses the points of the compass, particularly the west, to suggest more than geospatial direction.
100. Tolkien, *The Hobbit,* 223, 258.
101. Tolkien, *Return to Bag End,* 658.
102. My student, Chloe Vander Zwan, first drew my attention to this reading of divine intervention underlying Bilbo's being knocked unconscious.
103. Tolkien, *The Hobbit,* 94.
104. Tolkien, *The Peoples,* 4.
105. Tolkien, *The Fellowship of the Ring,* 303.
106. Tolkien, *The Silmarillion,* 361–62.
107. Tolkien, *The Letters,* 149.
108. Kreeft, *The Philosophy of Tolkien,* 60.
109. Davis, "Heroic Failure," 26.
110. Ryan, *Tolkien: Cult or Culture?,* 188.
111. Drury, "Providence at Elrond's Council," 8.
112. Rutledge, *The Battle for Middle-earth,* 27.
113. Tolkien, *The Fellowship of the Ring,* 97; Hammond and Scull, *The Lord of the Rings: A Reader's Companion,* 90.
114. Tolkien, *The Return of the King,* 229; Tolkien, *The Return of the Shadow,* 398.
115. Tolkien, *The Two Towers,* 36.
116. Tolkien, *The Two Towers,* 353, 367, 339.
117. Tolkien, *The Return of the King,* 66, 190; Tolkien, *The War of the Ring,* 305.
118. Tolkien, *The Return of the King,* 151, 309.
119. Tolkien, *The Two Towers,* 47.
120. Tolkien, *The Two Towers,* 54, 73, 75.
121. Tolkien, *The Two Towers,* 81.
122. Tolkien, *The Fellowship of the Ring,* 489, 501, 124.
123. Tolkien, *The Return of the King,* 381.
124. Hickman, "The Religious Ritual and Practice," 39–43; Tolkien, *The Return of the Shadow,* 212, 364.
125. Tolkien, *The Fellowship of the Ring,* 221.
126. Tolkien, *The Road Goes Ever On,* 71, 65; qtd. in Hammond and Scull, *The Lord of the Rings: A Reader's Companion,* 180.
127. Tolkien, *The Fellowship of the Ring,* 293, 289, 293.
128. Tolkien, *The Fellowship of the Ring,* 263.
129. Tolkien, *The Return of the Shadow,* 186, 214.

130. Kreeft, *The Philosophy of Tolkien,* 73.
131. Tolkien, *The Two Towers,* 418.
132. Palmer, *Visions of Paradise,* 22.
133. Tolkien, *The Two Towers,* 418.
134. Tolkien, *The Letters,* 385.
135. Milbank, *Chesterton and Tolkien,* 77.
136. Tolkien, *The Letters,* 278.
137. Startzman, "Goldberry and Galadriel," 11.
138. Kowalik, "Elbereth the Star-Queen," 93–113.
139. Tolkien, *The Return of the King,* 218, 234.
140. Tolkien, *The Return of the King,* 239.
141. Tolkien, *The Return of the King,* 244.
142. Tolkien, *The Silmarillion,* 19.
143. Tolkien, *The Silmarillion,* 36; Shippey, *The Road to Middle-earth,* 172.
144. Tolkien, *The Return of the King,* 506; Tolkien, *The Book of Lost Tales,* 2:158.
145. Tolkien, *The Silmarillion,* 8.
146. MacArthur, "The Mystery of the Ring's Destruction," 17–20; Tolkien, *The Fellowship of the Ring,* 296; Tolkien, *The Silmarillion,* 20; Dickerson. "Water, Ecology, and Spirituality," 28.
147. Tolkien, *The Fellowship of the Ring,* 504.
148. Tolkien, *The War of the Ring,* 145; Tolkien, *The Two Towers,* 20, 347; Tolkien, *The Treason,* 382.
149. Tolkien, *The Fellowship of the Ring,* 349.
150. Hartley, "A Wind from the West," 115.
151. Tolkien, *The Two Towers,* 142.
152. Tolkien, *The Return of the King,* 133, 137.
153. Dickerson, *Following Gandalf,* 194.
154. Tolkien, *The Silmarillion,* 9; Tolkien, *The Return of the King,* 135.
155. Tolkien, *The Return of the King,* 189, 150, 167, 191.
156. Tolkien, *The Return of the King,* 240.
157. Hartley, "A Wind from the West," 112.
158. Tolkien, *The Return of the King,* 260.
159. Tolkien, *The Return of the King,* 144.
160. Hammond and Scull, *The Lord of the Rings: A Reader's Companion,* 582.
161. Tolkien, *The Return of the King,* 279; Tolkien, qtd. in Hammond and Scull, *The Lord of the Rings: A Reader's Companion,* 747; Tolkien, *The Peoples,* 242.
162. Tolkien, *Sauron,* 6, 40. Words in brackets within this quotation indicate Christopher Tolkien's guess as to the meaning of his father's manuscript.
163. Tolkien, *The Return of the King,* 283; Tolkien, *The Silmarillion,* 377.
164. Tolkien, *The Return of the King,* 297; Hammond and Scull, *The Lord of the Rings: A Reader's Companion,* 630.
165. Tolkien, *Sauron,* 103; Tolkien, *The Return of the King,* 369; Tolkien, *Unfinished Tales,* 408.
166. Tolkien, *The Return of the King,* 370.

167. Hammond and Scull, *The Lord of the Rings: A Reader's Companion*, 664; Tolkien, *The Return of the King*, 370.
168. Garbowski, "Tolkien's Cosmic Eucatastrophe," 284.
169. Ryan, *Tolkien: Cult or Culture?*, 177.
170. Tolkien, *Morgoth's Ring*, 293.
171. Hartley, "A Wind from the West," 111.
172. Tolkien, *The Return of the King*, 286.
173. Klinger, "Tolkien's 'Strange Powers of the Mind,'" 80.
174. Flieger, *A Question of Time*, 179.
175. Schorr, "The Nature of Dreams," 46.
176. Hammond and Scull, *The Lord of the Rings: A Reader's Guide*, 326.
177. Tolkien, "Ósanwe-kenta," 31–32.
178. Tolkien, *The Silmarillion*, 21.
179. Flieger, *A Question of Time*, 192.
180. Tolkien, *The Book of Lost Tales*, 2:17.
181. Tolkien, *The Silmarillion*, 114, 57; Tolkien, *The Lays*, 245.
182. Grayson, "The Functions of Dreams," 30–32; Tolkien, *The Fellowship of the Ring*, 71; Tolkien, *The Return of the Shadow*, 374; Tolkien, *The Treason*, 34; Tolkien, *The Fellowship of the Ring*, 154.
183. Hammond and Scull, *The Lord of the Rings: A Reader's Companion*, 119.
184. Tolkien, *The Fellowship of the Ring*, 177, 153; Tolkien, *Sauron*, 53.
185. Flieger, *A Question of Time*, 189.
186. Flieger, *A Question of Time*, 167.
187. Amendt-Raduege, "Dream Visions," 47.
188. Schorr, "The Nature of Dreams," 21.
189. Tolkien, *The Fellowship of the Ring*, 307.
190. Amendt-Raduege, "Dream Visions," 47.
191. Tolkien, *The Two Towers*, 306.
192. Tolkien, *The Two Towers*, 417, 418.
193. Tolkien, *The Return of the King*, 272.
194. Tolkien, *The Treason*, 204; Tolkien, *The Return of the King*, 151, 422.
195. Tolkien, *The Return of the King*, 278.
196. Tolkien, *The Return of the King*, 63–64.
197. Tolkien, *The Return of the King*, 85.
198. Tolkien, *The Return of the King*, 444; Tolkien, *The Treason*, 142.
199. Tolkien, *The Return of the King*, 412, 141.
200. Tolkien, *The Two Towers*, 325.
201. Schorr, "The Nature of Dreams," 46.
202. Qtd. in Hammond and Scull, *The Lord of the Rings: A Reader's Companion*, 747; Tolkien, *The War of the Ring*, 386.
203. Hammond and Scull, *The Lord of the Rings: A Reader's Companion*, 584; Tolkien, *The Return of the King*, 288.
204. Tolkien, *The War of the Ring*, 396n21.
205. Aldrich, "The Sense of Time," 7.

206. Tolkien, *The Return of the King*, 419.
207. Tolkien, *The Return of the Shadow*, 264.
208. Tolkien, *The Return of the King*, 518.
209. Thum, "The 'Sub-Creation' of Galadriel, Arwen, and Éowyn," 236.
210. Palmer, *Visions of Paradise*, 22.
211. Tolkien, *The Silmarillion*, 26. My student, Katie Huffman, has suggested that the admiration, even reverence, that high Elves such as Galadriel display toward trees suggests an awareness that trees, even in the Third Age, possess a residue of the Valier who created them, the Vala who favored them, and the Maiar who inhabit and shepherd them. The army of trees at the Battle of the Hornburg illustrates this most dynamically.
212. Qtd. in Hammond and Scull, *The Lord of the Rings: A Reader's Companion*, 743; Tolkien, *Silmarillion*, 374.
213. Dubs, "Providence, Fate, and Chance," 137.
214. Drury, "Providence at Elrond's Council," 8–9.
215. Tolkien, *The Fellowship of the Ring*, 354, 526; Tolkien, *The Two Towers*, 266.
216. Clark, "J. R. R. Tolkien and the True Hero," 47.
217. Tolkien, *Unfinished Tales*, 361, 369n2.
218. Tolkien, *The Two Towers*, 281.
219. Filmer, "An Allegory Unveiled," 20.
220. Tolkien, *The Two Towers*, 246.
221. Rosebury, "Revenge and Moral Judgment," 19n16.
222. Tolkien, *The Return of the King*, 219; Tolkien, *Sauron*, 33; Tolkien, *The Two Towers*, 310; Tolkien, *The Fellowship of the Ring*, 354; Tolkien, *The Two Towers*, 313.
223. Tolkien, *The Two Towers*, 394, 395.
224. Tolkien, *The Two Towers*, 396.
225. Sarti, "Man in a Mortal World."
226. Tolkien, *The Return of the King*, 268, 270, 271.
227. Tolkien, *The Return of the King*, 274.
228. Rorabeck, *Tolkien's Heroic Quest*, 66.
229. Milbank, *Chesterton and Tolkien as Theologians*, 139.
230. Tolkien, *The Treason*, 208.
231. Wood, "Tolkien's Augustinian Understanding," 92.
232. New International Version; Abbott, "Tolkien's Monsters . . . (Part 3)," 57.
233. Tolkien, *The Letters*, 331.
234. Tolkien, *Sauron*, 5–6; Tolkien, *The Return of the Shadow*, 380.
235. Blackburn, "'Dangerous as a Guide to Deeds,'" 65.
236. Hibbs, "Providence and the Dramatic Unity," 170.
237. MacArthur, "The Mystery of the Ring's Destruction," 17–20.
238. Urang, *Shadows of Heaven*, 128.
239. Clark, "J. R. R. Tolkien and the True Hero," 48.
240. Tolkien, *The Letters*, 233, 234, 251, 252, 326.
241. Tolkien, *The Letters*, 326, 327.

242. Petty, *Tolkien in the Land of Heroes,* 93.
243. Tolkien, *The Letters,* 327, 234, 251–52.
244. Tolkien, *The Letters,* 253, 326.
245. Hood, "The Lidless Eye," 193, 198.
246. Cattaneo, "Divine Presence and Providence," 14.
247. Hutton, "The Pagan Tolkien," 39.
248. Mills, "The Writer of Our Story," 28.
249. Tolkien, qtd. in Hammond and Scull, *The Lord of the Rings: A Reader's Companion,* 262.
250. Petty, *Tolkien in the Land of Heroes,* 293.
251. Foster, "Levels of Interpretation," 22.

5. The Problem of Evil in Arda

1. Ellwood, "The Good Guys and the Bad Guys," 9.
2. Anonymous, Review of *The Lord of the Rings,* "The Saga of Middle-earth," 341.
3. Tolkien, *The Lord of the Rings,* 342.
4. Tolkien, *The Letters,* 197.
5. Shippey, *J. R. R. Tolkien,* xxx.
6. Flieger, *Splintered Light,* viii.
7. Rutledge, *The Battle for Middle-earth,* 25.
8. Tolkien, *The Book of Lost Tales,* 1:260; Tolkien, *The Book of Lost Tales,* 2:13, 24.
9. Tolkien, *The Silmarillion,* xii.
10. Kocher, *Master of Middle-earth,* 50.
11. Croft, "The Thread on Which Doom Hangs," 131–32.
12. Houghton and Keesee, "Tolkien, King Alfred, and Boethius," 131–59.
13. Glover, "The Christian Character," 3–8; Tolkien, *Morgoth's Ring,* 334.
14. Pearce, *Tolkien: Man and Myth,* 118.
15. Rosebury, qtd. in Hammond and Scull, *The Lord of the Rings: A Reader's Companion,* 256.
16. Treloar, "Tolkien and Christian Concepts of Evil," 59–60.
17. Shippey, *J. R. R. Tolkien,* 130.
18. Milbank, *Chesterton and Tolkien as Theologians,* 71.
19. Vink, "Fate and Doom in Tolkien," 5–13.
20. Tolkien, *Morgoth's Ring,* 402.
21. Tolkien, "Ósanwe-kenta," 26.
22. Tolkien, *Morgoth's Ring,* 217, 334, 402.
23. Tolkien, *The Silmarillion,* 6.
24. Tolkien, *Sauron,* 397.
25. Tolkien, *The Letters,* 286–87.
26. Tolkien, *Morgoth's Ring,* 400–401, 254–55.
27. Tolkien, *Morgoth's Ring,* 259, 255, 270, 271.
28. Tolkien, *Morgoth's Ring,* 254, 344.

29. Hood, "Nature and Technology," 8.
30. Tolkien, *The Book of Lost Tales,* 1:272.
31. Bullock, "The Importance of Free Will," 29; Tolkien, *The Book of Lost Tales,* 2:112.
32. Shippey, *J. R. R. Tolkien,* 130.
33. Tolkien, *The Letters,* 252; Tolkien, *Morgoth's Ring,* 334.
34. Shippey, *J. R. R. Tolkien,* 149.
35. Tolkien, *The Return of the Shadow,* 212, 364.
36. Rutledge, *The Battle for Middle-earth,* 85.
37. Dickerson, "Valar," 690.
38. Evans, "The Anthropology of Arda," 210.
39. Tolkien, *The Fellowship of the Ring,* 351.
40. Tolkien, *The Silmarillion,* 4.
41. Tolkien, *The Silmarillion,* 4.
42. Tolkien, *The Silmarillion,* 8; Tolkien, *Morgoth's Ring,* 396.
43. Rosebury, *Tolkien,* 189.
44. Tolkien, *The Letters,* 287.
45. Tolkien, *The Silmarillion,* 37.
46. Seeman, "Tolkien's Conception of Evil," 52–67.
47. Tolkien, *The Silmarillion,* 41.
48. Schroeder, "'It's Alive!'" 121.
49. Tolkien, *The Silmarillion,* 38.
50. Flieger, *Splintered Light,* 100.
51. Tolkien, *Morgoth's Ring,* 411; emphasis in the original.
52. Tolkien, *The Silmarillion,* 41.
53. Milbank, *Chesterton and Tolkien as Theologians,* 65.
54. Tolkien, *The Silmarillion,* 41–42.
55. Whitt, "Germanic Fate and Doom," 122.
56. Tolkien, *The Silmarillion,* 42–43.
57. Tolkien, *The Letters,* 287.
58. Tolkien, *The Silmarillion,* 20.
59. Tolkien, *The War of the Jewels,* 213.
60. Blacharska, "The Fallen," 118.
61. Tolkien, *Return to Bag End,* 565; Hammond and Scull, *The Lord of the Rings: A Reader's Companion,* 245.
62. Barajas-Garrido, "Perspectives on Reality," 51–59.
63. Tolkien, *The Lost Road,* 300.
64. Tolkien, *The War of the Jewels,* 213; Tolkien, *The Letters,* 287.
65. Tolkien, *The Silmarillion,* 41; emphasis added.
66. Tolkien, *The Letters,* 287.
67. Tolkien, *Morgoth's Ring,* 392.
68. Tolkien, "Notes on Orë," 15; Tolkien, *Morgoth's Ring,* 209–14.
69. Flieger, *Splintered Light,* 109.
70. Flieger, *Interrupted Music,* 53.

71. Tolkien, "Sir Gawain and the Green Knight," 95.
72. Tolkien, *The Two Towers,* 362.
73. Tolkien, *The Two Towers,* 253.
74. Tolkien, *The Fellowship of the Ring,* 520; Tolkien, *The War of the Ring,* 208.
75. Hammond and Scull, *The Lord of the Rings: A Reader's Companion,* 359.
76. Tolkien, *Tolkien on Fairy-stories,* 141.
77. Tolkien, *The Return of the King,* 191.
78. Tolkien, *The Lost Road,* 234.
79. Tolkien, *The Fellowship of the Ring,* 461.
80. Tolkien, *Unfinished Tales,* 408.
81. Croft, "The Thread on Which Doom Hangs," 139.
82. Croft, "The Thread on Which Doom Hangs," 141; emphasis in the original.
83. Blackburn, "'Dangerous as a Guide to Deeds,'" 63.
84. Stratyner, "ðe us ðas beagas geaf," 6.
85. Auden, "Good and Evil," 7.
86. Tolkein, *Mr. Baggins,* 326.
87. Tolkein, *Mr. Baggins,* 326.
88. Tolkein, *Morgoth's Ring,* 411; Tolkien, *The Two Towers,* 441; Tolkien, *The Return of the King,* 216.
89. Tolkien, *The Two Towers,* 28, 60, 68, 218; Tolkien, *The Shaping,* 136.
90. Rosebury, *Tolkien,* 45.
91. Rogers, *Evil, Eroticism, and Englishness,* 105.
92. Tolkien, *The Letters,* 228.
93. Tolkien, *The Shaping,* 110.
94. Crowe, "Making and Unmaking," 63.
95. Tolkien, *The Silmarillion,* 81.
96. Tolkien, *The Book of Lost Tales,* 2:1.
97. Petty, *Tolkien in the Land of Heroes,* 225.
98. Flieger, *Splintered Light,* 111.
99. Tolkien, *Morgoth's Ring,* 295.
100. Tolkien, *The Silmarillion,* 89–90.
101. Tolkien, *The Shaping,* 18; Tolkien, *The War of the Jewels,* 196.
102. Tolkien, *Morgoth's Ring,* 295–96. I have argued elsewhere that Tolkien assigns Ungoliant female gender in part because he feels irrationality more naturally aligns with femininity; see Fredrick and McBride, *Women among the Inklings.*
103. Tolkien, *The Letters,* 243; Tolkien, *Morgoth's Ring,* 396.
104. Hood, "Sauron and Dracula," 16.
105. Seeman, "Tolkien's Conception of Evil," 54.
106. Hood, "The Lidless Eye."
107. Crowe, "Making and Unmaking," 62; Tolkien, *The Book of Lost Tales,* 2:293.
108. Tolkien, *Morgoth's Ring,* 41, 395.
109. Tolkien, *Morgoth's Ring,* 395–97; Tolkien, *The Letters,* 243.
110. Tolkien, *The Two Towers,* 310, 355.
111. Lense, "Sauron Is Watching *You,*" 4.

112. Nagy, "A Body of Myth," 129.
113. Levitin, "Power in *The Lord of the Rings*," 13.
114. Tolkien, *The War of the Ring*, 365, 335.
115. Tolkien, *Morgoth's Ring*, 397.
116. Tolkien, *The Two Towers*, 423, 415, 422; Tolkien, *The War of the Ring*, 208.
117. Tolkien, *The Two Towers*, 422, 423.
118. Burns, "Eating, Devouring, Sacrifice," 108–14.
119. Tolkien, *The Two Towers*, 424.
120. Tolkien, *The Fellowship of the Ring*, 351.
121. Tolkien, *The Hobbit*, 272–73, 276.
122. Ryan, *Tolkien: Cult or Culture?*, 178.
123. Tolkien, *The Treason*, 212, 385.
124. I am indebted to my student, Marjorie Ellenwood, for drawing to my attention Galadriel's trajectory of rebellion and redemption.
125. Stratyner, "ðe us ðas beagas geaf," 7; Tolkien, *The Letters*, 292.
126. Tolkien, *The Peoples*, 225; Tolkien, *The Fellowship of the Ring*, 85, 87.
127. Crabbe, *J. R. R. Tolkien* (1981), 82.
128. Tolkien, *The Fellowship of the Ring*, 286; Tolkien, *The Treason*, 119; Tolkien, *The Two Towers*, 381.
129. Burke, "Fear and Horror," 47.
130. Tolkien, *The Two Towers*, 411; qtd. in Hammond and Scull, *The Lord of the Rings: A Reader's Companion*, 746; Tolkien, *The Letters*, 110; Tolkien, *The Return of the King*, 466, xii.
131. Hammond and Scull, *The Lord of the Rings: A Reader's Companion*, 746.
132. Purtill, *J. R. R. Tolkien*, 94.
133. Tolkien, *The Letters*, 221.
134. Abbott, "Tolkien's Monsters . . . (Part 2)," 45.
135. Tolkien, *The Letters*, 330.
136. Tolkien, *The Return of the King*, 512.
137. Tally, "Let Us Now Praise Famous Orcs," 27.
138. Tolkien, *The Book of Lost Tales*, 2:161; Tolkien, *The Letters*, 274; Tolkien, *The Return of the King*, 414.
139. Tolkien, *The Two Towers*, 26, 64; Colebatch, *Return of the Heroes*, 105; Tolkien, *The Lost Road*, 194; Tolkien, *The Return of the King*, 511; Tolkien, *The Peoples*, 65n16, 35, 42.
140. Tally, "Let Us Now Praise Famous Orcs," 17.
141. Colebatch, *Return of the Heroes*, 143–44.
142. Harvey, *The Song of Middle-earth*, 56.
143. Barajas-Garrido, "Perspectives on Reality," 51–59.
144. Chism, "Race and Ethnicity in Tolkien's Works," 556.
145. Tolkien, *The Return of the King*, 105; Tolkien, *Unfinished Tales*, 394; Tolkien, *The Return of the Shadow*, 362.
146. Mathews, *Lightning from a Clear Sky*, 35.
147. Tolkien, *The Two Towers*, 199.

148. Shippey, qtd. in Hammond and Scull, *The Lord of the Rings: A Reader's Companion*, 375.
149. Auden, "Good and Evil," 5; Tolkien, *The Letters*, 90.
150. Tolkien, *The Fellowship of the Ring*, 351.
151. Sturch, "Of Orcs and Other Oddities," 5.
152. Tolkien, *The Two Towers*, 441.
153. Auden, "Good and Evil," 5.
154. Birzer, *J. R. R. Tolkien's Sanctifying Myth*, 94.
155. Eggington, "Tolkien's Corrupt World," 22.
156. Kocher, *Master of Middle-earth*, 70–71.
157. Tolkien, *The Letters*, 195.
158. Tolkien, *Morgoth's Ring*, 409.
159. Rosebury, "Revenge and Moral Judgment," 2, 9–11.
160. Shippey, "Orcs, Wraiths, Wights," 244.
161. Colebatch, *Return of the Heroes*, 141.
162. Tolkien, *The Two Towers*, 395.
163. Shippey, "Orcs, Wraiths, Wights," 186, 184.
164. Shippey, "Orcs, Wraiths, Wights," 198.
165. Tneh, "The Human Image," 37.
166. Tally, "'Let Us Now Praise Famous Orcs,'" 23.
167. Hammond and Scull, *The Lord of the Rings: A Reader's Companion*, 390.
168. Tally, "Let Us Now Praise Famous Orcs," 19.
169. Tolkien, *The Return of the King*, 222.
170. Tolkien, *The Hobbit*, 88; Colebatch, *Return of the Heroes*, 141.
171. Tneh, "Orcs and Tolkien's Treatment of Evil," 37–43.
172. Tolkien, *The Book of Lost Tales*, 2:36; Tally, "Let Us Now Praise Famous Orcs," 25; Tolkien, *The Return of the King*, 233.
173. Tolkien, *The Peoples*, 414.
174. Tolkien, *Morgoth's Ring*, 419, 417–18.
175. Tolkien, *Morgoth's Ring*, 409.
176. Tally, "Let Us Now Praise Famous Orcs," 19; Tolkien, *The Letters*, 191.
177. Tolkien, *The Silmarillion*, 50.
178. Tolkien, *The Book of Lost Tales*, 2:347; Tolkien, *The Shaping*, 13.
179. Tolkien, *Unfinished Tales*, 401n5; Tolkien, *The Letters*, 178; Tolkien, *Morgoth's Ring*, 418.
180. Luling, "Those Awful Orcs," 5.
181. Tolkien, *Sauron*, 332; Tolkien, *The Lost Road*, 300.
182. Tolkien, *The Lost Road*, 177; Tolkien, *The Shaping*, 100.
183. Sturch, "Of Orcs and Other Oddities," 6.
184. Tolkien, *Morgoth's Ring*, 121, 123–24, 159, 195; Tolkien, *The Shaping*, 232–33, 352, 376; Tolkien, *Morgoth's Ring*, 413n10.
185. Tolkien, *Morgoth's Ring*, 410.
186. Tolkien, *Morgoth's Ring*, 410.
187. Tolkien, *The War of the Jewels*, 391.

188. Tolkien, *Morgoth's Ring*, 413n6.
189. Tolkien, *Morgoth's Ring*, 411.
190. Petty, *Tolkien in the Land of Heroes*, 46.
191. Colebatch, *Return of the Heroes*, 143–44.
192. Tolkien, *Morgoth's Ring*, 410, 74; Tolkien, *The Lost Road*, 255–56; Tolkien, *The War of the Jewels*, 15.
193. Partridge, "No Sex Please," 179–97.
194. Tolkien, *The Book of Lost Tales*, 2:12.
195. Tolkien, *The Peoples*, 36, 79–80; Tolkien, *Morgoth's Ring*, 406, 411, 414–18; Tolkien, *Unfinished Tales*, 431n7; Ruud, "The Voice of Saruman," 143; Tolkien, *The Two Towers*, 180.
196. Tolkien, *Morgoth's Ring*, 409.
197. Croft, "The Thread on Which Doom Hangs," 135.
198. Tolkien, *Morgoth's Ring*, 411.
199. Tolkien, *The Letters*, 152.
200. Shippey, qtd. in Hammond and Scull, *The Lord of the Rings: A Reader's Companion*, 255.
201. Harris, "The Psychology of Power," 50.
202. Tolkien, *The Letters*, 200.
203. Tolkien, *The Letters*, 88, 246, 116, 158.
204. Rogers, *Evil, Eroticism, and Englishness*, 100.
205. Carpenter, *Tolkien*, 230; Tolkien, *The War of the Ring*, 105; Hood, "Sauron and Dracula," 15.
206. Veldman, *Fantasy, the Bomb, and the Greening of Britain*, 109.
207. Tolkien, *The Letters*, 77, 88, 97, 105, 115.
208. Tolkien, *The War of the Jewels*, 413.
209. Tolkien, *The Letters*, 121, 246, 190, 146.
210. Tolkien, *The Silmarillion*, 204.
211. Tolkien, *The Return of the Shadow*, 41, 42.
212. Tolkien, *The Peoples*, 167–69, 233; Tolkien, *The Return of the Shadow*, 42; Tolkien, *The Treason*, 22; Tolkien, *The Return of the Shadow*, 321.
213. Tolkien, *Unfinished Tales*, 287, 295; Petty, *Tolkien in the Land of Heroes*, 92.
214. Tolkien, *The Letters*, 157; Tolkien, *The Return of the Shadow*, 397; Tolkien, *The Peoples*, 266.
215. Tolkien, *The War of the Ring*, 404.
216. Birzer, *J. R. R. Tolkien's Sanctifying Myth*, 104.
217. Tolkien, *The War of the Ring*, 400; Hood, "Sauron and Dracula," 15.
218. Shippey, *J. R. R. Tolkien*, 106. My student, Jason Wymore, has compared the impact of the One Ring with the impact of heroin, as described in William S. Burroughs's *Junky*.
219. Tolkien, *The Letters*, 152.
220. Tolkien, *The Silmarillion*, 356, 370. See also Tolkien, *The Return of the Shadow*, 260.
221. Tolkien, *Unfinished Tales*, 353, 358, 354.

222. Colebatch, *Return of the Heroes,* 32.
223. Hood, "Nature and Technology," 8.
224. Tolkien, *The Peoples,* 310; Tolkien, *Unfinished Tales,* 403n11.
225. Tolkien, *Unfinished Tales,* 396, 397; Tolkien, *The Two Towers,* 155.
226. Tolkien, *Unfinished Tales,* 398.
227. Walker, *The Power of Tolkien's Prose,* 64.
228. Tolkien, *The Two Towers,* 254–55, 260.
229. Tolkien, *The Two Towers,* 255; Tolkien, *The Return of the King,* 107.
230. Tolkien, *Unfinished Tales,* 271, 284; Tolkien, *The Treason,* 286.
231. World Health Organization, "F60.2: Dissocial personality disorder."

🖋 6. Death

1. Tolkien, *The Letters,* 246, 284, 236.
2. Tolkien, *Morgoth's Ring,* 315–16, 267.
3. Tolkien, *Morgoth's Ring,* 349, 250, 351.
4. Qtd. in Hammond and Scull, *The Lord of the Rings: A Reader's Guide,* 65.
5. Tolkien, *Morgoth's Ring,* 330, 349.
6. Tolkien, *Morgoth's Ring,* 308, 336–37.
7. Testi, "Tolkien's Legendarium," 48.
8. Tolkien, *Morgoth's Ring,* 312, 319; Tolkien, *The Letters,* 280.
9. Tolkien, *Sauron,* 338; Tolkien, *The Letters,* 151.
10. Fornet-Ponse, "'Strange and Free,'" 219.
11. Tolkien, *The Letters,* 151; Tolkien, *The Shaping,* 196; Tolkien, *Morgoth's Ring,* 212.
12. Tolkien, *Sauron,* 115–16; Tolkien, *The Peoples,* 235–36, 264.
13. Tolkien, *The Letters,* 237.
14. Tolkien, *The Letters,* 286; Tolkien, *Morgoth's Ring,* 218, 331.
15. Tolkien, *Morgoth's Ring,* 330–31.
16. Tolkien, *Morgoth's Ring,* 219, 223.
17. Tolkien, *The Silmarillion,* 227; Tolkien, *The Lays,* 305–6; Tolkien, *The Book of Lost Tales,* 1:77–78.
18. Tolkien, *Morgoth's Ring,* 339, 222–24.
19. Tolkien, *Morgoth's Ring,* 224; Tolkien, *The Two Towers,* 297–98.
20. Tolkien, *Morgoth's Ring,* 232.
21. Tolkien, *Morgoth's Ring,* 37.
22. Flieger, *A Question of Time,* 134.
23. Tolkien, *The Letters,* 189, 189n.
24. Tolkien, *Morgoth's Ring,* 21, 221–22.
25. Tolkien, *Morgoth's Ring,* 224, 216n, 233.
26. Tolkien, *Morgoth's Ring,* 361–63; Tolkien, *The Peoples,* 390n17.
27. Tolkien, *Mr. Baggins,* 433n42.
28. Tolkien, *Morgoth's Ring,* 363–64.

29. Tolkien, *The Shaping*, 121; Tolkien, *The War of the Jewels*, 67; Tolkien, *Morgoth's Ring*, 331, 267; Tolkien, *The Peoples*, 389n8; Tolkien, *Morgoth's Ring*, 222.

30. Tolkien, *The Book of Lost Tales*, 2:194–95; Tolkien, *Morgoth's Ring*, 378.

31. Tolkien, *Morgoth's Ring*, 339.

32. Tolkien, *Morgoth's Ring*, 222.

33. Tolkien, *Morgoth's Ring*, 236, 206.

34. Tolkien, *Morgoth's Ring*, 361.

35. Tolkien, *Morgoth's Ring*, 207, 237.

36. Tolkien, *Morgoth's Ring*, 239–47.

37. Tolkien, *Morgoth's Ring*, 242–44.

38. Tolkien, *Morgoth's Ring*, 248.

39. Tolkien, *Morgoth's Ring*, 249.

40. Tolkien, *Morgoth's Ring*, 250.

41. Aldrich, "The Sense of Time," 6, 9; emphasis in the original.

42. Tolkien, *The Peoples*, 225.

43. Williams, *Mere Humanity*, 122; emphasis in the original.

44. Tolkien, *The Lost Road*, 179.

45. Tolkien, *Morgoth's Ring*, 429.

46. Tolkien, *Morgoth's Ring*, 331; Tolkien, *The Letters*, 325; Tolkien, *Tolkien on Fairy-stories*, 75; Tolkien, *Morgoth's Ring*, 317.

47. Garbowski, *Recovery and Transcendence*, 180.

48. Tolkien, *Morgoth's Ring*, 315, 310; Tolkien, *The Silmarillion*, 38.

49. Flieger, *Splintered Light*, 144.

50. Tolkien, *The Silmarillion*, 327; Tolkien, *Morgoth's Ring*, 339, 309, 311, 314.

51. Tolkien, *Morgoth's Ring*, 315; Tolkien, *The Letters*, 286.

52. Tolkien, "Notes on Óre," 12.

53. Garbowski, "Eucatastrophe and the Gift of Ilúvatar," 26, 31.

54. Tolkien, *Sauron*, 365, 382.

55. Tolkien, *The Book of Lost Tales*, 1:78; Tolkien, *Unfinished Tales*, 23; Tolkien, *Morgoth's Ring*, 340; Tolkien, *The Lost Road*, 367; Tolkien, *The Book of Lost Tales*, 2:115.

56. Tolkien, *The Lost Road*, 271; Tolkien, *The Silmarillion*, 121; Tolkien, *The Lost Road*, 336, 271; Tolkien, *Sauron*, 333.

57. Tolkien, *The Silmarillion*, 326.

58. Hammond and Scull, *The Lord of the Rings: A Reader's Companion*, 702; Tolkien, *The Children of Hurin*, 252.

59. Tolkien, *Unfinished Tales*, 65; Tolkien, *The Shaping*, 356.

60. Tolkien, *Morgoth's Ring*, 427; Tolkien, *The Silmarillion*, 349; Tolkien, *Morgoth's Ring*, 428–30.

61. Tolkien, *The Return of the King*, 120, 157.

62. Tolkien, *The Silmarillion*, 325; Tolkien, *The Two Towers*, 363.

63. Tolkien, *Unfinished Tales*, 229, 235; Tolkien, *The Letters*, 205n; Tolkien, *Unfinished Tales*, 175; Tolkien, *The Lost Road*, 17, 23.

64. Tolkien, *The Lays*, 405; Tolkien, *The Silmarillion*, 197; Tolkien, *The Lays*, 201, 200.
65. Tolkien, *The Lays*, 323; Tolkien, *The Silmarillion*, 221.
66. Tolkien, *The Silmarillion*, 226–27.
67. Tolkien, *The War of the Jewels*, 69; Tolkien, *The Silmarillion*, 227; Tolkien, *Morgoth's Ring*, 340; Tolkien, *The Silmarillion*, 227.
68. Tolkien, *The Silmarillion*, 227.
69. Tolkien, *The Silmarillion*; Tolkien, *Morgoth's Ring*, 340.
70. Tolkien, *The Shaping*, 160.
71. Tolkien, *The Book of Lost Tales*, 2:241.
72. Tolkien, *The Silmarillion*, 228.
73. Flieger, *Splintered Light*, 143.
74. Tolkien, *The Silmarillion*, 292.
75. Tolkien, *The Silmarillion*; emphasis added.
76. Tolkien, *The Shaping*, 368.
77. Tolkien, *The Return of the Shadow*, 184.
78. Tolkien, *The Return of the King*, 388.
79. Shippey, *J. R. R. Tolkien*, 248.
80. Tolkien, *The Silmarillion*, 229.
81. Tolkien, *The Silmarillion*, 228; Tolkien, *The Fellowship of the Ring*, 261.
82. Tolkien, *The Silmarillion*, 303, 326.
83. Tolkien, *The Silmarillion*, 322; Tolkien, *Sauron*, 333.
84. Tolkien, *The Peoples*, 234, 257.
85. Tolkien, *The Peoples*, 262n6.
86. Tolkien, *The Return of the King*, 316; Tolkien, *The Peoples*, 265.
87. Tolkien, *The Return of the King*, 426–28; Hammond and Scull, *The Lord of the Rings: A Reader's Guide*, 701.
88. Tolkien, *The Return of the King*, 428.
89. Tolkien, *The Return of the King*, 468, 423.
90. Tolkien, *The Return of the King*, 425.
91. Tolkien, *The Letters*, 327; emphasis added.
92. Tolkien, *The Letters*, 327–28.
93. Tolkien, *The Return of the King*, 312; Tolkien, *The Letters*, 328, 411; Tolkien, *Morgoth's Ring*, 341; Nelson, "'The Halls of Waiting,'" 200–211.
94. Tolkien, *The Return of the King*, 384; Tolkien, *Sauron*, 132; Tolkien, *The Letters*, 198–99.
95. Tolkien, *The Return of the King*, 140.
96. Tolkien, *Sauron*, 336; Tolkien, *The Silmarillion*, 345.
97. Tolkien, *The Return of the King*, 64–65.
98. Amendt-Raduege, "Barrows, Wights, and Ordinary People," 147.
99. Tolkien, *The Return of the King*, 71–72, 74.
100. Tolkien, *The Return of the Shadow*, 118.
101. Tolkien, *The Return of the King*, 195.
102. Tolkien, *The Return of the King*, 398.

103. Perry, *Untangling Tolkien*, 98.
104. Amendt-Raduege, "Barrows, Wights, and Ordinary People," 139.
105. Stratyner, "ðe us ðas beagas geaf," 6.
106. Rawls, "The Rings of Power," 30.
107. Tolkien, *The Two Towers*, 382.
108. Davis, "Choosing to Die," 125–26.
109. Tolkien, *The Silmarillion*, 346.
110. Kocher, *Master of Middle-earth*, 57.
111. Kisor, "Incorporeality and Transformation," 22.
112. Shippey, *J. R. R. Tolkien*, 124.
113. Tolkien, *The Return of the King*, 146, 143.
114. Tolkien, *The Silmarillion*, 364; Tolkien, *The Return of the King*, 125.
115. Garbowski, "Tolkien's Cosmic Eucatastrophe," 284.
116. Tolkien, *The Return of the Shadow*, 225.
117. Kocher, *Master of Middle-earth*, 93.
118. Flieger, "The Body in Question," 15.
119. Tolkien, *The Hobbit*, 272; Tolkien, *The War of the Jewels*, 204.
120. Tolkien, *The Two Towers*, 441.
121. Tolkien, *The Book of Lost Tales*, 2:38.
122. Tolkien, *The Lays*, 303, 307.
123. Tolkien, *The Silmarillion*, 337, 353, 377.
124. Tolkien, *The Silmarillion*, 306; Tolkien, *Unfinished Tales*, 408.
125. Shippey, *J. R. R. Tolkien*, 127.

7. *Eucatastrophe,* Estel, *and the End of Arda*

1. Tolkien, *The Lost Road*, 79n12.
2. Tolkien, *Tolkien on Fairy-stories*, 97.
3. Tolkien, *The Letters*, 100.
4. Tolkien, *The Letters*, 101.
5. Tolkien, *Tolkien on Fairy-stories*, 75.
6. Drury, "Providence at Elrond's Council," 9.
7. Tolkien, qtd. in Hammond and Scull, *The Lord of the Rings: A Reader's Compannion*, 748.
8. Mende, "Gondolin, Minas Tirith and the Eucatastrophe," 40; Tolkien, *Morgoth's Ring*, 321.
9. Hyles, "On the Nature of Evil," 13.
10. Tolkien, *The Book of Lost Tales*, 1:247; Hammond and Scull, *The Lord of the Rings: A Reader's Companion*, 143; see also Kocher, *Master of Middle-earth*, 69.
11. Tolkien, *Tolkien on Fairy-stories*, 75.
12. Garbowski, "Eucatastrophe and the Gift of Ilúvatar," 25.
13. Tolkien, from his 1951 letter to Milton Waldman; qtd. in Hammond and Scull, *The Lord of the Rings: A Reader's Companion*, 673.

14. Tolkien, *The Book of Lost Tales,* 2:115; Tolkien, *The Book of Lost Tales,* 1:50.
15. Shippey, *J. R. R. Tolkien,* 150.
16. Tolkien, *The Letters,* 149; Birzer, *J. R. R. Tolkien's Sanctifying Myth,* 54.
17. Tolkien, *The Lost Road,* 266; Tolkien, *The Letters* 207; Tolkien, *The Book of Lost Tales,* 2:140; Tolkien, *The Lost Road,* 266; Tolkien, *Morgoth's Ring,* 405, 71, 322.
18. Tolkien, *Morgoth's Ring,* 94–95; Tolkien, *The Shaping,* 46–47.
19. Tolkien, *The Shaping,* 89; Tolkien, *The Return of the King,* 259; Tolkien, *The Shaping,* 90; Tolkien, *Morgoth's Ring,* 94–95.
20. Tolkien, *The Shaping,* 197–99; Tolkien, *The Lost Road,* 368.
21. Tolkien, *Morgoth's Ring,* 37; Tolkien, *The Book of Lost Tales,* 1:50, 57; Tolkien, *Morgoth's Ring,* 9.
22. Davis, "The Ainulindalë," 7.
23. Tolkien, *Morgoth's Ring,* 245.
24. Tolkien, *Morgoth's Ring,* 351; Tolkien, *The Silmarillion,* 38; Tolkien, *Morgoth's Ring,* 21.
25. Tolkien, *Morgoth's Ring,* 251, 319, 252, 319.
26. Tolkien, *Morgoth's Ring,* 405; Tolkien, *The Lost Road,* 160n16; Tolkien, *The Letters,* 287; Tolkien, *The War of the Jewels,* 204; Tolkien, *The Letters,* 419.
27. Shippey, *J. R. R. Tolkien,* 150.
28. Tolkien, *Morgoth's Ring,* 245, 204; Tolkien, *The Lost Road,* 176, 179; Tolkien, *The Book of Lost Tales,* 1:58.
29. Tolkien, *Sauron,* 346.
30. Tolkien, *The Letters,* 285; Tolkien, *Morgoth's Ring,* 338.
31. Tolkien, *The Letters,* 283.

Bibliography

Abbott, Joe. "Tolkien's Monsters: Concept and Function in *The Lord of the Rings* (Part 2): Shelob the Great." *Mythlore: A Journal of J. R. R. Tolkien, C. S. Lewis, Charles Williams and Mythopoeic Literature* 16, no. 2 (Winter 1989): 40–47.

———. "Tolkien's Monsters: Concept and Function in *The Lord of the Rings* (Part 3): Sauron." *Mythlore: A Journal of J. R. R. Tolkien, C. S. Lewis, Charles Williams and Mythopoeic Literature* 16, no. 3 (Spring 1990): 51–59.

Agøy, Nils Ivar, "The Fall and Man's Mortality: An Investigation of Some Theological Themes in J. R. R. Tolkien's 'Athrabeth Finrod ah Andreth.'" In *Between Faith and Fiction: Tolkien and the Powers of His World,* edited by Nils Ivar Agøy, 26. Arda Special 1. Proceedings of the Arda Symposium at the Second Tolkien Festival, Oslo, Aug. 1997. Uppsala, Sweden: Arda-Society, 1998.

Aldrich, Kevin. "The Sense of Time in J. R. R. Tolkien's *The Lord of the Rings.*" *Mythlore: A Journal of J. R. R. Tolkien, C. S. Lewis, Charles Williams and Mythopoeic Literature* 15, no. 1 (Autumn 1988): 5–9.

Amendt-Raduege, Amy M. "Barrows, Wights, and Ordinary People: The Unquiet Dead in J. R. R. Tolkien's *The Lord of the Rings.*" In *The Mirror Crack'd: Fear and Horror in J. R. R. Tolkien's Major Works,* edited by Lynn Forest-Hill, 139–50. Cambridge: Cambridge Scholars, 2008.

———. "Dream Visions in J. R. R. Tolkien's *The Lord of the Rings.*" In *Tolkien Studies: An Annual Scholarly Review* 3, edited by Douglas A. Anderson, Michael D. C. Drout, and Verlyn Flieger, 45–55. Morgantown: West Virginia Univ. Press, 2006.

Amison, Anne. "An Unexpected Guest." *Mythlore: A Journal of J. R. R. Tolkien, C. S. Lewis, Charles Williams and Mythopoeic Literature* 25, no. 1/2 (Fall/Winter 2006): 127–36.

Anonymous. Review of *The Lord of the Rings,* "The Saga of Middle-earth." *Times Literary Supplement,* Nov. 25, 1955, 704. Quoted in Wayne G. Hammond and Christina Scull, *The Lord of the Rings: A Reader's Guide,* 341. Boston: Houghton Mifflin, 2005.

Apeland, Kaj Andre. "The Forces of Evil." *Angerthas in English,* Aug. 1985. Oslo: Arthedain—The Tolkien Society of Norway.

———. "On Entering the Same River Twice: Mythology and Theology in the Silmarillion Corpus." In *Between Faith and Fiction: Tolkien and the Powers of His World,* edited by Nils Ivar Agøy, 44. Arda Special 1. Proceedings of the Arda Symposium at the Second Tolkien Festival, Oslo, Aug. 1997. Uppsala, Sweden: Arda-Society, 1998.

Auden, W. H. "Good and Evil in *The Lord of the Rings.*" *Tolkien Journal* 3, no. 1 (1967): 7.

Barajas-Garrido, Gerardo. "Perspectives on Reality in *Lord of the Rings.*" *Mallorn* 42 (Aug. 2004): 51–59.

Berman, Ruth. "Tolkien as a Child of *The Green Fairy Book.*" *Mythlore: A Journal of J. R. R. Tolkien, C. S. Lewis, Charles Williams, and Mythopoeic Literature* 26, no. 1/2 (Fall/Winter 2007): 127–35.

Birns, Nicholas. "The Enigma of Radagast: Revision, Melodrama, and Depth." *Mythlore: A Journal of J. R. R. Tolkien, C. S. Lewis, Charles Williams, and Mythopoeic Literature* 26, no. 1/2 (Fall 2007): 113–26.

Birzer, Bradley. "Eru." In *J. R. R. Tolkien Encyclopedia: Scholarship and Critical Assessment,* edited by Michael D. C. Drout, 171–72. New York: Routledge, 2007.

———. *J. R. R. Tolkien's Sanctifying Myth: Understanding Middle-earth.* Wilmington, DE: ISI, 2009.

Blacharska, Katarzzyna. "The Fallen: Milton's Satan and Tolkien's Melkor." In *"O, What a Tangled Web": Tolkien and Medieval Literature—A View from Poland,* edited by Barbara Kowalik, 115–43. Zurich: Walking Tree, 2013.

Blackburn, William. "'Dangerous as a Guide to Deeds': Politics in the Fiction of J. R. R. Tolkien." *Mythlore: A Journal of J. R. R. Tolkien, C. S. Lewis, Charles Williams, and Mythopoeic Literature* 15, no. 1 (Autumn 1988): 62–66.

Bossert, A. R. "'Surely You Don't Disbelieve': Tolkien and Pius X: Antimodernism in Middle-earth." *Mythlore: A Journal of J. R. R. Tolkien, C. S. Lewis, Charles Williams, and Mythopoeic Literature* 25, no. 1/2 (Fall/Winter 2006): 53–76.

Brackmann, Rebecca. "'Dwarves Are Not Heroes': Anti-Semitism and the Dwarves in Tolkien." *Mythlore: A Journal of J. R. R. Tolkien, C. S. Lewis, Charles Williams, and Mythopoeic Literature* 28, no. 3/4 (Spring/Summer 2010): 85–106.

Brawley, Chris. *Nature and the Numinous in Mythopoeic Fantasy Literature.* Jefferson, NC: McFarland, 2014.

Bridoux, Denis. "Of the Ainur and Their Relationships." *Amon Hen* 55 (Apr. 1982): 6–7.

Brooks, Kerry. "Tom Bombadil and the Journey for Middle-earth." *Mallorn: The Journal of the Tolkien Society* 55 (Winter 2014): 11–13.

Bruce, Alexander M. "The Fall of Gondolin and the Fall of Troy: Tolkien and Book II of *The Aeneid.*" *Mythlore: A Journal of J. R. R. Tolkien, C. S. Lewis, Charles Williams, and Mythopoeic Literature* 30, no. 3/4 (Spring/Summer 2012): 103–15.

Brueckner, Patrick. "Tolkien on Love: Concepts of 'Love' in *The Silmarillion* and *The Lord of the Rings.*" In *Tolkien and Modernity* 2, edited by Thomas Honegger and Frank Weinreich, 1–52. Zollikofen, Switzerland: Walking Tree, 2006.

Bullock, Richard P. "The Importance of Free Will in *The Lord of the Rings.*" *Mythlore: A Journal of J. R. R. Tolkien, C. S. Lewis, Charles Williams and Mythopoeic Literature* 11, no. 3 (Winter–Spring 1985): 29–30.

Burke, Jessica. "Fear and Horror: Monsters in Tolkien and *Beowulf.*" In *The Mirror Crack'd: Fear and Horror in J. R. R. Tolkien's Major Works,* edited by Lynn Forest-Hill, 15–52. Cambridge: Cambridge Scholars, 2008.

Burns, Marjorie J. "All in One, One in All." In *Between Faith and Fiction: Tolkien and the Powers of His World,* edited by Nils Ivar Agøy, 2–11. Arda Special 1. Proceedings of the Arda Symposium at the Second Tolkien Festival, Oslo, Aug. 1997. Uppsala, Sweden: Arda-Society, 1998.

————. "Eating, Devouring, Sacrifice and Ultimate Just Desserts." *Mallorn 33/ Mythlore 80—Proceedings of the J. R. R. Tolkien Centenary Conference, Keble College, Oxford, 1992,* edited by Patricia Reynolds and Glen H. Goodnight, 108–14. Altadena, CA: Mythopoeic Press, 1995.

————. "Norse and Christian Gods: The Integrative Theology of J. R. R. Tolkien." In *Tolkien and the Invention of Myth: A Reader,* edited by Jane Chance, 163–78. Lexington: Univ. of Kentucky Press, 2004.

————. *Perilous Realms: Celtic and Norse in Tolkien's Middle-earth.* Toronto: Univ. of Toronto Press, 2005.

Caldecott, Stratford. *Secret Fire: The Spiritual Vision of J R R Tolkien.* London: Darton, Longman, and Todd, 2003.

Campbell, Liam. "The Enigmatic Mr. Bombadil: Tom Bombadil's Role as a Representation of Nature in *The Lord of the Rings.*" In *Middle-earth and Beyond: Essays on the World of J. R. R. Tolkien,* edited by Kathleen Dubs and Janka Kaščáková, 41–65. Newcastle-upon-Tyne, UK: Cambridge Scholars, 2010.

Carpenter, Humphrey. *Tolkien.* Boston: Houghton Mifflin, 1977.

Cattaneo, Davide. "Divine Presence and Providence in *The Lord of the Rings.*" In *Tolkien 2005: The Ring Goes Ever On—Proceedings,* edited by Sarah Wells, 12–14. Celebrating 50 Years of *The Lord of the Rings.* Aston Univ., Birmingham, Aug. 11–15, 2005. Coventry, UK: The Tolkien Society, 2008.

Chism, Christine. "Race and Ethnicity in Tolkien's Works." In *J. R. R. Tolkien Encyclopedia: Scholarship and Critical Assessment,* edited by Michael D. C. Drout, 556. New York: Routledge, 2007.

Clark, George. "J. R. R. Tolkien and the True Hero." In *J. R. R. Tolkien and His Literary Resonances,* edited by George Clark and Daniel Timmons, 39–51. Westport, CT: Greenwood, 2000.

Colebatch, Hal G. P. *Return of the Heroes:* The Lord of the Rings, Star Wars, Harry Potter, *and Social Conflict.* 2nd ed. Christchurch, New Zealand: Cybereditions, 2003.

Coombs, Jenny, and Marc Read. "Valaquanta: Of the Energy of the Valar." *Mallorn: The Journal of the Tolkien Society* 28 (Sept. 1991): 29–35.

Crabbe, Kathryn F. *J. R. R. Tolkien.* New York: Frederick Ungar, 1981. Rpt. in *Contemporary Literary Criticism,* edited by Daniel G. Marowski and Roger Matuz. Vol. 38. Detroit: Gale, 1986. *Artemis Literary Sources.*

———. *J. R. R. Tolkien*. Rev. ed. New York: Continuum, 1988.

Croft, Janet Brennan. "The Thread on Which Doom Hangs: Free Will, Disobedience, and Eucatastrophe." *Mythlore: A Journal of J. R. R. Tolkien, C. S. Lewis, Charles Williams and Mythopoeic Literature* 29, no. 1/2 (Fall/Winter 2010): 131–49.

Crowe, Edith L. "Making and Unmaking in Middle-earth and Elsewhere." *Mythlore: A Journal of J. R. R. Tolkien, C. S. Lewis, Charles Williams and Mythopoeic Literature* 23, no. 3 (Summer 2001): 56–69.

Curry, Patrick. *Defending Middle-earth: Tolkien: Myth and Modernity*. Boston: Houghton Mifflin, 2004.

Davis, Bill. "Choosing to Die: The Gift of Mortality in Middle-earth." In The Lord of the Rings *and Philosophy: One Book to Rule Them All*, edited by Gregory Bassham and Eric Bronson, 123–36. Chicago: Open Court, 2003.

Davis, Howard. "The Ainulindalë; Music of Creation." *Mythlore: A Journal of J. R. R. Tolkien, C. S. Lewis, Charles Williams and Mythopoeic Literature* 9, no. 2 (Summer 1982): 6–10.

Davis, John. "Heroic Failure and the Will of God in *The Lord of the Rings*." *Amon Hen* 211 (May 2008): 26.

Deyo, Steven Mark. "Wyrd and Will: Fate, Fatalism and Free Will in the Northern Elegy and J. R. R. Tolkien." *Mythlore: A Journal of J. R. R. Tolkien, C. S. Lewis, Charles Williams and Mythopoeic Literature* 14, no. 3 (Spring 1988): 59–62.

Dickerson, Matthew T. *Following Gandalf: Epic Battles and Moral Victory in* The Lord of the Rings. Grand Rapids, MI: Brazos, 2003.

———. "Valar." In *J. R. R. Tolkien Encyclopedia: Scholarship and Critical Assessment*, edited by Michael D. C. Drout, 689–90. New York: Routledge, 2007.

———. "Water, Ecology, and Spirituality in Tolkien's Middle-earth." In *Light Beyond All Shadow: Religious Experience in Tolkien's Work*, edited by Paul E. Kerry and Sandra Miesel, 15–32. Madison, TN: Fairleigh Dickinson Univ. Press, 2011.

———, and Jonathan Evans. *Ents, Elves, and Eriador: The Environmental Vision of J. R. R. Tolkien*. Lexington: Univ. of Kentucky Press, 2006.

Drout, Michael D. C., ed. *J. R. R. Tolkien Encyclopedia: Scholarship and Critical Assessment*. New York: Routledge, 2007.

Drury, Roger. "Providence at Elrond's Council." *Mythlore: A Journal of J. R. R. Tolkien, C. S. Lewis, Charles Williams and Mythopoeic Literature* 7, no. 3 (Autumn 1980): 8–9.

Dubs, Kathleen E. "Providence, Fate, and Chance: Boethian Philosophy in *The Lord of the Rings*." In *Tolkien and the Invention of Myth: A Reader*, edited by Jane Chance, 133–42. Lexington: Univ. of Kentucky Press, 2004.

Duriez, Colin. *Tolkien and* The Lord of the Rings: *A Guide to Middle-earth*. Mahwah, NJ: HiddenSpring, 2001.

Eden, Bradford Lee. "Elves." In *J. R. R. Tolkien Encyclopedia: Scholarship and Critical Assessment*, edited by Michael D. C. Drout, 150–52. New York: Routledge, 2007.

———. "Music in Middle-earth." In *J. R. R. Tolkien Encyclopedia: Scholarship and Critical Assessment*, edited by Michael D. C. Drout, 444–45. New York: Routledge, 2007.

———. "The 'Music of the Spheres': Relationships between Tolkien's Silmarillion and Medieval Cosmological and Religious Theory." In *Tolkien the Medievalist,* edited by Jane Chance, 183–93. London: Routledge, 2003.

Eggington, Mark. "Tolkien's Corrupt World." *Amon Hen* 164 (July 2000): 22.

Elam, Michael David. "The Ainulindalë and J. R. R. Tolkien's Beautiful Sorrow in Christian Tradition." *Seven: An Anglo-American Literary Review* 28 (2011): 61–78.

Ellwood, Gracía Fay. "The Good Guys and the Bad Guys." *Tolkien Journal* 3, no. 4 (Nov. 1969): 11.

Evans, Jonathan. "The Anthropology of Arda: Creation, Theology, and the Race of Men." In *Tolkien the Medievalist,* edited by Jane Chance, 194–224. New York: Routledge, 2003.

Filmer, Kath. "An Allegory Unveiled: A Reading of *The Lord of the Rings.*" *Mythlore: A Journal of J. R. R. Tolkien, C. S. Lewis, Charles Williams and Mythopoeic Literature* 13, no. 4 (Summer 1987): 19–21.

Fisher, Jason. "Three Rings for—Whom Exactly?" *Tolkien Studies: An Annual Scholarly Review* 5, edited by Douglas A. Anderson, Michael D. C. Drout, and Verlyn Flieger, 99–108. Morgantown: West Virginia Univ. Press, 2008.

———. "Tolkien's Fortunate Fall and the Third Theme of Ilúvatar." In *Truths Breathed Through Silver: The Inklings' Moral and Mythopoeic Legacy,* edited by Jonathan B. Himes, 93–109. Newcastle, UK: Cambridge Scholars, 2008.

Flieger, Verlyn. "The Body in Question: The Unhealed Wounds of Frodo Baggins." In *The Body in Tolkien's Legendarium: Essays on Middle-earth Corporeality,* edited by Christopher Vaccaro, 12–19. Jefferson, NC: McFarland, 2013.

———. "The Curious Incident of the Dream at the Barrow: Memory and Reincarnation in Middle-earth." In *Tolkien Studies: An Annual Scholarly Review* 4, edited by Douglas A. Anderson, Michael D. C. Drout, and Verlyn Flieger, 99–112. Morgantown: West Virginia Univ. Press, 2007.

———. *Interrupted Music: The Making of Tolkien's Mythology.* Kent, OH: Kent State Univ. Press, 2005.

———. *A Question of Time: J. R. R. Tolkien's Road to Faërie.* Kent, OH: Kent State Univ. Press, 1997.

———. *Splintered Light: Logos and Language in Tolkien's World.* Rev. ed. Kent, OH: Kent State Univ. Press, 2002.

———. "Tolkien and the Philosophy of Language." In *Tolkien and Philosophy,* edited by Roberto Arduini and Claudio A. Testi, 73–84. Zurich: Walking Tree, 2014.

Fornet-Ponse, Thomas. "Freedom and Providence as Anti-Modern Elements?" In *Tolkien and Modernity,* edited by Frank Weinreich and Thomas Honegger, 177–206. Zurich: Walking Tree, 2006.

———. "'Strange and Free': Some Aspects of the Nature of Elves and Men." In *Tolkien Studies: An Annual Scholarly Review* 7, edited by Douglas A. Anderson, Michael D. C. Drout, and Verlyn Flieger, 67–89. Morgantown: West Virginia Univ. Press, 2010.

Foster, Bob. "Letter." *Tolkien Journal* 3, no. 2 (1967): 19–20.

———. "Levels of Interpretation." *Tolkien Journal* 15 (Summer 1972): 22.

Foster, Robert. *The Complete Guide to Middle-earth: From* The Hobbit *to* The Silmarillion. New York: Del Ray, 1978.

Fredrick, Candice, and Sam McBride. *Women among the Inklings: Gender, C. S. Lewis, J. R. R. Tolkien, and Charles Williams.* Westport, CT: Greenwood Press, 2001.

Fuller, Edmund. "The Lord of the Hobbits: J. R. R. Tolkien." In *Understanding* The Lord of the Rings: *The Best of Tolkien Criticism,* edited by Rose A. Zimbardo and Neil D. Isaacs, 16–30. Boston: Houghton Mifflin, 2004.

Garbowski, Christopher. "Eucatastrophe and the Gift of Ilúvatar in Middle-earth." *Mallorn* 35 (Sept. 1997): 25–32.

———. "Middle-earth." In *J. R. R. Tolkien Encyclopedia: Scholarship and Critical Assessment,* edited by Michael D. C. Drout, 422–27. New York: Routledge, 2007.

———. *Recovery and Transcendence for the Contemporary Mythmaker: The Spiritual Dimension in the Works of J. R. R. Tolkien.* 2nd ed. Cormarë Series No. 7. Zurich: Walking Tree, 2004.

———. "Tolkien's Cosmic Eucatastrophe: From Ragnarok to Joyous Subcreation." *Inklings-Jahrbuch* 18 (2000): 272–89.

Garth, John. *Tolkien and the Great War: The Threshold of Middle-earth.* Boston: Houghton Mifflin, 2003.

Gee, Henry. *The Science of Middle-earth.* Cold Spring Harbor, NY: Cold Spring Press, 2004.

Glover, Willis B. "The Christian Character of Tolkien's Invented Worlds." *Mythlore: A Journal of J. R. R. Tolkien, C. S. Lewis, Charles Williams and Mythopoeic Literature* 3, no. 2 (1975): 3–8.

Goñi, Luis. "Reflections from the White Tower: Concerning Power and Magic." *Nolmë* 4 (May 2008): 14.

Grayson, David. "The Functions of Dreams in *The Lord of the Rings.*" *Amon Hen* 207 (Sept. 2007): 30–32.

Green, William H. "The Ring at the Centre: *Ēaca* in *The Lord of the Rings.*" *Mythlore: A Journal of J. R. R. Tolkien, C. S. Lewis, Charles Williams and Mythopoeic Literature* 4, no. 2 (Dec. 1976): 17–19.

Grotta, Daniel. *J. R. R. Tolkien: Architect of Middle-earth.* Philadelphia: Running Press, 1992.

Hammond, Wayne G., and Christina Scull. *The Lord of the Rings: A Reader's Companion.* Boston: Houghton Mifflin, 2005.

Hargrove, Gene. "Tom Bombadil." In *J. R. R. Tolkien Encyclopedia: Scholarship and Critical Assessment,* edited by Michael D. C. Drout, 670–71. New York: Routledge, 2007.

———. "Who Is Tom Bombadil?" *The Home Page of Eugene C. Hargrove.* https://itservices.cas.unt.edu/-hargrove/index.html.

Harris, Mason. "The Psychology of Power in Tolkien's *The Lord of the Rings,* Orwell's *1984* and LeGuin's *A Wizard of Earthsea.*" *Mythlore: A Journal of J. R. R. Tolkien, C. S. Lewis, Charles Williams and Mythopoeic Literature* 15, no. 1 (Autumn 1988): 46–56.

Hart, Trevor. "Tolkien, Creation and Creativity." In *Tree of Tales: Tolkien, Literature, and Theology,* edited by Trevor Hart and Ivan Khovacs, 39–53. Waco, TX: Baylor Univ. Press, 2007.

Hartley, Gregory. "A Wind from the West: The Role of the Holy Spirit in Tolkien's Middle-earth." *Christianity and Literature* 62, no. 1 (Autumn 2012): 95–120.

Harvey, David. *The Song of Middle-earth: J. R. R. Tolkien's Themes, Symbols and Myths.* London: George Allen and Unwin, 1985.

Hibbs, Thomas. "Providence and the Dramatic Unity of *The Lord of the Rings.*" In The Lord of the Rings *and Philosophy: One Book to Rule Them All,* edited by Gregory Bassham and Eric Bronson, 167–78. Chicago: Open Court, 2003.

Hickman, Michael R. "The Religious Ritual and Practice of the Elves of Middle-earth at the Time of the War of the Ring." *Mallorn: The Journal of the Tolkien Society* 26 (Sept. 1989): 39–43.

Hood, Gwyneth. "The Lidless Eye and the Long Burden: The Struggle Between Good and Evil in Tolkien's *The Lord of the Rings.*" PhD diss., Univ. of Michigan, 1984.

———. "Nature and Technology: Angelic and Sacrificial Strategies in Tolkien's *The Lord of the Rings.*" *Mythlore: A Journal of J. R. R. Tolkien, C. S. Lewis, Charles Williams and Mythopoeic Literature* 19, no. 4 (Autumn 1993): 6–12.

———. "Sauron and Dracula." *Mythlore: A Journal of J. R. R. Tolkien, C. S. Lewis, Charles Williams and Mythopoeic Literature* 14, no. 2 (Winter 1987): 11–17.

Houghton, John William, and Neal K. Keesee. "Tolkien, King Alfred, and Boethius: Platonist Views of Evil in *The Lord of the Rings.*" In *Tolkien Studies: An Annual Scholarly Review* 2, edited by Douglas A. Anderson, Michael D. C. Drout, and Verlyn Flieger, 131–59. Morgantown: West Virginia Univ. Press, 2005.

Hughes, Daniel. "Pieties and Giant Forms in *The Lord of the Rings.*" In *Shadows of Imagination: The Fantasies of C. S. Lewis, J. R. R. Tolkien, and Charles Williams,* new ed., edited by Mark R. Hillegas, 81–96. Carbondale: Southern Illinois Univ. Press, 1979.

Hutton, Ronald. "The Pagan Tolkien." In *The Ring and the Cross: Christianity and* The Lord of the Rings, edited by Paul E. Kerry, 57–70. Madison, WI: Fairleigh Dickinson Univ. Press, 2011.

Hyles, Vernon. "On the Nature of Evil: The Cosmic Myths of Lewis, Tolkien and Williams." *Mythlore: A Journal of J. R. R. Tolkien, C. S. Lewis, Charles Williams and Mythopoeic Literature* 13, no. 4 (Summer 1987): 9–13, 17.

Johnson, Janice. "The Celeblain of Celeborn and Galadriel." *Mythlore: A Journal of J. R. R. Tolkien, C. S. Lewis, Charles Williams and Mythopoeic Literature* 9, no. 2 (Summer 1982): 11–19.

Jones, Christine. "The Rise of the Lord of the Rings: A Synopsis of the Ancient Annals." *Tolkien Journal* 3, no .3 (Summer 1968): 4–10.

Kane, Douglas Charles. *Arda Reconstructed: The Creation of the Published Silmarillion.* Bethlehem, PA: Lehigh Univ. Press, 2009.

Kaufmann, U. Milo. "Aspects of the Paradisiacal in Tolkien's Work." In *A Tolkien Compass,* edited by Jared Lobdell, 156–67. New York: Ballantine, 1975.

Kilby, Clyde S. *Tolkien and the Silmarillion.* Wheaton, IL: Harold Shaw, 1976.

Kisor, Yvette. "Incorporeality and Transformation in *The Lord of the Rings.*" In *The Body in Tolkien's Legendarium: Essays on Middle-earth Corporeality,* edited by Christopher Vaccaro, 20–39. Jefferson, NC: McFarland, 2013.

Klinger, Judith. "Hidden Paths of Time: March 13th and the Riddles of Shelob's Lair." In *Tolkien and Modernity 2,* edited by Thomas Honegger and Frank Weinreich, 143–209. Zollikofen, Switzerland: Walking Tree, 2006.

———. "Tolkien's 'Strange Powers of the Mind': Dreams, Visionary History and Authorship." In *Sub-creating Middle-earth: Constructions of Authorship and the Works of J. R. R. Tolkien,* edited by Judith Klinger, 43–106. Zollikofen, Switzerland: Walking Tree, 2012.

Knight, Gareth. *The Magical World of the Inklings: J. R. R. Tolkien, C. S. Lewis, Charles Williams, Owen Barfield.* Longmead, Shaftesbury, UK: Element Books, 1990.

Kocher, Paul. "Ilúvatar and the Secret Fire." *Mythlore: A Journal of J. R. R. Tolkien, C. S. Lewis, Charles Williams, and Mythopoeic Literature* 12, no. 1 (Autumn 1985): 36–37.

———. *Master of Middle-earth: The Fiction of J. R. R. Tolk ien.* New York: Ballantine, 1972.

Kosyfi, Martha. "Ancient Greek Gods and the Valar." *Silver Leaves* 1(Fall 2007): 47–51.

Kowalik, Barbara. "Elbereth the Star-Queen Seen in the Light of Medieval Marian Devotion." In *"O, What a Tangled Web": Tolkien and Medieval Literature—A View from Poland,* edited by Barbara Kowalik, 93–113. Zurich: Walking Tree, 2013.

Kreeft, Peter. "Afterward: The Wonder of The Silmarillion." In *Shadows of Imagination: The Fantasies of C. S. Lewis, J. R. R. Tolkien, and Charles Williams,* new ed., edited by Mark R. Hillegas, 161–78. Carbondale: Southern Illinois Univ. Press, 1979.

———. *The Philosophy of Tolkien: The Worldview Behind* The Lord of the Rings. San Francisco: Ignatius, 2005.

Krueger, Heidi. "The Shaping of 'Reality' in Tolkien's Works: An Aspect of Tolkien and Modernity." In *Tolkien and Modernity 2,* edited by Thomas Honegger and Frank Weinreich, 233–72. Zollikofen, Switzerland: Walking Tree, 2006.

Larsen, Kristine. "[V]Arda Marred: The Evolution of the Queen of the Stars." *Mallorn: The Journal of the Tolkien Society* 45 (Spring 2008): 31–36.

Lense, Edward. "Sauron Is Watching *You:* The Role of the Great Eye in *The Lord of the Rings.*" *Mythlore: A Journal of J. R. R. Tolkien, C. S. Lewis, Charles Williams, and Mythopoeic Literature* 4, no. 1 (Sept. 1976): 3–6.

Levitin, Alexis. "Power in *The Lord of the Rings.*" *Orcrist* 4 (1969–70): 13.

Lewis, Alex. "The Breaking of Frodo." *Amon Hen* 79 (Mar. 1986): 17–18.

Lewis, C. S. *The Collected Letters of C. S. Lewis.* Vol. 2, edited by Walter Hooper. New York: HarperCollins, 2004.

———. *The Discarded Image: An Introduction to Medieval and Renaissance Literature.* Cambridge: Cambridge Univ. Press, 1964.

———. *Mere Christianity.* New York: Macmillan, 1943.

———. *Perelandra.* New York: Macmillan, 1944.

Lobdell, Jared. *The World of the Rings: Language, Religion, and Adventure in Tolkien.* Chicago: Open Court, 2004.

———. "Ymagynatyf and J. R. R. Tolkien's Roman Catholicism, Catholic Theology, and Religion in *The Lord of the Rings.*" In *Light Beyond All Shadow: Religious Experience in Tolkien's Work,* edited by Paul E. Kerry and Sandra Miesel, 15–32. Madison, TN: Fairleigh Dickinson Univ. Press, 2011.

"*The Lord of the Rings.*" *Times Literary Supplement,* Dec. 9, 1955, 743. Quoted in Wayne G. Hammond and Christina Scull, *The Lord of the Rings: A Reader's Guide,* 342. Boston: Houghton Mifflin, 2005.

Loy, David R., and Linda Goodhew. *The Dharma of Dragons and Daemons: Buddhist Themes in Modern Fantasy.* Boston: Wisdom, 2004.

Luling, Virginia. "Those Awful Orcs." *Amon Hen* 48 (Dec. 1980): 5.

Lynch, James. "The Literary Banquet and the Eucharistic Feast: Tradition in Tolkien." *Mythlore: A Journal of J. R. R. Tolkien, C. S. Lewis, Charles Williams and Mythopoeic Literature* 5, no. 2 (Autumn 1978): 15–16.

MacArthur, Chris. "The Mystery of the Ring's Destruction." *Amon Hen* 224 (July 2010): 17–20.

Madsen, Catherine. "Eru Erased: The Minimalist Cosmology of *The Lord of the Rings.*" In *The Ring and the Cross: Christianity and* The Lord of the Rings, edited by Paul Kerry, 152–69. Lanham, MD: Rowman and Littlefield, 2011.

———. "Light from an Invisible Lamp: Natural Religion in *The Lord of the Rings.*" *Mythlore: A Journal of J. R. R. Tolkien, C. S. Lewis, Charles Williams, and Mythopoeic Literature* 14, no. 3 (Spring 1988): 43–47.

Masson, Pat. "Mythology and the Silmarillion." *Amon Hen* 42 (Dec. 1979): 5–6.

Mathews, Richard. *Lightning from a Clear Sky: Tolkien, the Trilogy, and* The Silmarillion. San Bernardino, CA: Borgo, 1978.

McBride, Sam. "Stewards of Arda: Creation and Sustenance in J. R. R. Tolkien's Legendarium." In *Ecotheology in the Humanities: An Interdisciplinary Approach to Understanding the Divine and Nature,* edited by Melissa Brotton, 139–55. Lanham, MD: Lexington, 2016.

McIntosh, Jonathan. "Ainulindalë: Tolkien, St. Thomas, and the Metaphysics of the Music." In *Music in Middle-earth,* edited by Heidi Steimel and Friedhelm Schneidewind, 53–74. Zurich: Walking Tree, 2010.

———. *The Flame Imperishable: Tolkien, St. Thomas, and the Metaphysics of Faërie.* Kettering, OH: Angelico, 2017.

Mende, Lisa Anne. "Gondolin, Minas Tirith and the Eucatastrophe." *Mythlore: A Journal of J. R. R. Tolkien, C. S. Lewis, Charles Williams, and Mythopoeic Literature* 13, no. 2 (Winter 1986): 37–40.

"Menel a Ril." *Hobbitzine: Nazg* (June 1967): [8].

Milbank, Alison. *Chesterton and Tolkien as Theologians: The Fantasy of the Real.* London: T & T Clark, 2009.

Millen, Robert. "The Istari: A Look at a Middle-earth Enigma." *Amon Hen* (Oct. 1975): 9–10.

Mills, David. "The Writer of Our Story: Divine Providence in *The Lord of the Rings.*" *Touchstone* (Feb. 2002): 22–28.

Moorman, Charles. "'Now Entertain Conjecture of a Time'—The Fictive Worlds of C. S. Lewis and J. R. R. Tolkien." In *Shadows of Imagination: The Fantasies of C. S. Lewis, J. R. R. Tolkien, and Charles Williams,* new ed., edited by Mark R. Hillegas, 59–69. Carbondale: Southern Illinois Univ. Press, 1979.

Moseley, Charles. *J. R. R. Tolkien.* Plymouth, UK: Northcote House, 1997.

Murphy, David. Letter to the Editor. *Mythlore: A Journal of J. R. R. Tolkien, C. S. Lewis, Charles Williams, and Mythopoeic Literature* 5, no. 2 (Autumn 1978): 25–26.

Musk, Simon. "Tom Bombadil." *Minas Tirith Evening Star* 9, no. 11 (Oct. 1980): 13.

Nagy, Gergely. "A Body of Myth: Representing Sauron in *The Lord of the Rings.*" In *The Body in Tolkien's Legendarium: Essays on Middle-earth Corporeality,* edited by Christopher Vaccaro, 119–32. Jefferson, NC: McFarland, 2013.

———. "Saving the Myths: The Re-creation of Mythology in Plato and Tolkien." In *Tolkien and the Invention of Myth: A Reader,* edited by Jane Chance, 81–100. Lexington: Univ. of Kentucky Press, 2004.

Nance, O. V. "A Solution to the Tom Bombadil Problem." *Amon Hen* 193 (May 2005): 10–13.

Naveh, Reuven. "Tonality, Atonality, and the 'Ainulindalë.'" In *Music in Middle-earth,* edited by Heidi Steimel and Friedhelm Schneidewind, 29–52. Zurich: Walking Tree, 2010.

Nelson, Charles W. "'The Halls of Waiting': Death and Afterlife in Middle Earth." *Journal of the Fantastic in the Arts* 9, no. 3 (1998): 200–211.

Okunishi, Takashi. "Olórin." *Amon Hen* 50 (May 1981): 37.

Olszanski, Tadeusx Andrzej. "Evil and the Evil One in Tolkien's Theology." *Mallorn 33/Mythlore 80—Proceedings of the J. R. R. Tolkien Centenary Conference, Keble College, Oxford, 1992,* edited by Patricia Reynolds and Glen H. Goodnight, 298. Altadena, CA: Mythopoeic Press, 1995.

Ozment, Nicholas. "Prospero's Books, Gandalf's Staff: The Ethics of Magic in Shakespeare and Tolkien." In *Tolkien and Shakespeare: Essays on Shared Themes and Language,* edited by Janet Brennan Croft, 177–95. Jefferson, NC: McFarland, 2007.

Palmer, Bruce. *Visions of Paradise in* The Lord of the Rings. Kansas City, MO: T-K Graphics, 1976.

Partridge, Brenda. "No Sex Please—We're Hobbits: The Construction of Female Sexuality in *The Lord of the Rings.*" In *This Far Land,* edited by Robert Giddings, 179–97. London: Vision, 1984.

Pearce, Joseph. "The Hidden Evangelism in Tolkien's Work." *The Canadian C. S. Lewis Journal* 97 (Spring 2000): 32.

———. *Tolkien: Man and Myth.* San Francisco: Ignatius, 1998.

Pedersen, Kusumita. "The 'Divine Passive' in *The Lord of the Rings.*" *Mallorn: The Journal of the Tolkien Society* 51 (Spring 2011): 23–27.

Percival, Mike. "Of the Maiar." *Anor* 17 (1988): 5–12.

Perry, Michael W. *Untangling Tolkien.* Seattle: Inklings Books, 2006.

Petty, Anne C. *One Ring to Bind Them All: Tolkien's Mythology.* Tuscaloosa: Univ. of Alabama Press, 2002.

———. *Tolkien in the Land of Heroes: Discovering the Human Spirit.* Cold Spring Harbor, NY: Cold Spring Press, 2003.

Purdy, Margaret R. Letter to the Editor. *Mythlore: A Journal of J. R. R. Tolkien, C. S. Lewis, Charles Williams, and Mythopoeic Literature* 9, no. 4 (Winter 1983): 34–36.

Purtill, Richard. *J. R. R. Tolkien: Myth, Morality and Religion.* San Francisco: Ignatius, 1984.

———. *The Lord of the Elves and Eldils: Fantasy and Philosophy in C. S. Lewis and J. R. R. Tolkien.* Grand Rapids, MI: Zondervan, 1974.

Randolph, Burt. "The Singular Incompetence of the Valar," *Tolkien Journal* 3, no. 3 (Summer 1968): 11–13.

Rawls, Melanie. "The Rings of Power." *Mythlore: A Journal of J. R. R. Tolkien, C. S. Lewis, Charles Williams, and Mythopoeic Literature* 11, no. 2 (Autumn 1984): 29–32.

Reynolds, Patricia. "Funeral Customs in Tolkien's Fiction." *Mythlore: A Journal of J. R. R. Tolkien, C. S. Lewis, Charles Williams and Mythopoeic Literature* 19, no. 2 (Spring 1993): 45–53.

Ring, David. "Ad Valar Defendendi." *Tolkien Journal* 15 (Summer 1972): 18.

Roberts, Adam. "The One Ring." In *Reading* The Lord of the Rings: *New Writings on Tolkien's Classic,* edited by Robert Eaglestone, 59–70. London: Continuum, 2005.

———. *The Riddles of* The Hobbit. London: Palgrave Macmillan, 2013.

Rogers, Ted. *Evil, Eroticism, and Englishness in the Works of the British Literary Club: The Inklings: C. S. Lewis, J. R. R. Tolkien, and Charles Williams.* Saarbrücken, Germany: VDM Verlag Dr. Müller, 2008.

Rorabeck, Robert. *Tolkien's Heroic Quest.* Maidstone, UK: Crescent Moon, 2008.

Rosebury, Brian. "Revenge and Moral Judgment in Tolkien." In *Tolkien Studies: An Annual Scholarly Review* 5, edited by Douglas A. Anderson, Michael D. C. Drout, and Verlyn Flieger, 1–20. Morgantown: West Virginia Univ. Press, 2008.

———. *Tolkien: A Cultural Phenomenon.* Houndmills, UK: Palgrave Macmillan, 2003.

Rosman, Adam. "Gandalf as Torturer: The Ticking Bomb Terrorist and Due Process in J. R. R. Tolkien's *The Lord of the Rings.*" *Mallorn: The Journal of the Tolkien Society* 43 (July 2005): 38–42.

Rossi, Lee D. *The Politics of Fantasy: C. S. Lewis and J. R. R. Tolkien.* Ann Arbor, MI: UMI Dissertation Services, 1984.

Rutledge, Fleming. *The Battle for Middle-earth: Tolkien's Divine Design in* The Lord of the Rings. Grand Rapids, MI: William B. Eerdmans, 2004.

Ruud, Jay. *Critical Companion to J. R. R. Tolkien: A Literary Reference to His Life and Work.* New York: Facts on File, 2011.

———. "The Voice of Saruman: Wizards and Rhetoric in *The Two Towers.*" *Mythlore: A Journal of J. R. R. Tolkien, C. S. Lewis, Charles Williams, and Mythopoeic Literature* 28, no. 3/4 (Spring/Summer 2010): 141–52.

Ryan, J. S. *Tolkien: Cult or Culture?* Armidale, New South Wales: Univ. of New England, 1969.

————. *Tolkien's View: Windows into his World*. Zurich: Walking Tree, 2009.

Sabo, Deborah. "Archaeology and the Sense of History in J. R. R. Tolkien's Middle-earth." *Mythlore: A Journal of J. R. R. Tolkien, C. S. Lewis, Charles Williams and Mythopoeic Literature* 26, no. 1/2 (Fall/Winter 2007): 91–112.

Sammons, Martha C. *War of the Fantasy Worlds: C. S. Lewis and J. R. R. Tolkien on Art and Imagination*. Santa Barbara, CA: Praeger, 2010.

Sarti, Ronald Christopher. "Man in a Mortal World: J. R. R. Tolkien and *The Lord of the Rings*." PhD diss., Indiana Univ., May 1984.

Schorr, Karl. "The Nature of Dreams in *The Lord of the Rings*." *Mythlore: A Journal of J. R. R. Tolkien, C. S. Lewis, Charles Williams and Mythopoeic Literature* 10, no. 2 (Summer 1983): 21–46.

Schroeder, Sharin. "'It's Alive!': Tolkien's Monster on the Screen." In *Picturing Tolkien: Essays on Peter Jackson's* The Lord of the Rings *Film Trilogy*, edited by Janice M. Bogstad and Philip E. Kaveny, 116–38. Jefferson, NC: McFarland, 2011.

Scull, Christina, and Wayne G. Hammond. *The J. R. R. Tolkien Companion and Guide: Chronology*. Boston: Houghton Mifflin, 2006.

————. *The J. R. R. Tolkien Companion and Guide: Reader's Guide*. Boston: Houghton Mifflin, 2006.

Seeman, Chris. "Tolkien's Conception of Evil: An Anthropological Perspective." *Arda 1988–1991*. Annual of Arda Research (1994): 52–67.

Shippey, Tom. *J. R. R. Tolkien: Author of the Century*. Boston: Houghton Mifflin, 2000.

————. "Mythology, Germanic." In *J. R. R. Tolkien Encyclopedia: Scholarship and Critical Assessment*, edited by Michael D. C. Drout, 449–50. New York: Routledge, 2007.

————. "Orcs, Wraiths, Wights: Tolkien's Images of Evil." *Roots and Branches: Selected Papers on Tolkien*, 243–66. Zollikofen, Switzerland: Walking Tree, 2007.

————. *The Road to Middle-earth*. Boston: Houghton Mifflin, 1983.

Sly, Debbie. "Weaving Nets of Gloom: 'Darkness Profound' in Tolkien and Milton." In *J. R. R. Tolkien and His Literary Resonances*, edited by George Clark and Daniel Timmons, 109–19. Westport, CT: Greenwood, 2000.

Sookoo, L. Lara. "Animals in Tolkien's Works." In *J. R. R. Tolkien Encyclopedia: Scholarship and Critical Assessment*, edited by Michael D. C. Drout, 19–21. New York: Routledge, 2007.

Stanton, Michael N. *Hobbits, Elves, and Wizards: Exploring the Wonders and Worlds of J. R. R. Tolkien's* The Lord of the Rings. New York: Palgrave, 2001.

Startzman, L. Eugene. "Goldberry and Galadriel: The Quality of Joy." *Mythlore: A Journal of J. R. R. Tolkien, C. S. Lewis, Charles Williams and Mythopoeic Literature* 16, no. 2 (Winter 1989): 5–13.

Stevenson, Jeffrey. "T.B. or not T.B.: That Is the Question." *Amon Hen* 196 (Nov. 2005): 16–21.

Stoddard, William H. "Symbelmynë: Mortality and Memory in Middle-earth." *Mythlore: A Journal of J. R. R. Tolkien, C. S. Lewis, Charles Williams, and Mythopoeic Literature* 29, no. 1/2 (Fall/Winter 2010): 151–59.

Stratyner, Leslie. "ðe us ðas beagas geaf (He Who Gave Us These Rings): Sauron and the Perversion of Anglo-Saxon Ethos." *Mythlore: A Journal of J. R. R. Tolkien, C. S. Lewis, Charles Williams and Mythopoeic Literature* 16, no. 1 (Autumn 1989): 5–8.

Sturch, Richard. "Of Orcs and Other Oddities." *Amon Hen* 46 (Sept. 1980): 5.

Tally, Robert T. "Let Us Now Praise Famous Orcs: Simple Humanity in Tolkien's Inhuman Creatures." *Mythlore: A Journal of J. R. R. Tolkien, C. S. Lewis, Charles Williams, and Mythopoeic Literature* 29, no. 1/2 (2010): 17–28.

Testi, Claudio A. "Tolkien's *Legendarium* as a *Meditation Mortis*." *The Broken Scythe: Death and Immortality in the Works of J. R. R. Tolkien*, edited by Roberto Arduini and Claudio A. Testi, 39–68. Zurich: Walking Tree Publishers, 2012.

Thum, Maureen. "The 'Sub-Creation' of Galadriel, Arwen, and Éowyn; Women of Power in Tolkien's and Jackson's *The Lord of the Rings*." In *Tolkien on Film: Essays on Peter Jackson's* The Lord of the Rings, edited by Janet Brennan Croft, 231–56. Altadena, CA: Mythopoeic Press, 2004.

Tneh, David. "The Human Image and the Interrelationship of the Orcs, Elves and Men." *Mallorn: The Journal of the Tolkien Society* 55 (Winter 2014): 35–39.

———. "Orcs and Tolkien's Treatment of Evil." *Mallorn: The Journal of the Tolkien Society* 52 (Autumn 2011): 37–43.

Tolkien, J. R. R. "The Adventures of Tom Bombadil." In *The Tolkien Reader*, 11–16. New York: Ballantine, 1966.

———. *The Annotated Hobbit*. Edited by Douglas A. Anderson. Boston: Houghton Mifflin, 2002.

———. *The Book of Lost Tales: Part 1*. Edited by Christopher Tolkien. Vol. 1, *The History of Middle-earth*. New York: Ballantine, 1983.

———. *The Book of Lost Tales: Part 2*. Edited by Christopher Tolkien. Vol. 2, *The History of Middle-earth*. New York: Ballantine, 1984.

———. *The Children of Hurin*. Edited by Christopher Tolkien. Boston: Houghton Mifflin, 2007.

———. *Farmer Giles of Ham*. In *Smith of Wootton Major and Farmer Giles of Ham*, 61–156. New York: Ballantine, 1969.

———. "Fate and Free Will." Edited by Carl F. Hostetter. *Tolkien Studies: An Annual Scholarly Review* 6, edited by Douglas A. Anderson, Michael D. C. Drout, and Verlyn Flieger, 183–88. Morgantown: West Virginia Univ. Press, 2009.

———. *The Fellowship of the Ring*. New York: Ballantine Books, 1965.

———. "From 'Quendi and Eldar,' Appendix D." Edited by Carl F. Hostetter. *Vinyar Tengwar* 39 (July 1998): 4–20.

———. *The Hobbit*. New York: Ballantine Books, 1966.

———. *The Lays of Beleriand*. Edited by Christopher Tolkien. Vol. 3, *The History of Middle-earth*. New York: Ballantine, 1985.

———. *The Legend of Sigurd and Gudrun*. Edited by Christopher Tolkien. Boston: Houghton Mifflin, 2009.

———. *The Letters of J. R. R. Tolkien*. Edited by Humphrey Carpenter. Boston: Houghton Mifflin, 1981.

————. *The Lost Road and Other Writings.* Edited by Christopher Tolkien. Vol. 5, *The History of Middle-earth.* New York: Ballantine, 1987.

————. *The Monsters and the Critics and Other Essays.* Edited by Christopher Tolkien. London: Harper Collins, 2006.

————. *Morgoth's Ring: The Later Silmarillion, Part 1.* Edited by Christopher Tolkien. Vol. 10, *The History of Middle-earth.* Boston: Houghton Mifflin, 1993.

————. *Mr. Baggins: The History of the Hobbit, Part 1.* Edited by John D. Rateliff. Boston: Houghton Mifflin, 2007.

————. "Notes on Óre." *Vinyar Tengwar* 41 (July 2000): 11–19.

————. "Ósanwe-kenta." Edited by Carl F. Hostetter. *Vinyar Tengwar* 39 (July 1998): 21–34.

————. *The Peoples of Middle-earth.* Edited by Christopher Tolkien. Vol. 12, *The History of Middle-earth.* Boston: Houghton Mifflin, 1996.

————. *The Return of the King.* New York: Ballantine Books, 1965.

————. *The Return of the Shadow: The History of The Lord of the Rings, Part 1.* Edited by Christopher Tolkien. Vol. 6, *The History of Middle-earth.* London: Unwin Hyman, 1988.

————. *Return to Bag End: The History of the Hobbit, Part 2.* Edited by John D. Rateliff. Boston: Houghton Mifflin, 2007.

————. *The Road Goes Ever On.* 2nd ed. Boston: Houghton Mifflin, 1978.

————. *Sauron Defeated: The End of the Third Age: The History of The Lord of the Rings, Part 4.* Edited by Christopher Tolkien. Vol. 9, *The History of Middle-earth.* Boston: Houghton Mifflin, 1992.

————. *The Shaping of Middle-earth.* Edited by Christopher Tolkien. Vol. 4, *The History of Middle-earth.* New York: Ballantine, 1986.

————. *The Silmarillion.* Edited by Christopher Tolkien. New York: Ballantine, 1977.

————. "Sir Gawain and the Green Knight." In *The Monsters and the Critics and Other Essays,* edited by Christopher Tolkien. London: Harper Collins, 2006.

————. *Tolkien on Fairy-stories.* Expanded ed. Edited by Verlyn Flieger and Douglas A. Anderson. London: Harper Collins, 2008.

————. *The Treason of Isengard: The History of The Lord of the Rings, Part 2.* Edited by Christopher Tolkien. Vol. 7, *The History of Middle-earth.* Boston: Houghton Mifflin, 1989

————. *The Two Towers.* New York: Ballantine, 1965.

————. *Unfinished Tales of Númenor and Middle-earth.* Edited by Christopher Tolkien. New York: Ballantine, 1980.

————. *The War of the Jewels: The Later Silmarillion, Part 2.* Edited by Christopher Tolkien. Vol. 11, *The History of Middle-earth.* Boston: Houghton Mifflin, 1994.

————. *The War of the Ring: The History of The Lord of the Rings, Part 3.* Edited by Christopher Tolkien. Vol. 8, *The History of Middle-earth.* Boston: Houghton Mifflin, 1990.

Treloar, John L. "Tolkien and Christian Concepts of Evil: Apocalypse and Privation." *Mythlore: A Journal of J. R. R. Tolkien, C. S. Lewis, Charles Williams and Mythopoeic Literature* 15, no. 2 (Winter 1988): 57–60.

Treschow, Michael, and Mark Duckworth. "Bombadil's Role in *The Lord of the Rings*." *Mythlore: A Journal of J. R. R. Tolkien, C. S. Lewis, Charles Williams and Mythopoeic Literature* 252, no. 1/2 (Fall/Winter 2006): 175–96.

Upstone, Sara. "Applicability and Truth in *The Hobbit, The Lord of the Rings,* and *The Silmarillion*." *Mythlore: A Journal of J. R. R. Tolkien, C. S. Lewis, Charles Williams and Mythopoeic Literature* 23, no. 4 (Fall/Winter 2002): 50–66.

Urang, Gunnar. *Shadows of Heaven: Religion and Fantasy in the Writing of C. S. Lewis, Charles Williams, and J. R. R. Tolkien.* Philadelphia: Pilgrim Publishing, 1971.

Vaccaro, Christopher. "Rings." In *J. R. R. Tolkien Encyclopedia: Scholarship and Critical Assessment,* edited by Michael D. C. Drout, 571–72. New York: Routledge, 2007.

Vanhecke, Johan. "Old Tom Bombadil was a . . ." *Amon Hen* 43 (Jan. 1980): 6–7.

Veldhoen, Bart. "J. R. R. Tolkien, philologist and Holist." *Lembas* Extra (2004): 1–14.

Veldman, Merideth. *Fantasy, the Bomb, and the Greening of Britain: Romantic Protest, 1945–1980.* Cambridge: Univ. Press, 1994.

Vincent, Alana M. *Culture, Communion and Recovery: Tolkienian Fairy-Story and Inter-Religious Exchange.* Newcastle upon Tyne, UK: Cambridge Scholars, 2012.

Vink, Renee. "Fate and Doom in Tolkien." *Lembas* Extra (1986): 5–13.

Walker, Steve. *The Power of Tolkien's Prose: Middle-earth's Magical Style.* New York: Palgrave Macmillan, 2009.

Walter, Brian D. "The Grey Pilgrim: Gandalf and the Challenges of Characterization in Middle-earth." In *Picturing Tolkien: Essays on Peter Jackson's* The Lord of the Rings *Film Trilogy,* edited by Janice M. Bogstad and Philip E. Kaveny, 194–215. Jefferson, NC: McFarland, 2011.

Watkins, Zach. "Satan and The Silmarillion: John Milton's Angelic Decline in J. R. R. Tolkien's Melkor." *The Grey Book: Online Journals of Middle-earth* 1 (2005). https://www.unm.edu/-tolkien/Greybook/vol1/satan.pdf.

Wheeler, Ron. "Providence and Choice in the Fiction of C. S. Lewis, J. R. R. Tolkien, and Charles Williams: Embracing the Infinite Recesses." PhD diss. prospectus, Marquette Univ.

Whitt, Richard J. "Germanic Fate and Doom in J. R. R. Tolkien's The Silmarillion." *Mythlore: A Journal of J. R. R. Tolkien, C. S. Lewis, Charles Williams, and Mythopoeic Literature* 29, no. 1/2 (Fall/Winter 2010): 115–29.

Whittingham, Elizabeth A. *The Evolution of Tolkien's Mythology: A Study of the History of Middle-earth.* Jefferson, NC: McFarland, 2008.

Williams, Donald T. "The Everlasting Hobbit: Perspectives on the Human in Tolkien's Mythos." In *Tolkien 2005: The Ring Goes Even On—Proceedings,* edited by Sarah Wells, 2–11. The Tolkien Society. Aston Univ., Birmingham, Aug. 11–15, 2005. Coventry: The Tolkien Society, 2008.

———. *Mere Humanity: G. K. Chesterton, C. S. Lewis, and J. R. R. Tolkien on the Human Condition.* Nashville, TN: Broadman and Homan, 2006.

Williams, Madawc. "Death in Aman." *Amon Hen* 48 (Dec. 1980): 7–8.

Williamson, James T. "Emblematic Bodies: Tolkien and the Depiction of Female Physical Presence." In *The Body in Tolkien's Legendarium: Essays on Middle-earth Corporeality,* edited by Christopher Vaccaro, 134–56. Jefferson, NC: McFarland, 2013.

Wood, Ralph. "Tolkien's Augustinian Understanding of Good and Evil: Why *The Lord of the Rings* Is Not Manichean." In *Tree of Tales: Tolkien, Literature, and Theology,* edited by Trevor Hart and Ivan Khovacs, 85–102. Waco, TX: Baylor Univ. Press, 2007.

Wood, Steve. "The Silmarillion." *Amon Hen* 29 (1978): 12.

World Health Organization. "F60.2: Dissocial Personality Disorder." In *The ICD-10 Classification of Mental and Behavioural Disorders: Diagnostic Criteria for Research.* World Health Organization, 1993. https://www.who.int/classifications/icd/en/GRNBOOK.pdf.

Wright, Marjorie Evelyn. "The Vision of Cosmic Order in the Oxford Mythmakers." In *Imagination and the Spirit: Essays in Literature and the Christian Faith Presented to Clyde S. Kilby,* edited by Charles A. Huttar, 259–76. Grand Rapids, MI: William B. Eerdmans, 1971.

Zaleski, Philip, and Carol Zaleski. *The Fellowship: The Literary Lives of the Inklings: J. R. R. Tolkien, C. S. Lewis, Owen Barfield, Charles Williams.* New York: Farrar, Straus and Giroux, 2015.

Index